VIZ GRAPHIC NOVEL

MAISON IKKOKU ™

BEDSIDE MANNERS

STORY AND ART BY
RUMIKO TAKAHASHI

CONTENTS

This volume contains MAISON IKKOKU PART FIVE #1,
through #4 plus one episode from
Animerica, Anime & Manga Monthly, Vol. 3, No. 10 in their entirety.

Story & Art by Rumiko Takahashi
*
English Adaptation by Gerard Jones

Translation/Mari Morimoto
Touch-Up Art & Lettering/Wayne Truman
Cover Design/Viz Graphics
Editor/Trish Ledoux
Assistant Editors/Annette Roman & Toshifumi Yoshida

Director of Sales & Marketing/Oliver Chin
Editor-in-Chief/Satoru Fujii
Publisher/Seiji Horibuchi
*

Printed in Canada
*
Published by Viz Communications, Inc.
P.O. Box 77010
San Francisco, CA 94107
*
10 9 8 7 6 5 4 3
Third printing, August 1999

Vizit us at www.viz.com and our online magazines at www.j-pop.com,
www.animerica-mag.com and www.pulp-mag.com!

Get your free Viz Shop-By-Mail catalog!
(800) 394-3042 or fax (415) 546-7086

PART ONE

WELL, WELL, WELL

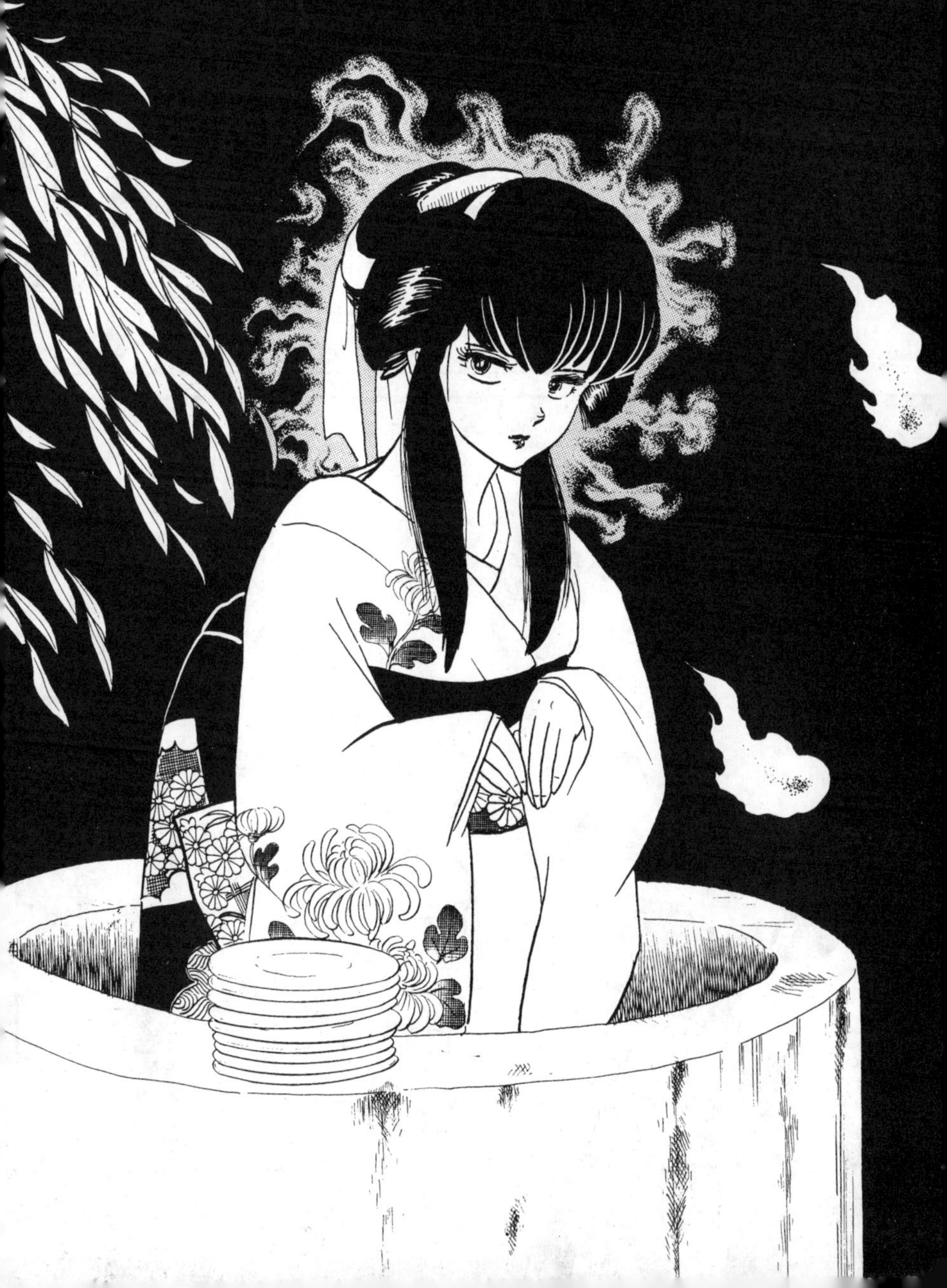

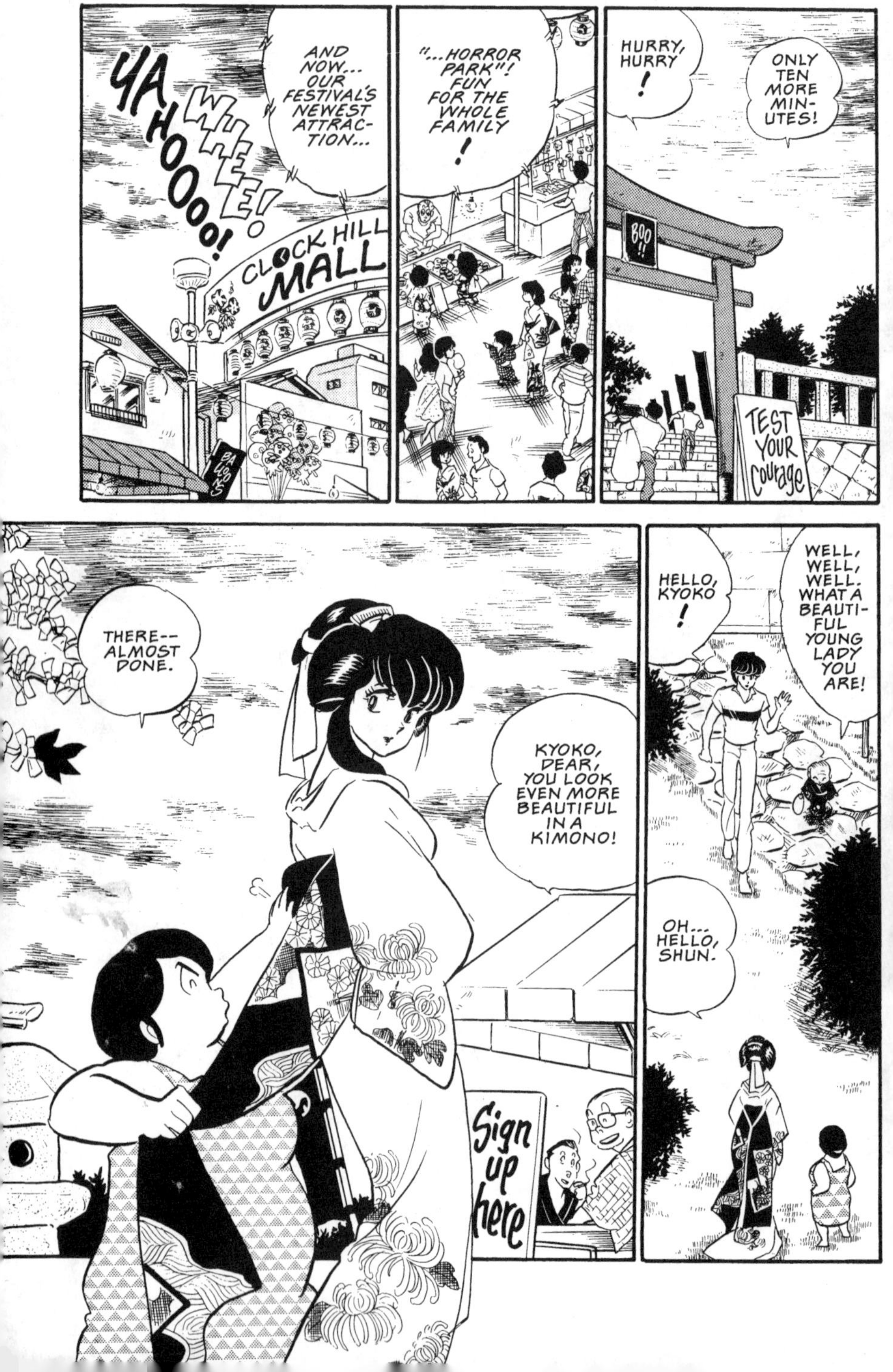
YAHOOOOO!
WHEE!
AND NOW... OUR FESTIVAL'S NEWEST ATTRACTION...
CLOCK HILL MALL
BALLOONS
"...HORROR PARK"! FUN FOR THE WHOLE FAMILY!
HURRY, HURRY!
ONLY TEN MORE MIN-UTES!
BOO!!
TEST YOUR Courage
THERE--ALMOST DONE.
KYOKO, DEAR, YOU LOOK EVEN MORE BEAUTIFUL IN A KIMONO!
Sign up here
HELLO, KYOKO!
WELL, WELL, WELL. WHAT A BEAUTI-FUL YOUNG LADY YOU ARE!
OH... HELLO, SHUN.

YOU MUST BE "OKIKU-SAN," THE GHOST OF THAT LADY WHO FELL IN THE HOLE.

OOHOO HOO HOO!

OOOH, HOW DID YOU GUESS?

SOUNDS LIKE YOU'RE GETTING INTO IT.

WHERE'S MY GRANDSON?

HE'S OVER IN THE MAKEUP AREA, GETTING HIS FACE DONE UP.

A "CAT DEMON."

QUIT FIDGETING! GEEZ!

SEE? IT'S SMUDGED AGAIN!

HMM...

HEY! HEY! YOTSUYA!

IT OCCURRED TO ME THAT A LINE BELOW HIS EYES... LIKE SO...

HEY, THAT'S ACTUALLY PRETTY COOL!

YOU SEE? HIS EVIL IS THUS REVEALED.

OKAY... THEN I'VE GOTTA DO THIS... LIKE SO...

THEN I SHALL...

WHAT AM I, AN EASEL?!

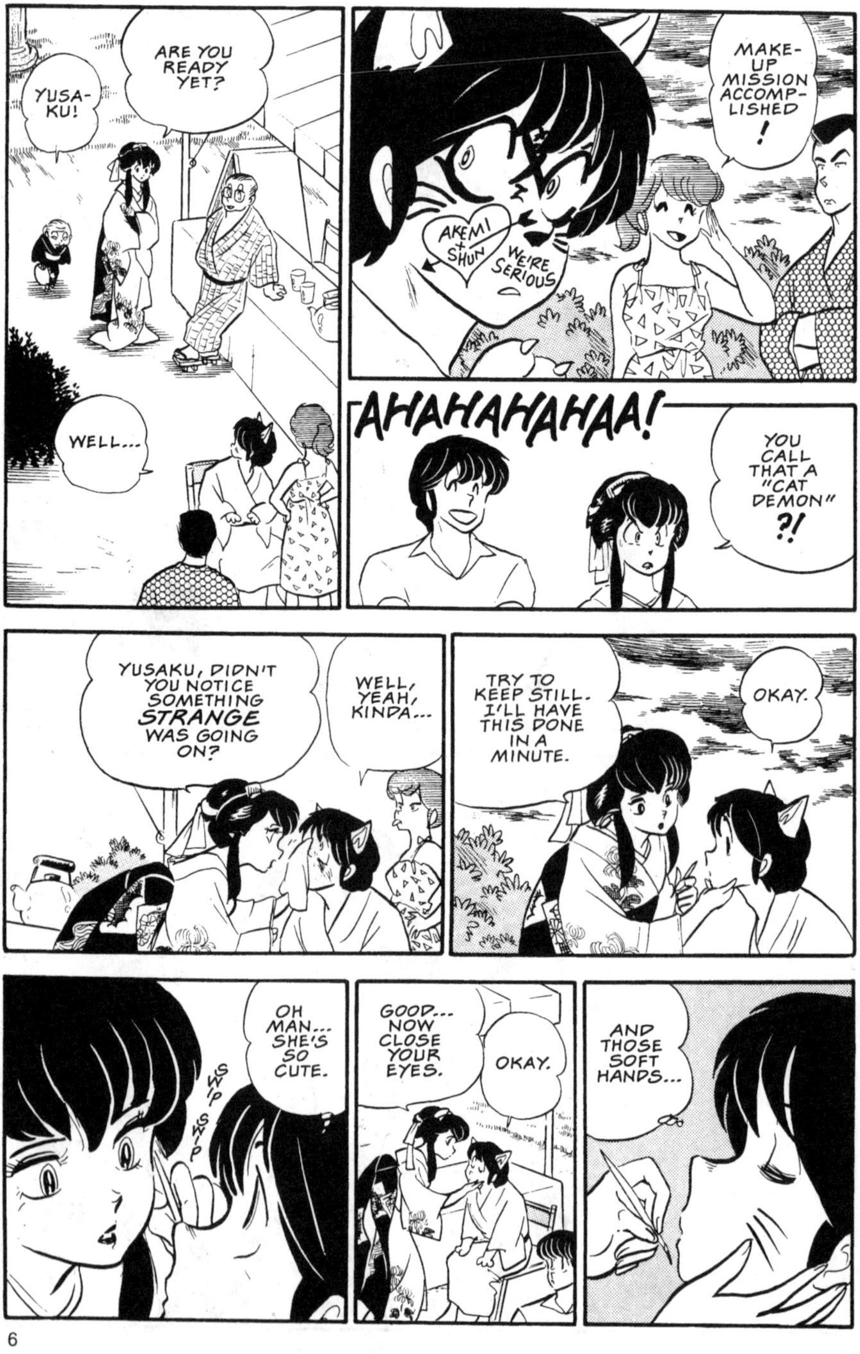
YUSAKU!
ARE YOU READY YET?
WELL...
MAKE-UP MISSION ACCOMPLISHED!
AKEMI + SHUN
WE'RE SERIOUS
AHAHAHAHAA!
YOU CALL THAT A "CAT DEMON"?!
YUSAKU, DIDN'T YOU NOTICE SOMETHING STRANGE WAS GOING ON?
WELL, YEAH, KINDA...
TRY TO KEEP STILL. I'LL HAVE THIS DONE IN A MINUTE.
OKAY.
OH MAN... SHE'S SO CUTE.
SWIP SWIP
GOOD... NOW CLOSE YOUR EYES.
OKAY.
AND THOSE SOFT HANDS...

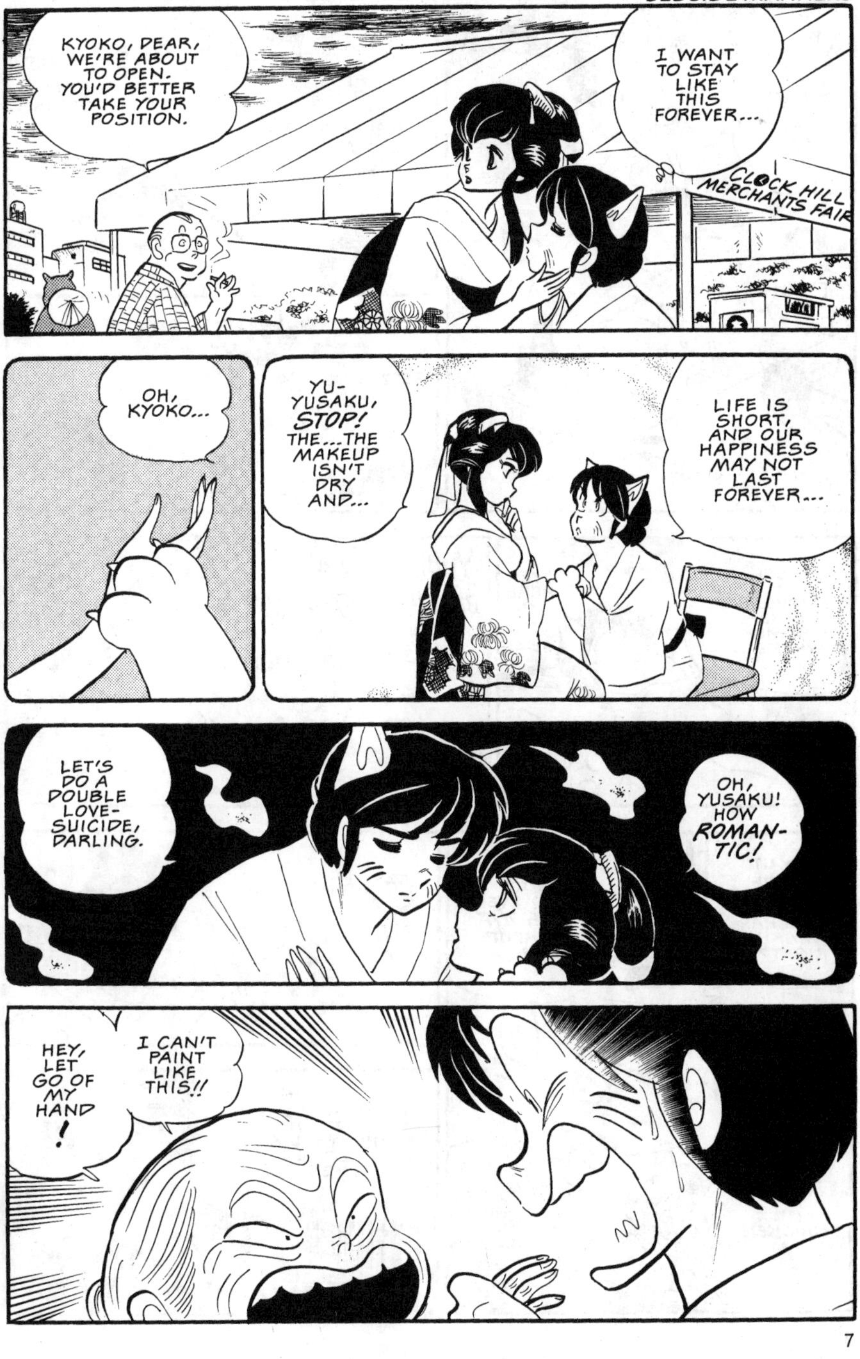
KYOKO, DEAR, WE'RE ABOUT TO OPEN. YOU'D BETTER TAKE YOUR POSITION.
I WANT TO STAY LIKE THIS FOREVER...
CLOCK HILL MERCHANTS FAIR
OH, KYOKO...
YU-YUSAKU, STOP! THE... THE MAKEUP ISN'T DRY AND...
LIFE IS SHORT, AND OUR HAPPINESS MAY NOT LAST FOREVER...
LET'S DO A DOUBLE LOVE-SUICIDE, DARLING.
OH, YUSAKU! HOW ROMAN-TIC!
HEY, LET GO OF MY HAND!
I CAN'T PAINT LIKE THIS!!

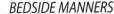

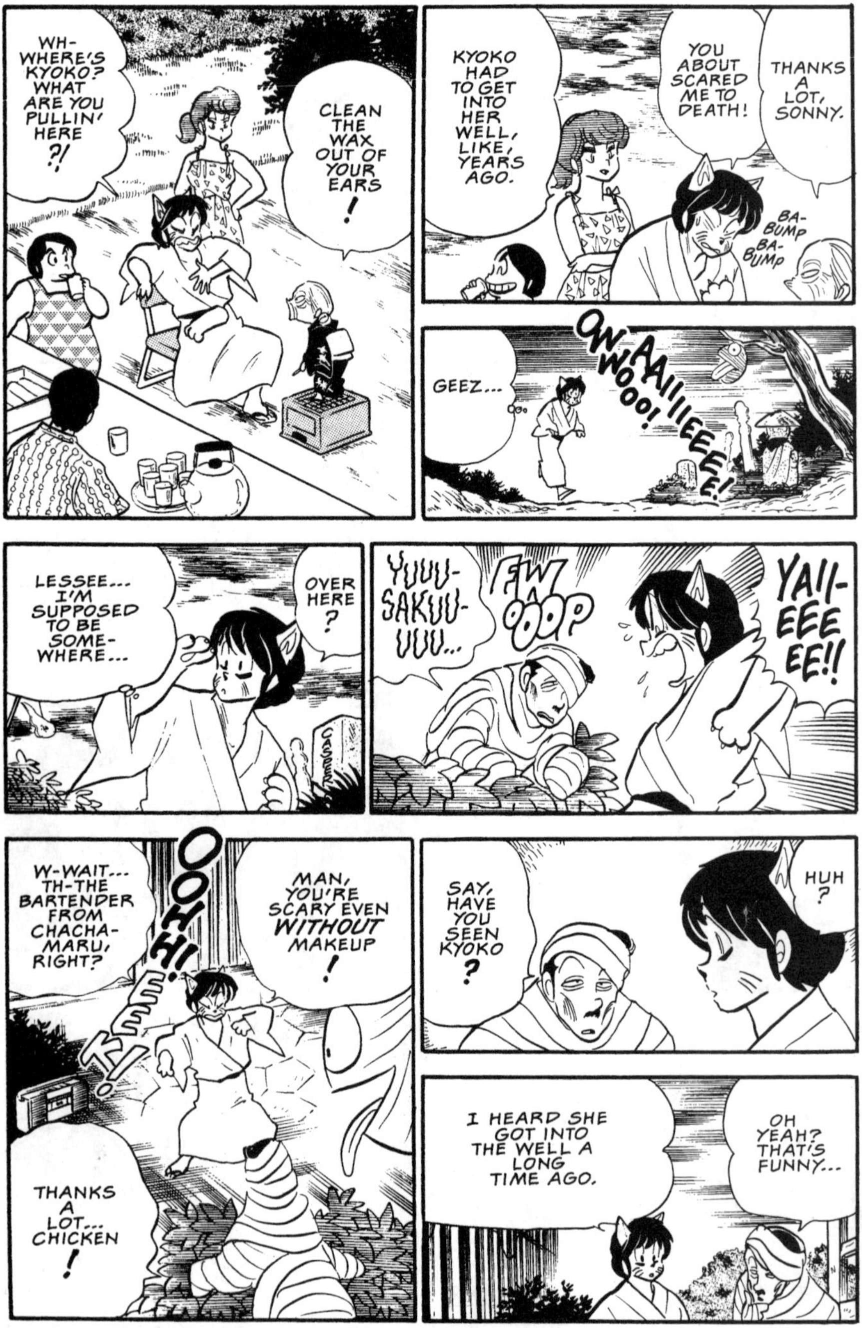
WH- WHERE'S KYOKO? WHAT ARE YOU PULLIN' HERE ?!
CLEAN THE WAX OUT OF YOUR EARS !
KYOKO HAD TO GET INTO HER WELL, LIKE, YEARS AGO.
YOU ABOUT SCARED ME TO DEATH!
THANKS A LOT, SONNY.
BA-BUMP BA-BUMP
GEEZ...
OWAAIIIIEEEEE!
WOOO!
LESSEE... I'M SUPPOSED TO BE SOME-WHERE...
OVER HERE ?
YUUU-SAKUU-UUU...
FWOOP
YAII-EEEEE!!
W-WAIT... TH-THE BARTENDER FROM CHACHA-MARU, RIGHT?
OOHH!
EEEK!
MAN, YOU'RE SCARY EVEN WITHOUT MAKEUP !
THANKS A LOT... CHICKEN !
SAY, HAVE YOU SEEN KYOKO ?
HUH ?
I HEARD SHE GOT INTO THE WELL A LONG TIME AGO.
OH YEAH? THAT'S FUNNY...

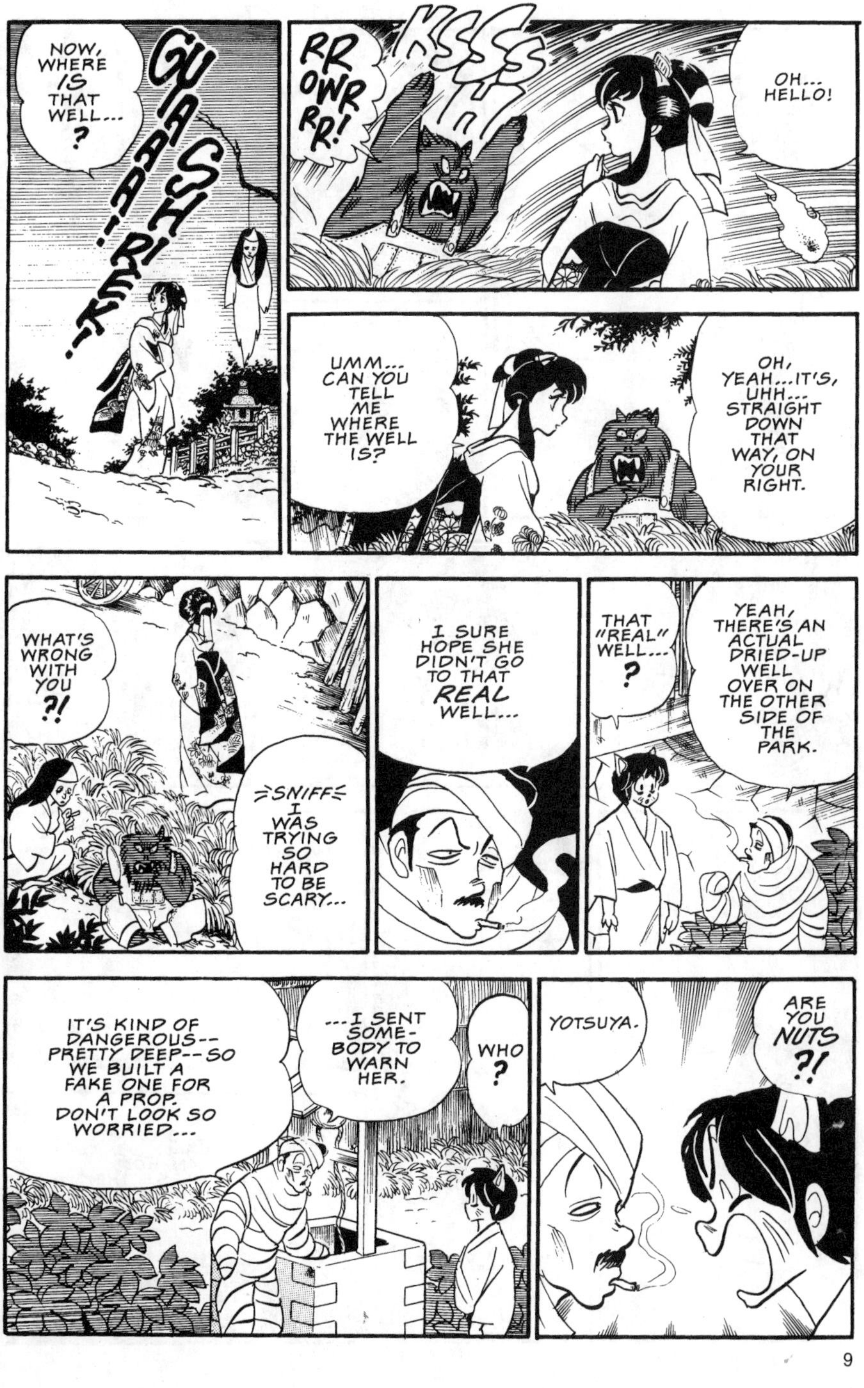
NOW, WHERE IS THAT WELL...?
GUAAAAH! SHRIEK!
RRROWRRR!
KSSSS
OH... HELLO!
UMM... CAN YOU TELL ME WHERE THE WELL IS?
OH, YEAH...IT'S, UHH... STRAIGHT DOWN THAT WAY, ON YOUR RIGHT.
WHAT'S WRONG WITH YOU?!
=SNIFF= I WAS TRYING SO HARD TO BE SCARY...
I SURE HOPE SHE DIDN'T GO TO THAT REAL WELL...
THAT "REAL" WELL...?
YEAH, THERE'S AN ACTUAL DRIED-UP WELL OVER ON THE OTHER SIDE OF THE PARK.
IT'S KIND OF DANGEROUS--PRETTY DEEP--SO WE BUILT A FAKE ONE FOR A PROP. DON'T LOOK SO WORRIED...
...I SENT SOMEBODY TO WARN HER.
WHO?
YOTSUYA.
ARE YOU NUTS?!

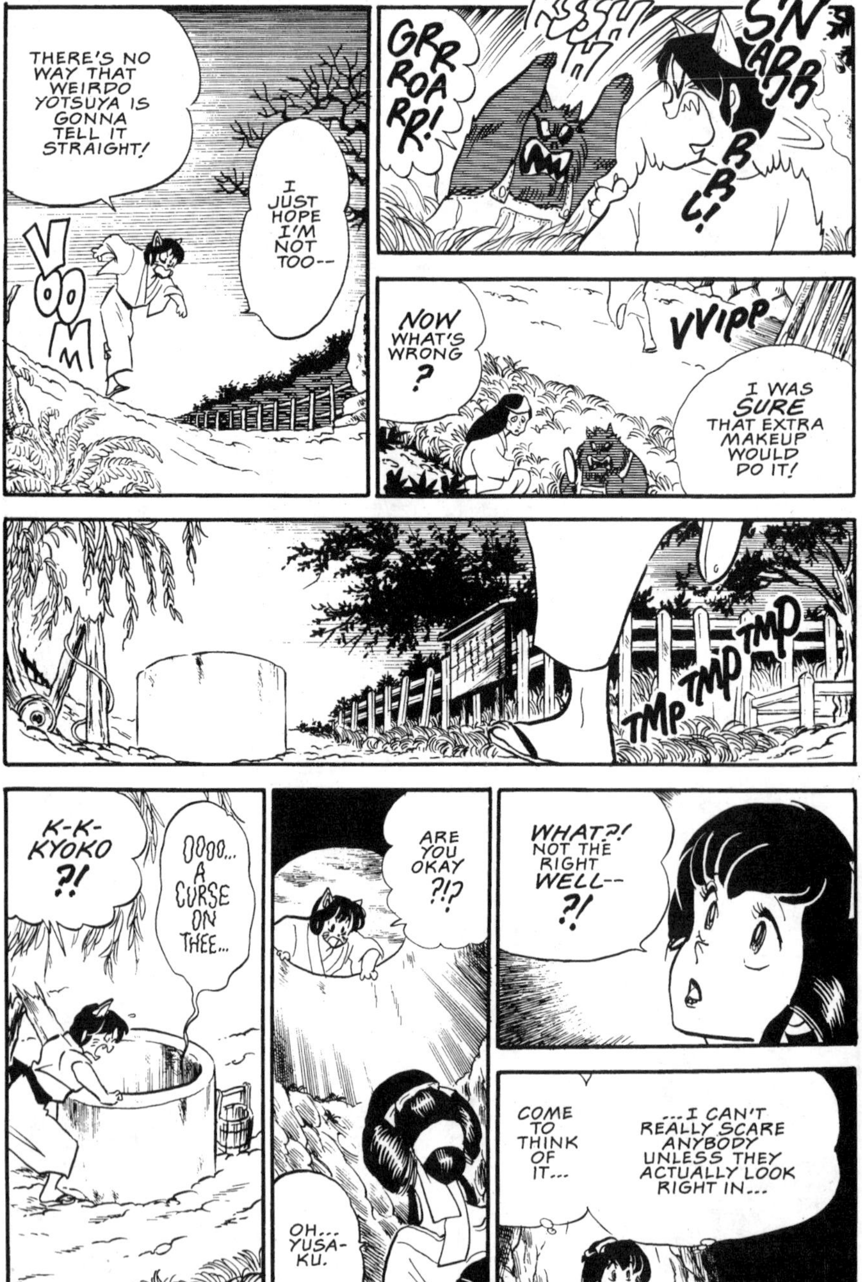

THERE'S NO WAY THAT WEIRDO YOTSUYA IS GONNA TELL IT STRAIGHT!
VOOM
I JUST HOPE I'M NOT TOO--
KSSSH
GRR ROARR!
SNARRRL!
NOW WHAT'S WRONG?
VVIPP
I WAS SURE THAT EXTRA MAKEUP WOULD DO IT!
TMP TMP TMP TMP
K-K-KYOKO?!
OOOO... A CURSE ON THEE...
ARE YOU OKAY?!?
OH... YUSAKU.
WHAT?! NOT THE RIGHT WELL--?!
COME TO THINK OF IT...
...I CAN'T REALLY SCARE ANYBODY UNLESS THEY ACTUALLY LOOK RIGHT IN...

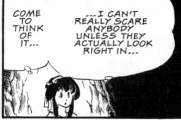

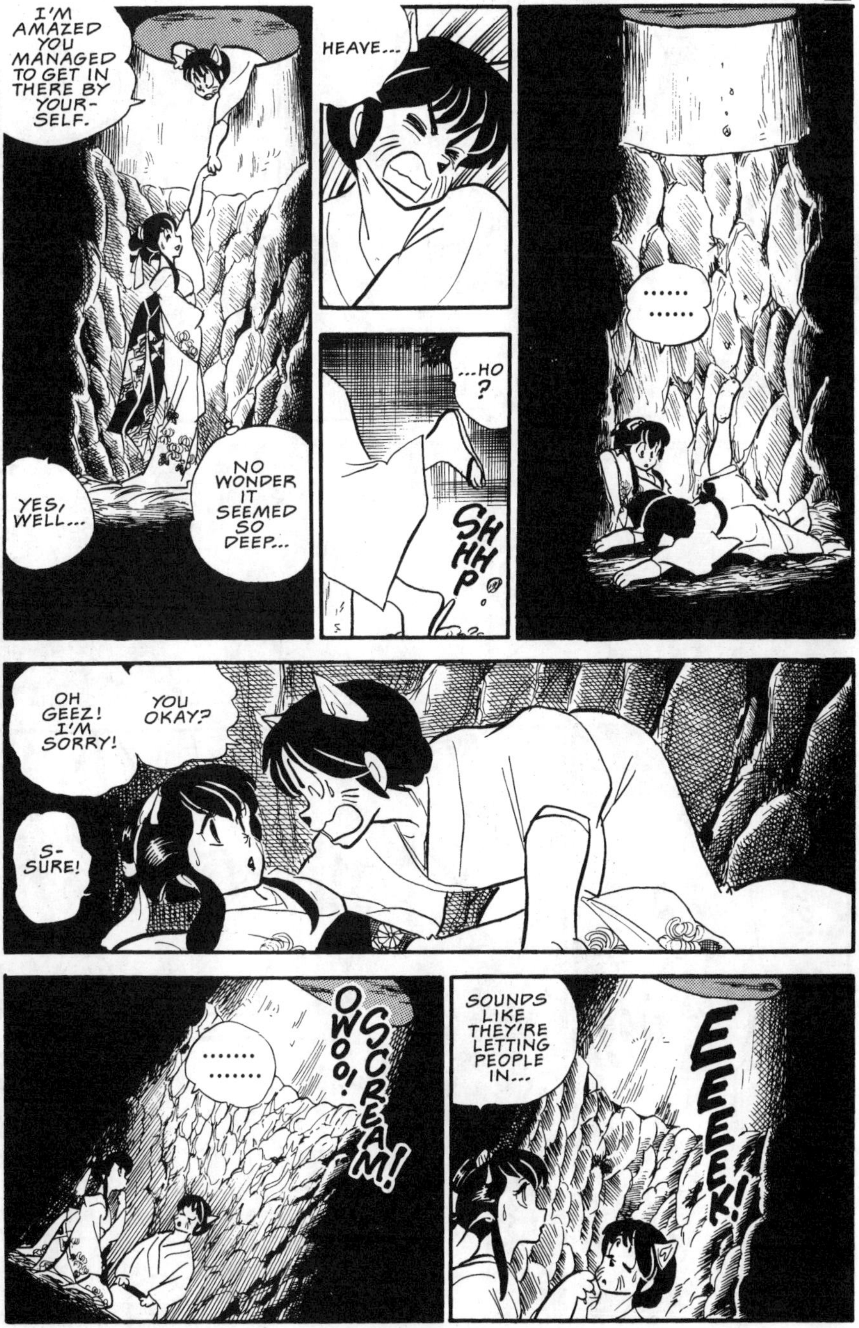
I'M AMAZED YOU MANAGED TO GET IN THERE BY YOURSELF.
YES, WELL...
NO WONDER IT SEEMED SO DEEP...
HEAVE...
...HO?
SHHHP
......
......
OH GEEZ! I'M SORRY!
YOU OKAY?
S-SURE!
....
....
OWOO!
SCREAM!
SOUNDS LIKE THEY'RE LETTING PEOPLE IN...
EEEEEK!

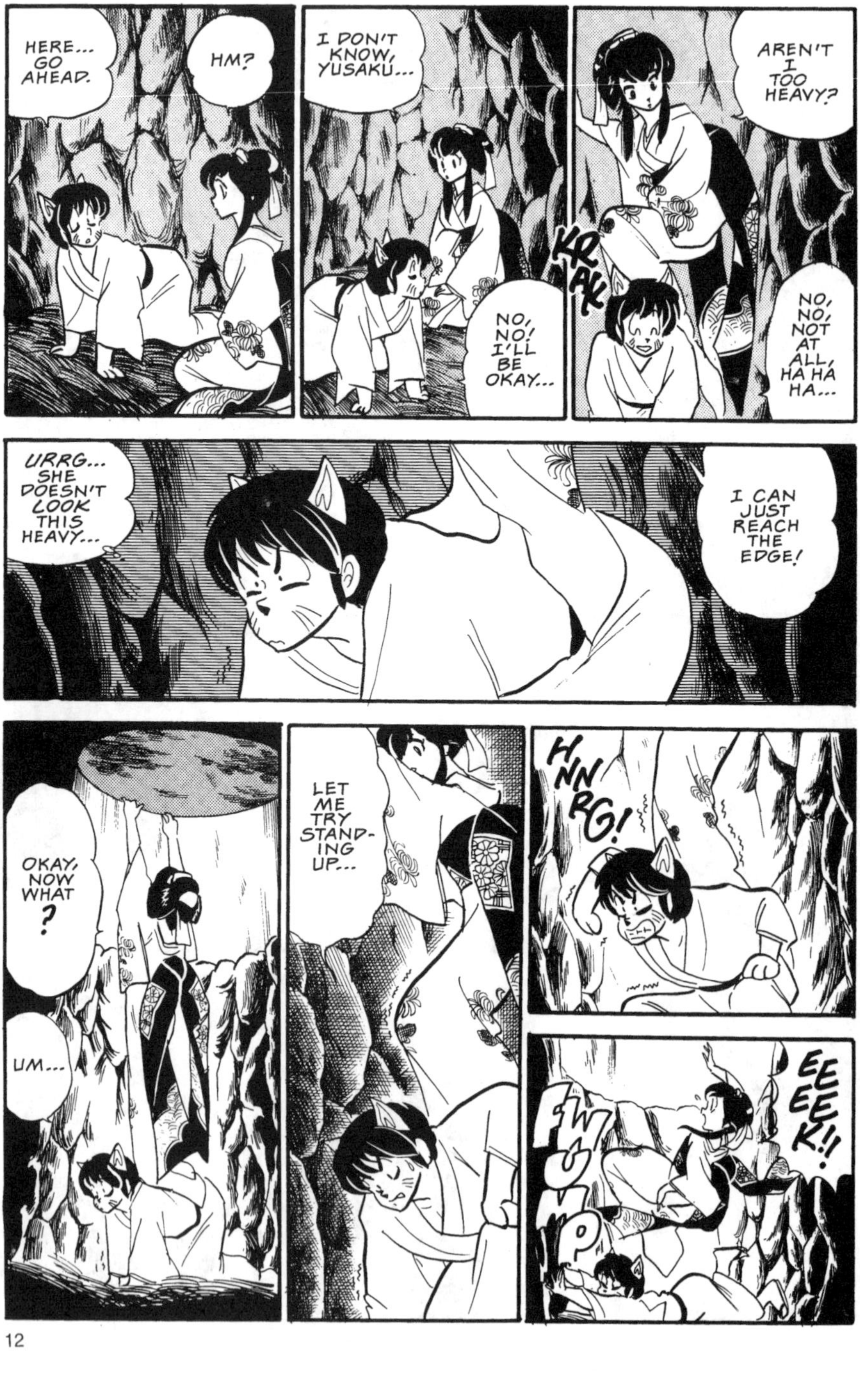

HERE... GO AHEAD.
HM?
I DON'T KNOW, YUSAKU...
NO, NO! I'LL BE OKAY...
AREN'T I TOO HEAVY?
KRAKK
NO, NO, NOT AT ALL, HA HA HA...
URRG... SHE DOESN'T LOOK THIS HEAVY...
I CAN JUST REACH THE EDGE!
OKAY, NOW WHAT?
UM...
LET ME TRY STANDING UP...
HNNRG!
FWUMP
EEEEK!!

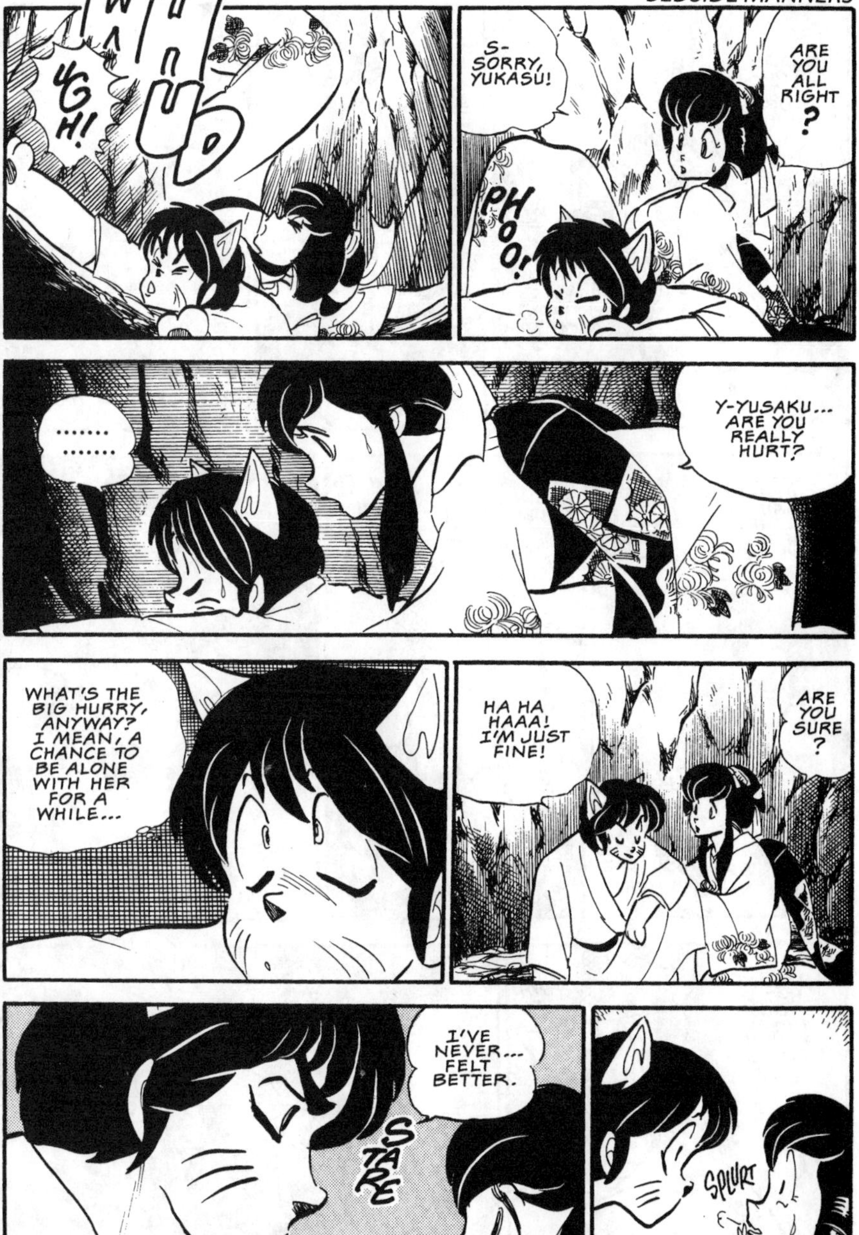
WHUD
UGH!
S-SORRY, YUKASU!
ARE YOU ALL RIGHT?
PHOO!
....
....
Y-YUSAKU... ARE YOU REALLY HURT?
WHAT'S THE BIG HURRY, ANYWAY? I MEAN, A CHANCE TO BE ALONE WITH HER FOR A WHILE...
HA HA HAAA! I'M JUST FINE!
ARE YOU SURE?
I'VE NEVER... FELT BETTER.
STARE
SPLURT

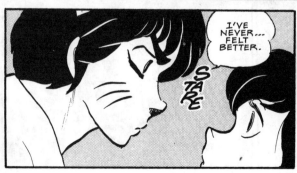

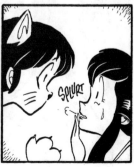

GUESS I LOOK PRETTY STUPID, HUH?

HEE HEE SNORT HEE

I...I'M SORRY, BUT...

GOOD EVENING. ENJOYING YOURSELVES?

HEY!!

THIS IS ALL YOUR FAULT, YOU--!

SHH HHH!

YUSAKU, PUT YOUR HANDS AGAINST THE SIDE OF THE WELL.

EX- CELLENT. NOW BRACE YOUR- SELF.

"BRACE MY--"?

HUH? LIKE THIS?

......

......

.....

.....

H-HEY! WHAT DO YOU THINK YOU'RE DOING-- ?!

SHH HHH!

ST RE C

OW

KI! EE

SHRRIEE

AHH!

THANK YOU FOR YOUR KIND ASSISTANCE IN FULFILLING MY DESIRES. GOODBYE.

WHAT?!..

MR. YOT-SUYA! DON'T YOU DARE--

FEAR NOT.

I SHALL RETURN WITH THE OTHERS.

THAT RAT!

WELL, AT LEAST HELP IS ON THE WAY, RIGHT?

I WONDER WHERE KYOKO'S HIDING...?

HWOOOO AIIIEEEE! MOANNNN

MR. MITAKA, OVER HERE!

SHE'S WHERE? DOWN A REAL WELL?!?

THIS WAY.

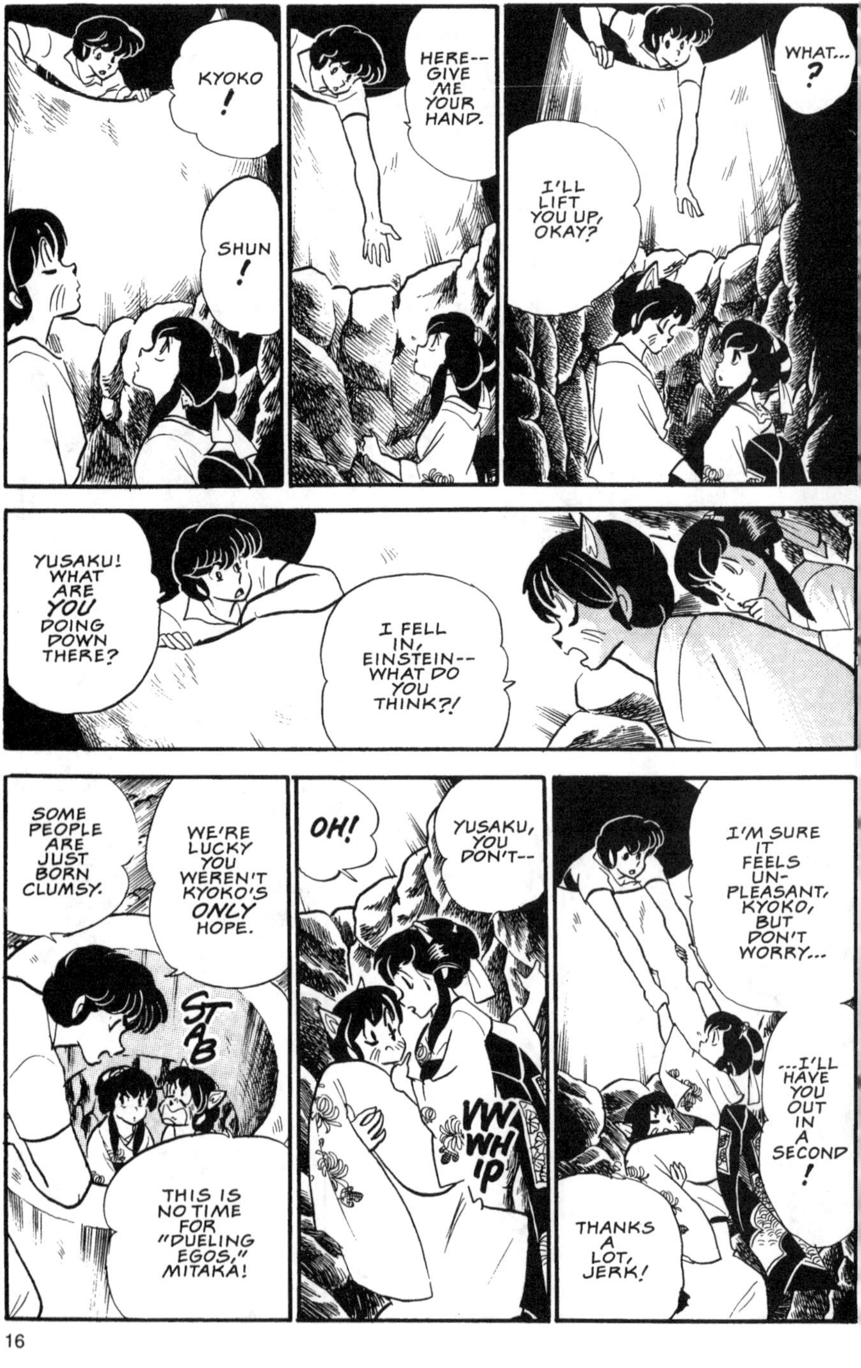
KYOKO!
SHUN!
HERE--GIVE ME YOUR HAND.
WHAT...?
I'LL LIFT YOU UP, OKAY?
YUSAKU! WHAT ARE YOU DOING DOWN THERE?
I FELL IN, EINSTEIN--WHAT DO YOU THINK?!
SOME PEOPLE ARE JUST BORN CLUMSY.
WE'RE LUCKY YOU WEREN'T KYOKO'S ONLY HOPE.
STAB
THIS IS NO TIME FOR "DUELING EGOS," MITAKA!
OH!
YUSAKU, YOU DON'T--
VWWHIP
I'M SURE IT FEELS UN-PLEASANT, KYOKO, BUT DON'T WORRY...
...I'LL HAVE YOU OUT IN A SECOND!
THANKS A LOT, JERK!

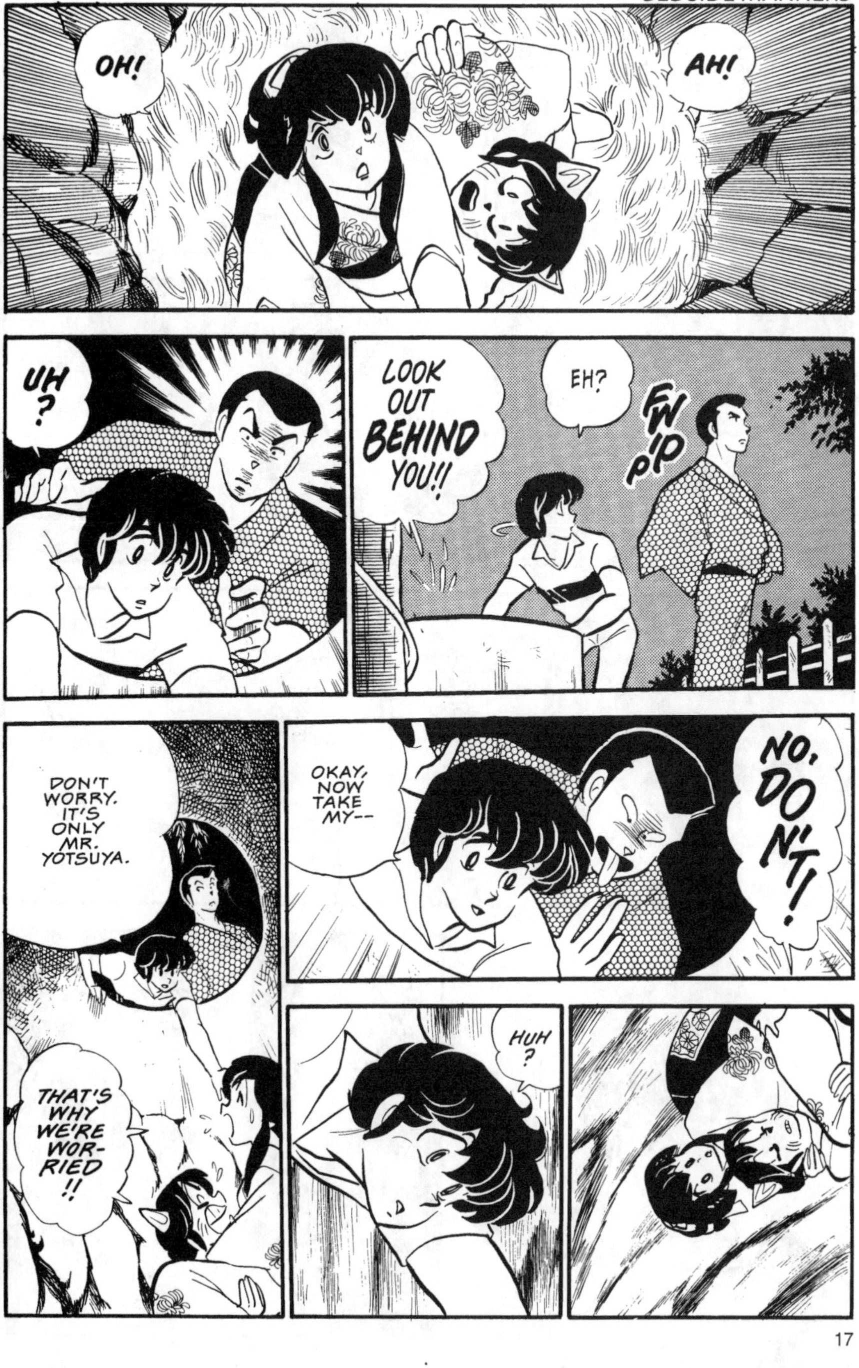
OH!
AH!
UH ?
LOOK OUT BEHIND YOU!!
EH?
FWIP
DON'T WORRY. IT'S ONLY MR. YOTSUYA.
THAT'S WHY WE'RE WOR-RIED !!
OKAY, NOW TAKE MY--
NO, DON'T!
HUH ?

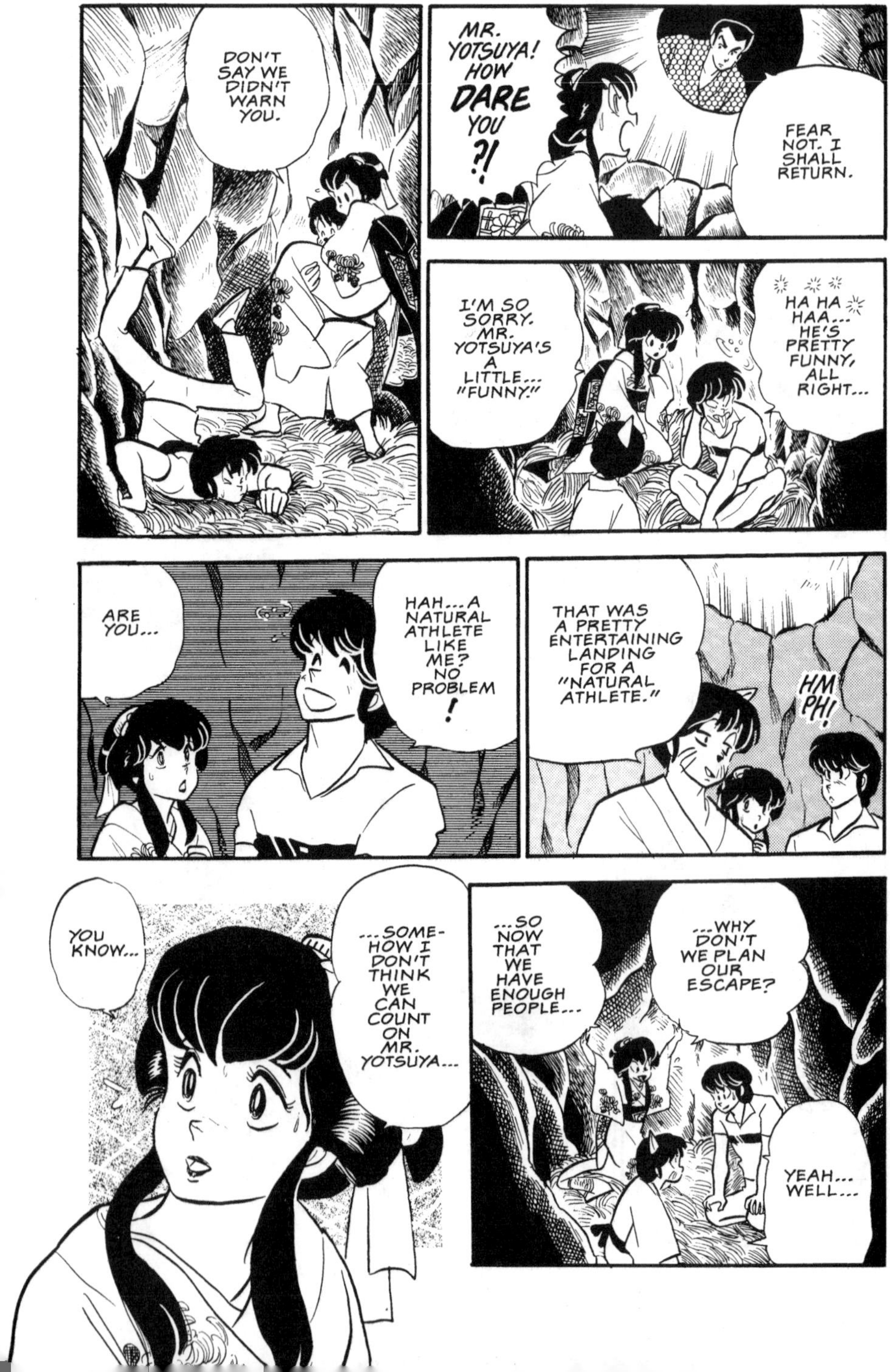
DON'T SAY WE DIDN'T WARN YOU.
MR. YOTSUYA! HOW DARE YOU ?!
FEAR NOT. I SHALL RETURN.
I'M SO SORRY. MR. YOTSUYA'S A LITTLE... "FUNNY."
HA HA HAA... HE'S PRETTY FUNNY, ALL RIGHT...
ARE YOU...
HAH... A NATURAL ATHLETE LIKE ME? NO PROBLEM !
THAT WAS A PRETTY ENTERTAINING LANDING FOR A "NATURAL ATHLETE."
HMPH!
YOU KNOW...
...SOMEHOW I DON'T THINK WE CAN COUNT ON MR. YOTSUYA...
...SO NOW THAT WE HAVE ENOUGH PEOPLE...
...WHY DON'T WE PLAN OUR ESCAPE?
YEAH... WELL...

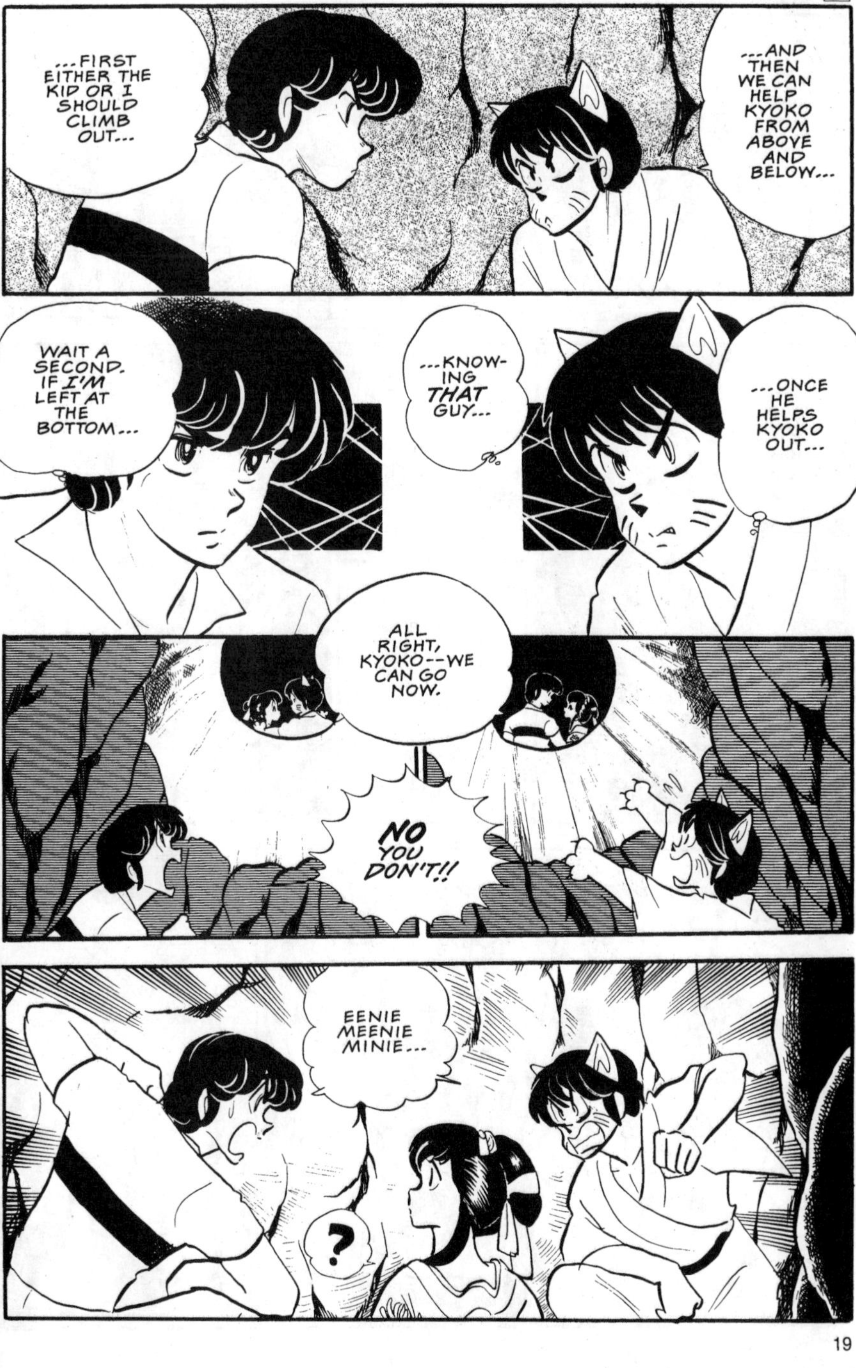
...FIRST EITHER THE KID OR I SHOULD CLIMB OUT...
...AND THEN WE CAN HELP KYOKO FROM ABOVE AND BELOW...
WAIT A SECOND. IF I'M LEFT AT THE BOTTOM...
...KNOWING THAT GUY...
...ONCE HE HELPS KYOKO OUT...
ALL RIGHT, KYOKO--WE CAN GO NOW.
NO YOU DON'T!!
EENIE MEENIE MINIE...
?

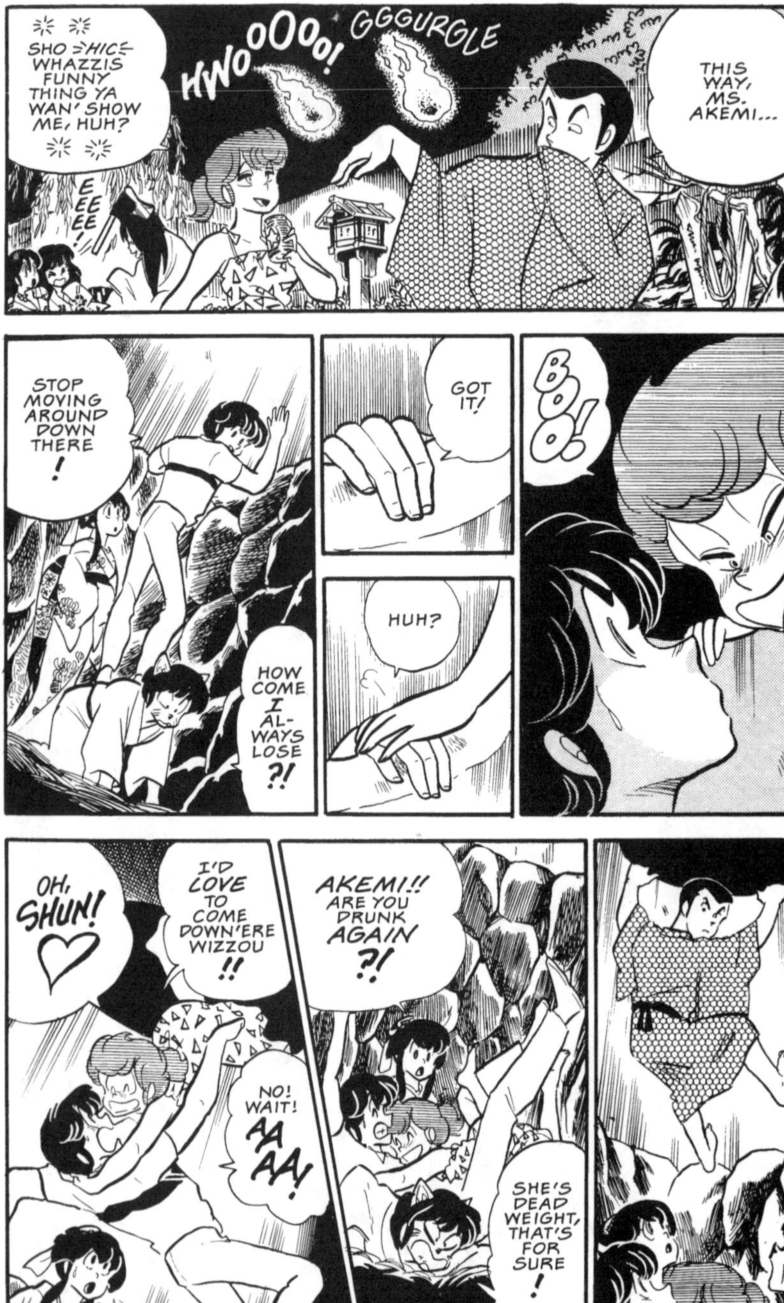
SHO =HIC= WHAZZIS FUNNY THING YA WAN' SHOW ME, HUH?
EEEEE!
HWOoOOo!
GGGURGLE
THIS WAY, MS. AKEMI...
STOP MOVING AROUND DOWN THERE!
HOW COME I ALWAYS LOSE?!
GOT IT!
HUH?
BOOO!
OH, SHUN!
I'D LOVE TO COME DOWN'ERE WIZZOU!!
NO! WAIT! AAAA!
AKEMI!! ARE YOU DRUNK AGAIN?!
SHE'S DEAD WEIGHT, THAT'S FOR SURE!

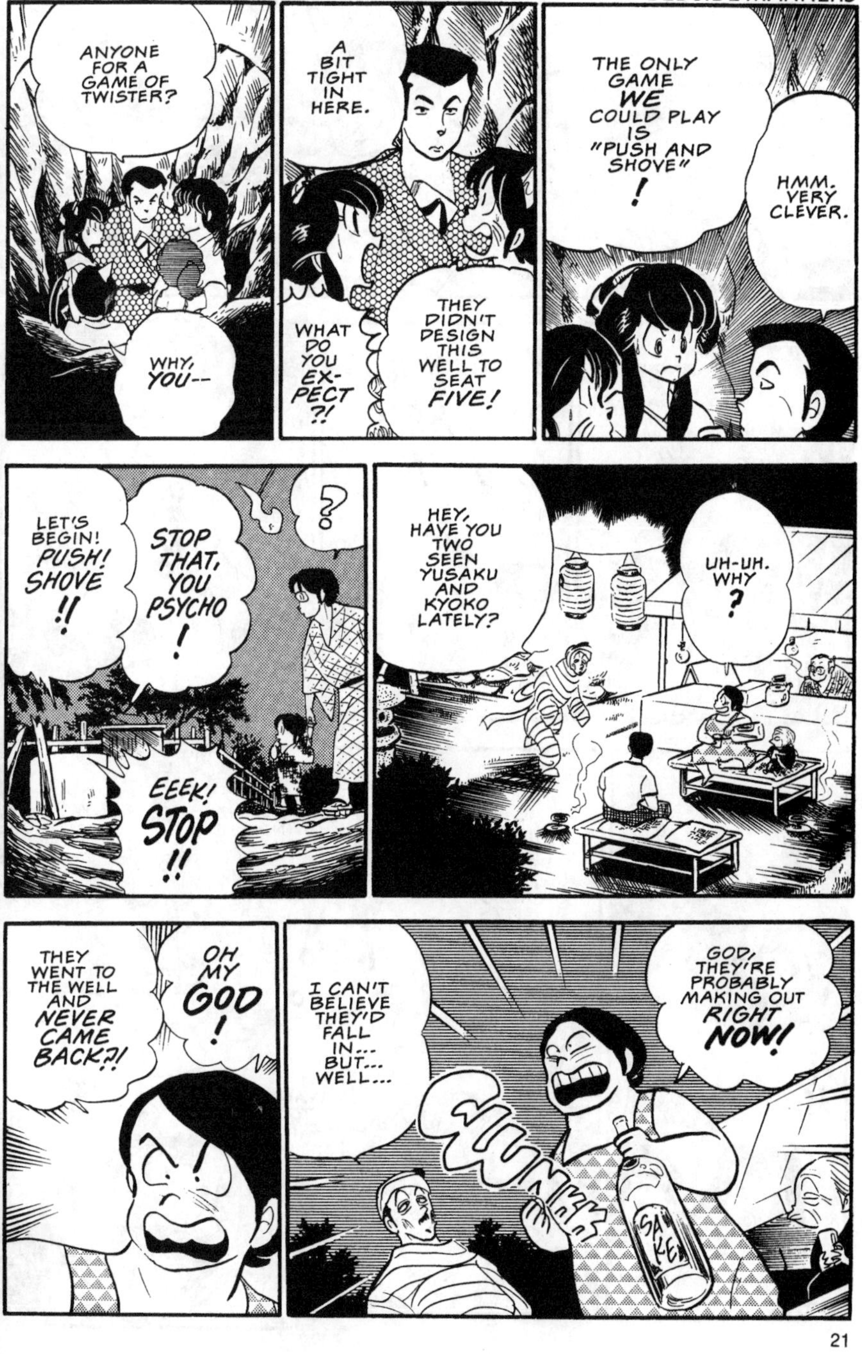
ANYONE FOR A GAME OF TWISTER?
WHY, YOU--
A BIT TIGHT IN HERE.
WHAT DO YOU EX-PECT?!
THEY DIDN'T DESIGN THIS WELL TO SEAT FIVE!
THE ONLY GAME WE COULD PLAY IS "PUSH AND SHOVE"!
HMM. VERY CLEVER.
LET'S BEGIN! PUSH! SHOVE!!
STOP THAT, YOU PSYCHO!
?
EEEK! STOP!!
HEY, HAVE YOU TWO SEEN YUSAKU AND KYOKO LATELY?
UH-UH. WHY?
THEY WENT TO THE WELL AND NEVER CAME BACK?!
OH MY GOD!
I CAN'T BELIEVE THEY'D FALL IN... BUT... WELL...
GOD, THEY'RE PROBABLY MAKING OUT RIGHT NOW!
SAKE

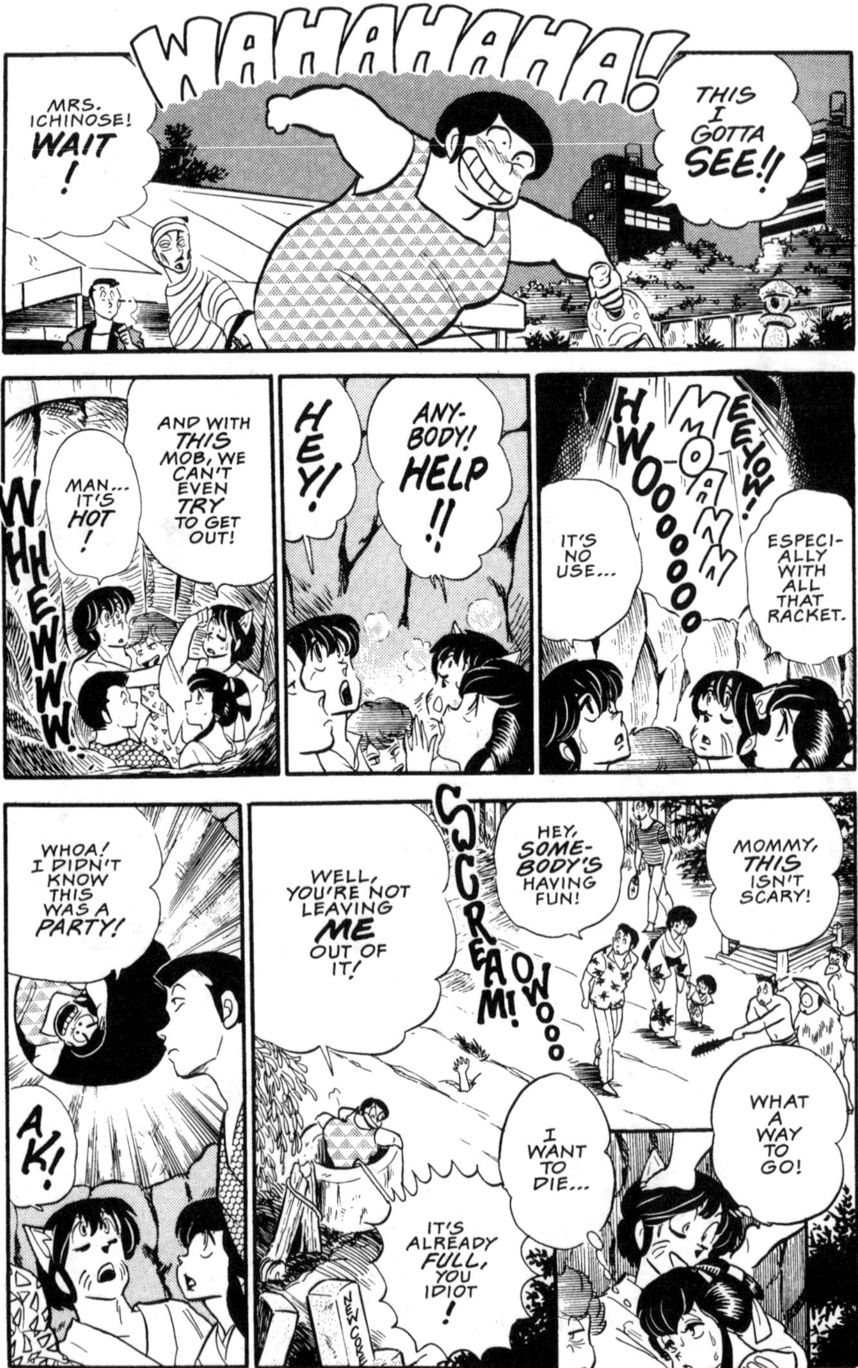
WAHAHAHAHA!
MRS. ICHINOSE! WAIT!
THIS I GOTTA SEE!!
WHHEWWWW!
MAN... IT'S HOT!
AND WITH THIS MOB, WE CAN'T EVEN TRY TO GET OUT!
HEY!
ANY-BODY! HELP!!
HWOOOOOOOO
MEEYOW!
MO-OANNN
IT'S NO USE...
ESPECI-ALLY WITH ALL THAT RACKET.
WHOA! I DIDN'T KNOW THIS WAS A PARTY!
AK!
WELL, YOU'RE NOT LEAVING ME OUT OF IT!
SCREAM!
OWOOOO
HEY, SOMEBODY'S HAVING FUN!
MOMMY, THIS ISN'T SCARY!
WHAT A WAY TO GO!
I WANT TO DIE...
IT'S ALREADY FULL, YOU IDIOT!
NEW COKE

PART TWO

PRUNE-FACED CUPID

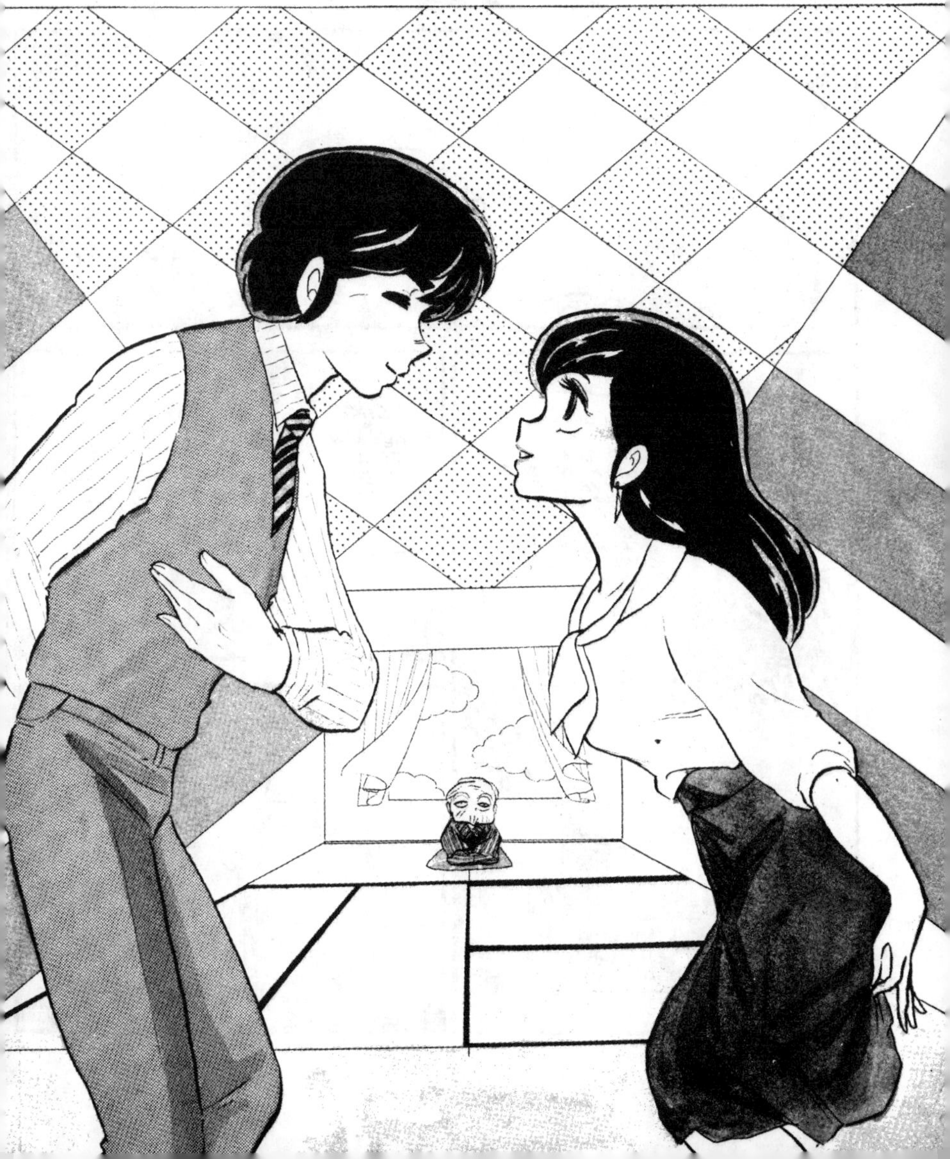

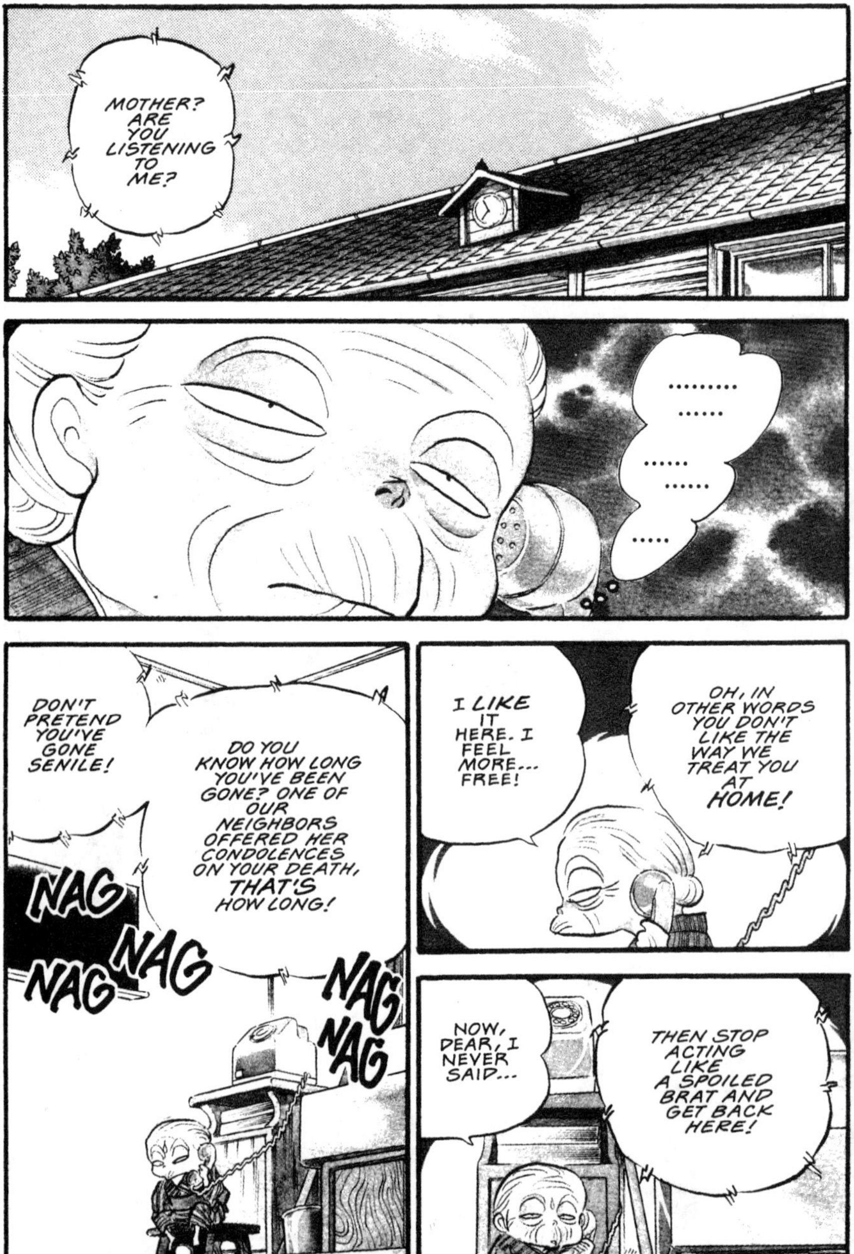
MOTHER? ARE YOU LISTENING TO ME?
....
....
.....
DON'T PRETEND YOU'VE GONE SENILE!
DO YOU KNOW HOW LONG YOU'VE BEEN GONE? ONE OF OUR NEIGHBORS OFFERED HER CONDOLENCES ON YOUR DEATH, THAT'S HOW LONG!
NAG
NAG NAG
NAG NAG
I LIKE IT HERE. I FEEL MORE... FREE!
OH, IN OTHER WORDS YOU DON'T LIKE THE WAY WE TREAT YOU AT HOME!
NOW, DEAR, I NEVER SAID...
THEN STOP ACTING LIKE A SPOILED BRAT AND GET BACK HERE!

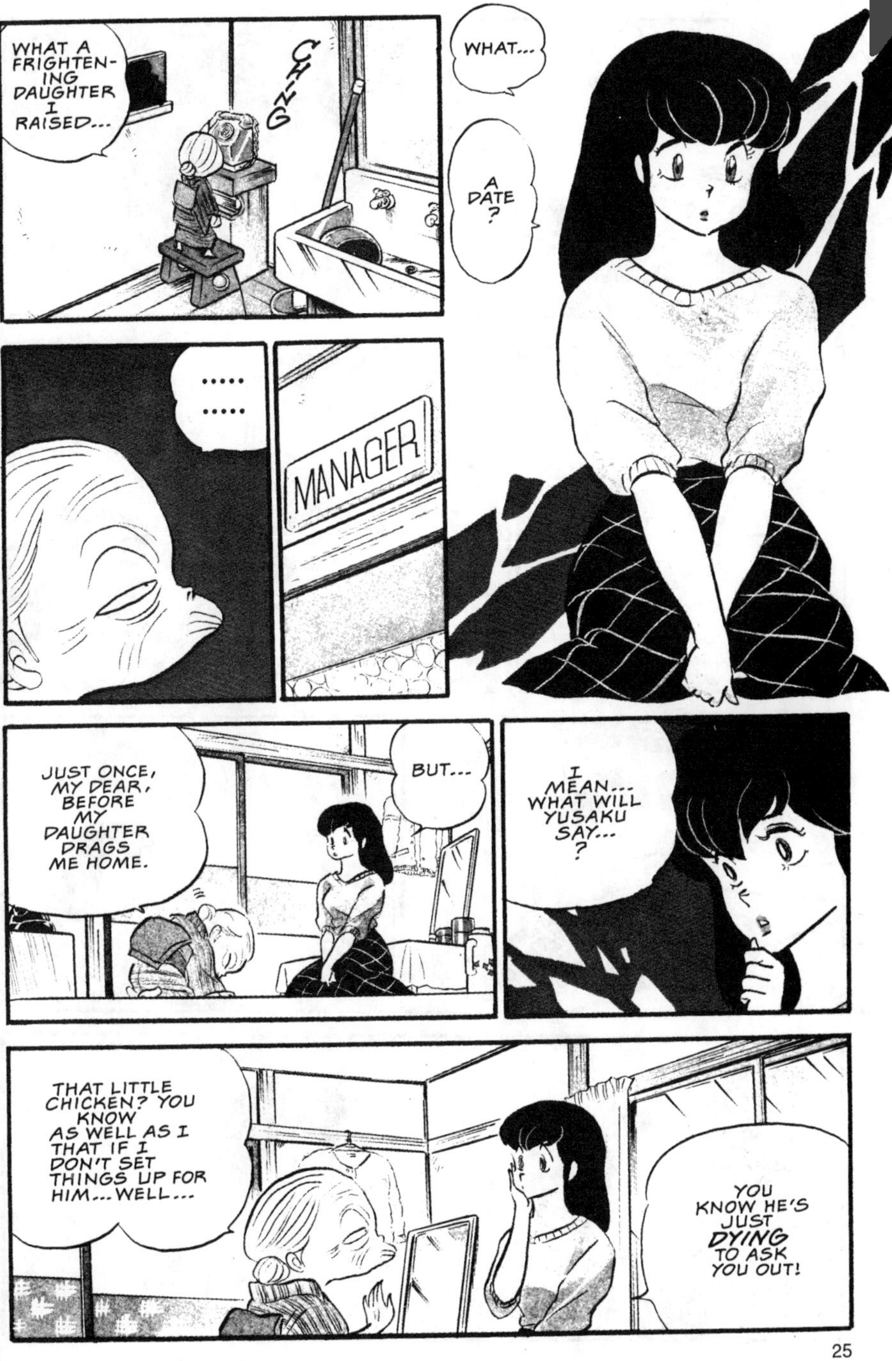
WHAT A FRIGHTENING DAUGHTER I RAISED...
CHING
WHAT...
A DATE?
......
......
MANAGER
JUST ONCE, MY DEAR, BEFORE MY DAUGHTER DRAGS ME HOME.
BUT...
I MEAN... WHAT WILL YUSAKU SAY...?
THAT LITTLE CHICKEN? YOU KNOW AS WELL AS I THAT IF I DON'T SET THINGS UP FOR HIM... WELL...
YOU KNOW HE'S JUST *DYING* TO ASK YOU OUT!

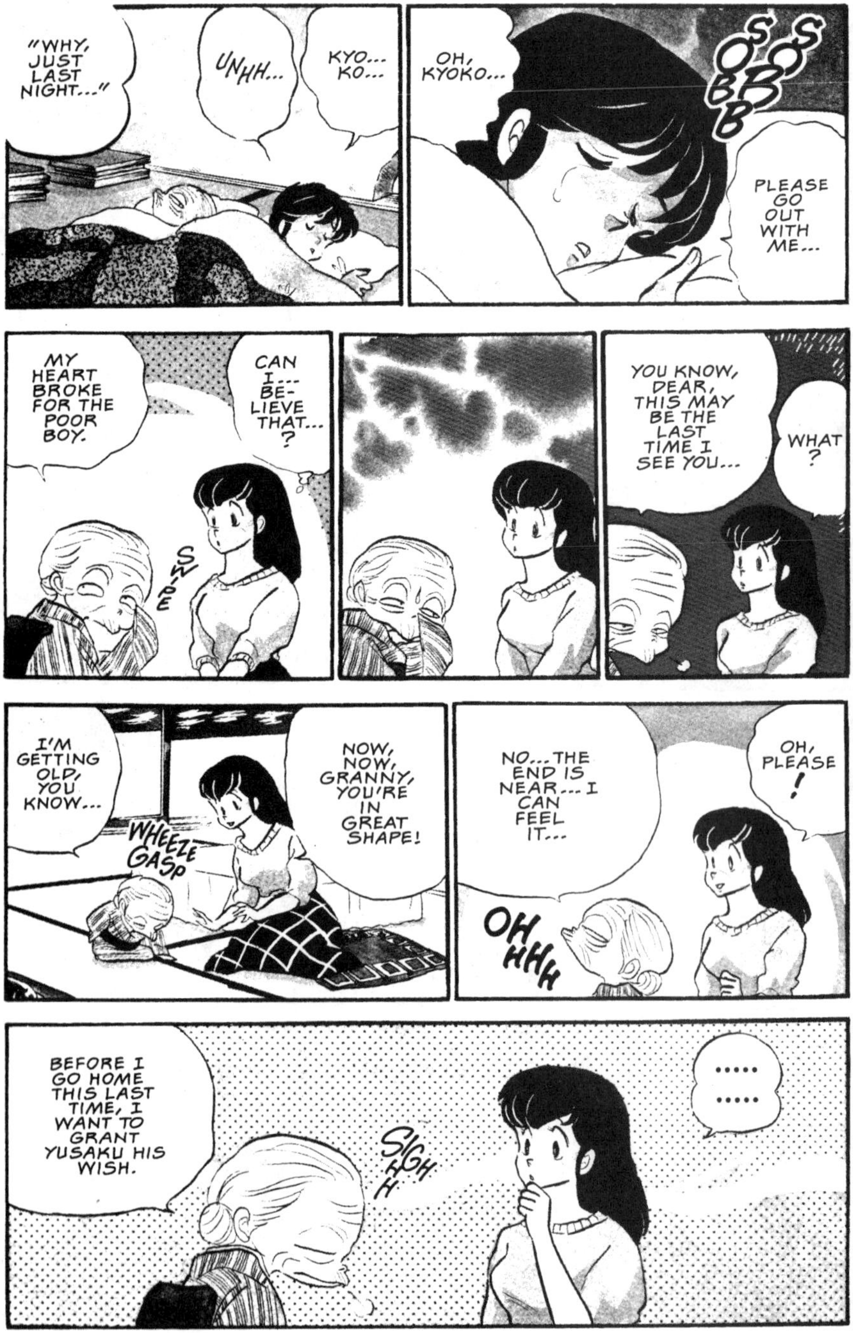
"WHY, JUST LAST NIGHT..."
UNHH...
KYO... KO...
OH, KYOKO...
SOB SOB
PLEASE GO OUT WITH ME...
MY HEART BROKE FOR THE POOR BOY.
CAN I... BE-LIEVE THAT...?
SWIPE
YOU KNOW, DEAR, THIS MAY BE THE LAST TIME I SEE YOU...
WHAT?
I'M GETTING OLD, YOU KNOW...
WHEEZE GASP
NOW, NOW, GRANNY, YOU'RE IN GREAT SHAPE!
NO...THE END IS NEAR... I CAN FEEL IT...
OH, PLEASE!
OHHHH
BEFORE I GO HOME THIS LAST TIME, I WANT TO GRANT YUSAKU HIS WISH.
SIGHHH
......
......

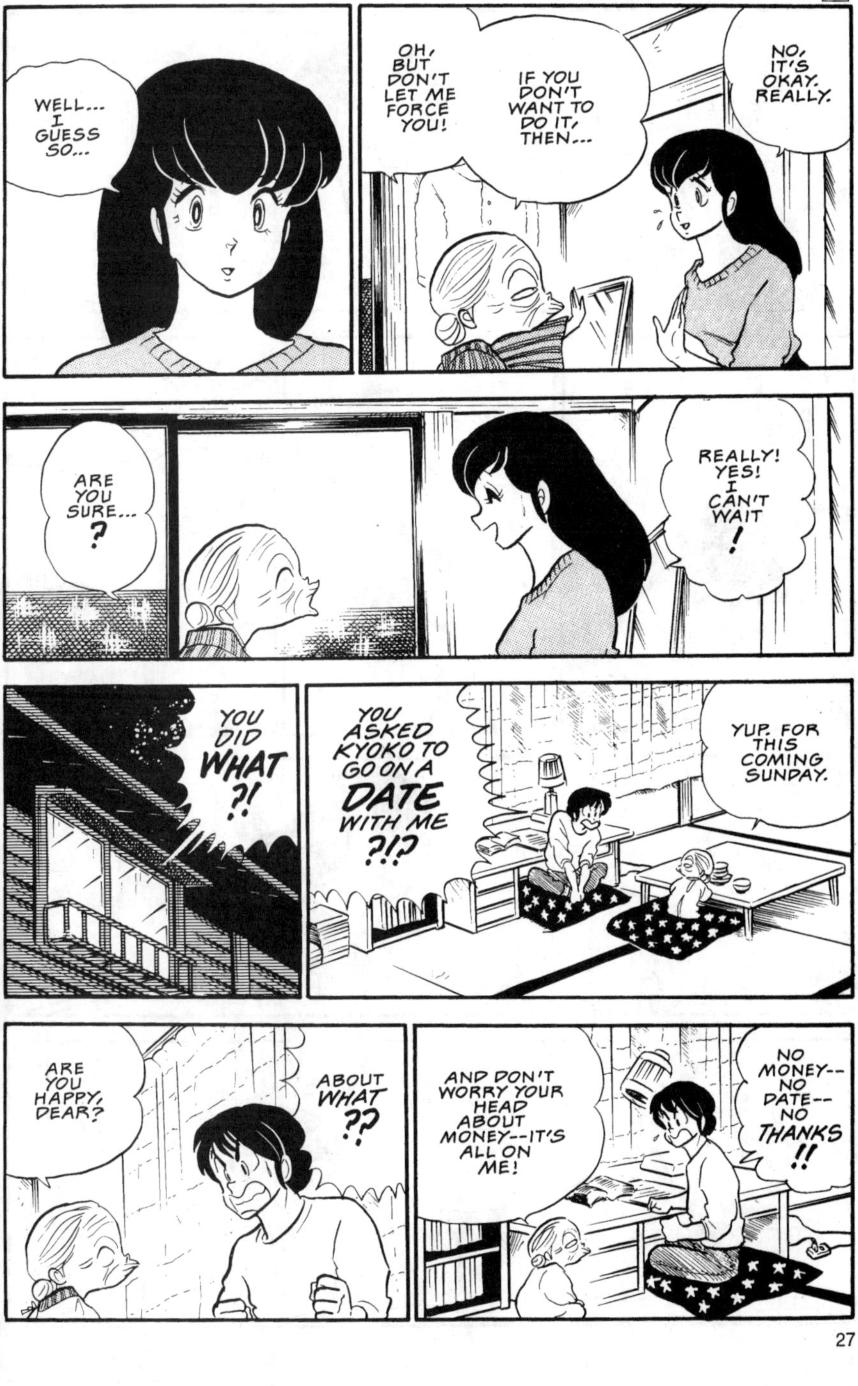
WELL... I GUESS SO...
OH, BUT DON'T LET ME FORCE YOU!
IF YOU DON'T WANT TO DO IT, THEN...
NO, IT'S OKAY. REALLY.
ARE YOU SURE...?
REALLY! YES! I CAN'T WAIT!
YOU DID WHAT?!
YOU ASKED KYOKO TO GO ON A DATE WITH ME?!?
YUP. FOR THIS COMING SUNDAY.
ARE YOU HAPPY, DEAR?
ABOUT WHAT??
AND DON'T WORRY YOUR HEAD ABOUT MONEY--IT'S ALL ON ME!
NO MONEY--NO DATE--NO THANKS!!

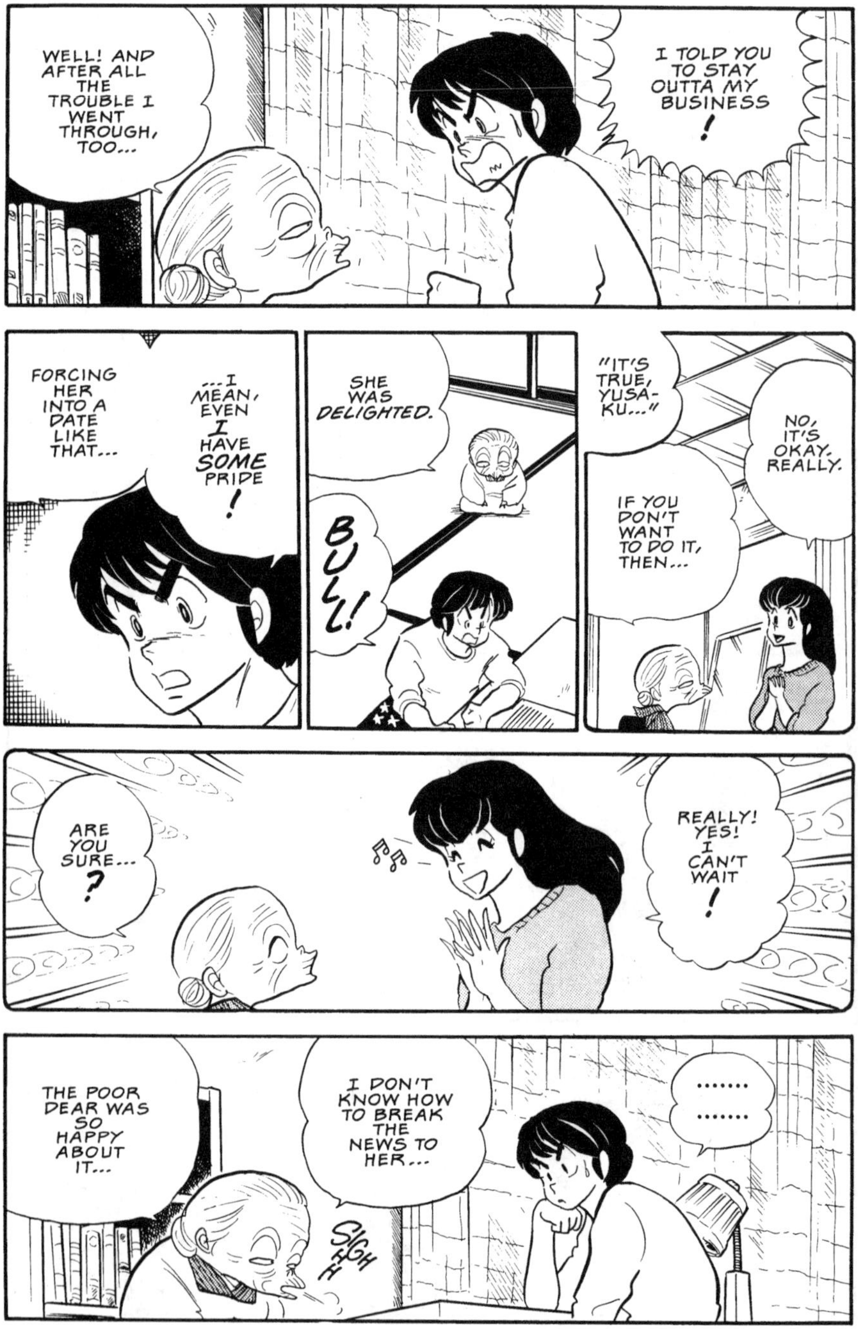
WELL! AND AFTER ALL THE TROUBLE I WENT THROUGH, TOO...
I TOLD YOU TO STAY OUTTA MY BUSINESS!
FORCING HER INTO A DATE LIKE THAT...
...I MEAN, EVEN I HAVE SOME PRIDE!
SHE WAS DELIGHTED.
BULL!
"IT'S TRUE, YUSAKU..."
NO, IT'S OKAY. REALLY.
IF YOU DON'T WANT TO DO IT, THEN...
ARE YOU SURE...?
REALLY! YES! I CAN'T WAIT!
THE POOR DEAR WAS SO HAPPY ABOUT IT...
I DON'T KNOW HOW TO BREAK THE NEWS TO HER...
SIGHHH
....
....

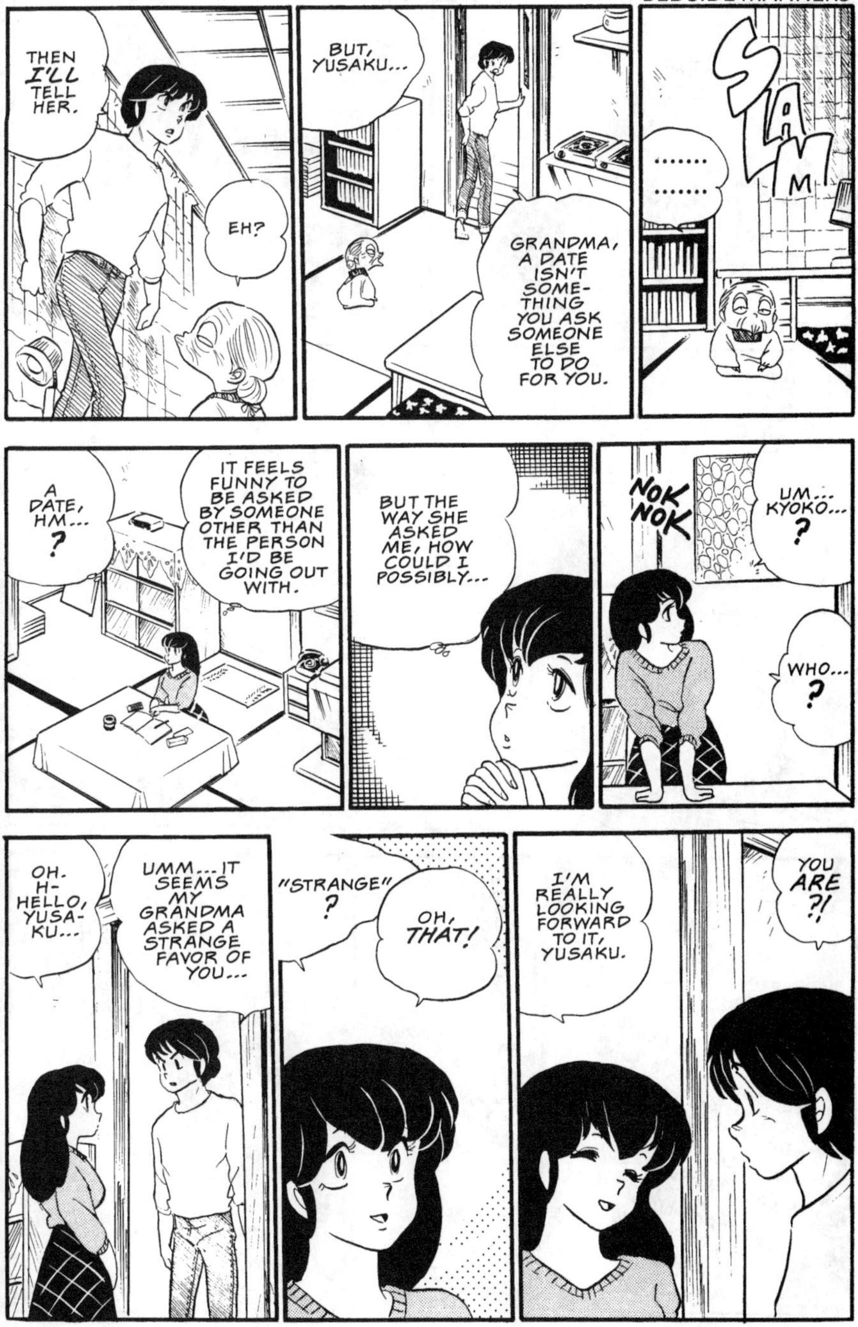
THEN I'LL TELL HER.
EH?
BUT, YUSAKU...
GRANDMA, A DATE ISN'T SOME-THING YOU ASK SOMEONE ELSE TO DO FOR YOU.
SLAMM
....
....
A DATE, HM...?
IT FEELS FUNNY TO BE ASKED BY SOMEONE OTHER THAN THE PERSON I'D BE GOING OUT WITH.
BUT THE WAY SHE ASKED ME, HOW COULD I POSSIBLY...
NOK NOK
UM... KYOKO...?
WHO...?
OH. H-HELLO, YUSAKU...
UMM... IT SEEMS MY GRANDMA ASKED A STRANGE FAVOR OF YOU...
"STRANGE"?
OH, THAT!
I'M REALLY LOOKING FORWARD TO IT, YUSAKU.
YOU ARE?!

I MEAN... SO AM I!

I WONDER WHAT I SHOULD WEAR...

HEH!

UMM... DID YOU WANT TO SAY SOMETHING?

OH, NOTHING, NOTHING! FORGET IT!

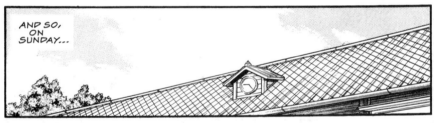

"I TOLD YOU TO STAY OUTTA MY BUSINESS," HE SAYS. BAH!

YOU ARE A LUCKY FOOL, YUSAKU GODAI.

AND SO, ON SUNDAY...

12:30 p.m. Movie Miyugi Theater—tickets in jacket pocket

2:30 p.m. Late Lunch Restaurant Kala Kala—reservations for two in name of Godai

4:00 p.m. Afternoon Tea Cafe Kul Kul

6:00 p.m. Pre-Dinner Drinks—Yukio's Dew Drop Inn

WHAT THE HECK IS THIS?!

YOUR SCHEDULE.

GIVE ME A BREAK!!

THEM'S THAT GOT THE GOLD, MAKES THE RULES! THAT'S THE GOLDEN RULE, KIDDO!

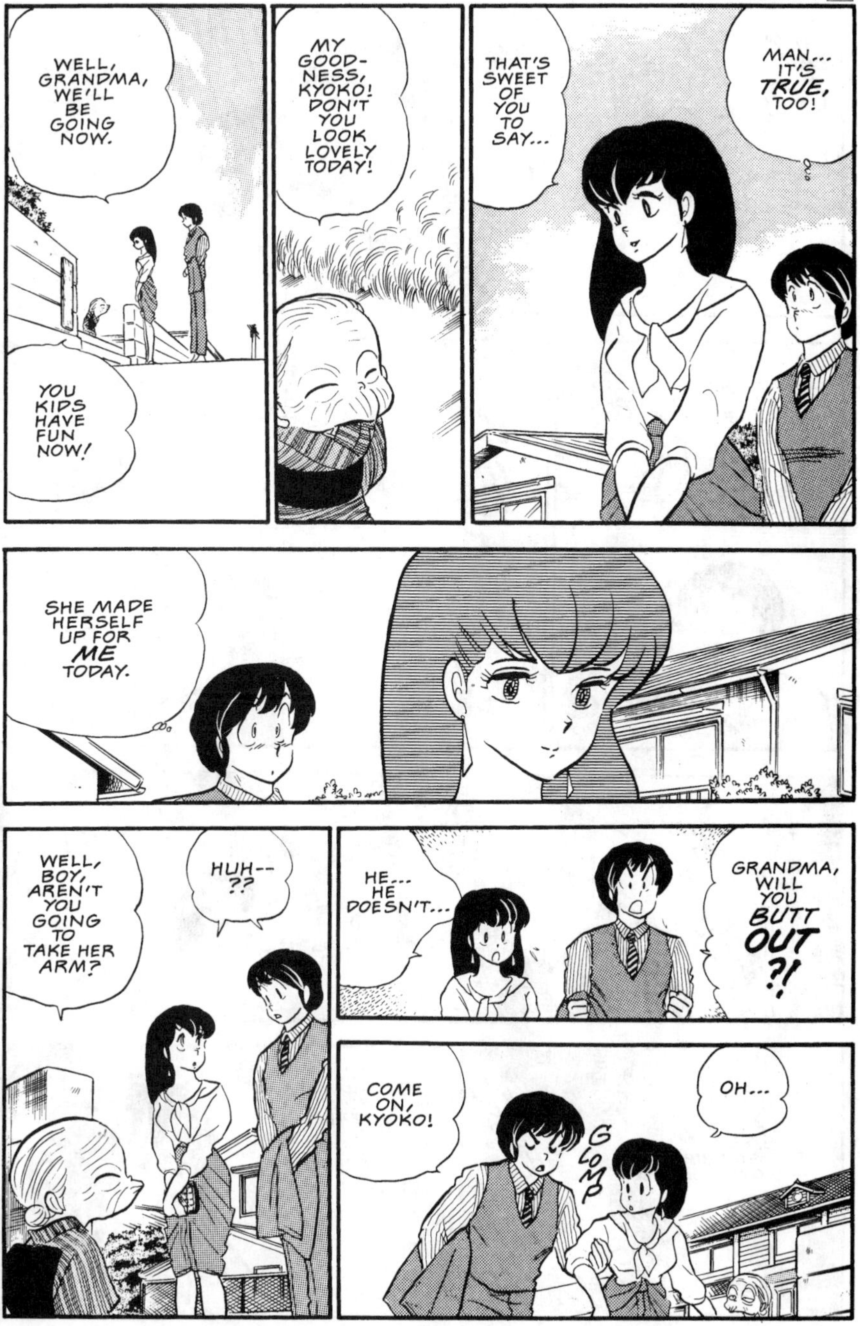
WELL, GRANDMA, WE'LL BE GOING NOW.
YOU KIDS HAVE FUN NOW!
MY GOODNESS, KYOKO! DON'T YOU LOOK LOVELY TODAY!
THAT'S SWEET OF YOU TO SAY...
MAN... IT'S TRUE, TOO!
SHE MADE HERSELF UP FOR ME TODAY.
WELL, BOY, AREN'T YOU GOING TO TAKE HER ARM?
HUH-- ??
HE... HE DOESN'T...
GRANDMA, WILL YOU BUTT OUT ?!
COME ON, KYOKO!
GLOMP
OH...

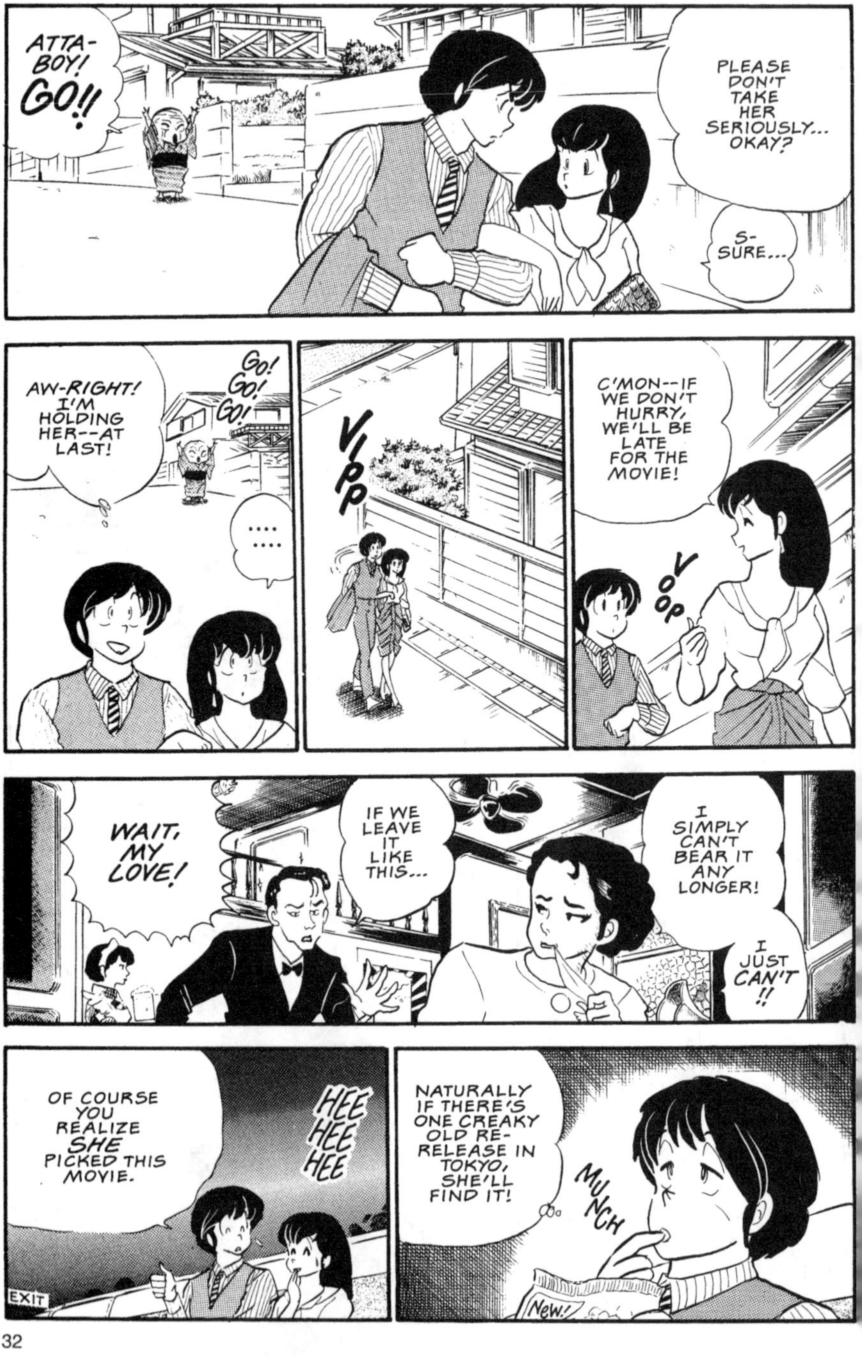
ATTA-BOY! GO!!
PLEASE DON'T TAKE HER SERIOUSLY... OKAY?
S-SURE...
AW-RIGHT! I'M HOLDING HER--AT LAST!
GO! GO! GO!
....
....
VIPP
C'MON--IF WE DON'T HURRY, WE'LL BE LATE FOR THE MOVIE!
VOOP
WAIT, MY LOVE!
IF WE LEAVE IT LIKE THIS...
I SIMPLY CAN'T BEAR IT ANY LONGER!
I JUST CAN'T!!
OF COURSE YOU REALIZE SHE PICKED THIS MOVIE.
HEE HEE HEE
EXIT
NATURALLY IF THERE'S ONE CREAKY OLD RE-RELEASE IN TOKYO, SHE'LL FIND IT!
MUNCH
NEW!

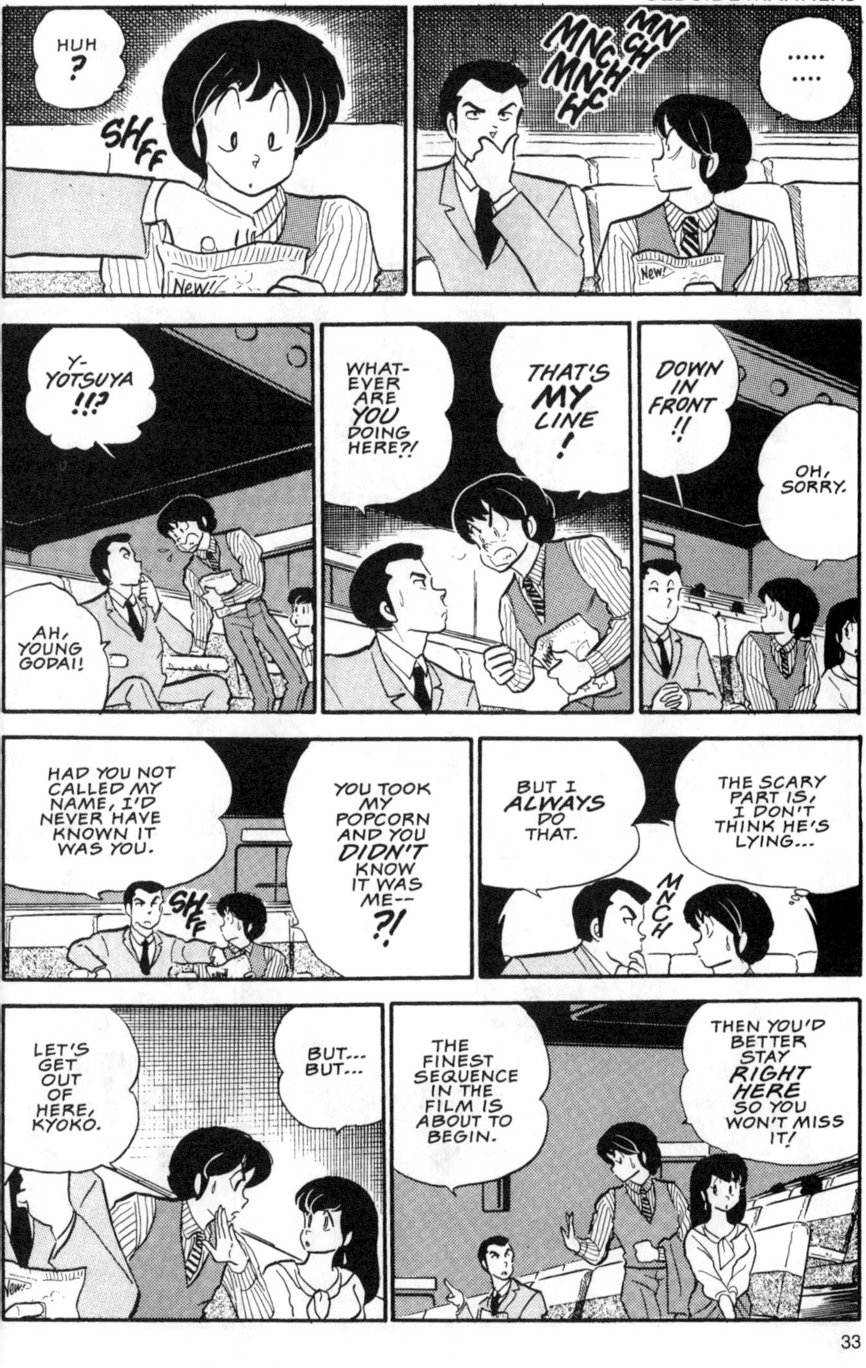
HUH ?
SHFF
MNCH MNCH MNCH MNCH
.....
....
Y-YOTSUYA !!?
AH, YOUNG GODAI!
WHATEVER ARE YOU DOING HERE?!
THAT'S MY LINE !
DOWN IN FRONT !!
OH, SORRY.
HAD YOU NOT CALLED MY NAME, I'D NEVER HAVE KNOWN IT WAS YOU.
SHFF
YOU TOOK MY POPCORN AND YOU DIDN'T KNOW IT WAS ME-- ?!
BUT I ALWAYS DO THAT.
MNCH
THE SCARY PART IS, I DON'T THINK HE'S LYING...
LET'S GET OUT OF HERE, KYOKO.
BUT... BUT...
THE FINEST SEQUENCE IN THE FILM IS ABOUT TO BEGIN.
THEN YOU'D BETTER STAY RIGHT HERE SO YOU WON'T MISS IT!

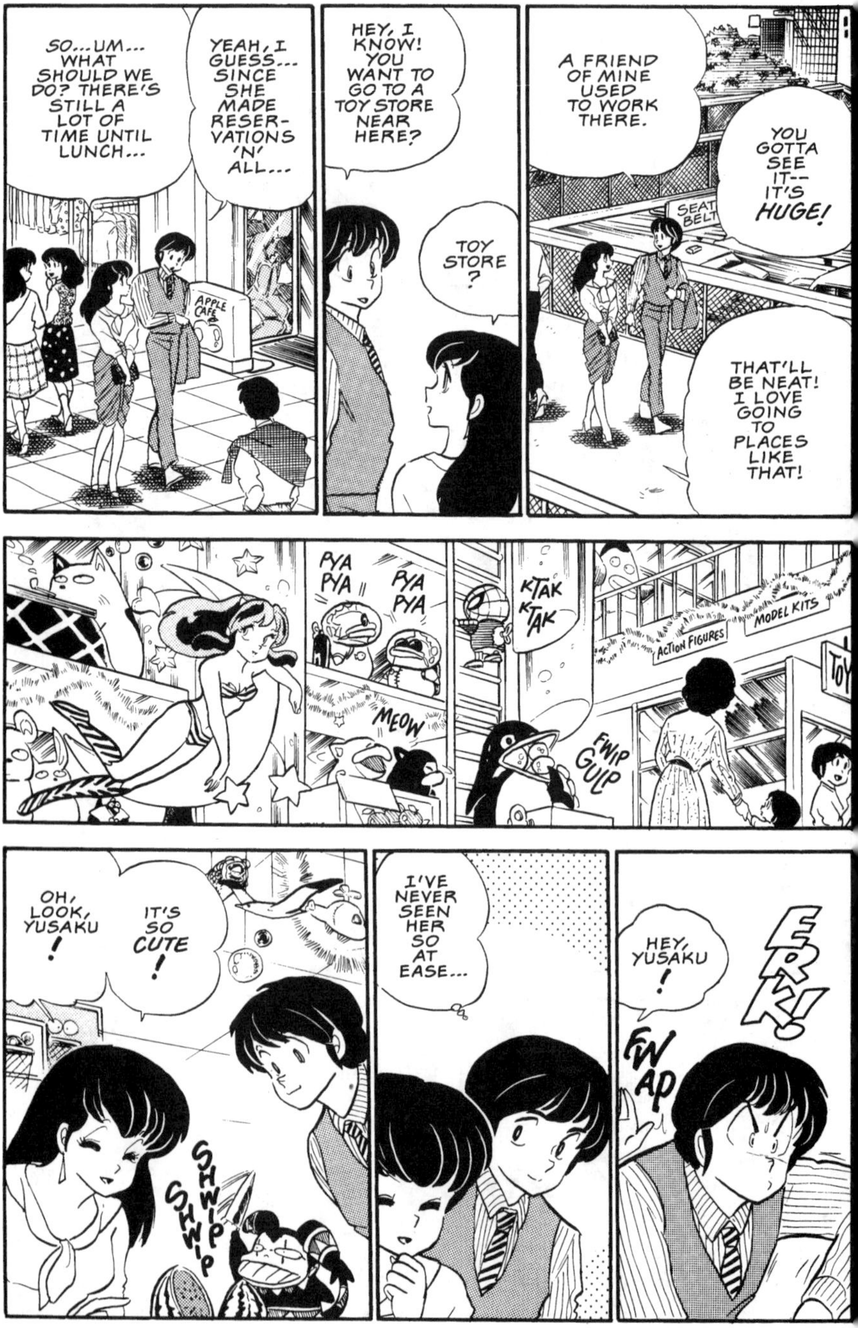
SO...UM... WHAT SHOULD WE DO? THERE'S STILL A LOT OF TIME UNTIL LUNCH...
YEAH, I GUESS... SINCE SHE MADE RESER-VATIONS 'N' ALL...
APPLE CAFE
HEY, I KNOW! YOU WANT TO GO TO A TOY STORE NEAR HERE?
TOY STORE ?
A FRIEND OF MINE USED TO WORK THERE.
YOU GOTTA SEE IT-- IT'S HUGE!
SEAT BELT
THAT'LL BE NEAT! I LOVE GOING TO PLACES LIKE THAT!
PYA PYA
PYA PYA
MEOW
KTAK KTAK
FWIP GULP
ACTION FIGURES
MODEL KITS
OH, LOOK, YUSAKU!
IT'S SO CUTE!
SHWIP SHWIP SHWIP
I'VE NEVER SEEN HER SO AT EASE...
HEY, YUSAKU!
FWAP
ERK!

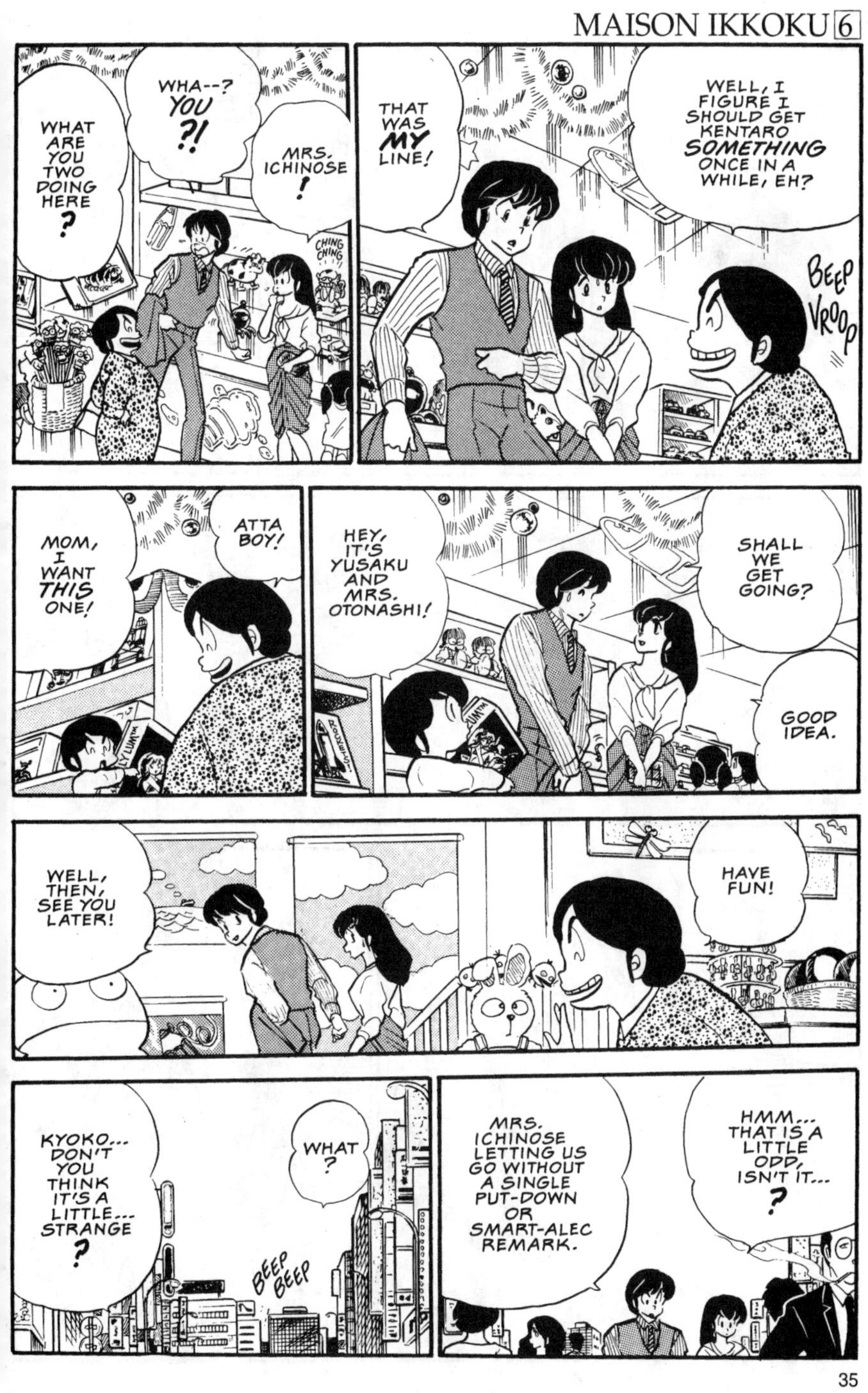
WHAT ARE YOU TWO DOING HERE?
WHA--? YOU?!
MRS. ICHINOSE!
CHING CHING
THAT WAS MY LINE!
WELL, I FIGURE I SHOULD GET KENTARO SOMETHING ONCE IN A WHILE, EH?
BEEP VROOP
MOM, I WANT THIS ONE!
ATTA BOY!
HEY, IT'S YUSAKU AND MRS. OTONASHI!
SHALL WE GET GOING?
GOOD IDEA.
WELL, THEN, SEE YOU LATER!
HAVE FUN!
KYOKO... DON'T YOU THINK IT'S A LITTLE... STRANGE?
WHAT?
BEEP BEEP
MRS. ICHINOSE LETTING US GO WITHOUT A SINGLE PUT-DOWN OR SMART-ALEC REMARK.
HMM... THAT IS A LITTLE ODD, ISN'T IT...?

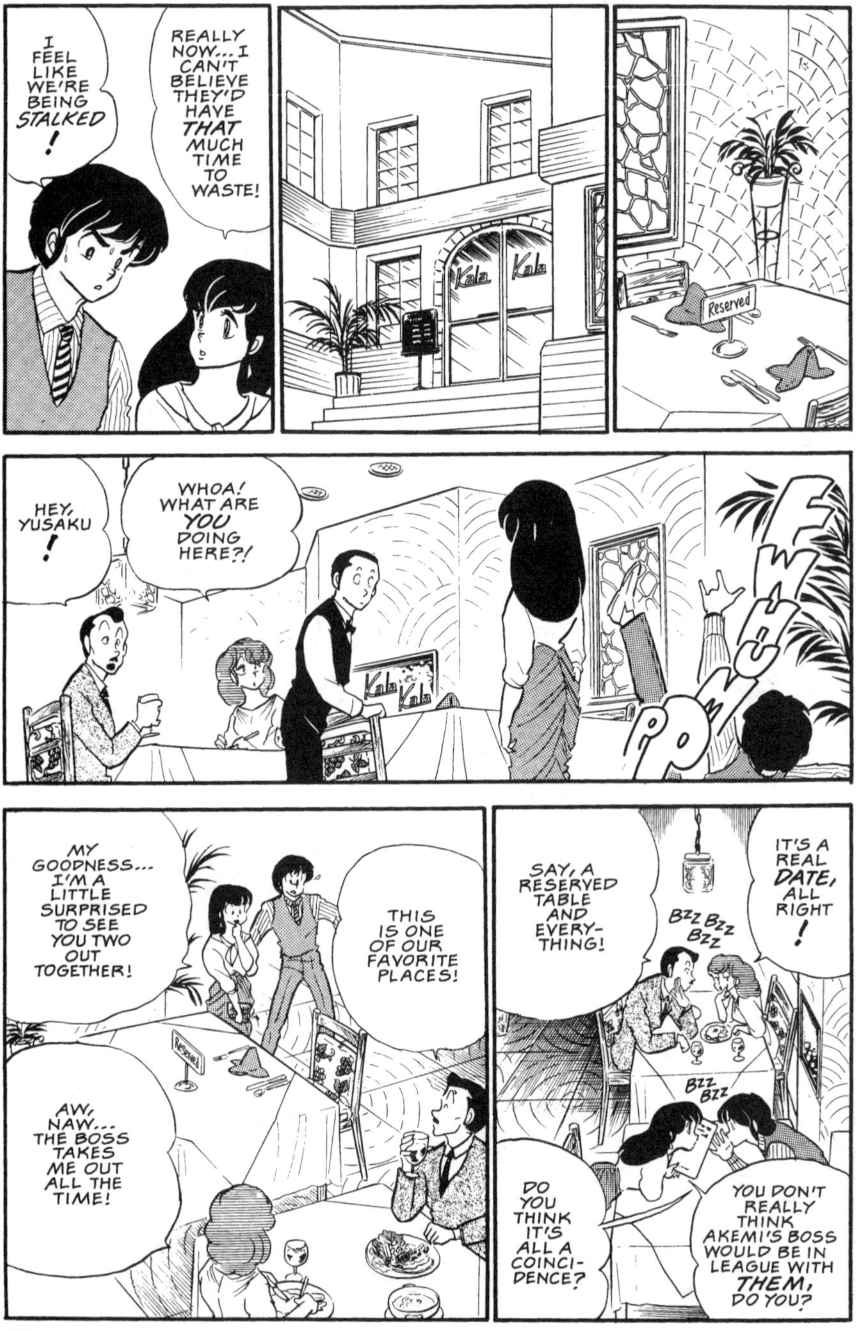
I FEEL LIKE WE'RE BEING STALKED!
REALLY NOW... I CAN'T BELIEVE THEY'D HAVE THAT MUCH TIME TO WASTE!
Kala Kala
Reserved
HEY, YUSAKU!
WHOA! WHAT ARE YOU DOING HERE?!
Kala Kala
MY GOODNESS... I'M A LITTLE SURPRISED TO SEE YOU TWO OUT TOGETHER!
THIS IS ONE OF OUR FAVORITE PLACES!
Reserved
AW, NAW... THE BOSS TAKES ME OUT ALL THE TIME!
SAY, A RESERVED TABLE AND EVERYTHING!
IT'S A REAL DATE, ALL RIGHT!
BZZ BZZ BZZ
BZZ BZZ
DO YOU THINK IT'S ALL A COINCIDENCE?
YOU DON'T REALLY THINK AKEMI'S BOSS WOULD BE IN LEAGUE WITH THEM, DO YOU?

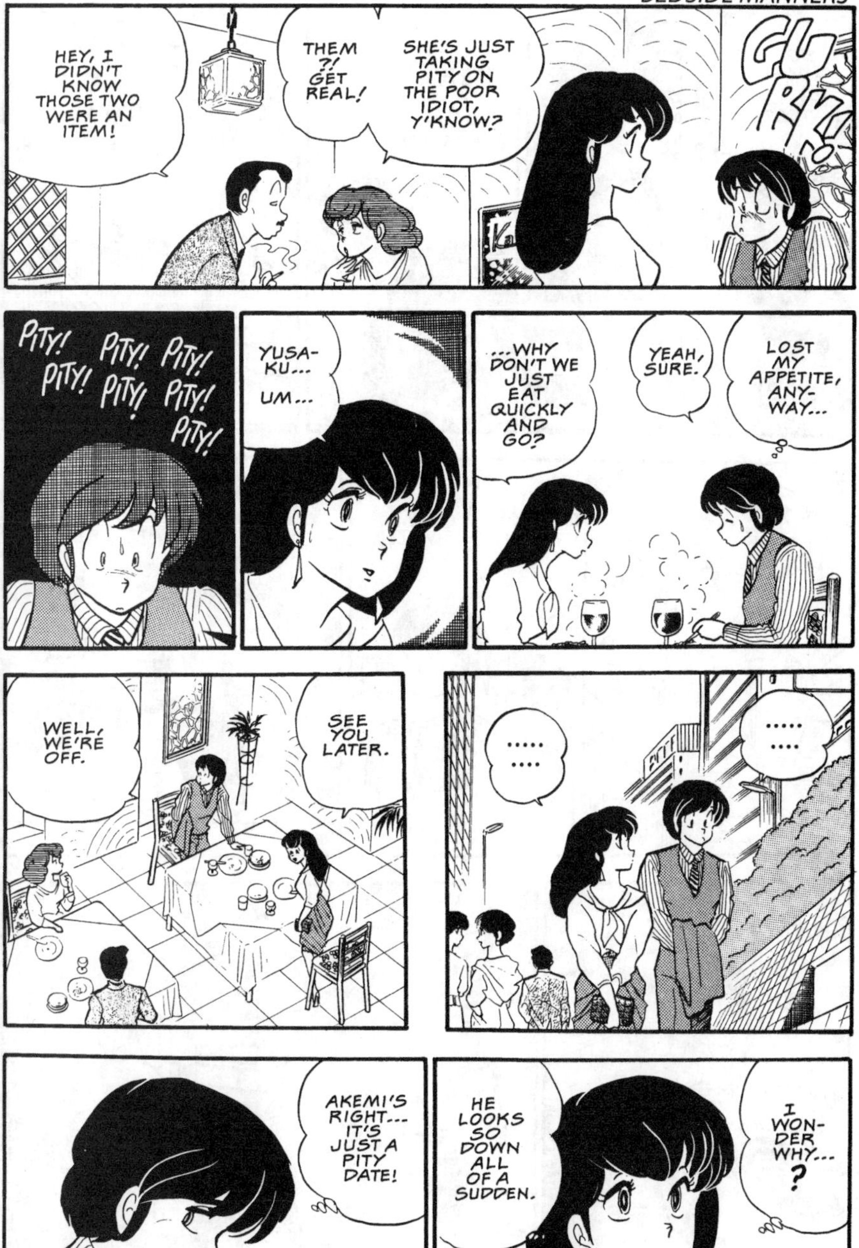
HEY, I DIDN'T KNOW THOSE TWO WERE AN ITEM!
THEM ?! GET REAL!
SHE'S JUST TAKING PITY ON THE POOR IDIOT, Y'KNOW?
GU RK!
PITY! PITY! PITY! PITY! PITY! PITY! PITY!
YUSAKU... UM...
...WHY DON'T WE JUST EAT QUICKLY AND GO?
YEAH, SURE.
LOST MY APPETITE, ANYWAY...
WELL, WE'RE OFF.
SEE YOU LATER.
....
....
AKEMI'S RIGHT... IT'S JUST A PITY DATE!
HE LOOKS SO DOWN ALL OF A SUDDEN.
I WONDER WHY...?

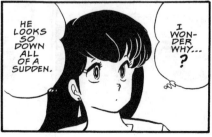

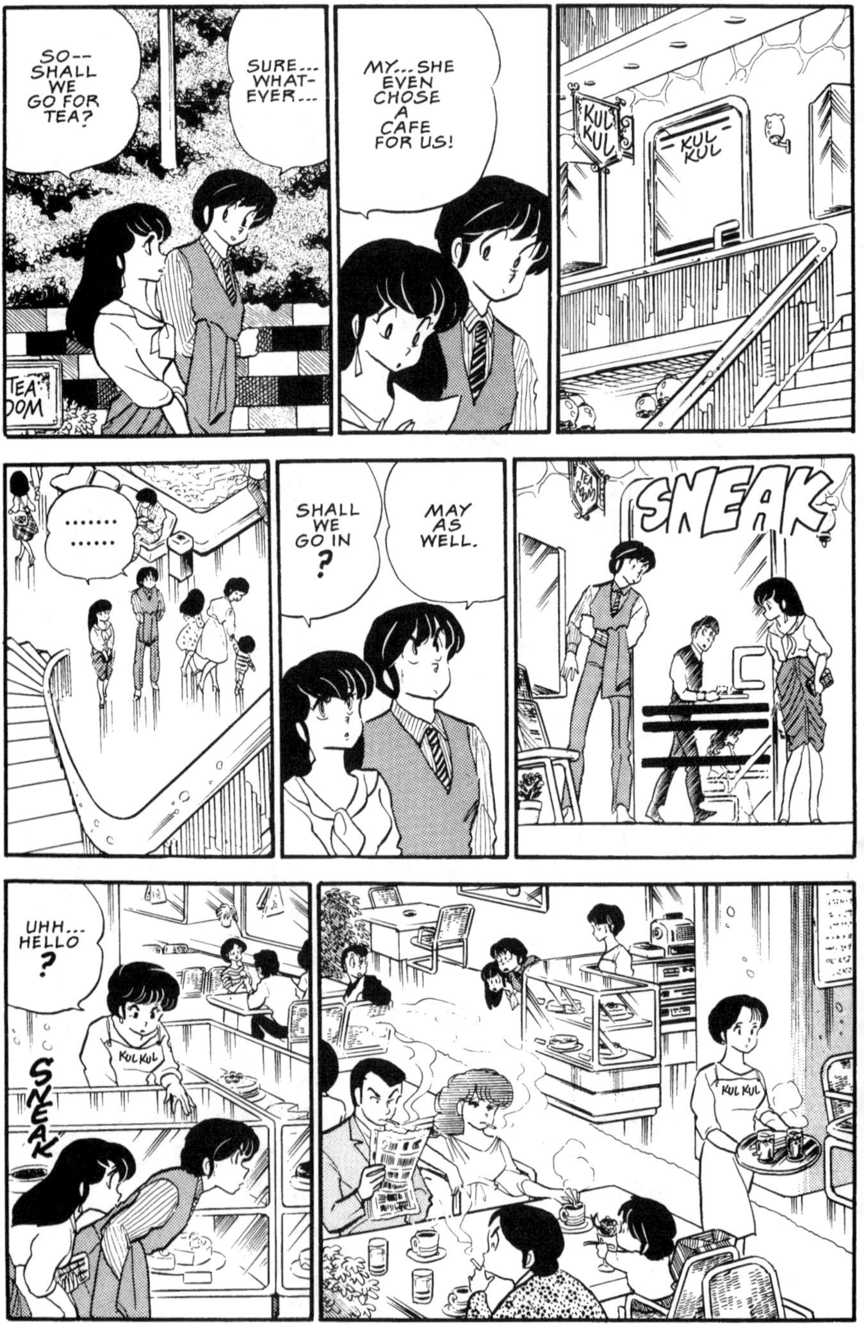
SO-- SHALL WE GO FOR TEA?
SURE... WHATEVER...
MY... SHE EVEN CHOSE A CAFE FOR US!
KUL KUL
KUL KUL
....
......
SHALL WE GO IN ?
MAY AS WELL.
SNEAK
UHH... HELLO ?
KUL KUL
SNEAK
KUL KUL

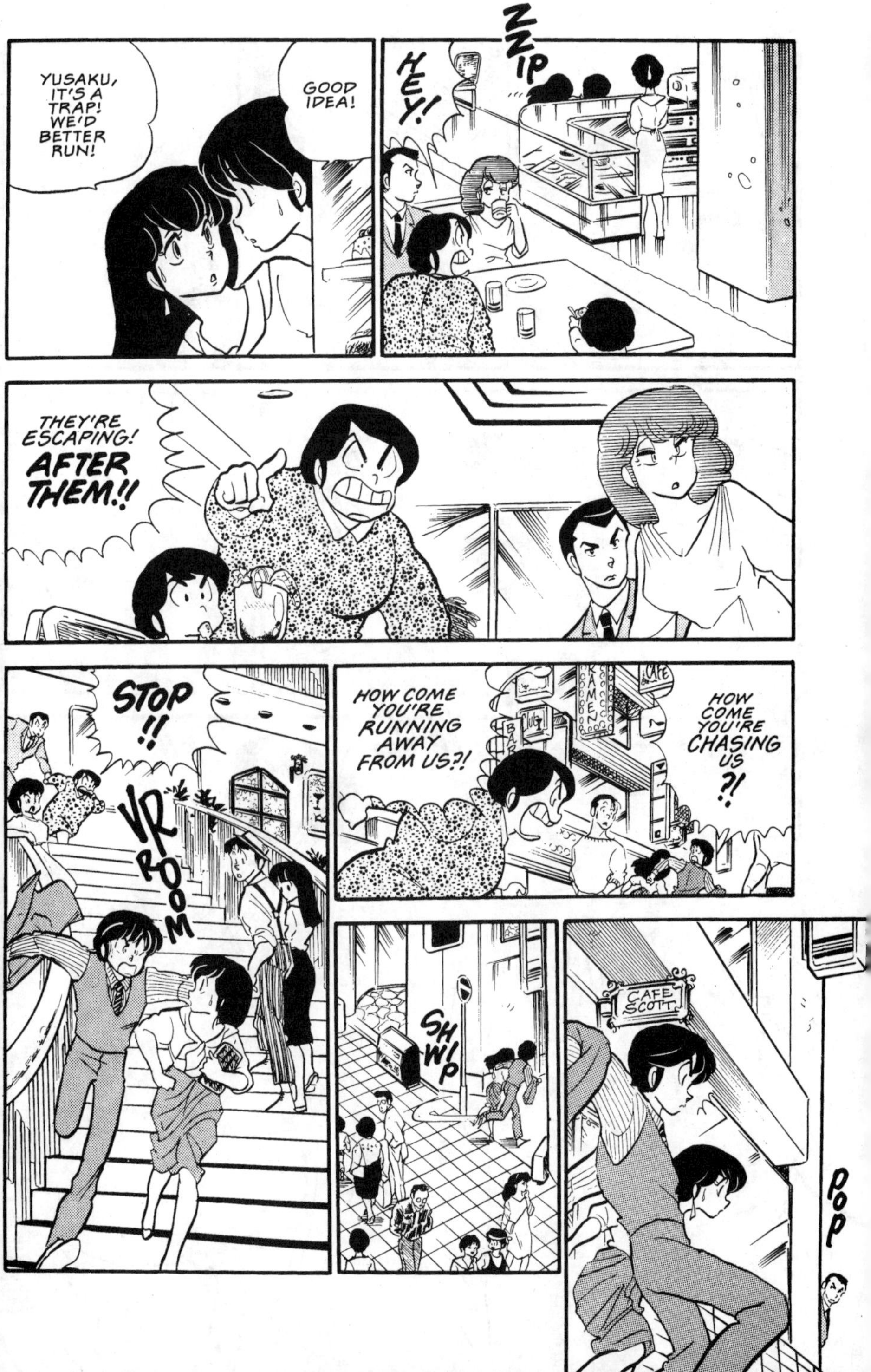
YUSAKU, IT'S A TRAP! WE'D BETTER RUN!
GOOD IDEA!
HEY!
ZZIP
THEY'RE ESCAPING! AFTER THEM!!
STOP!!
VROOOM
HOW COME YOU'RE RUNNING AWAY FROM US?!
HOW COME YOU'RE CHASING US?!
RAMEN
CAFE
BAR
SHWIP
CAFE SCOTT
POP

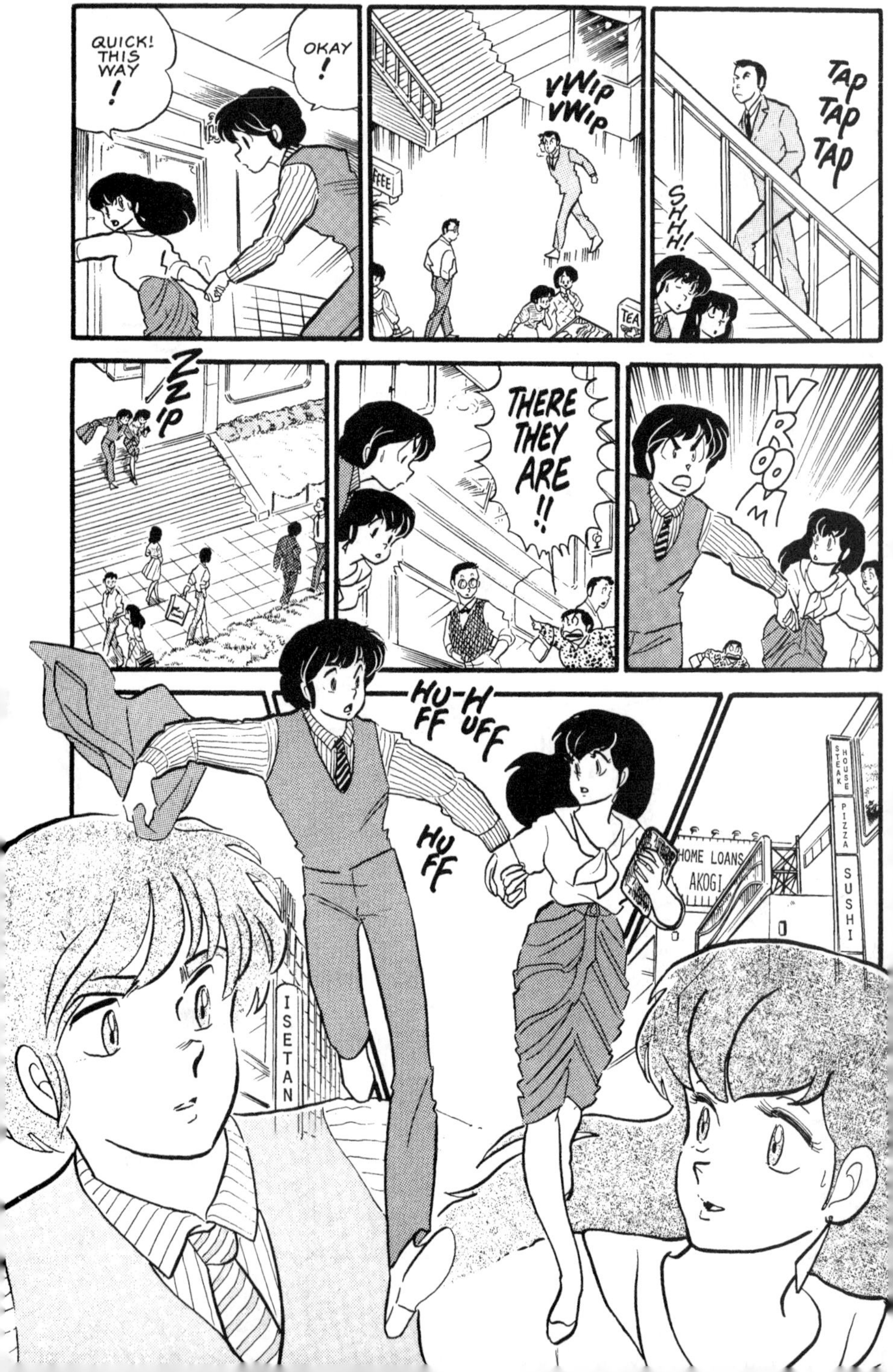
QUICK! THIS WAY!
OKAY!
VWIP VWIP
COFFEE
TEA
TAP TAP TAP
SHHH!
ZZIP
THERE THEY ARE!!
VROOM
HU-HFF UFF
HUFF
STEAK HOUSE
PIZZA
SUSHI
HOME LOANS AKOGI
ISETAN

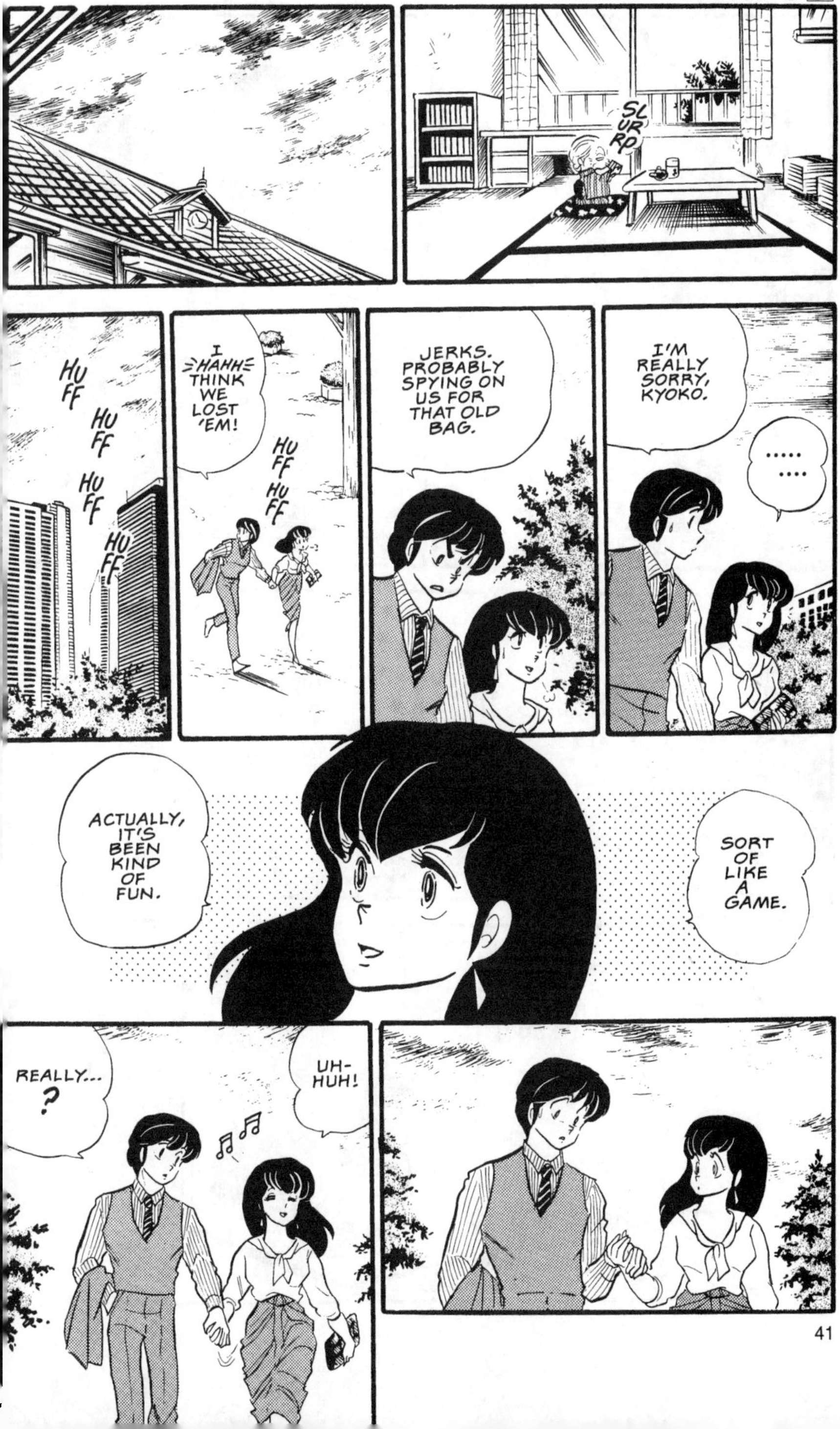
SLURP
HUFF HUFF HUFF HUFF
I =HAHH= THINK WE LOST 'EM!
HUFF HUFF
JERKS. PROBABLY SPYING ON US FOR THAT OLD BAG.
I'M REALLY SORRY, KYOKO.
....
ACTUALLY, IT'S BEEN KIND OF FUN.
SORT OF LIKE A GAME.
REALLY... ?
UH-HUH!

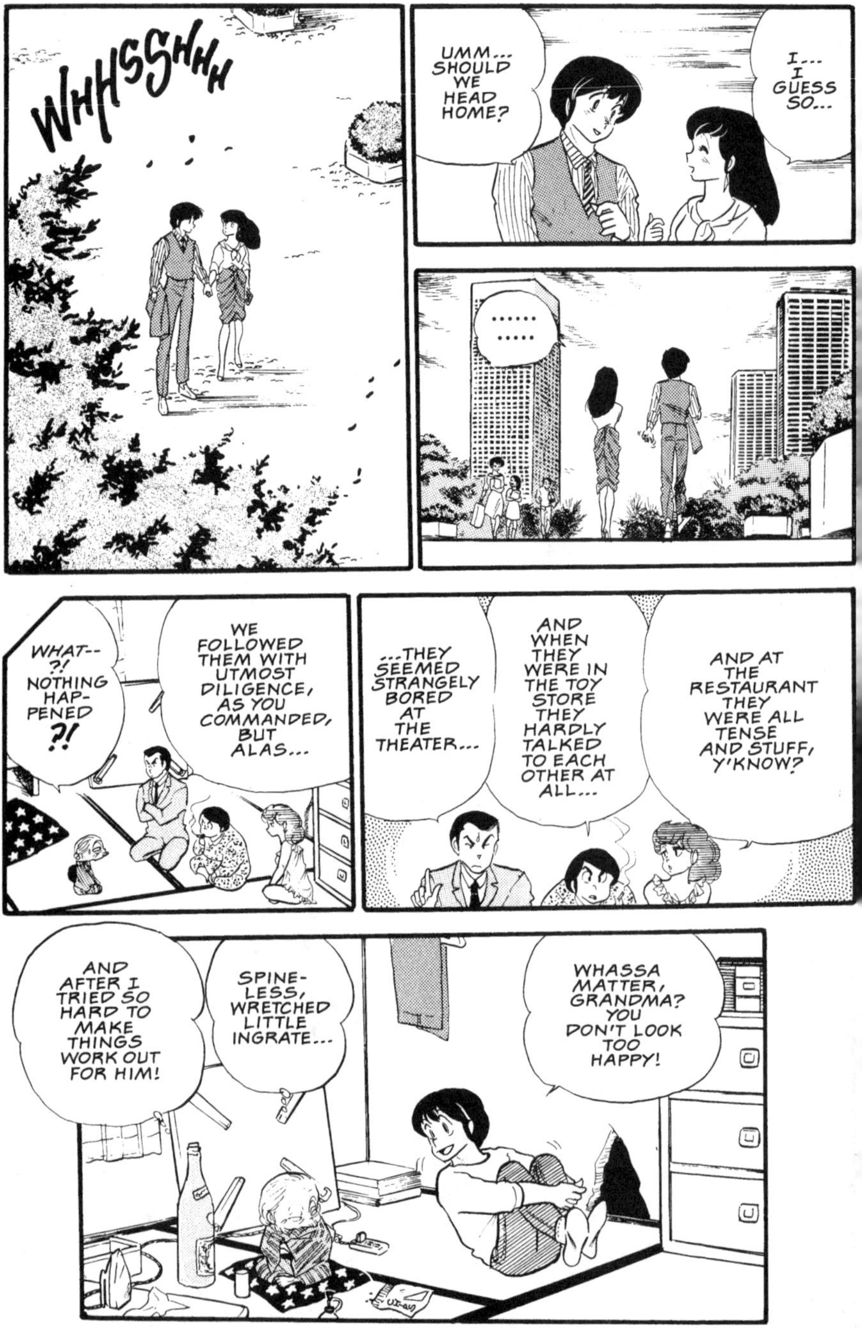
WHHSSHHH
UMM... SHOULD WE HEAD HOME?
I... I GUESS SO...
....
WHAT--?! NOTHING HAPPENED?!
WE FOLLOWED THEM WITH UTMOST DILIGENCE, AS YOU COMMANDED, BUT ALAS...
...THEY SEEMED STRANGELY BORED AT THE THEATER...
AND WHEN THEY WERE IN THE TOY STORE THEY HARDLY TALKED TO EACH OTHER AT ALL...
AND AT THE RESTAURANT THEY WERE ALL TENSE AND STUFF, Y'KNOW?
AND AFTER I TRIED SO HARD TO MAKE THINGS WORK OUT FOR HIM!
SPINELESS, WRETCHED LITTLE INGRATE...
WHASSA MATTER, GRANDMA? YOU DON'T LOOK TOO HAPPY!

PART THREE

FAREWELL ON PLATFORM 18

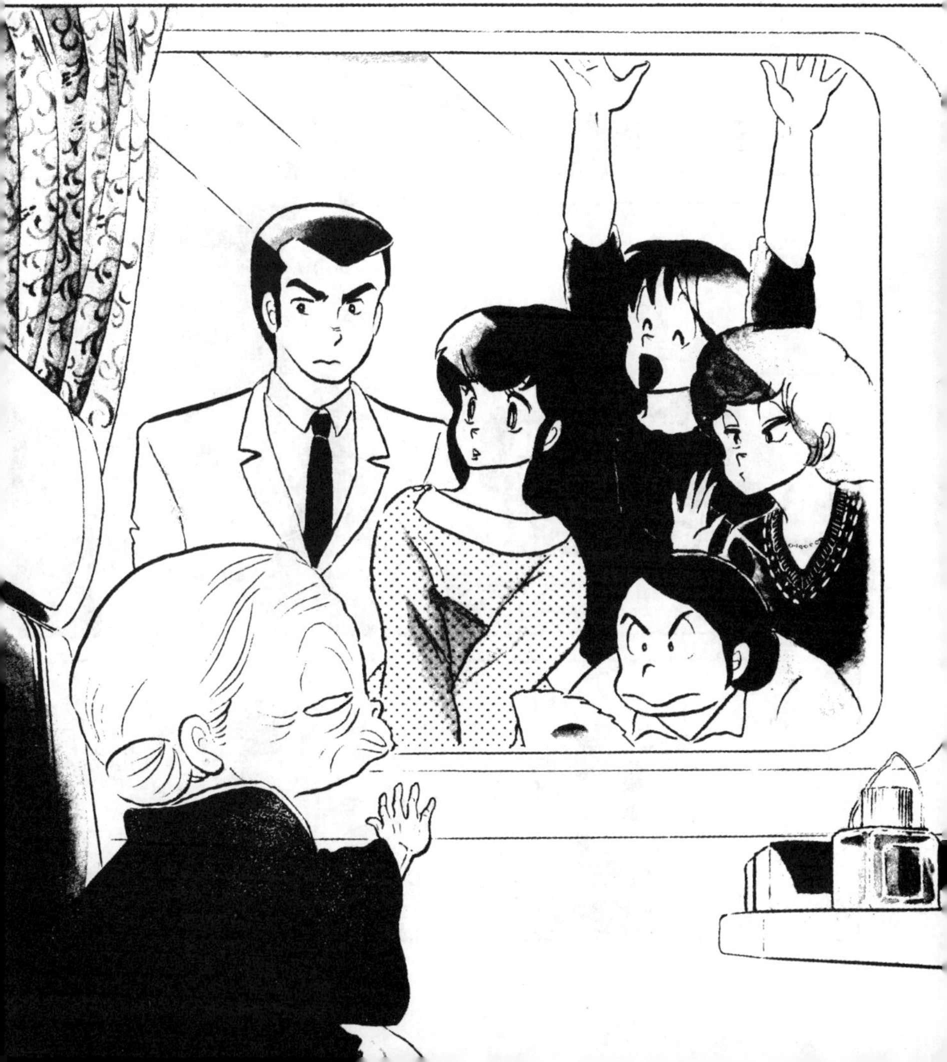

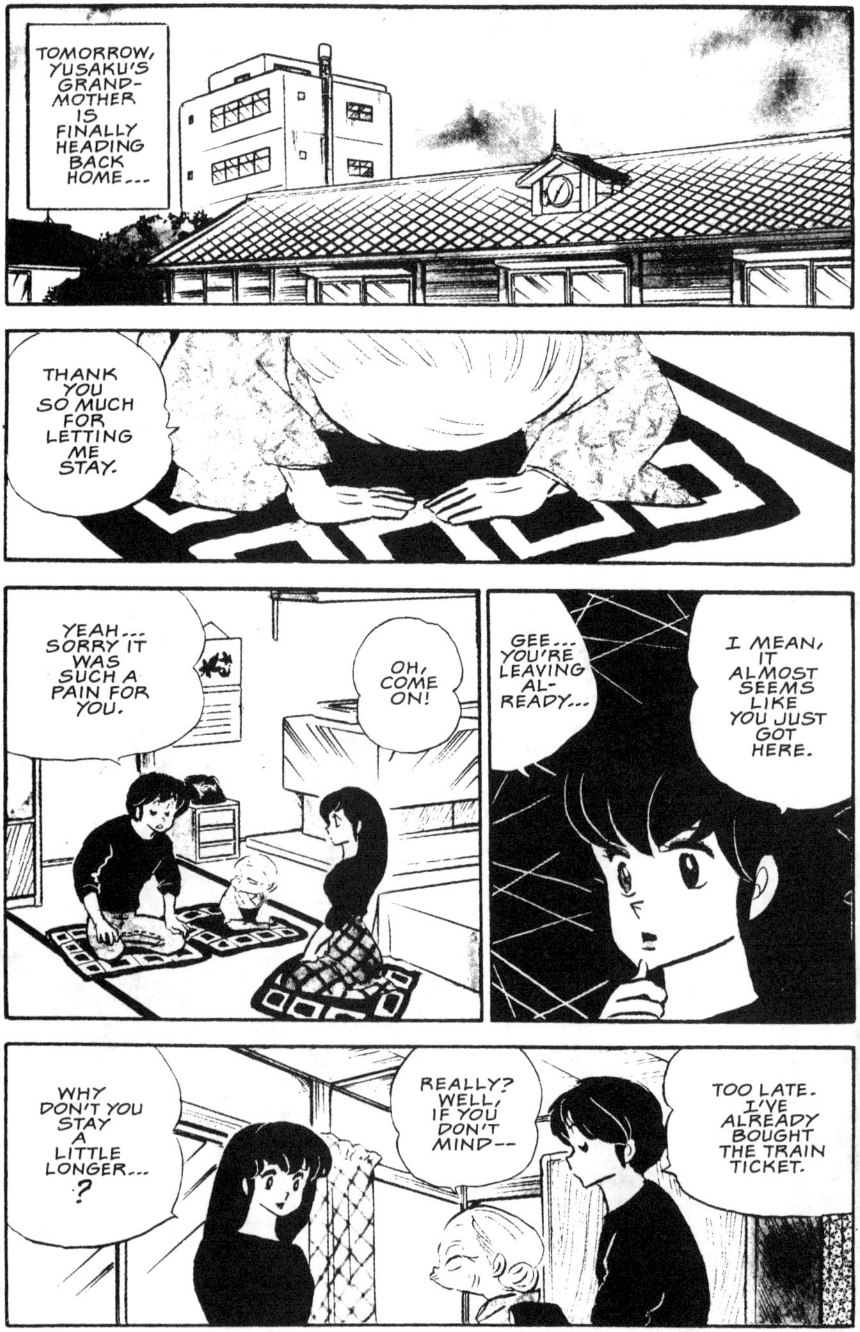
TOMORROW, YUSAKU'S GRAND-MOTHER IS FINALLY HEADING BACK HOME...
THANK YOU SO MUCH FOR LETTING ME STAY.
YEAH... SORRY IT WAS SUCH A PAIN FOR YOU.
OH, COME ON!
GEE... YOU'RE LEAVING AL-READY...
I MEAN, IT ALMOST SEEMS LIKE YOU JUST GOT HERE.
WHY DON'T YOU STAY A LITTLE LONGER...?
REALLY? WELL, IF YOU DON'T MIND--
TOO LATE. I'VE ALREADY BOUGHT THE TRAIN TICKET.

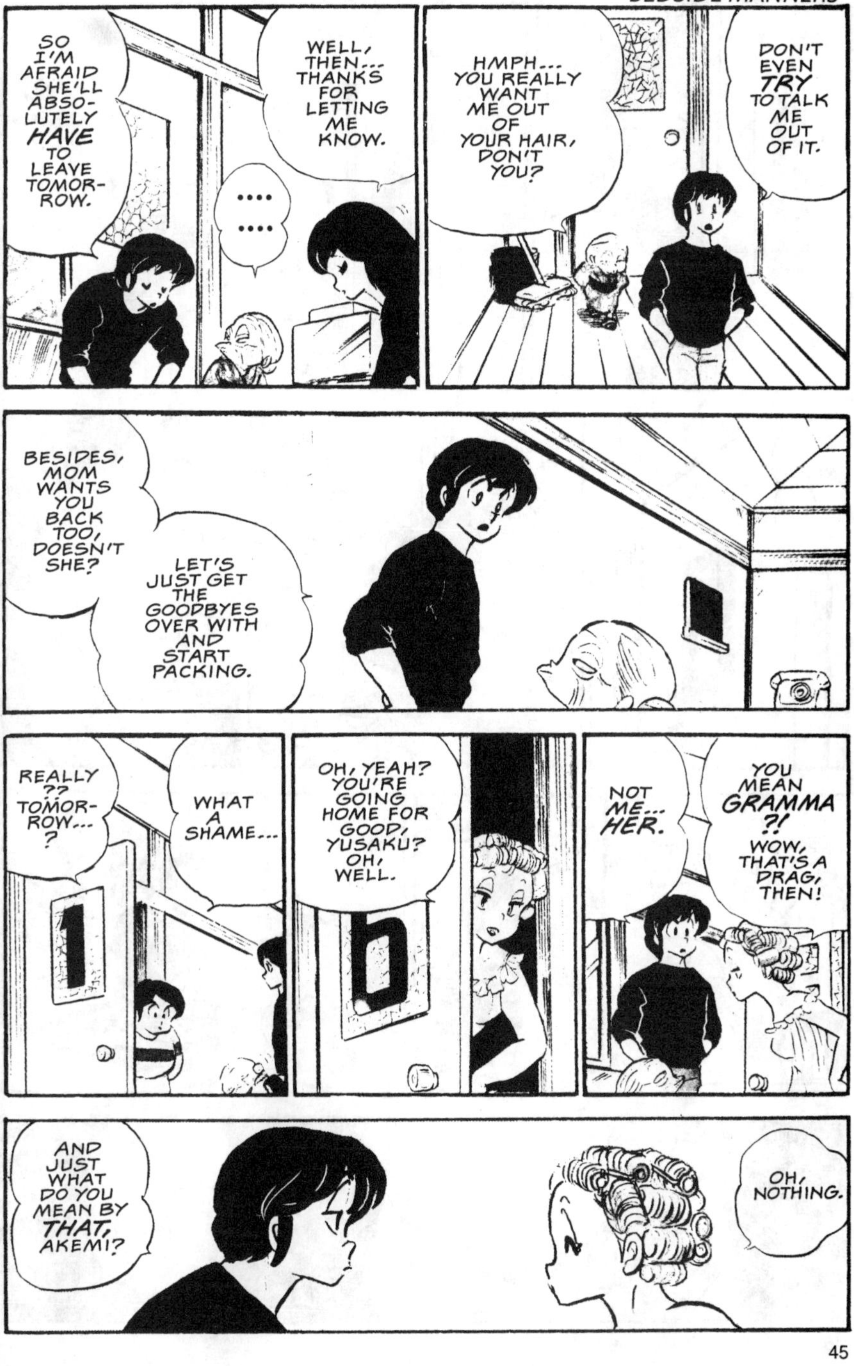
SO I'M AFRAID SHE'LL ABSOLUTELY *HAVE* TO LEAVE TOMORROW.
WELL, THEN... THANKS FOR LETTING ME KNOW.
....
HMPH... YOU REALLY WANT ME OUT OF YOUR HAIR, DON'T YOU?
DON'T EVEN *TRY* TO TALK ME OUT OF IT.
BESIDES, MOM WANTS YOU BACK TOO, DOESN'T SHE?
LET'S JUST GET THE GOODBYES OVER WITH AND START PACKING.
REALLY?? TOMORROW...?
WHAT A SHAME...
OH, YEAH? YOU'RE GOING HOME FOR GOOD, YUSAKU? OH, WELL.
NOT *ME*... *HER*.
YOU MEAN *GRAMMA* ?! WOW, THAT'S A DRAG, THEN!
AND JUST WHAT DO YOU MEAN BY *THAT*, AKEMI?
OH, NOTHING.

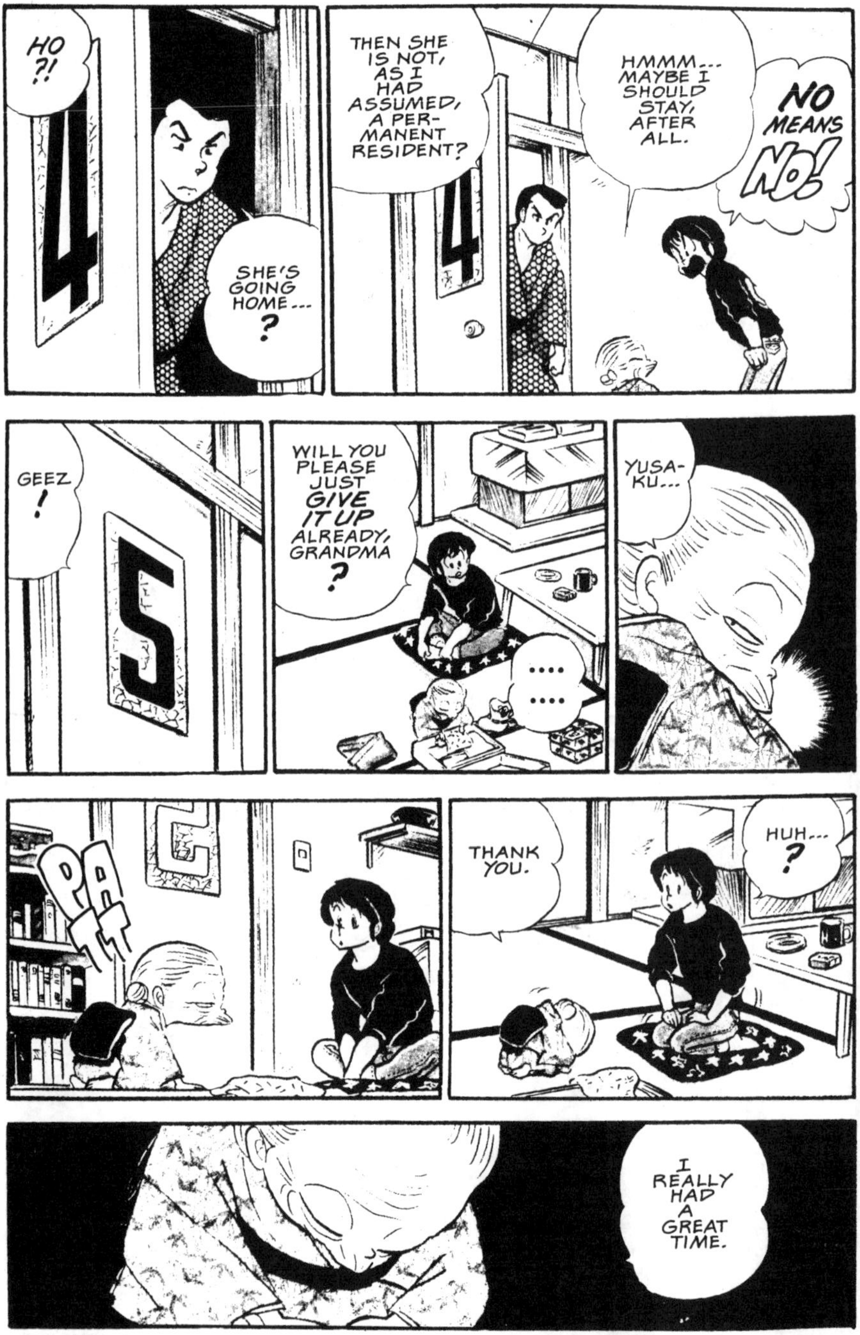
HO ?!
SHE'S GOING HOME... ?
THEN SHE IS NOT, AS I HAD ASSUMED, A PERMANENT RESIDENT?
HMMM... MAYBE I SHOULD STAY, AFTER ALL.
NO MEANS NO!
GEEZ !
WILL YOU PLEASE JUST GIVE IT UP ALREADY, GRANDMA ?
....
....
YUSAKU...
PA TT
THANK YOU.
HUH... ?
I REALLY HAD A GREAT TIME.

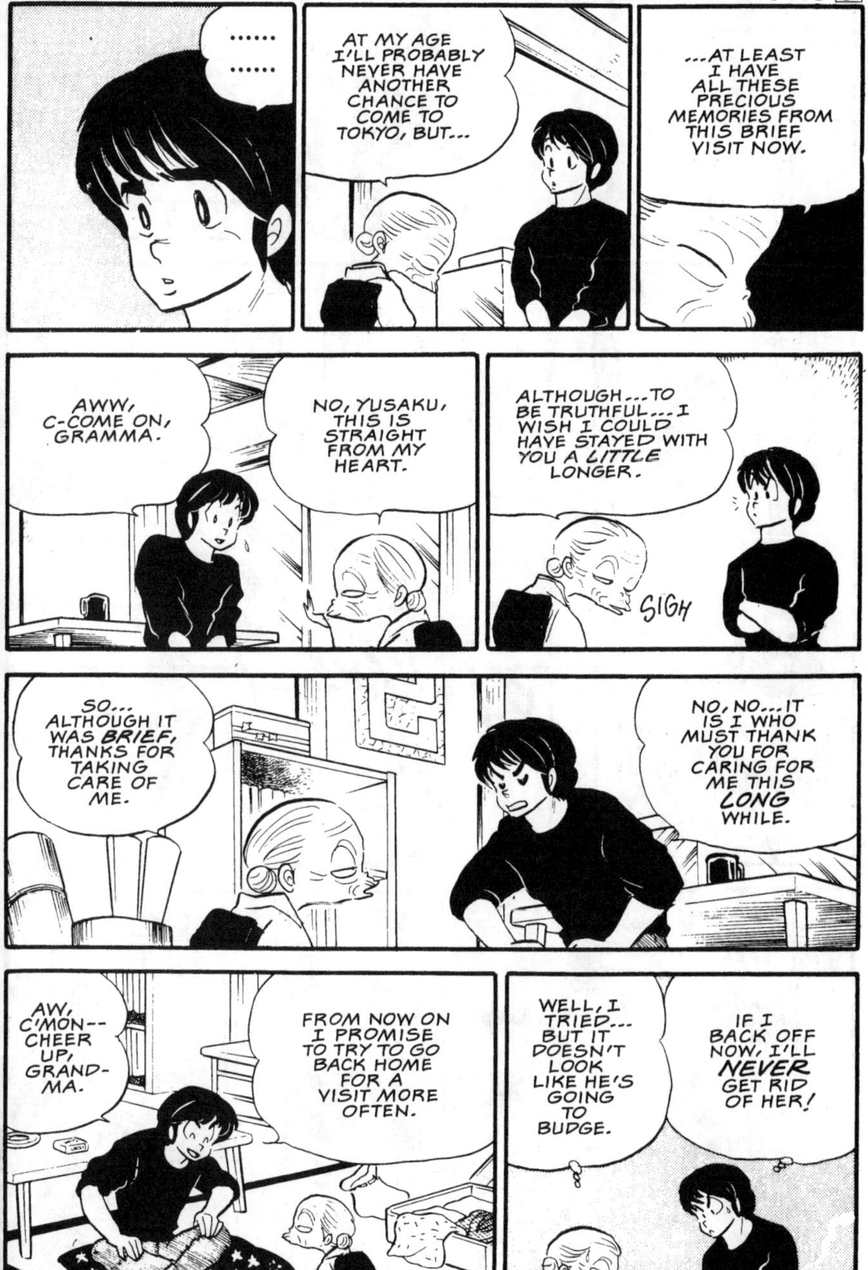
......
......
AT MY AGE I'LL PROBABLY NEVER HAVE ANOTHER CHANCE TO COME TO TOKYO, BUT...
...AT LEAST I HAVE ALL THESE PRECIOUS MEMORIES FROM THIS BRIEF VISIT NOW.
AWW, C-COME ON, GRAMMA.
NO, YUSAKU, THIS IS STRAIGHT FROM MY HEART.
ALTHOUGH...TO BE TRUTHFUL...I WISH I COULD HAVE STAYED WITH YOU A LITTLE LONGER.
SIGH
SO... ALTHOUGH IT WAS BRIEF, THANKS FOR TAKING CARE OF ME.
NO, NO...IT IS I WHO MUST THANK YOU FOR CARING FOR ME THIS LONG WHILE.
AW, C'MON--CHEER UP, GRAND-MA.
FROM NOW ON I PROMISE TO TRY TO GO BACK HOME FOR A VISIT MORE OFTEN.
WELL, I TRIED... BUT IT DOESN'T LOOK LIKE HE'S GOING TO BUDGE.
IF I BACK OFF NOW, I'LL NEVER GET RID OF HER!

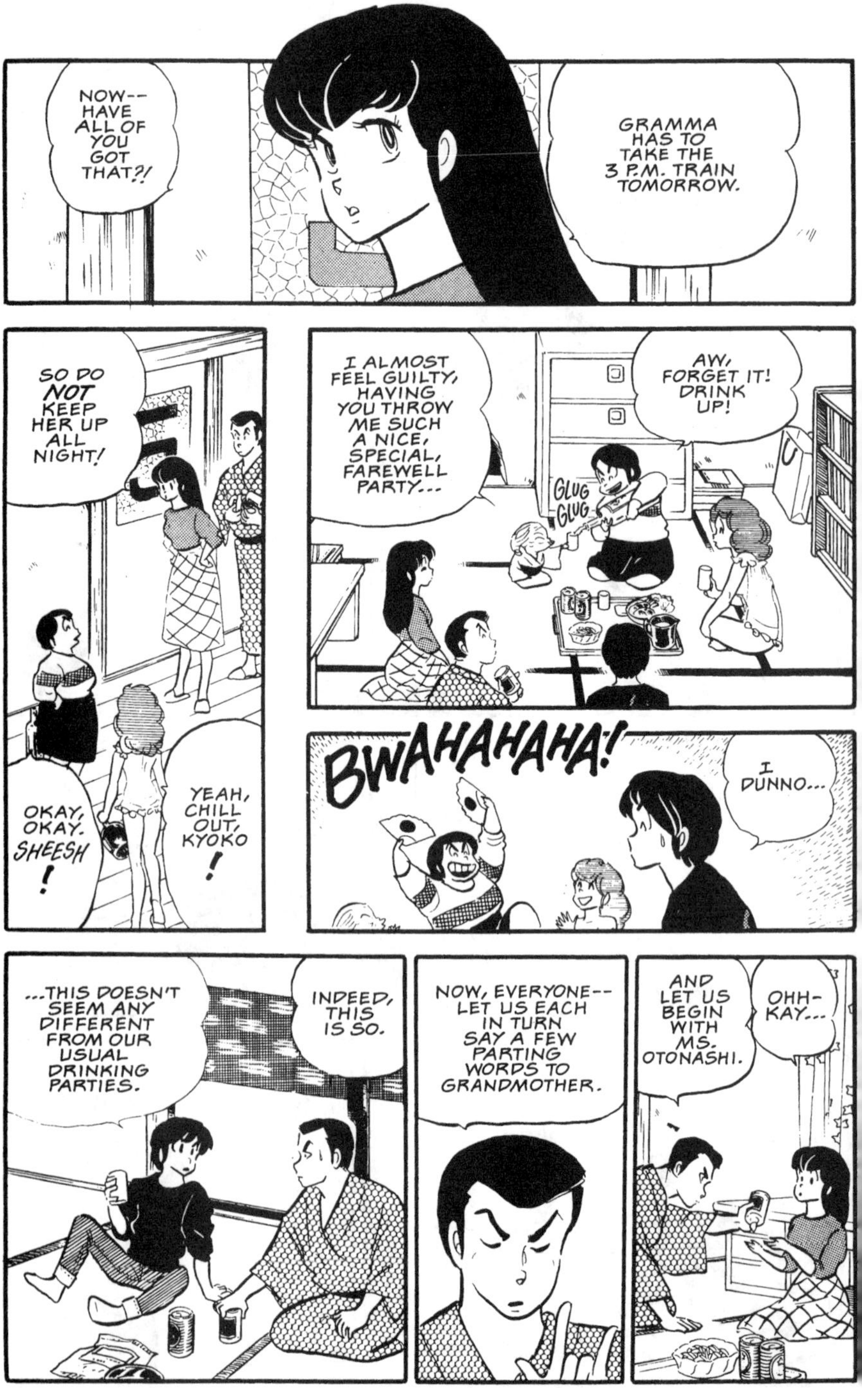
NOW-- HAVE ALL OF YOU GOT THAT?!
GRAMMA HAS TO TAKE THE 3 P.M. TRAIN TOMORROW.
SO DO NOT KEEP HER UP ALL NIGHT!
OKAY, OKAY. SHEESH!
YEAH, CHILL OUT, KYOKO!
I ALMOST FEEL GUILTY, HAVING YOU THROW ME SUCH A NICE, SPECIAL, FAREWELL PARTY...
AW, FORGET IT! DRINK UP!
GLUG GLUG
BWAHAHAHA!
I DUNNO...
...THIS DOESN'T SEEM ANY DIFFERENT FROM OUR USUAL DRINKING PARTIES.
INDEED, THIS IS SO.
NOW, EVERYONE-- LET US EACH IN TURN SAY A FEW PARTING WORDS TO GRANDMOTHER.
AND LET US BEGIN WITH MS. OTONASHI.
OHH-KAY...

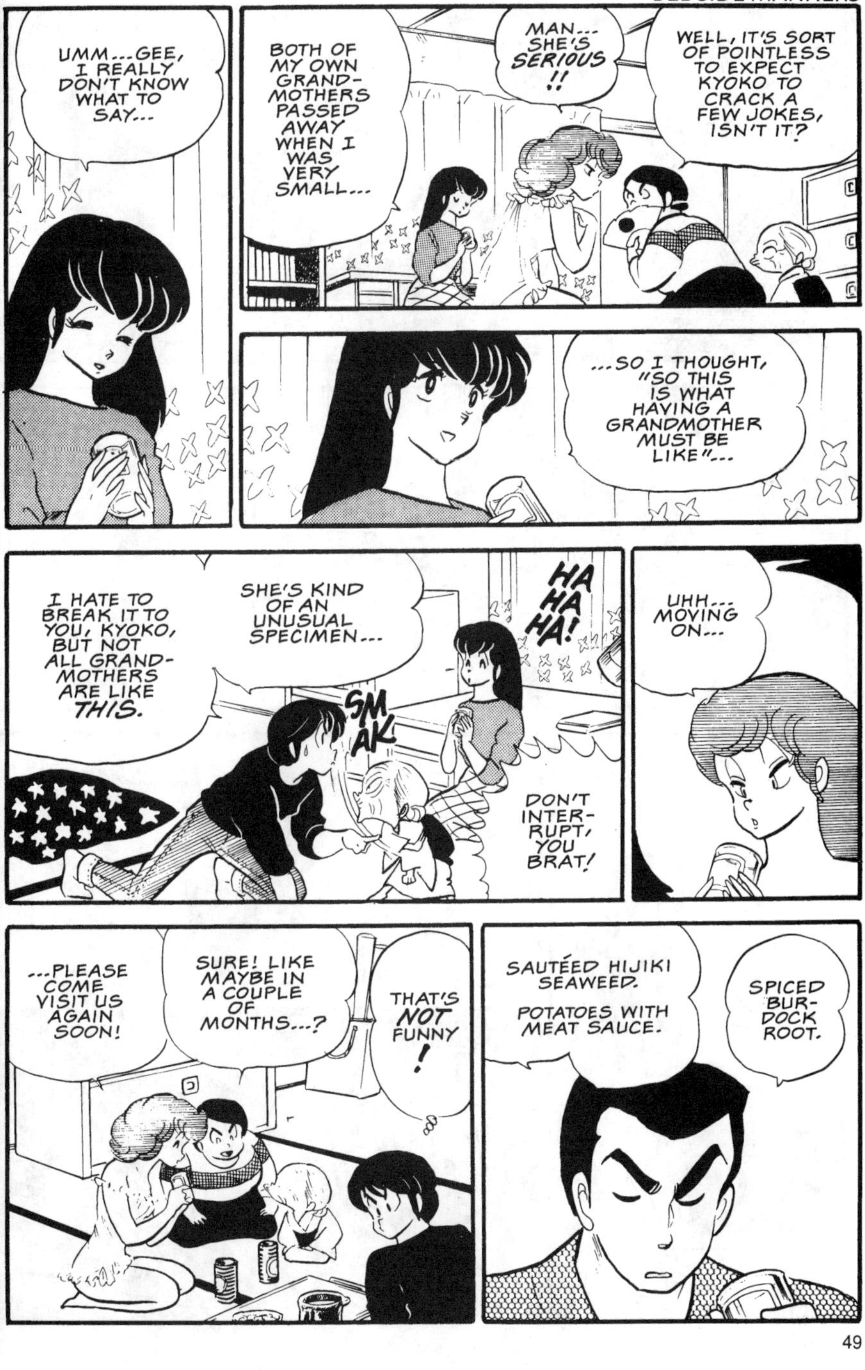
UMM...GEE, I REALLY DON'T KNOW WHAT TO SAY...
BOTH OF MY OWN GRAND-MOTHERS PASSED AWAY WHEN I WAS VERY SMALL...
MAN... SHE'S SERIOUS!!
WELL, IT'S SORT OF POINTLESS TO EXPECT KYOKO TO CRACK A FEW JOKES, ISN'T IT?
...SO I THOUGHT, "SO THIS IS WHAT HAVING A GRANDMOTHER MUST BE LIKE"...
I HATE TO BREAK IT TO YOU, KYOKO, BUT NOT ALL GRAND-MOTHERS ARE LIKE THIS.
SHE'S KIND OF AN UNUSUAL SPECIMEN...
HA HA HA!
SMAK
DON'T INTER-RUPT, YOU BRAT!
UHH... MOVING ON...
...PLEASE COME VISIT US AGAIN SOON!
SURE! LIKE MAYBE IN A COUPLE OF MONTHS...?
THAT'S NOT FUNNY!
SAUTÉED HIJIKI SEAWEED.
POTATOES WITH MEAT SAUCE.
SPICED BUR-DOCK ROOT.

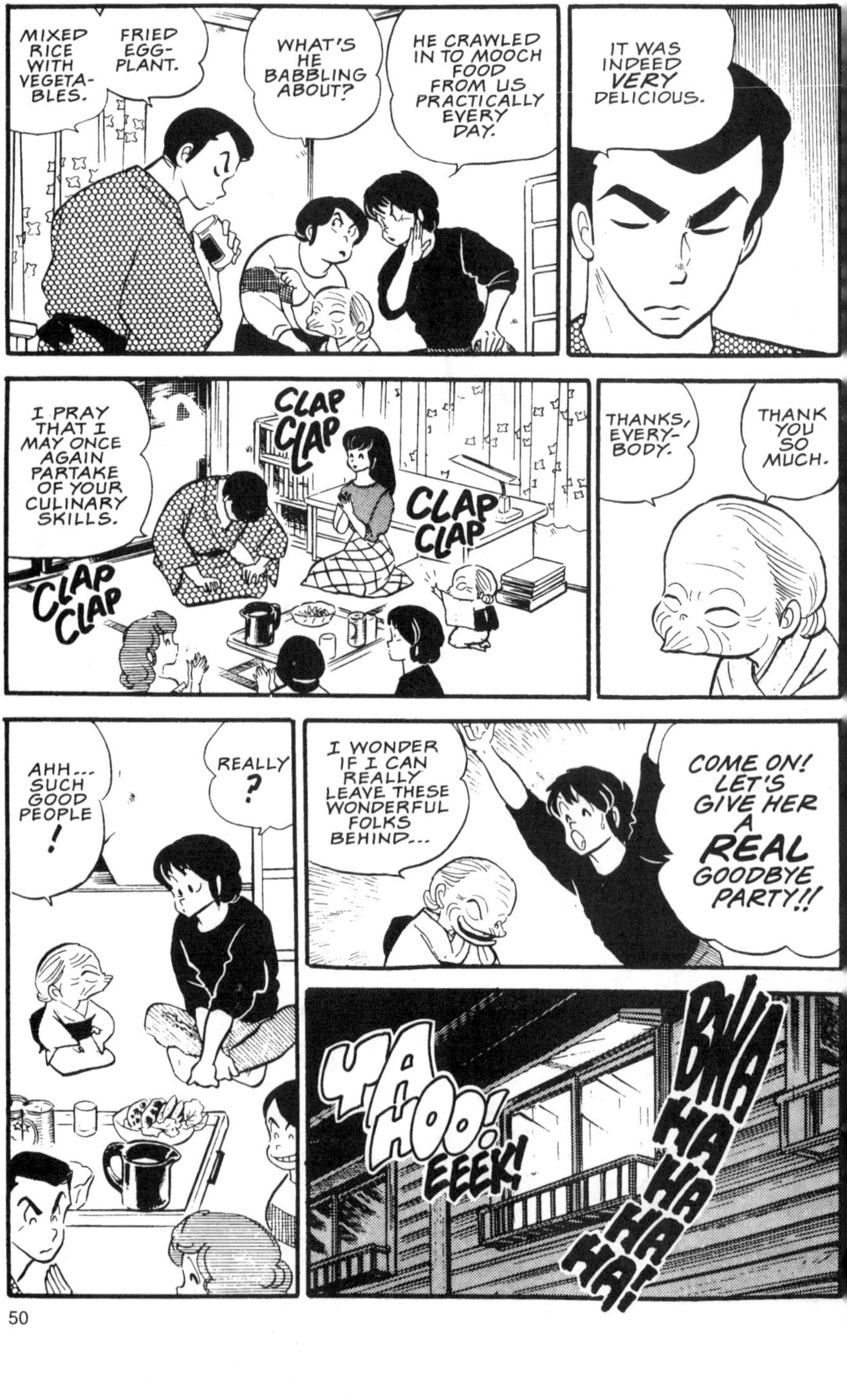
MIXED RICE WITH VEGETABLES.
FRIED EGG-PLANT.
WHAT'S HE BABBLING ABOUT?
HE CRAWLED IN TO MOOCH FOOD FROM US PRACTICALLY EVERY DAY.
IT WAS INDEED VERY DELICIOUS.
I PRAY THAT I MAY ONCE AGAIN PARTAKE OF YOUR CULINARY SKILLS.
CLAP CLAP
CLAP CLAP
CLAP CLAP
THANKS, EVERYBODY.
THANK YOU SO MUCH.
AHH... SUCH GOOD PEOPLE!
REALLY?
I WONDER IF I CAN REALLY LEAVE THESE WONDERFUL FOLKS BEHIND...
COME ON! LET'S GIVE HER A REAL GOODBYE PARTY!!
YAHOO!
EEEK!
BWAHAHAHAHA!

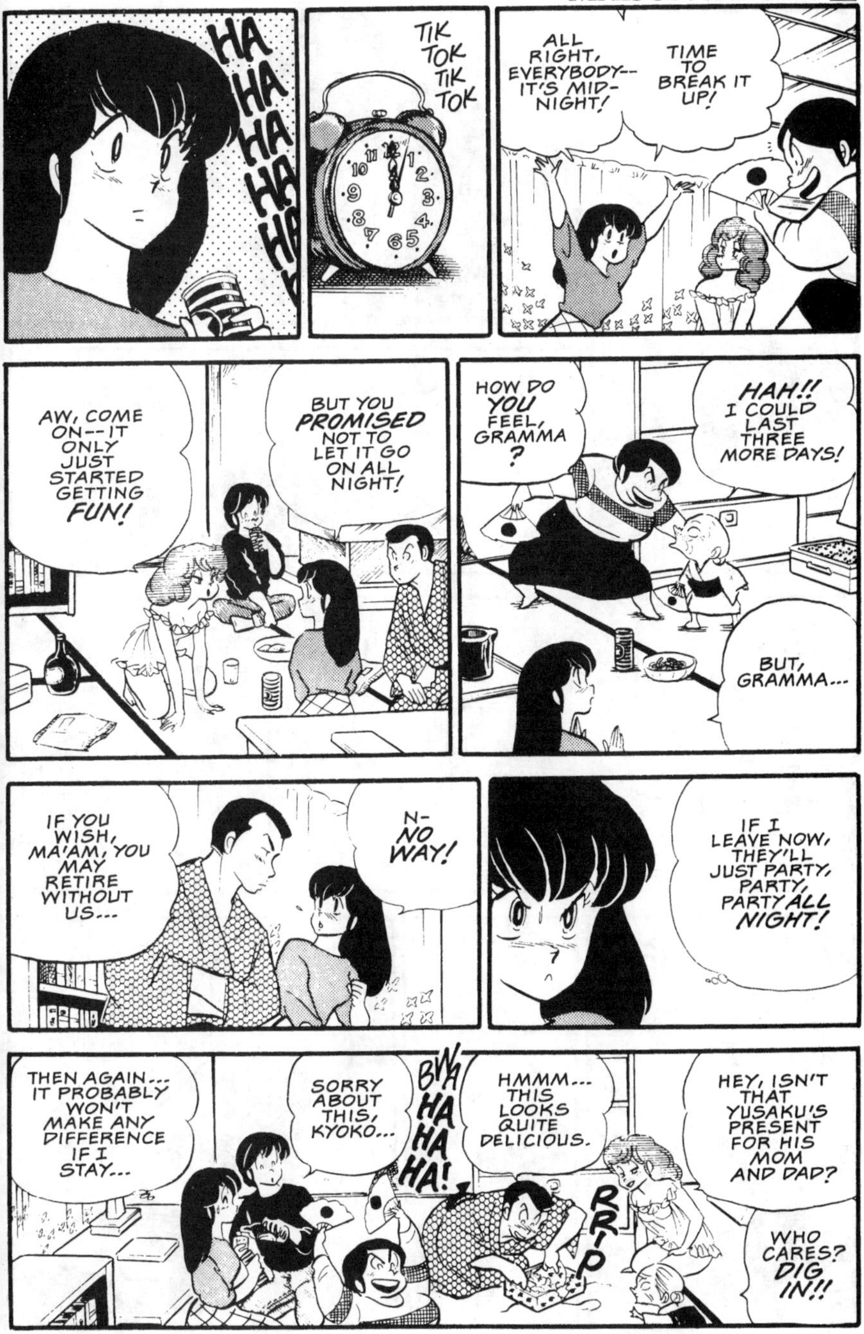
HA HA HA HA HA HA
TIK TOK TIK TOK
ALL RIGHT, EVERYBODY-- IT'S MID-NIGHT!
TIME TO BREAK IT UP!
AW, COME ON-- IT ONLY JUST STARTED GETTING FUN!
BUT YOU PROMISED NOT TO LET IT GO ON ALL NIGHT!
HOW DO YOU FEEL, GRAMMA?
HAH!! I COULD LAST THREE MORE DAYS!
BUT, GRAMMA...
IF YOU WISH, MA'AM, YOU MAY RETIRE WITHOUT US...
N-NO WAY!
IF I LEAVE NOW, THEY'LL JUST PARTY, PARTY, PARTY ALL NIGHT!
THEN AGAIN... IT PROBABLY WON'T MAKE ANY DIFFERENCE IF I STAY...
SORRY ABOUT THIS, KYOKO...
BWA HA HA HA!
HMMM... THIS LOOKS QUITE DELICIOUS.
RRIP
HEY, ISN'T THAT YUSAKU'S PRESENT FOR HIS MOM AND DAD?
WHO CARES? DIG IN!!

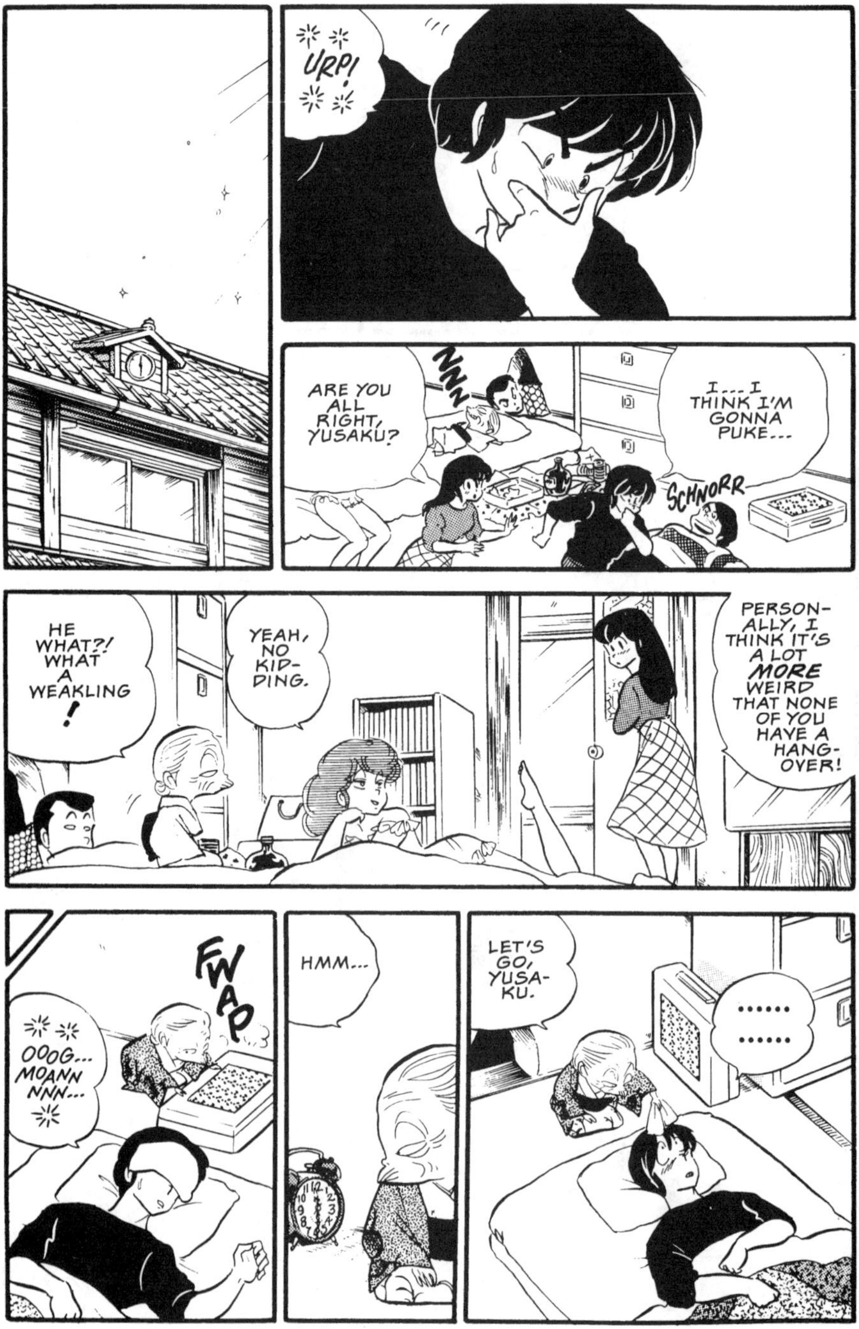

URP!
ARE YOU ALL RIGHT, YUSAKU?
ZZZ
I... I THINK I'M GONNA PUKE...
SCHNORR
HE WHAT?! WHAT A WEAKLING!
YEAH, NO KID-DING.
PERSON-ALLY, I THINK IT'S A LOT **MORE** WEIRD THAT NONE OF YOU HAVE A HANG-OVER!
FWAP
OOOG... MOANN NNN...
HMM...
LET'S GO, YUSA-KU.
......
......

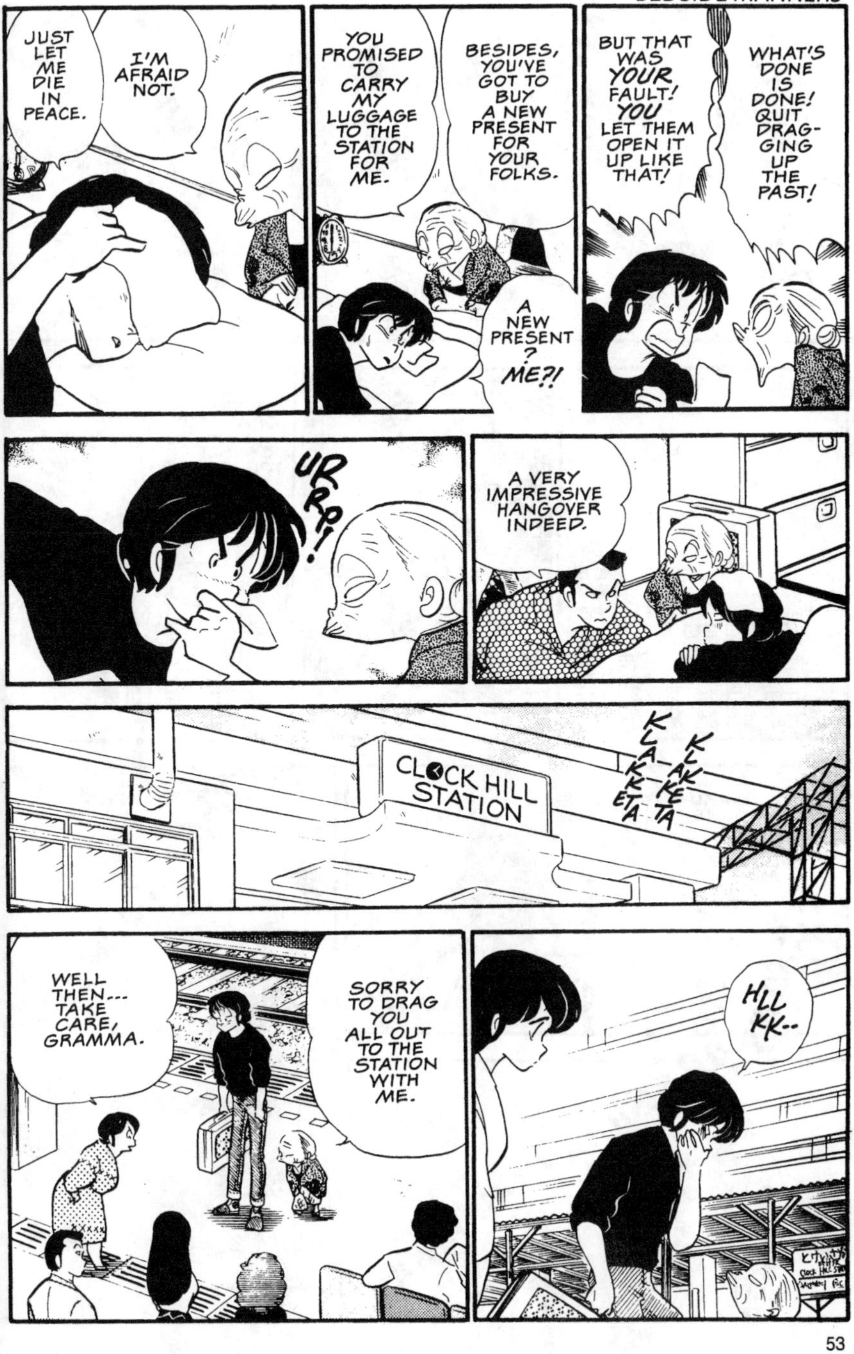
JUST LET ME DIE IN PEACE.
I'M AFRAID NOT.
YOU PROMISED TO CARRY MY LUGGAGE TO THE STATION FOR ME.
BESIDES, YOU'VE GOT TO BUY A NEW PRESENT FOR YOUR FOLKS.
A NEW PRESENT? ME?!
BUT THAT WAS YOUR FAULT! YOU LET THEM OPEN IT UP LIKE THAT!
WHAT'S DONE IS DONE! QUIT DRAGGING UP THE PAST!
URRP!
A VERY IMPRESSIVE HANGOVER INDEED.
CLOCK HILL STATION
KLAKKETA
KLAKKETA
WELL THEN... TAKE CARE, GRAMMA.
SORRY TO DRAG YOU ALL OUT TO THE STATION WITH ME.
HLLKK..

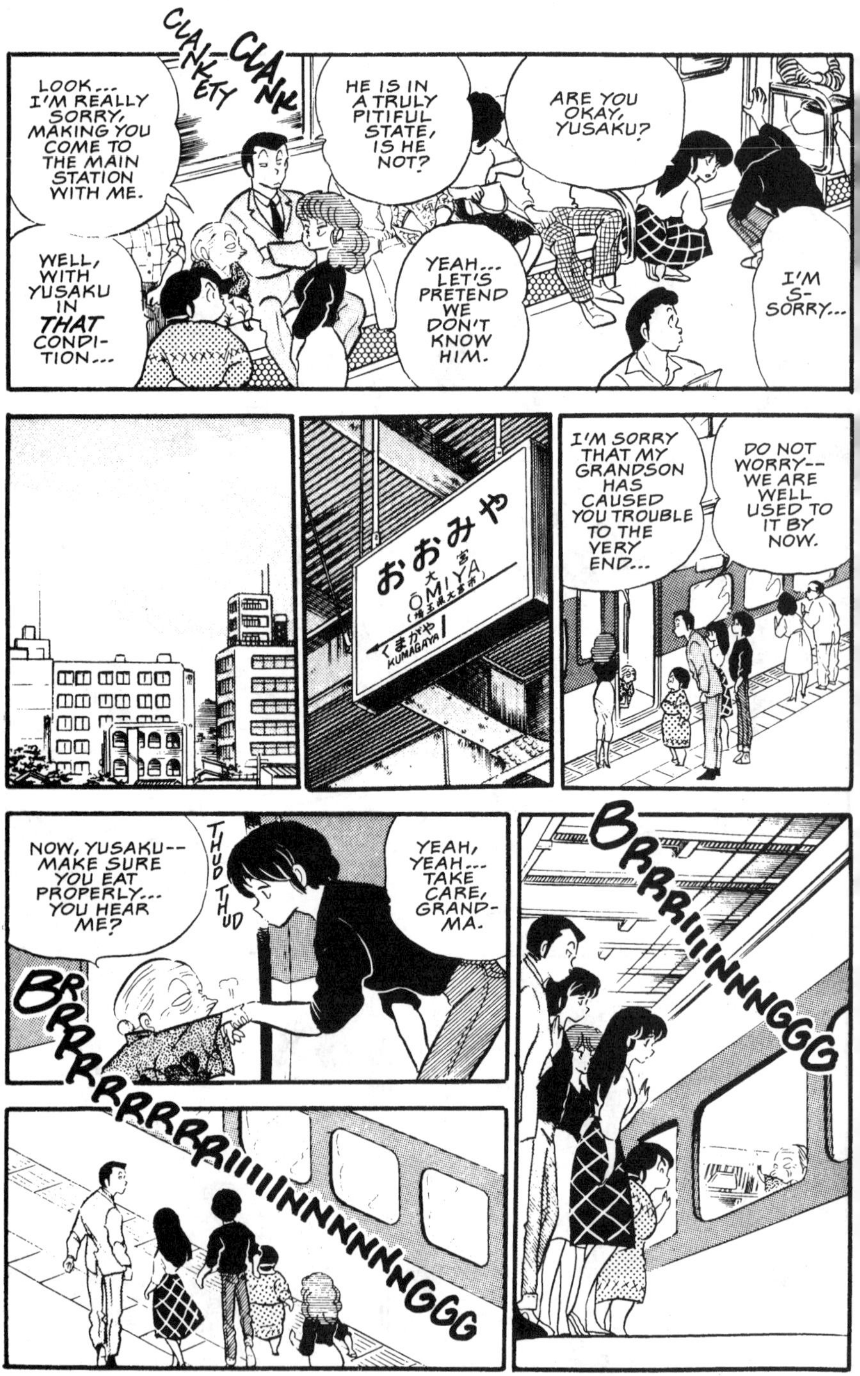
CLANK-CLANKETY-CLANK
LOOK... I'M REALLY SORRY, MAKING YOU COME TO THE MAIN STATION WITH ME.
WELL, WITH YUSAKU IN THAT CONDITION...
HE IS IN A TRULY PITIFUL STATE, IS HE NOT?
YEAH... LET'S PRETEND WE DON'T KNOW HIM.
ARE YOU OKAY, YUSAKU?
I'M S-SORRY...
おおみや
大宮
ŌMIYA
くまがや
KUMAGAYA
I'M SORRY THAT MY GRANDSON HAS CAUSED YOU TROUBLE TO THE VERY END...
DO NOT WORRY-- WE ARE WELL USED TO IT BY NOW.
NOW, YUSAKU-- MAKE SURE YOU EAT PROPERLY... YOU HEAR ME?
THUD THUD
YEAH, YEAH... TAKE CARE, GRANDMA.
BRRRRRRRRRIIIIINNNNNNNNNGGG
BRRRIIIIINNNGGG

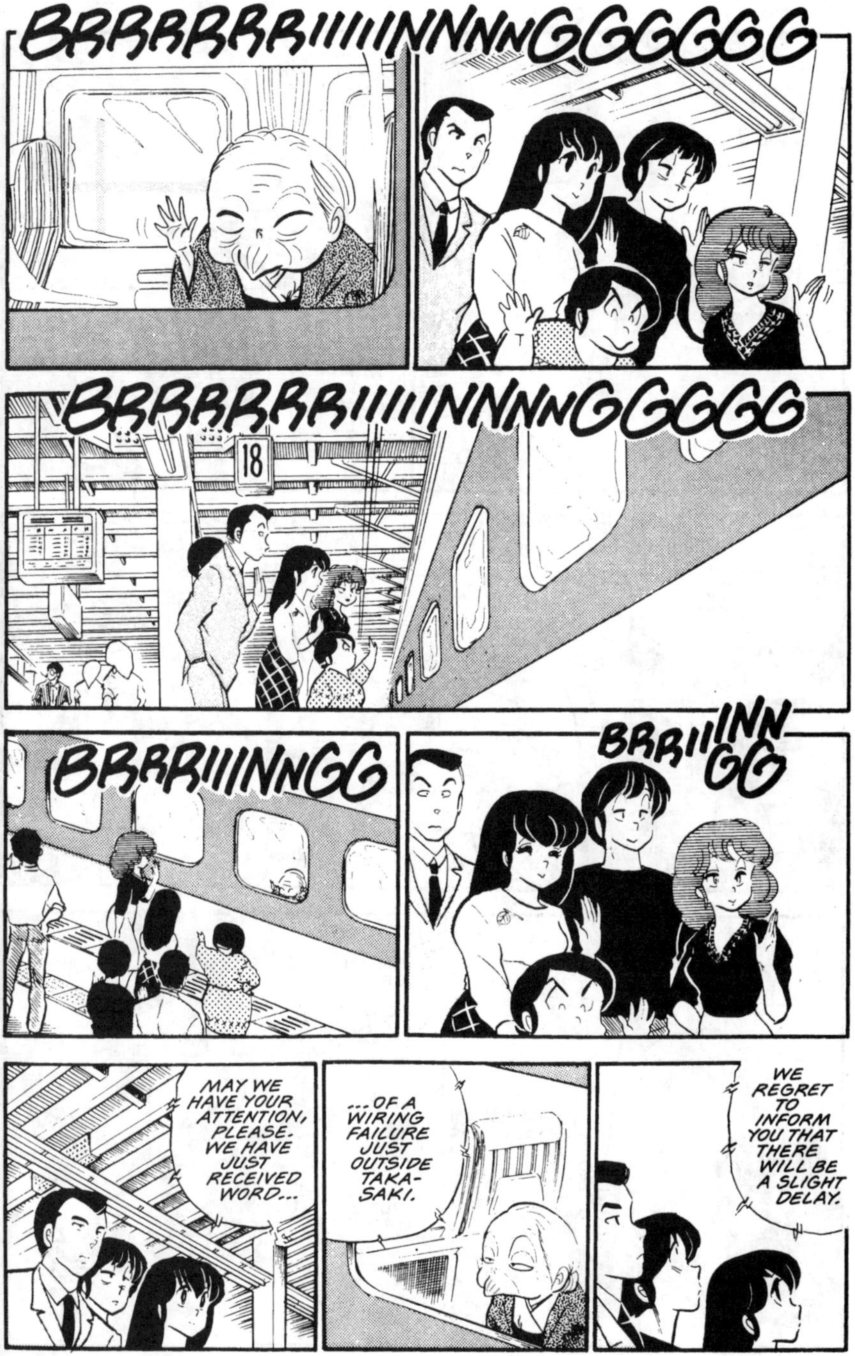
BRRRRRRIIIIINNNNGGGGGG
BRRRRRRIIIIINNNNGGGGG
BRRRIIINNGG
BRRIIINN GG
MAY WE HAVE YOUR ATTENTION, PLEASE. WE HAVE JUST RECEIVED WORD...
...OF A WIRING FAILURE JUST OUTSIDE TAKA-SAKI.
WE REGRET TO INFORM YOU THAT THERE WILL BE A SLIGHT DELAY.

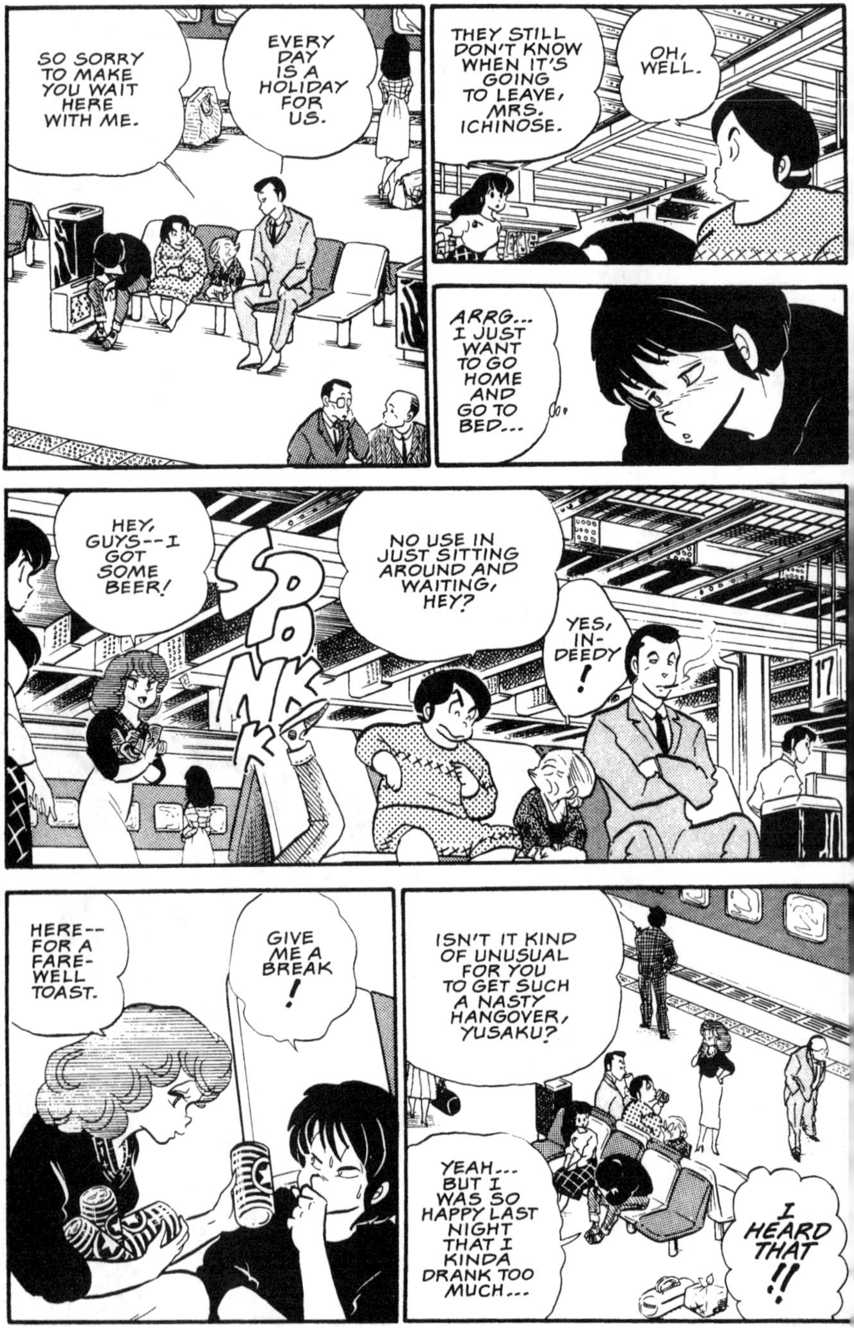
SO SORRY TO MAKE YOU WAIT HERE WITH ME.
EVERY DAY IS A HOLIDAY FOR US.
THEY STILL DON'T KNOW WHEN IT'S GOING TO LEAVE, MRS. ICHINOSE.
OH, WELL.
ARRG... I JUST WANT TO GO HOME AND GO TO BED...
HEY, GUYS--I GOT SOME BEER!
SPONK
NO USE IN JUST SITTING AROUND AND WAITING, HEY?
YES, IN-DEEDY!
HERE--FOR A FARE-WELL TOAST.
GIVE ME A BREAK!
ISN'T IT KIND OF UNUSUAL FOR YOU TO GET SUCH A NASTY HANGOVER, YUSAKU?
YEAH... BUT I WAS SO HAPPY LAST NIGHT THAT I KINDA DRANK TOO MUCH...
I HEARD THAT!!

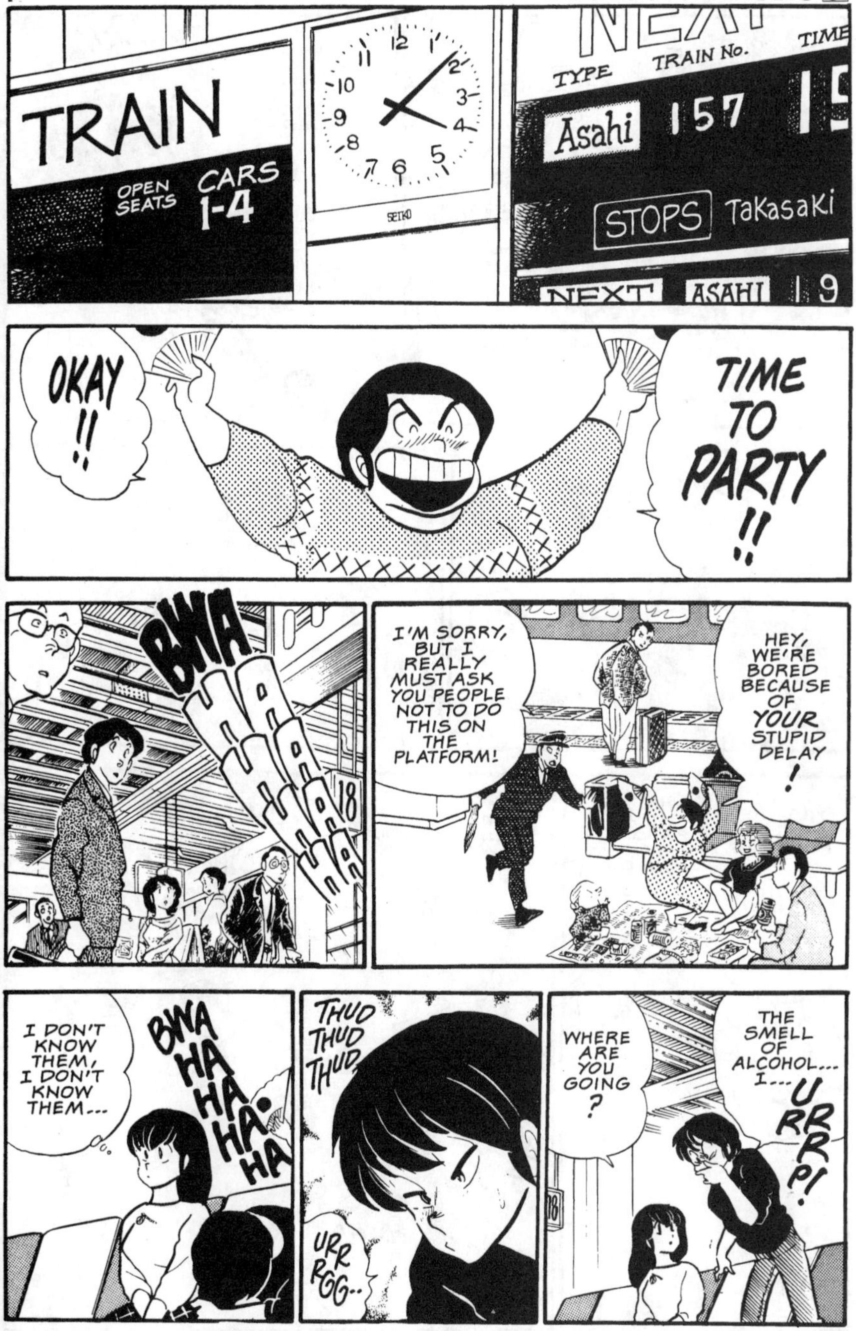
TRAIN
OPEN SEATS
CARS 1-4
SEIKO
NEXT
TYPE
TRAIN No.
TIME
Asahi
157
STOPS
TaKasaKi
NEXT
ASAHI
OKAY !!
TIME TO PARTY !!
BWA HA HA HA HA
18
I'M SORRY, BUT I REALLY MUST ASK YOU PEOPLE NOT TO DO THIS ON THE PLATFORM!
HEY, WE'RE BORED BECAUSE OF YOUR STUPID DELAY!
I DON'T KNOW THEM, I DON'T KNOW THEM...
BWA HA HA HA HA
THUD THUD THUD
URR RGG..
WHERE ARE YOU GOING?
THE SMELL OF ALCOHOL... I...
URRP!

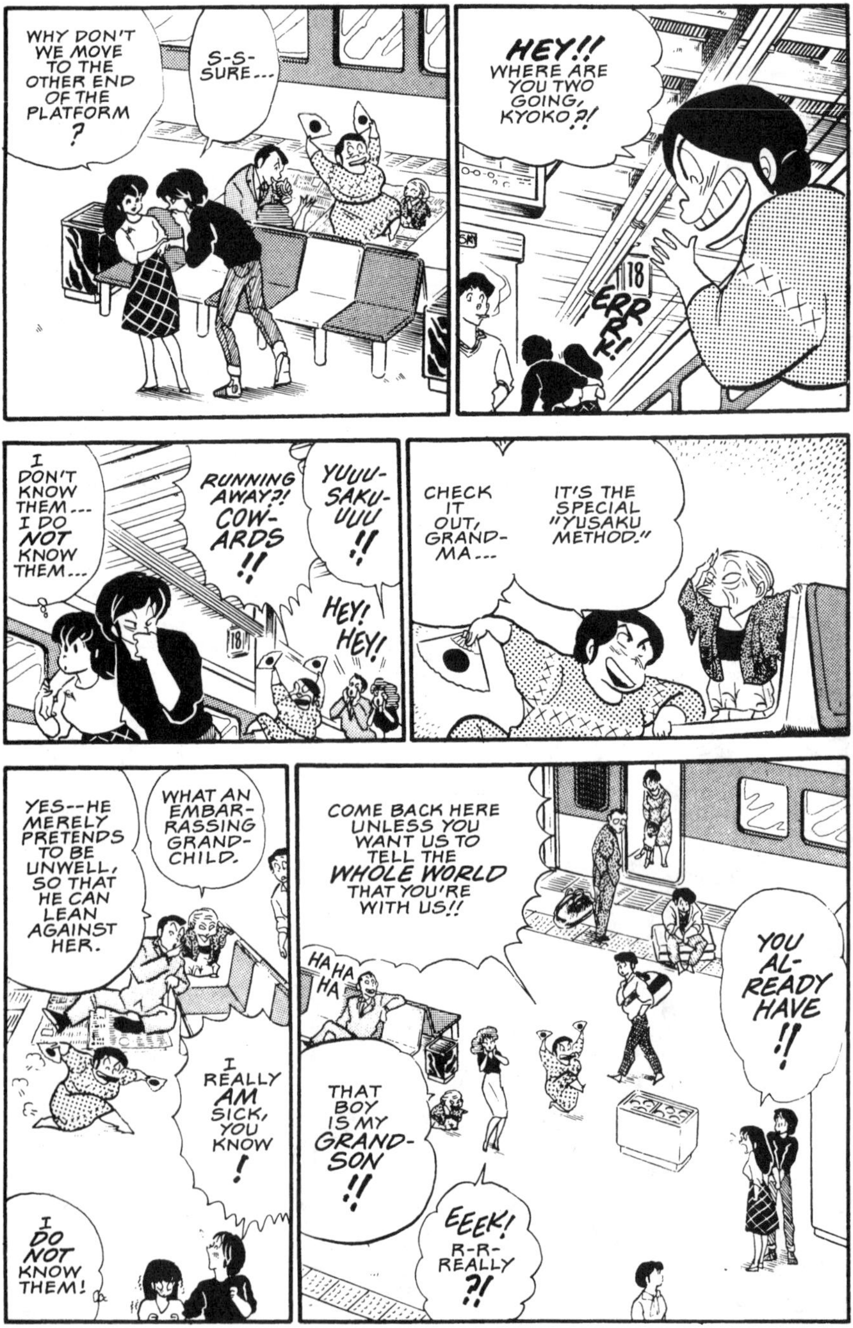
WHY DON'T WE MOVE TO THE OTHER END OF THE PLATFORM?
S-S-SURE...
HEY!! WHERE ARE YOU TWO GOING, KYOKO?!
ERRRK!
I DON'T KNOW THEM... I DO NOT KNOW THEM...
RUNNING AWAY?! COWARDS!!
YUUU-SAKU-UUU!!
HEY! HEY!
CHECK IT OUT, GRANDMA...
IT'S THE SPECIAL "YUSAKU METHOD."
YES--HE MERELY PRETENDS TO BE UNWELL, SO THAT HE CAN LEAN AGAINST HER.
WHAT AN EMBARRASSING GRANDCHILD.
I REALLY AM SICK, YOU KNOW!
I DO NOT KNOW THEM!
COME BACK HERE UNLESS YOU WANT US TO TELL THE WHOLE WORLD THAT YOU'RE WITH US!!
HA HA HA
YOU ALREADY HAVE!!
THAT BOY IS MY GRANDSON!!
EEEK! R-R-REALLY?!

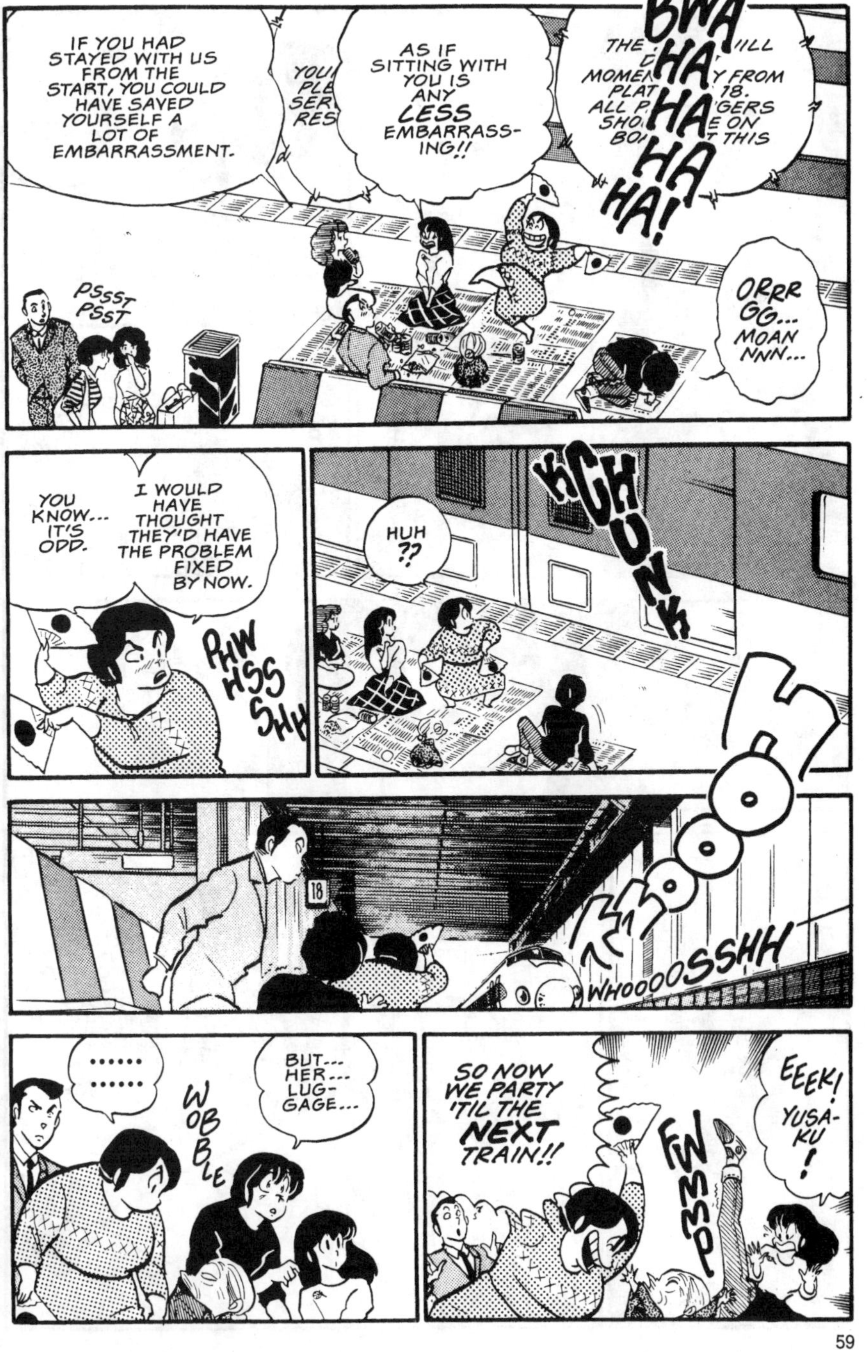

IF YOU HAD STAYED WITH US FROM THE START, YOU COULD HAVE SAVED YOURSELF A LOT OF EMBARRASSMENT.
YOU PLE SER RES
AS IF SITTING WITH YOU IS ANY LESS EMBARRASSING!!
THE ILL D MOMEN Y FROM PLAT 18. ALL P GERS SHO E ON BO T THIS
BWA HA HA HA HA!
PSSST PSST
ORRR GG... MOAN NNN...
YOU KNOW... IT'S ODD.
I WOULD HAVE THOUGHT THEY'D HAVE THE PROBLEM FIXED BY NOW.
PHW HSS SHH
HUH ??
K'CHUNK
WHOOOOSSHH
......
......
BUT... HER... LUGGAGE...
WOBBLE
SO NOW WE PARTY 'TIL THE NEXT TRAIN!!
FWMMP
EEEK! YUSAKU!

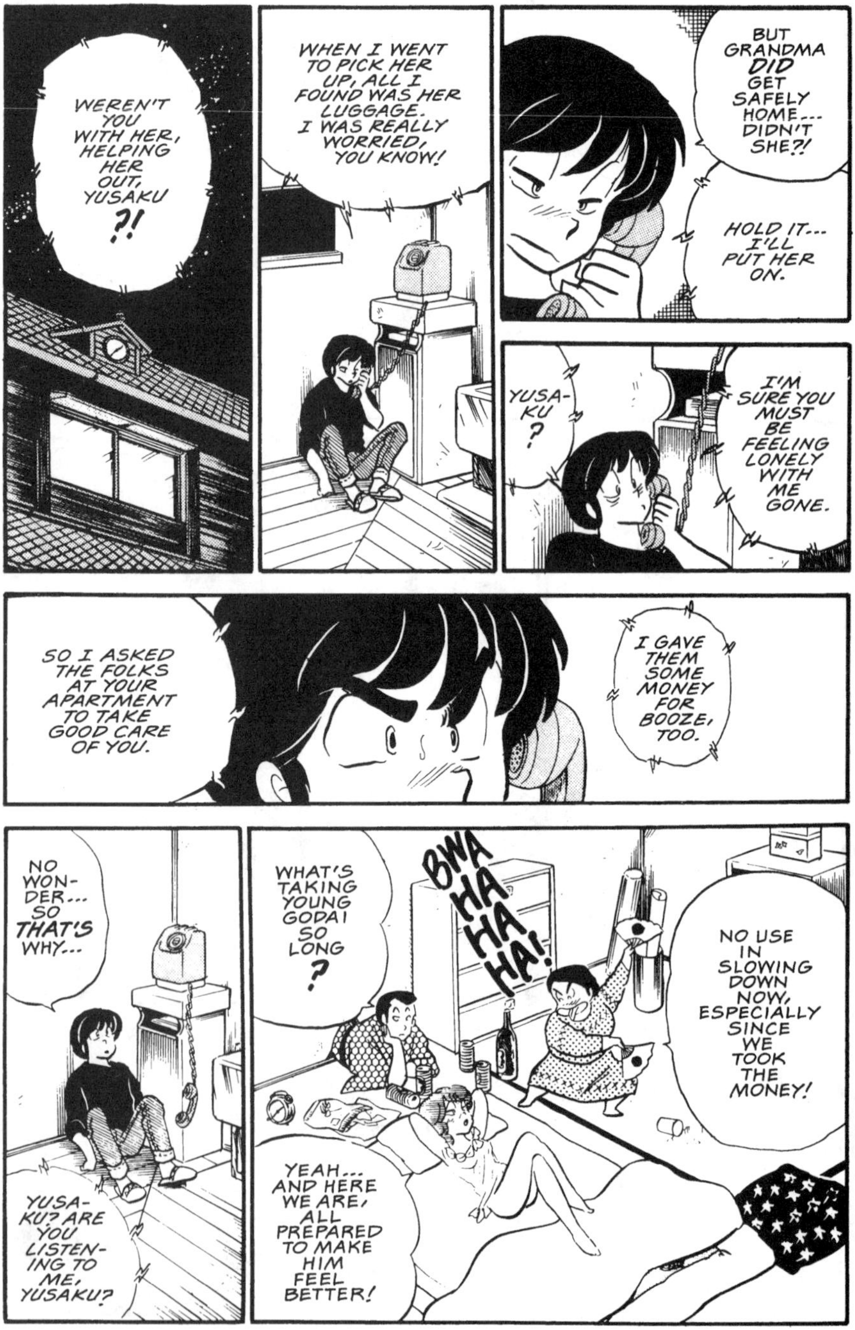
WEREN'T YOU WITH HER, HELPING HER OUT, YUSAKU ?!
WHEN I WENT TO PICK HER UP, ALL I FOUND WAS HER LUGGAGE. I WAS REALLY WORRIED, YOU KNOW!
BUT GRANDMA DID GET SAFELY HOME... DIDN'T SHE?!
HOLD IT... I'LL PUT HER ON.
YUSA-KU ?
I'M SURE YOU MUST BE FEELING LONELY WITH ME GONE.
SO I ASKED THE FOLKS AT YOUR APARTMENT TO TAKE GOOD CARE OF YOU.
I GAVE THEM SOME MONEY FOR BOOZE, TOO.
NO WON-DER... SO THAT'S WHY...
YUSA-KU? ARE YOU LISTEN-ING TO ME, YUSAKU?
WHAT'S TAKING YOUNG GODAI SO LONG ?
BWA HA HA HA!
NO USE IN SLOWING DOWN NOW, ESPECIALLY SINCE WE TOOK THE MONEY!
YEAH... AND HERE WE ARE, ALL PREPARED TO MAKE HIM FEEL BETTER!

PART FOUR

MR. ICHINOSE GETS LAID OFF

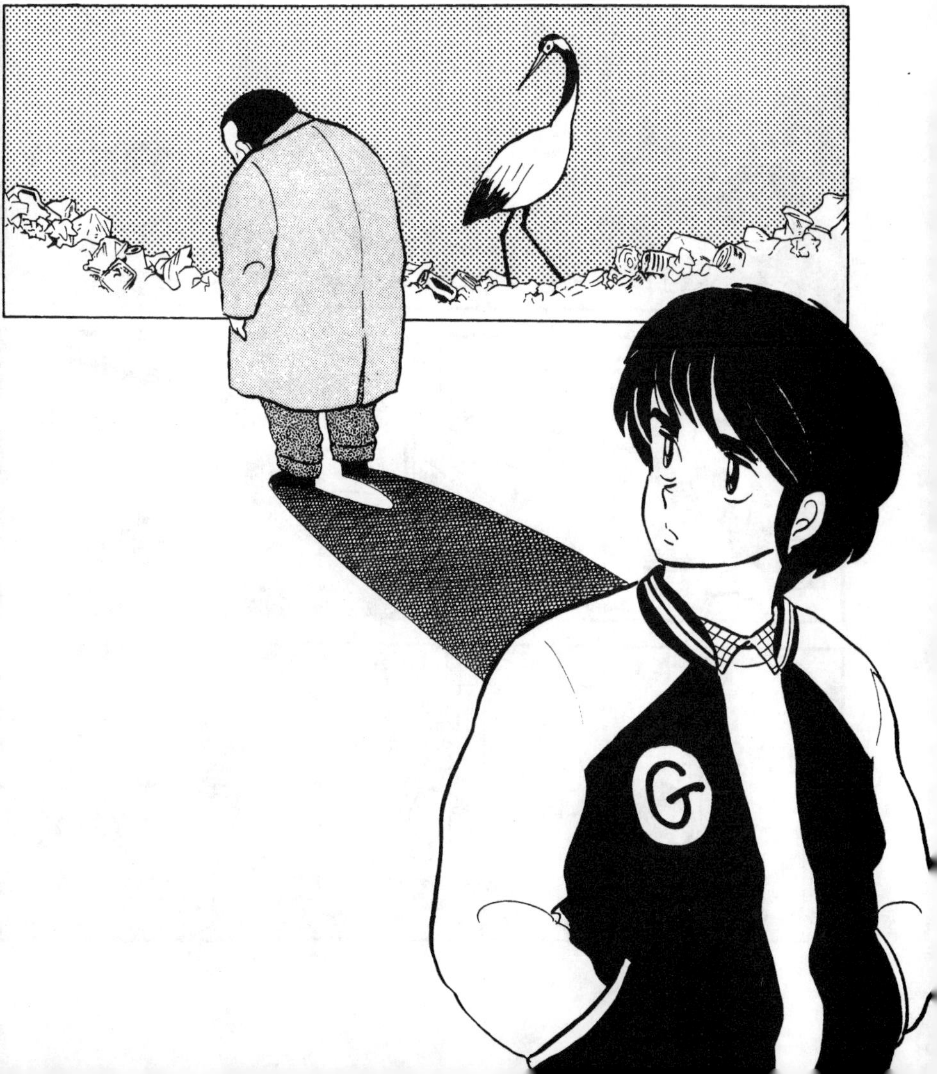

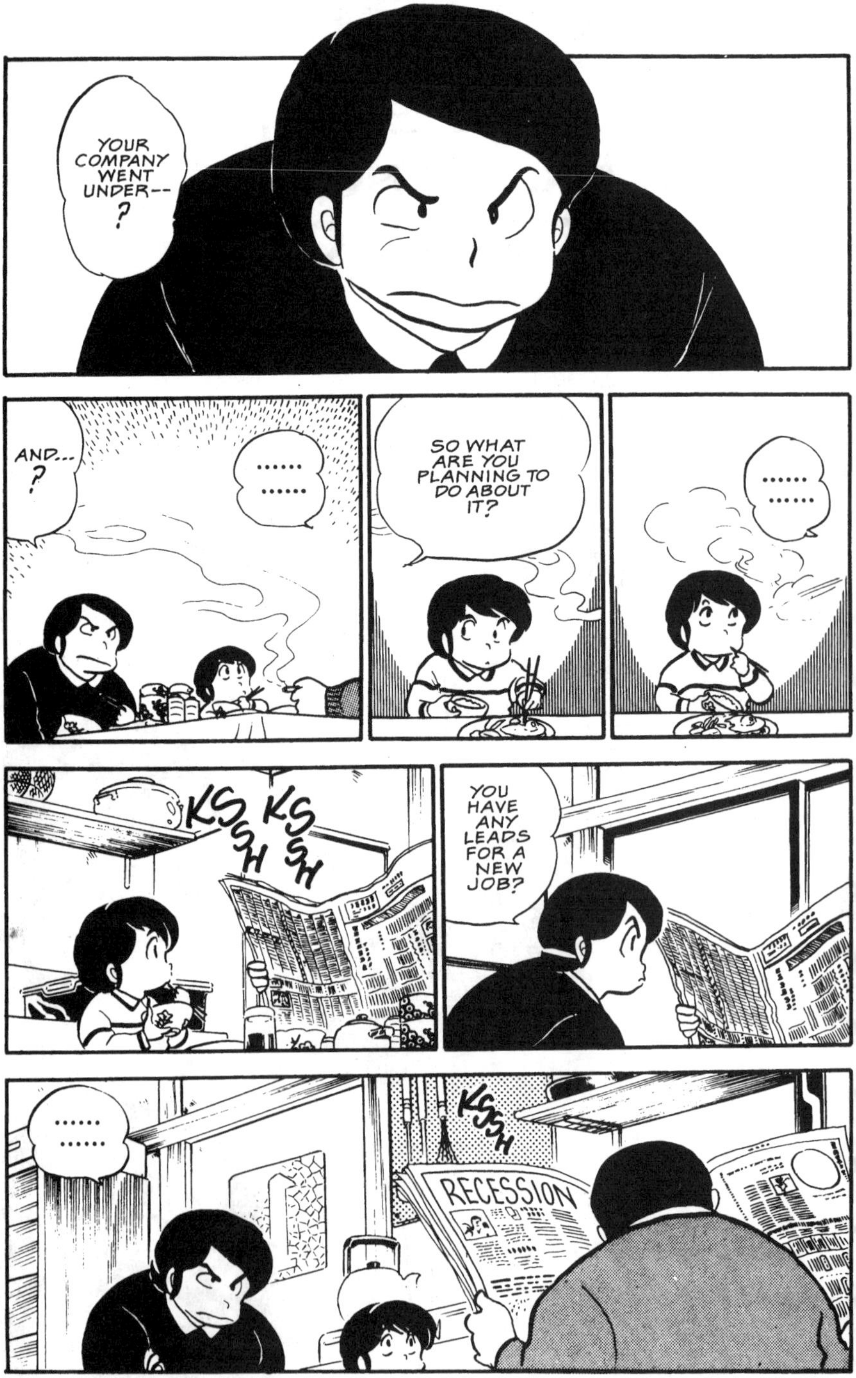
YOUR COMPANY WENT UNDER-- ?
AND... ?
......
......
SO WHAT ARE YOU PLANNING TO DO ABOUT IT?
......
......
KSSH KSSH
YOU HAVE ANY LEADS FOR A NEW JOB?
......
......
KSSH
RECESSION

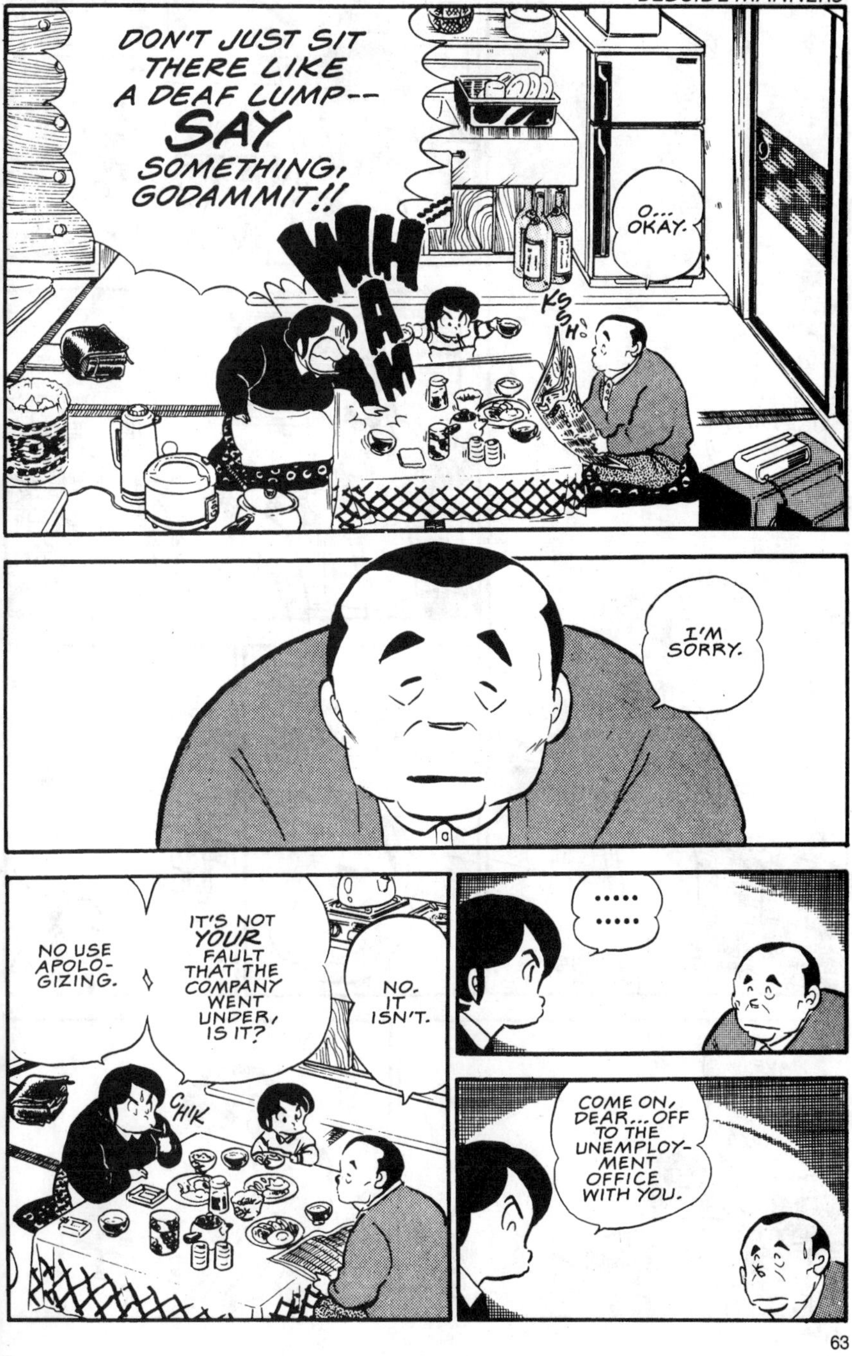
DON'T JUST SIT THERE LIKE A DEAF LUMP-- SAY SOMETHING, GODAMMIT!!
WHAM
KSSH
O... OKAY.
I'M SORRY.
NO USE APOLO-GIZING.
IT'S NOT YOUR FAULT THAT THE COMPANY WENT UNDER, IS IT?
NO. IT ISN'T.
CHIK
....
COME ON, DEAR... OFF TO THE UNEMPLOY-MENT OFFICE WITH YOU.

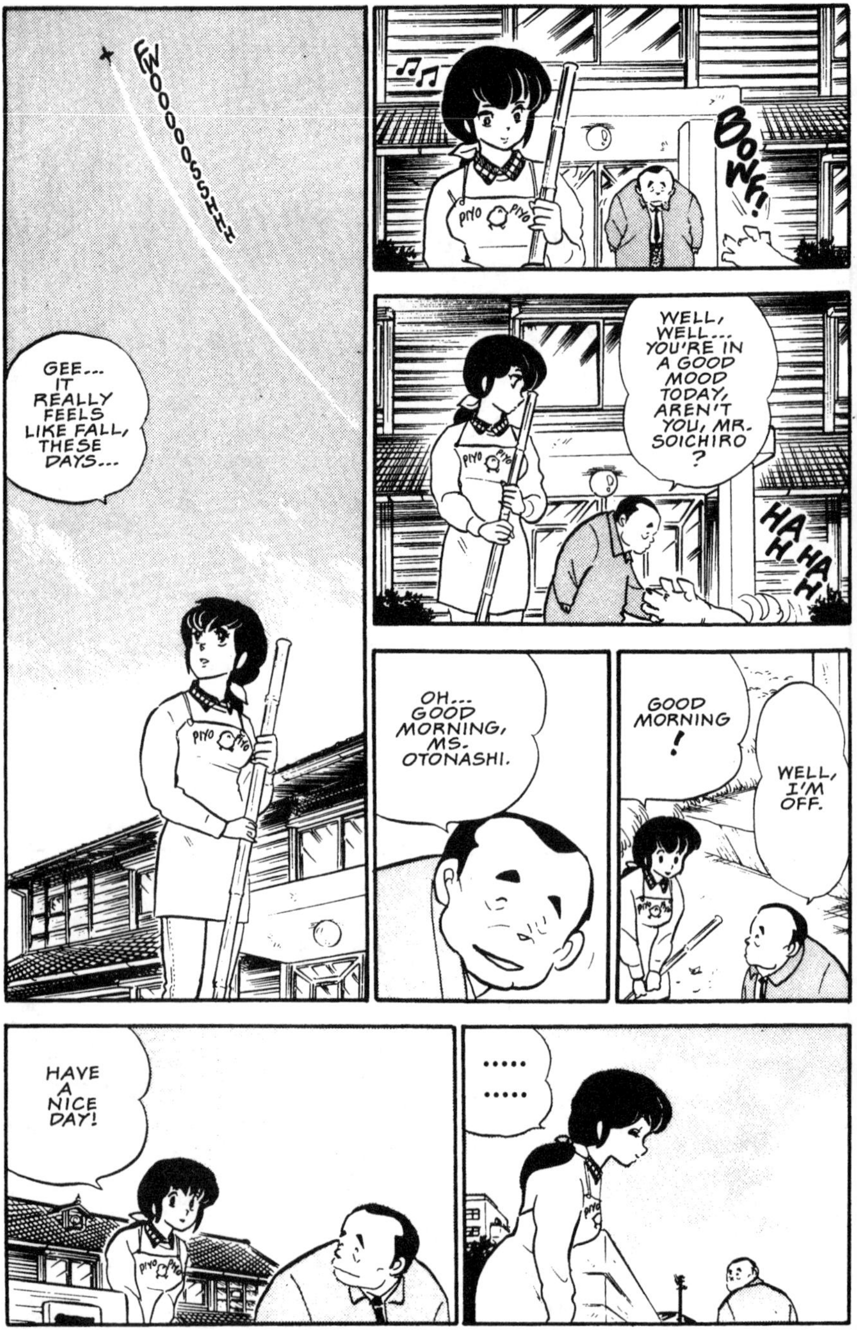
FWOOOOOSSHHH
GEE... IT REALLY FEELS LIKE FALL, THESE DAYS...
BOWF!
WELL, WELL... YOU'RE IN A GOOD MOOD TODAY, AREN'T YOU, MR. SOICHIRO?
HAH HAH HAH
OH... GOOD MORNING, MS. OTONASHI.
GOOD MORNING!
WELL, I'M OFF.
HAVE A NICE DAY!
......
......

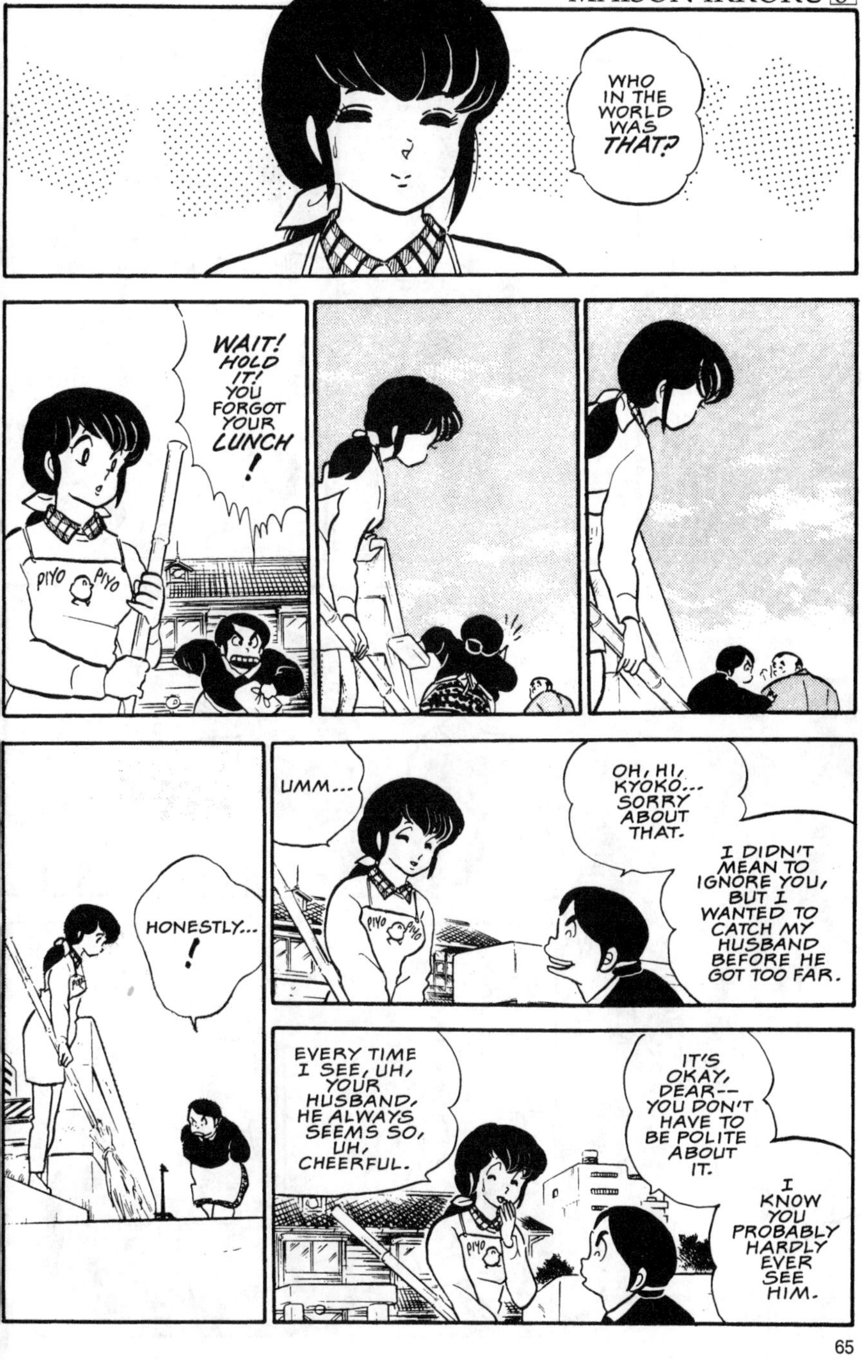
WHO IN THE WORLD WAS THAT?
WAIT! HOLD IT! YOU FORGOT YOUR LUNCH!
PIYO PIYO
HONESTLY...!
UMM...
OH, HI, KYOKO... SORRY ABOUT THAT.
I DIDN'T MEAN TO IGNORE YOU, BUT I WANTED TO CATCH MY HUSBAND BEFORE HE GOT TOO FAR.
EVERY TIME I SEE, UH, YOUR HUSBAND, HE ALWAYS SEEMS SO, UH, CHEERFUL.
IT'S OKAY, DEAR-- YOU DON'T HAVE TO BE POLITE ABOUT IT.
I KNOW YOU PROBABLY HARDLY EVER SEE HIM.

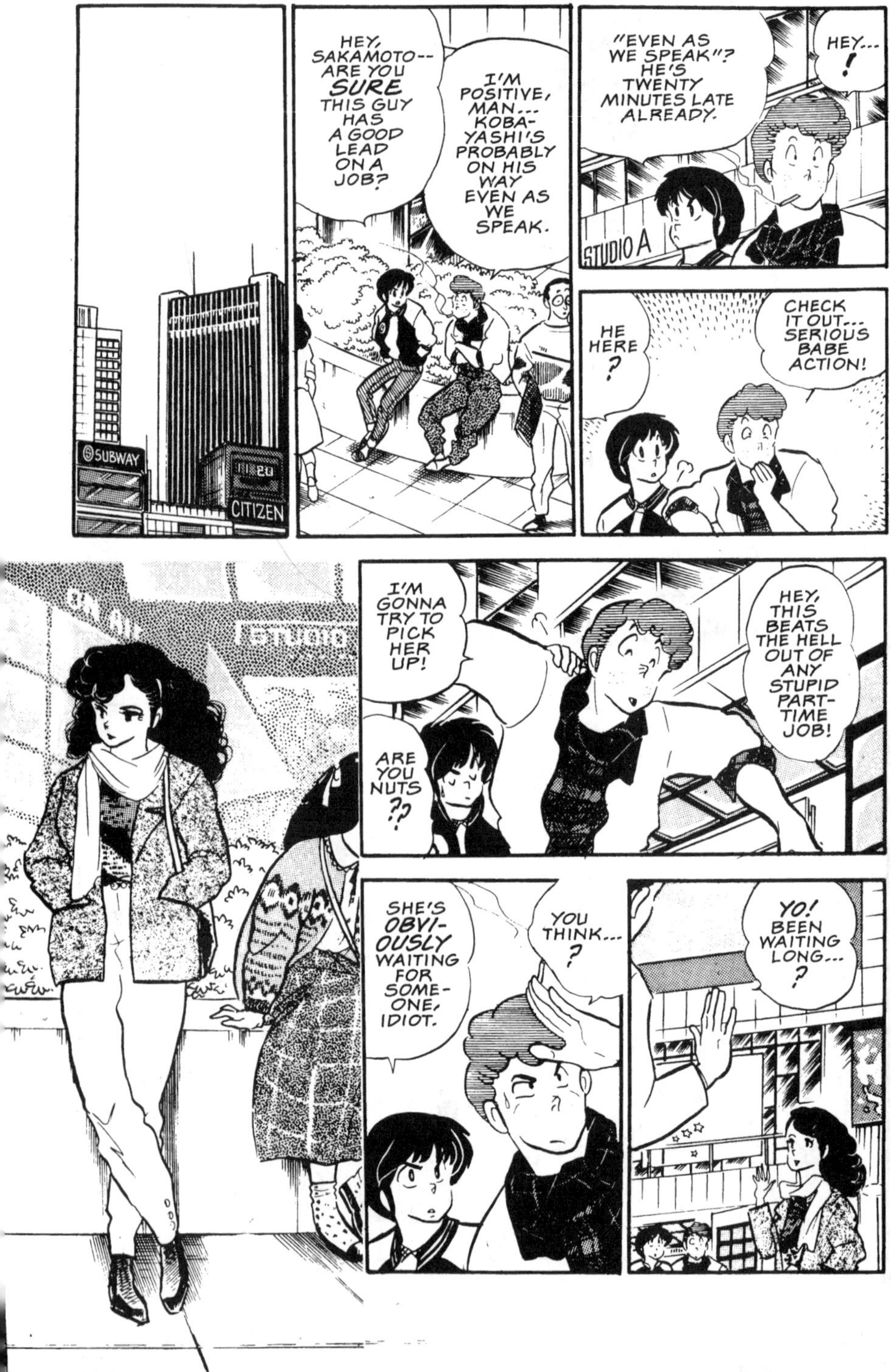
SUBWAY
11:20
CITIZEN
HEY, SAKAMOTO-- ARE YOU SURE THIS GUY HAS A GOOD LEAD ON A JOB?
I'M POSITIVE, MAN... KOBAYASHI'S PROBABLY ON HIS WAY EVEN AS WE SPEAK.
"EVEN AS WE SPEAK"? HE'S TWENTY MINUTES LATE ALREADY.
HEY...!
STUDIO A
HE HERE?
CHECK IT OUT... SERIOUS BABE ACTION!
I'M GONNA TRY TO PICK HER UP!
ARE YOU NUTS??
HEY, THIS BEATS THE HELL OUT OF ANY STUPID PART-TIME JOB!
SHE'S OBVIOUSLY WAITING FOR SOMEONE, IDIOT.
YOU THINK...?
YO! BEEN WAITING LONG...?

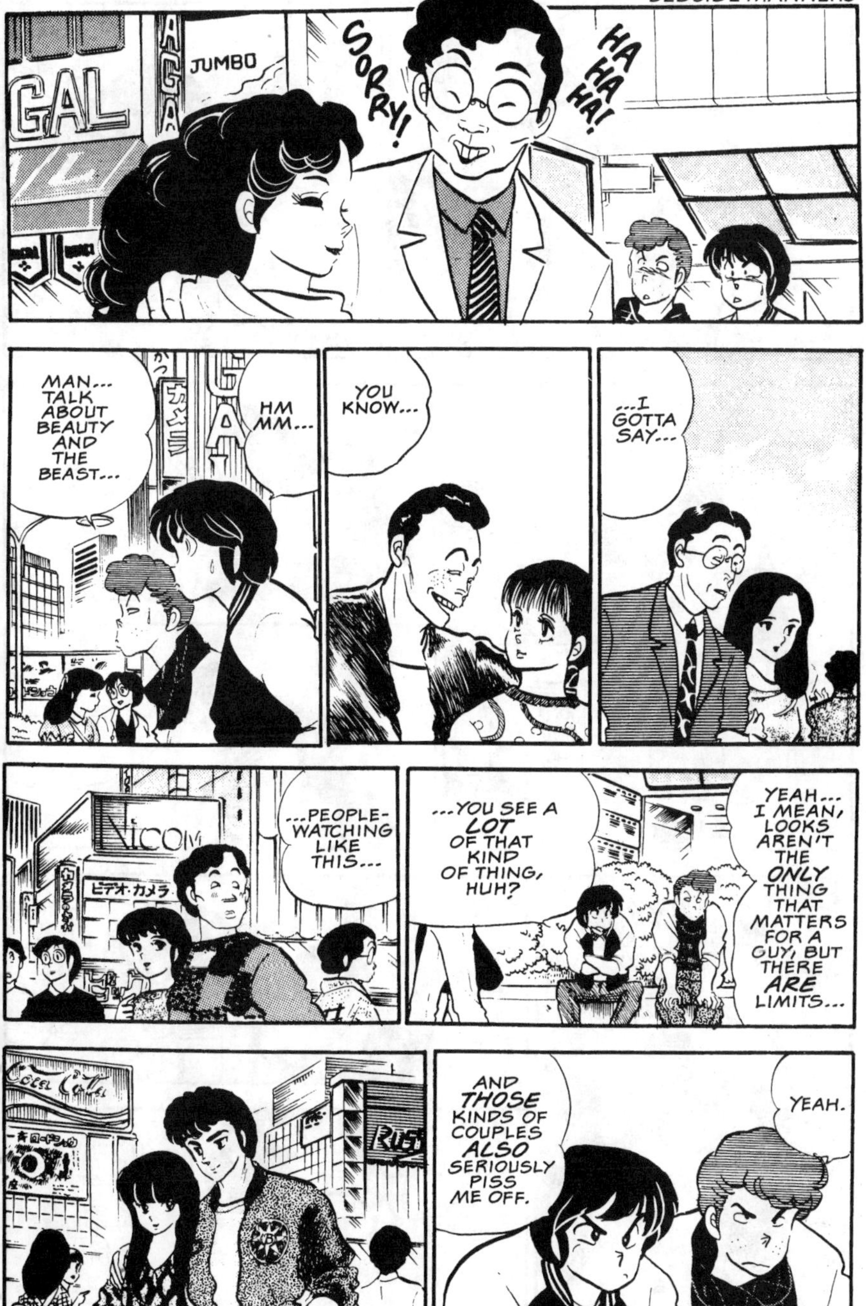
JUMBO
GAL
SORRY!
HA HA HA!
MAN... TALK ABOUT BEAUTY AND THE BEAST...
HM MM...
YOU KNOW...
...I GOTTA SAY...
...PEOPLE-WATCHING LIKE THIS...
NICOM
ビデオ・カメラ
...YOU SEE A LOT OF THAT KIND OF THING, HUH?
YEAH... I MEAN, LOOKS AREN'T THE ONLY THING THAT MATTERS FOR A GUY, BUT THERE ARE LIMITS...
AND THOSE KINDS OF COUPLES ALSO SERIOUSLY PISS ME OFF.
YEAH.

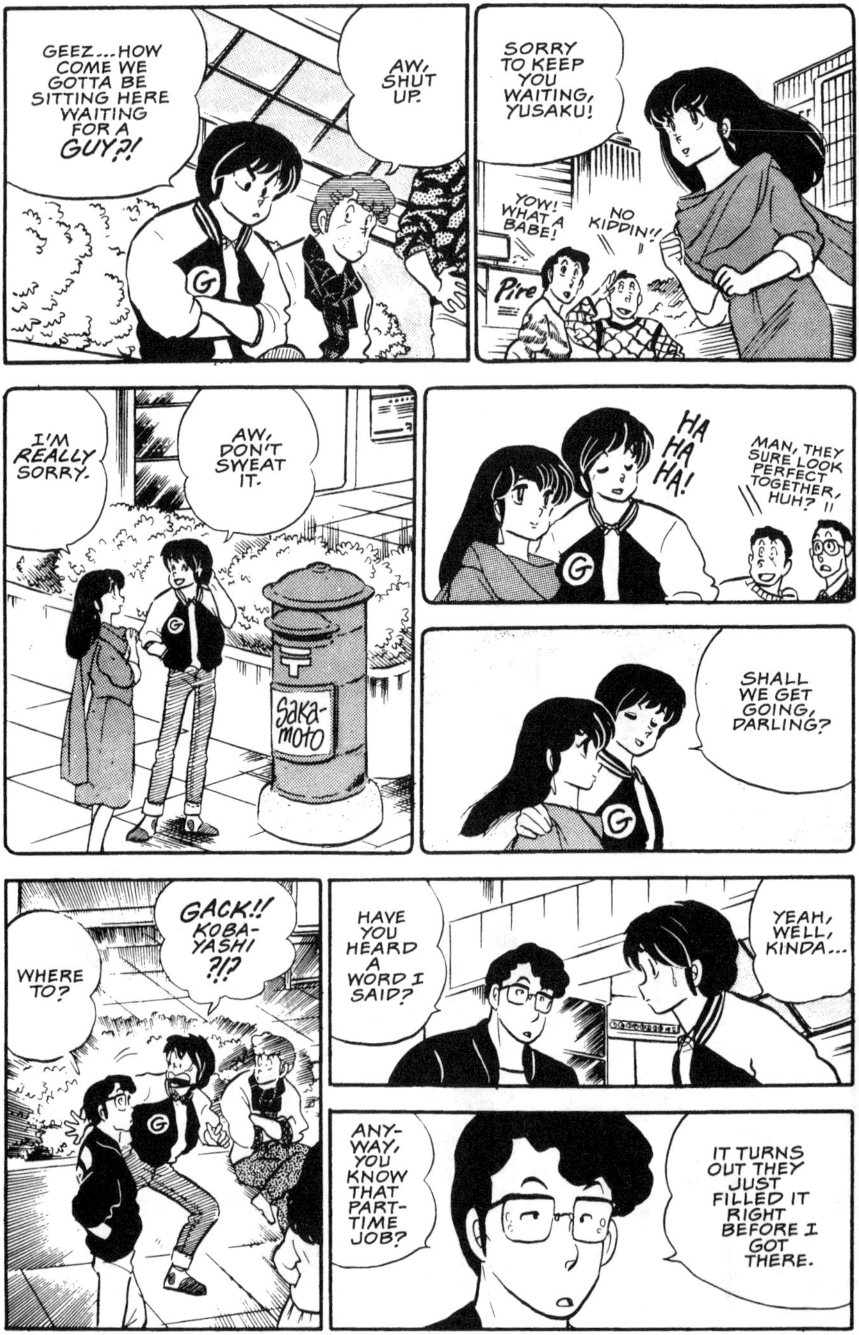
GEEZ...HOW COME WE GOTTA BE SITTING HERE WAITING FOR A GUY?!
AW, SHUT UP.
SORRY TO KEEP YOU WAITING, YUSAKU!
YOW! WHAT A BABE!
NO KIDDIN'!
Pire
I'M REALLY SORRY.
AW, DON'T SWEAT IT.
SAKA-MOTO
HA HA HA!
MAN, THEY SURE LOOK PERFECT TOGETHER, HUH?
SHALL WE GET GOING, DARLING?
WHERE TO?
GACK!! KOBA-YASHI ?!?
HAVE YOU HEARD A WORD I SAID?
YEAH, WELL, KINDA...
ANY-WAY, YOU KNOW THAT PART-TIME JOB?
IT TURNS OUT THEY JUST FILLED IT RIGHT BEFORE I GOT THERE.

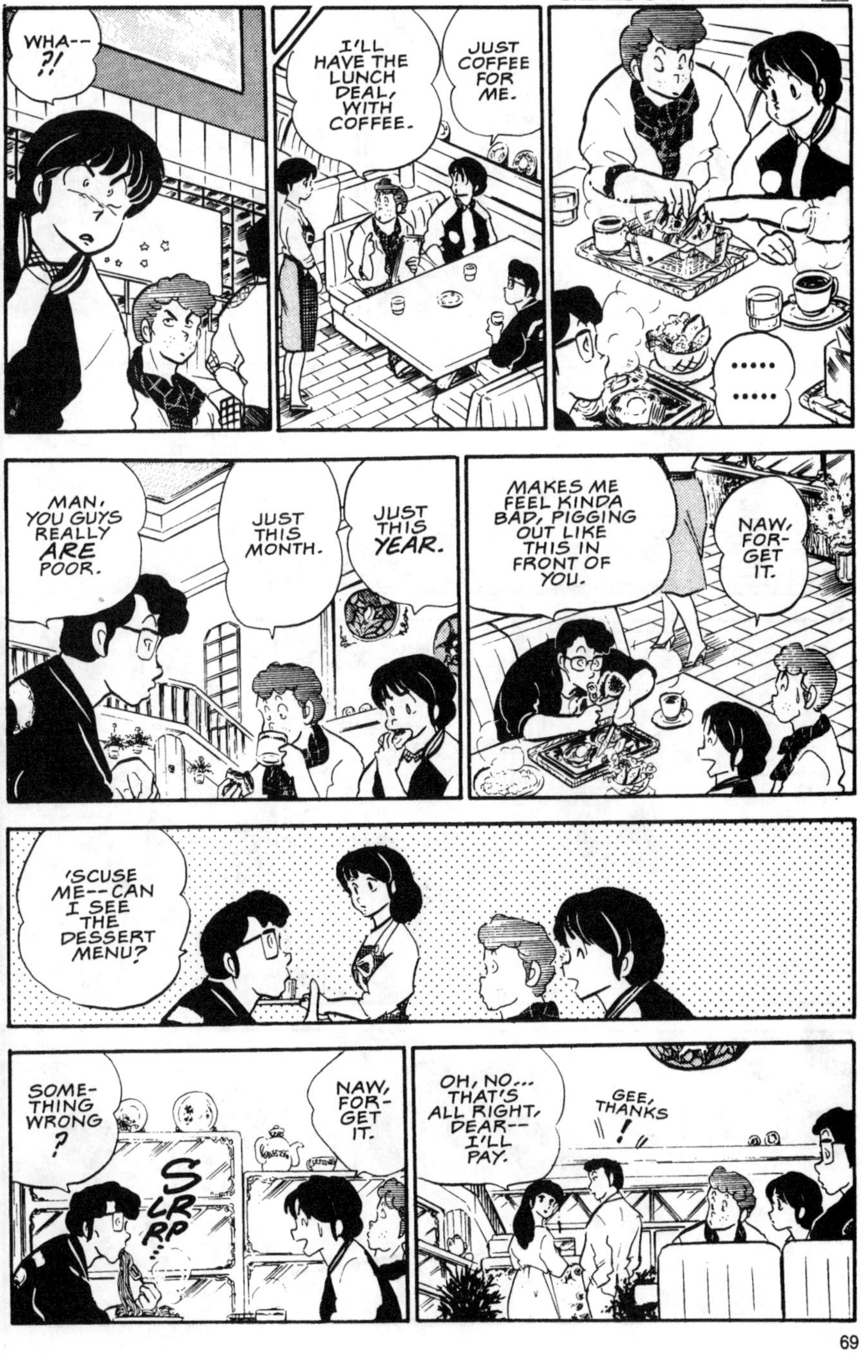
WHA-- ?!
I'LL HAVE THE LUNCH DEAL, WITH COFFEE.
JUST COFFEE FOR ME.
....
MAN, YOU GUYS REALLY ARE POOR.
JUST THIS MONTH.
JUST THIS YEAR.
MAKES ME FEEL KINDA BAD, PIGGING OUT LIKE THIS IN FRONT OF YOU.
NAW, FOR-GET IT.
'SCUSE ME--CAN I SEE THE DESSERT MENU?
SOME-THING WRONG?
SLRRP
NAW, FOR-GET IT.
OH, NO... THAT'S ALL RIGHT, DEAR-- I'LL PAY.
GEE, THANKS!

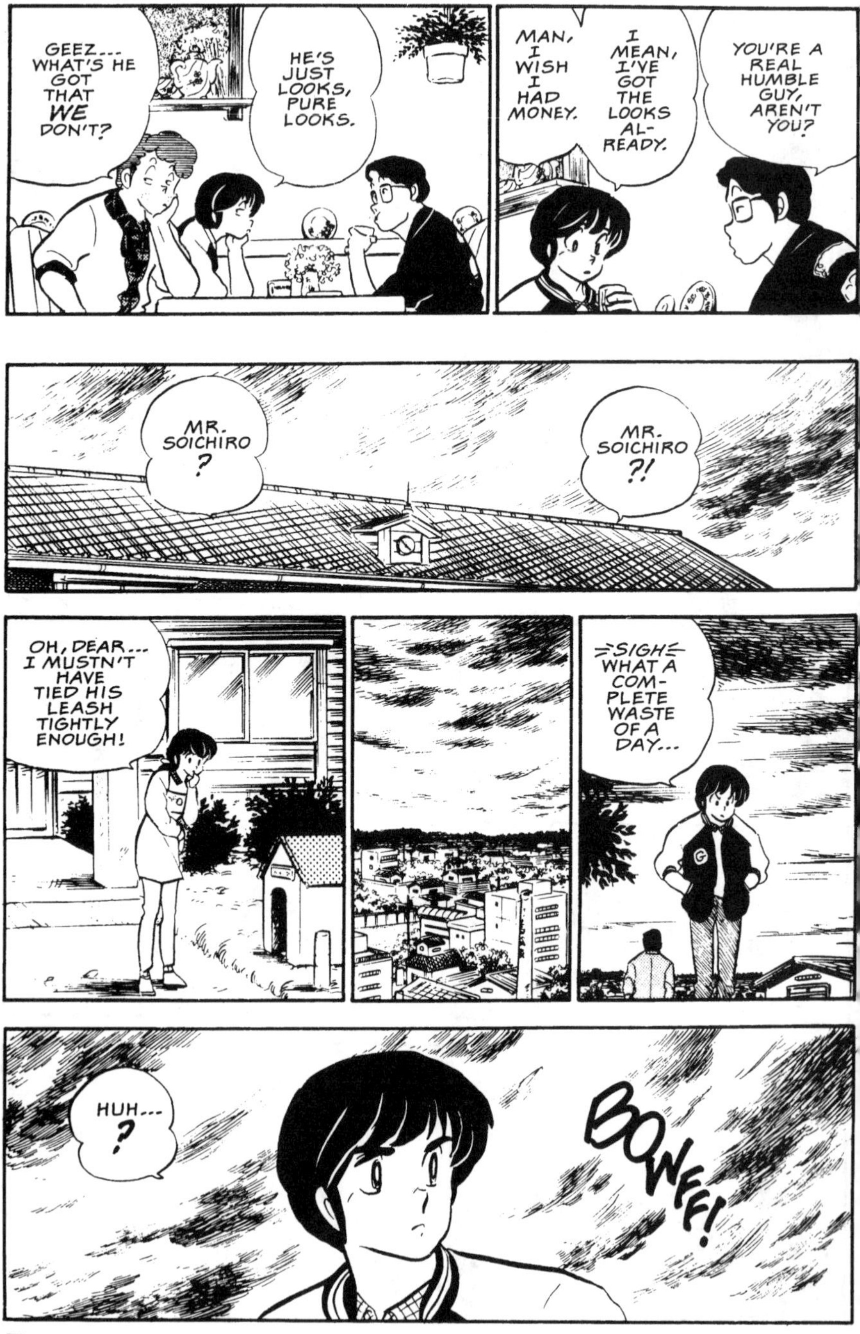
GEEZ... WHAT'S HE GOT THAT WE DON'T?
HE'S JUST LOOKS, PURE LOOKS.
MAN, I WISH I HAD MONEY.
I MEAN, I'VE GOT THE LOOKS AL-READY.
YOU'RE A REAL HUMBLE GUY, AREN'T YOU?
MR. SOICHIRO?
MR. SOICHIRO?!
OH, DEAR... I MUSTN'T HAVE TIED HIS LEASH TIGHTLY ENOUGH!
SIGH WHAT A COM-PLETE WASTE OF A DAY...
HUH...?
BOWFF!

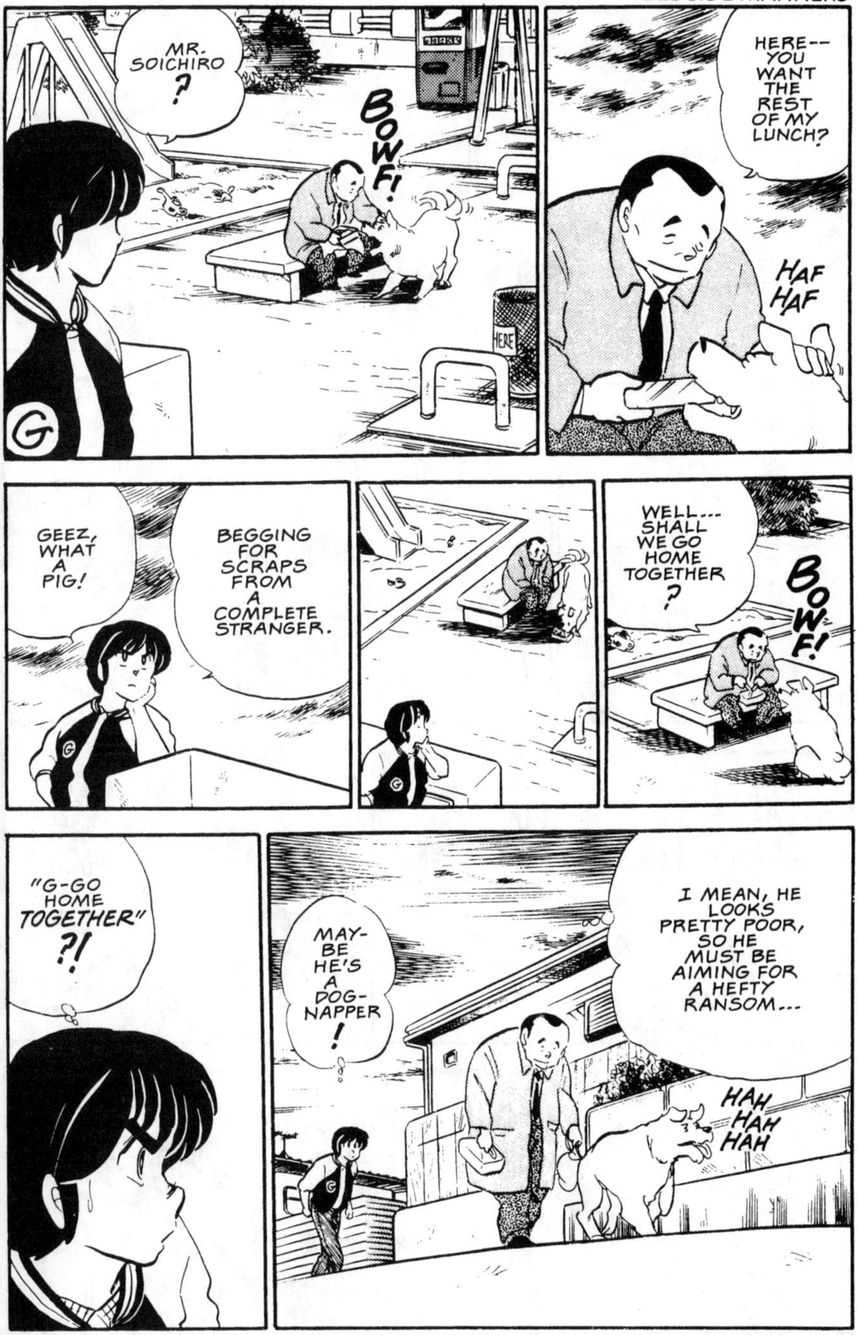
MR. SOICHIRO?
BOWF!
HERE-- YOU WANT THE REST OF MY LUNCH?
HAF HAF
GEEZ, WHAT A PIG!
BEGGING FOR SCRAPS FROM A COMPLETE STRANGER.
WELL... SHALL WE GO HOME TOGETHER?
BOWF!
"G-GO HOME TOGETHER"?!
MAY-BE HE'S A DOG-NAPPER!
I MEAN, HE LOOKS PRETTY POOR, SO HE MUST BE AIMING FOR A HEFTY RANSOM...
HAH HAH HAH

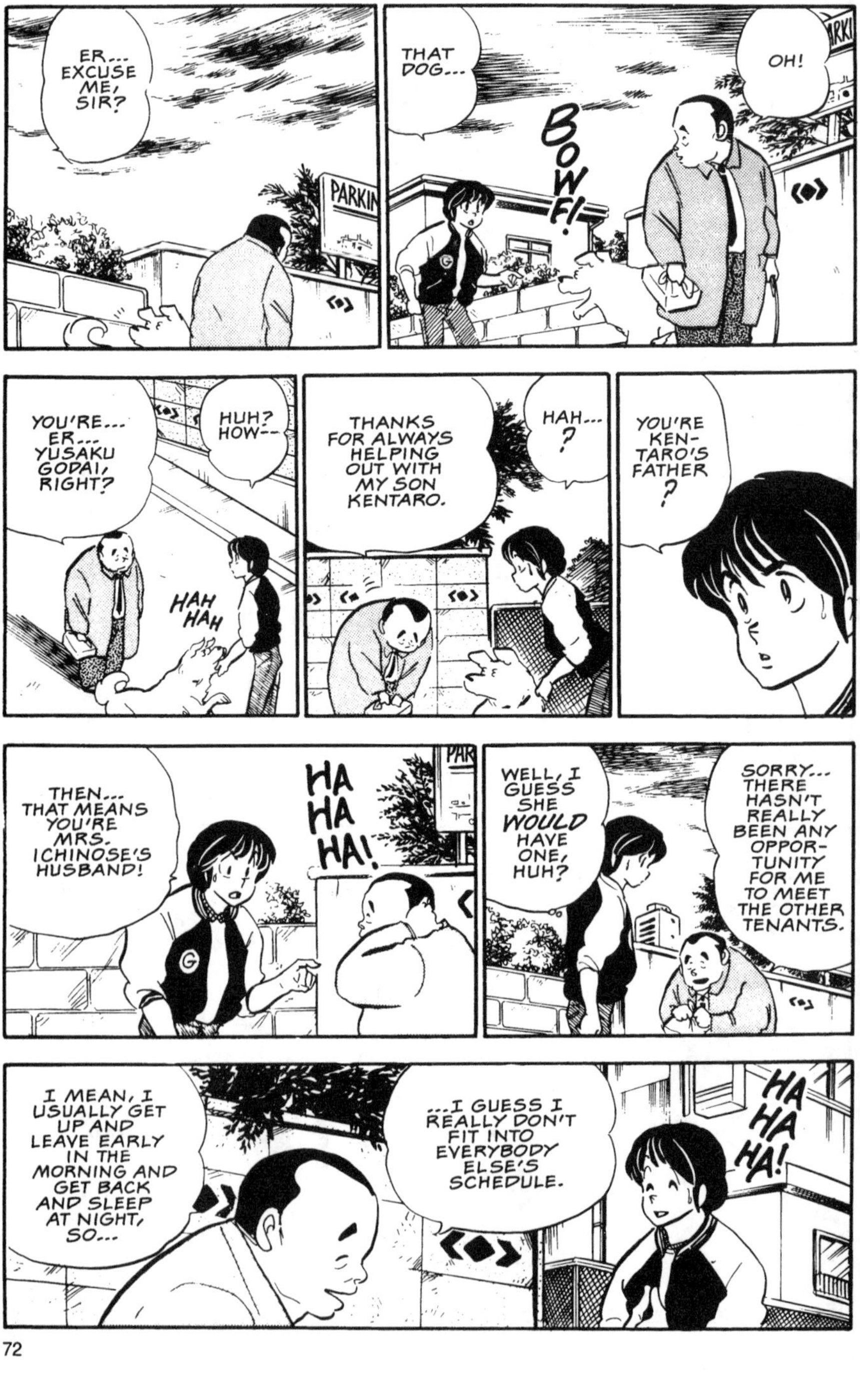
ER... EXCUSE ME, SIR?
THAT DOG...
BOWF!
OH!
YOU'RE... ER... YUSAKU GODAI, RIGHT?
HUH? HOW--
HAH HAH
THANKS FOR ALWAYS HELPING OUT WITH MY SON KENTARO.
HAH... ?
YOU'RE KEN-TARO'S FATHER ?
THEN... THAT MEANS YOU'RE MRS. ICHINOSE'S HUSBAND!
HA HA HA!
WELL, I GUESS SHE WOULD HAVE ONE, HUH?
SORRY... THERE HASN'T REALLY BEEN ANY OPPOR-TUNITY FOR ME TO MEET THE OTHER TENANTS.
I MEAN, I USUALLY GET UP AND LEAVE EARLY IN THE MORNING AND GET BACK AND SLEEP AT NIGHT, SO...
...I GUESS I REALLY DON'T FIT INTO EVERYBODY ELSE'S SCHEDULE.
HA HA HA!

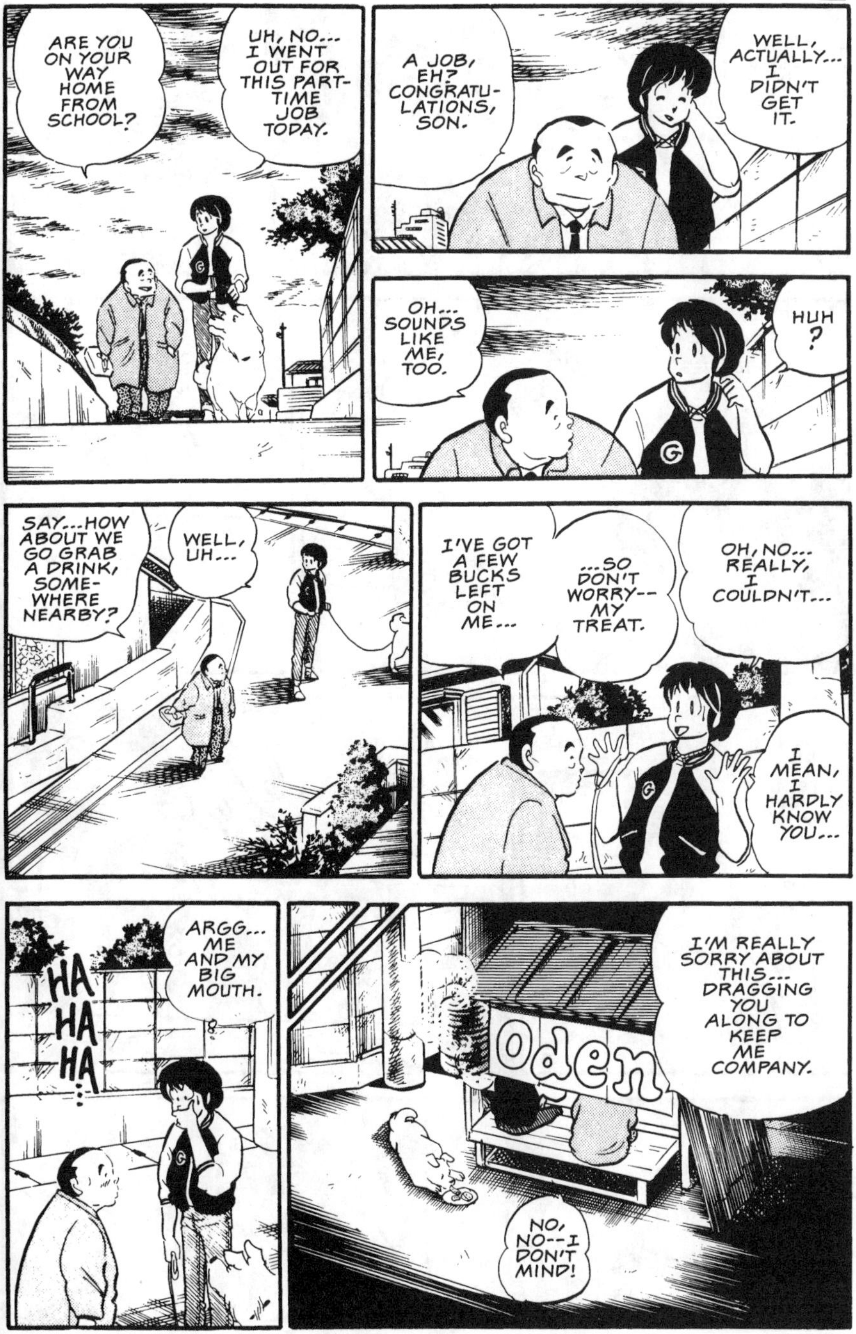
ARE YOU ON YOUR WAY HOME FROM SCHOOL?
UH, NO... I WENT OUT FOR THIS PART-TIME JOB TODAY.
A JOB, EH? CONGRATULATIONS, SON.
WELL, ACTUALLY... I DIDN'T GET IT.
OH... SOUNDS LIKE ME, TOO.
HUH?
SAY...HOW ABOUT WE GO GRAB A DRINK, SOMEWHERE NEARBY?
WELL, UH...
I'VE GOT A FEW BUCKS LEFT ON ME...
...SO DON'T WORRY--MY TREAT.
OH, NO... REALLY, I COULDN'T...
I MEAN, I HARDLY KNOW YOU...
HA HA HA...
ARGG... ME AND MY BIG MOUTH.
I'M REALLY SORRY ABOUT THIS... DRAGGING YOU ALONG TO KEEP ME COMPANY.
Oden
NO, NO--I DON'T MIND!

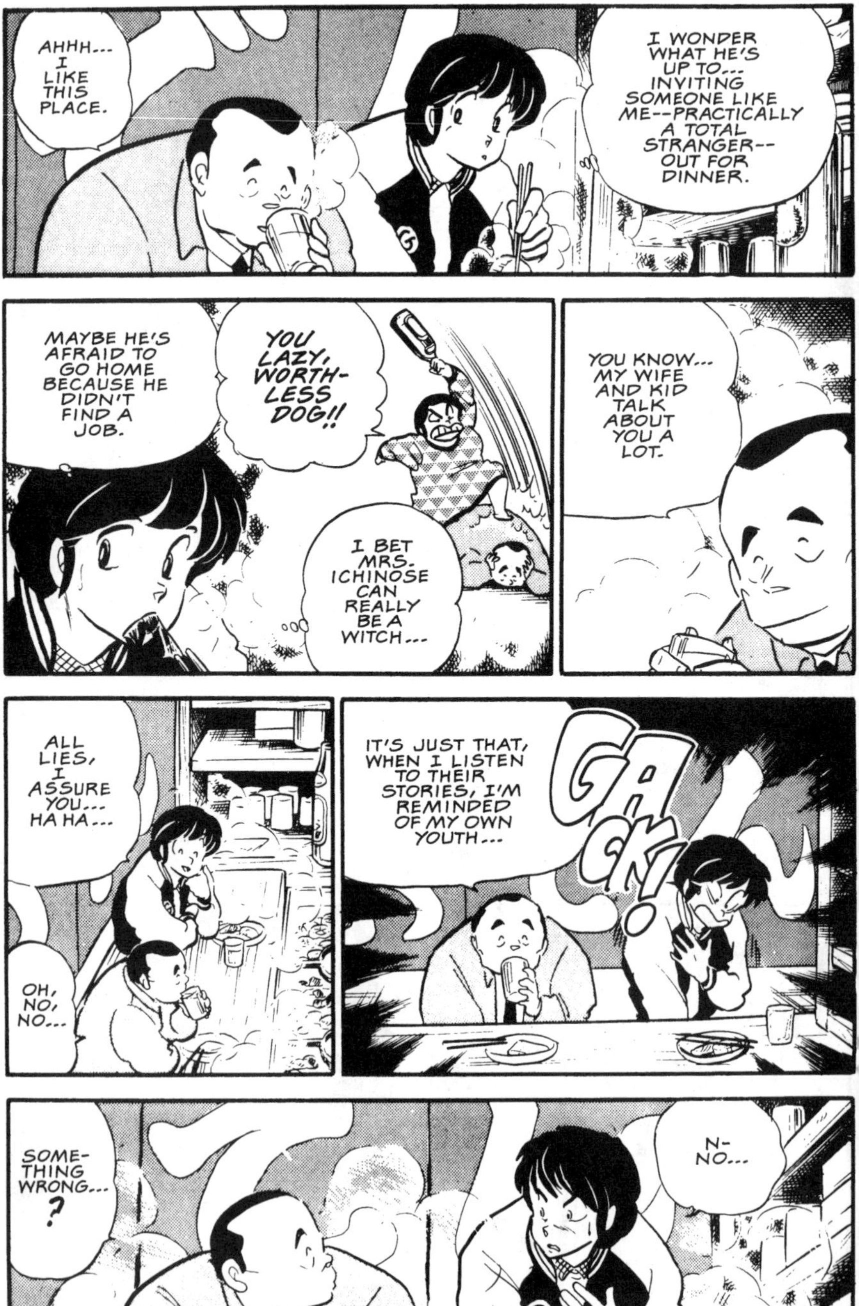

AHHH... I LIKE THIS PLACE.
I WONDER WHAT HE'S UP TO... INVITING SOMEONE LIKE ME--PRACTICALLY A TOTAL STRANGER--OUT FOR DINNER.
MAYBE HE'S AFRAID TO GO HOME BECAUSE HE DIDN'T FIND A JOB.
YOU LAZY, WORTH-LESS DOG!!
I BET MRS. ICHINOSE CAN REALLY BE A WITCH...
YOU KNOW... MY WIFE AND KID TALK ABOUT YOU A LOT.
ALL LIES, I ASSURE YOU... HA HA...
OH, NO, NO...
IT'S JUST THAT, WHEN I LISTEN TO THEIR STORIES, I'M REMINDED OF MY OWN YOUTH...
GACK!
SOME-THING WRONG...?
N-NO...

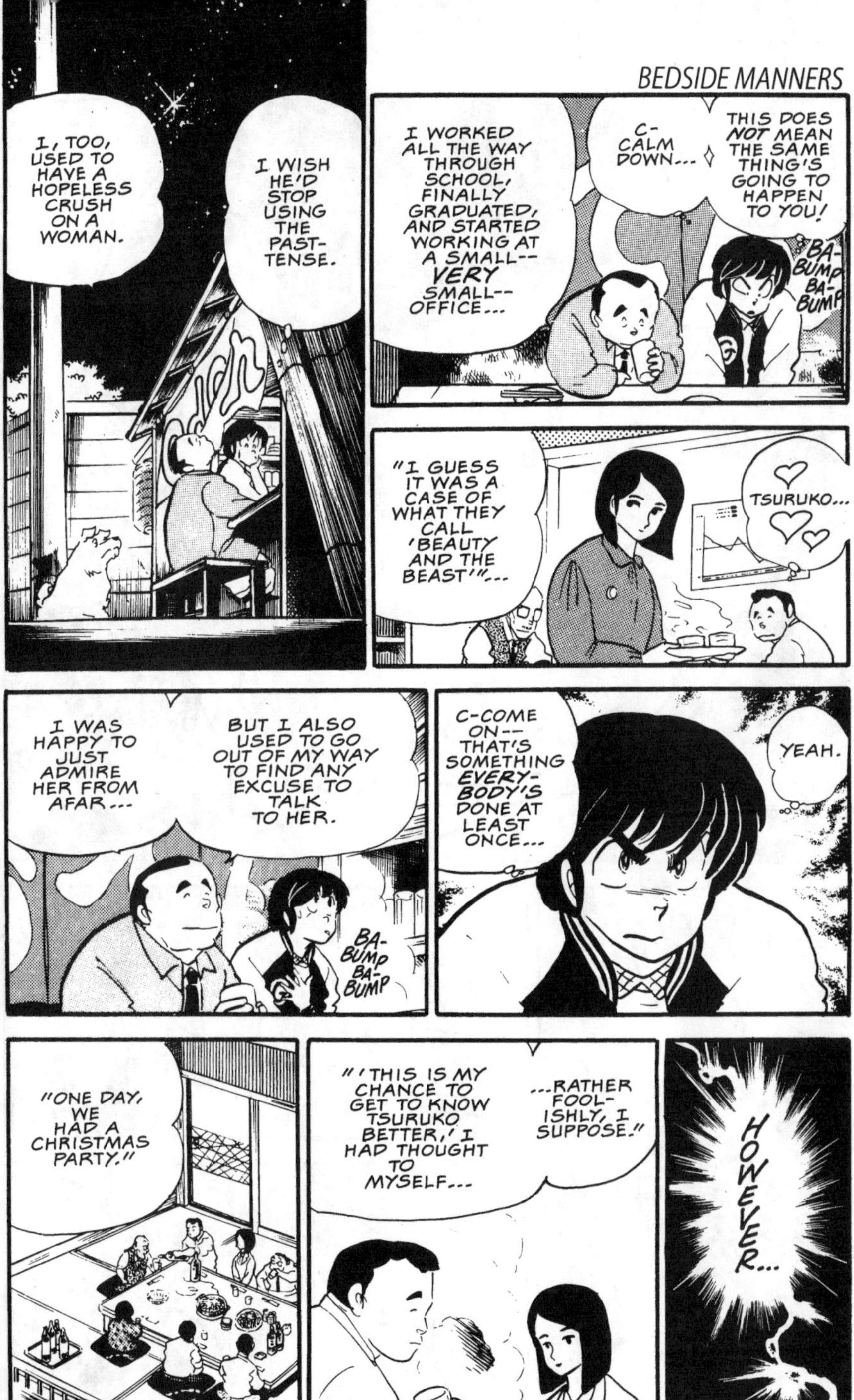
I, TOO, USED TO HAVE A HOPELESS CRUSH ON A WOMAN.
I WISH HE'D STOP USING THE PAST-TENSE.
I WORKED ALL THE WAY THROUGH SCHOOL, FINALLY GRADUATED, AND STARTED WORKING AT A SMALL-- VERY SMALL-- OFFICE...
C-CALM DOWN...
THIS DOES NOT MEAN THE SAME THING'S GOING TO HAPPEN TO YOU!
BA-BUMP BA-BUMP
"I GUESS IT WAS A CASE OF WHAT THEY CALL 'BEAUTY AND THE BEAST'"...
TSURUKO...
I WAS HAPPY TO JUST ADMIRE HER FROM AFAR...
BUT I ALSO USED TO GO OUT OF MY WAY TO FIND ANY EXCUSE TO TALK TO HER.
BA-BUMP BA-BUMP
C-COME ON-- THAT'S SOMETHING EVERY-BODY'S DONE AT LEAST ONCE...
YEAH.
"ONE DAY, WE HAD A CHRISTMAS PARTY."
"'THIS IS MY CHANCE TO GET TO KNOW TSURUKO BETTER,' I HAD THOUGHT TO MYSELF...
...RATHER FOOL-ISHLY, I SUPPOSE."
HOWEVER...

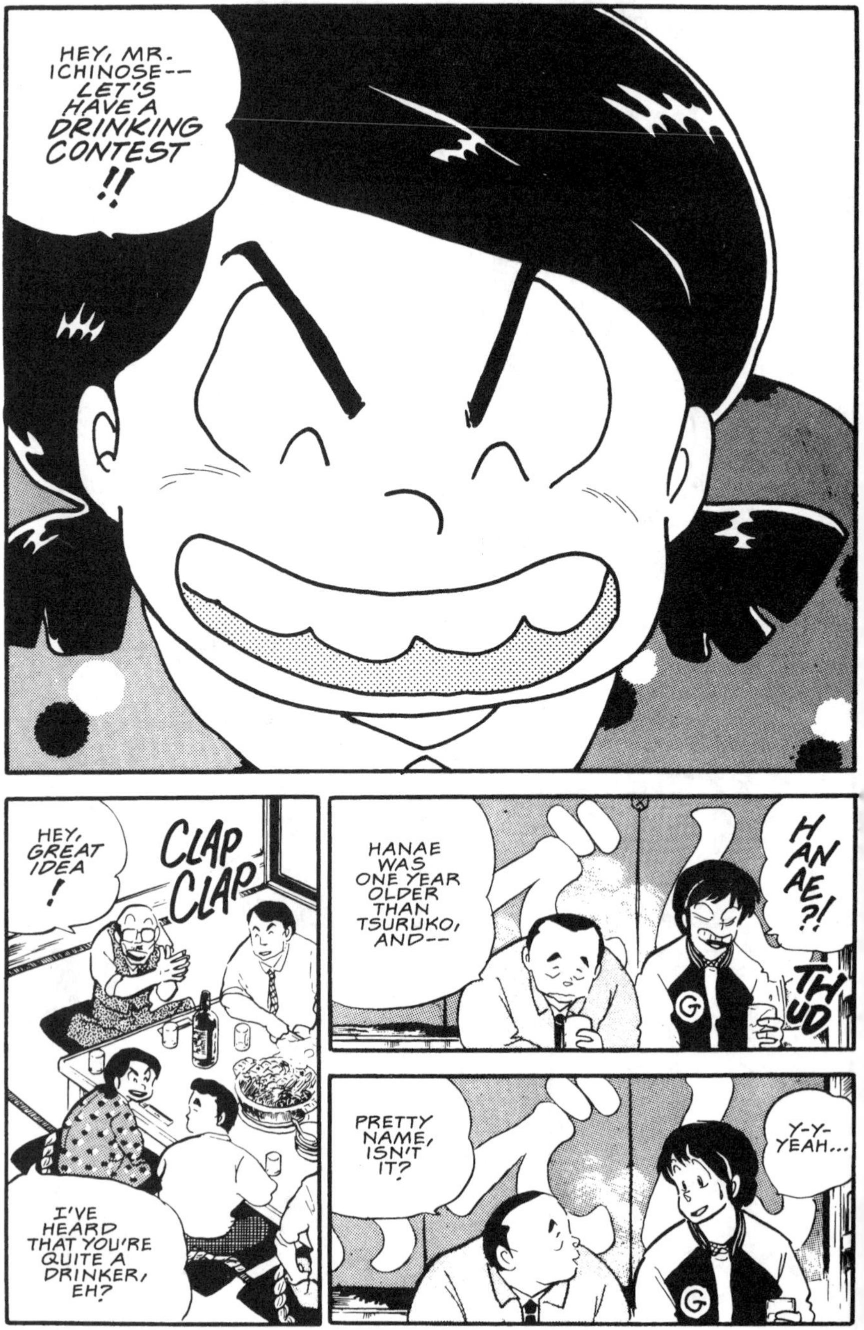
HEY, MR. ICHINOSE-- LET'S HAVE A DRINKING CONTEST!!
HEY, GREAT IDEA!
CLAP CLAP
I'VE HEARD THAT YOU'RE QUITE A DRINKER, EH?
HANAE WAS ONE YEAR OLDER THAN TSURUKO, AND--
HANAE?!
THUD
PRETTY NAME, ISN'T IT?
Y-Y-YEAH...

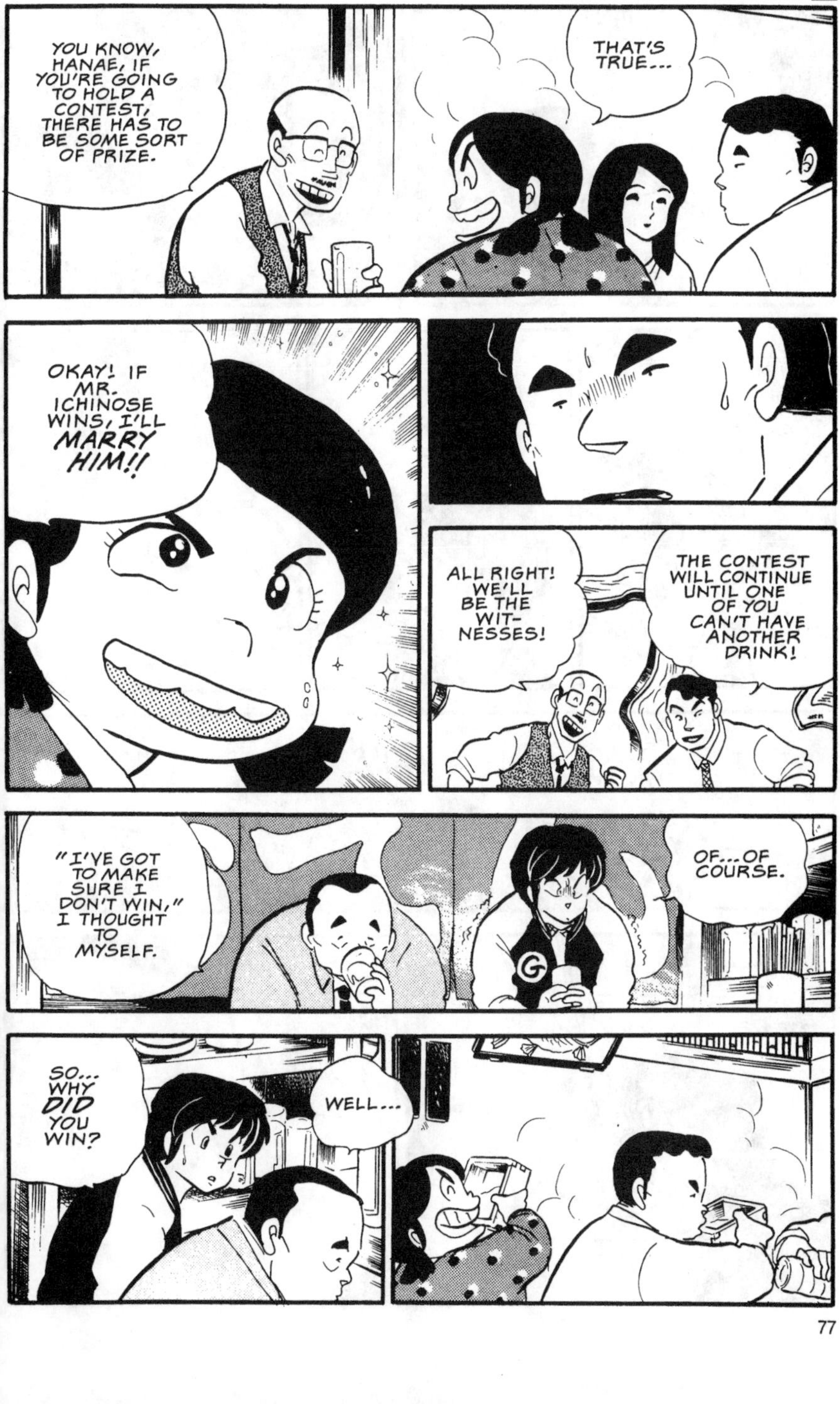
YOU KNOW, HANAE, IF YOU'RE GOING TO HOLD A CONTEST, THERE HAS TO BE SOME SORT OF PRIZE.
THAT'S TRUE...
OKAY! IF MR. ICHINOSE WINS, I'LL MARRY HIM!!
ALL RIGHT! WE'LL BE THE WIT-NESSES!
THE CONTEST WILL CONTINUE UNTIL ONE OF YOU CAN'T HAVE ANOTHER DRINK!
"I'VE GOT TO MAKE SURE I DON'T WIN," I THOUGHT TO MYSELF.
OF...OF COURSE.
SO... WHY DID YOU WIN?
WELL...

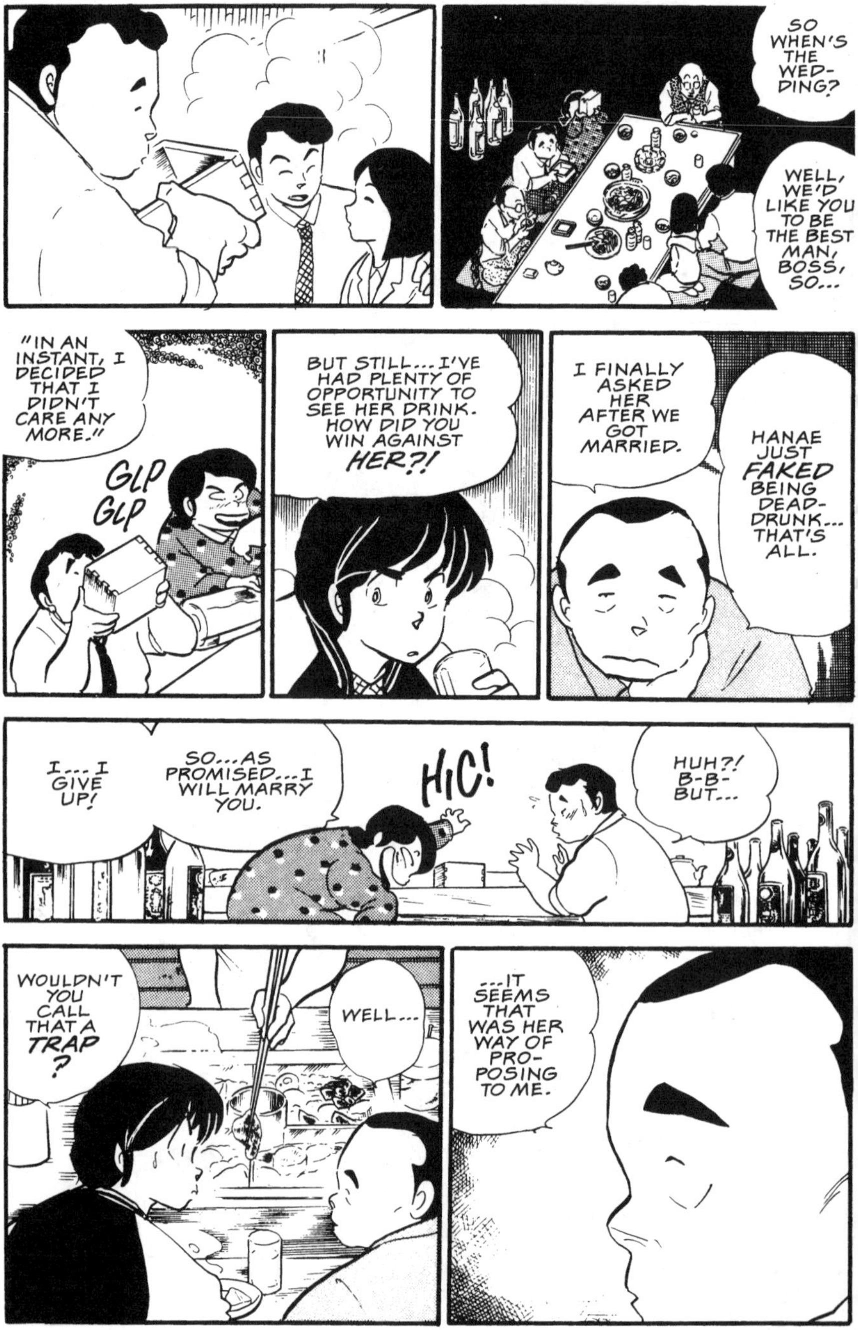
SO WHEN'S THE WED-DING?
WELL, WE'D LIKE YOU TO BE THE BEST MAN, BOSS, SO...
"IN AN INSTANT, I DECIDED THAT I DIDN'T CARE ANY MORE."
GLP GLP
BUT STILL... I'VE HAD PLENTY OF OPPORTUNITY TO SEE HER DRINK. HOW DID YOU WIN AGAINST HER?!
I FINALLY ASKED HER AFTER WE GOT MARRIED.
HANAE JUST FAKED BEING DEAD-DRUNK... THAT'S ALL.
I... I GIVE UP!
SO... AS PROMISED... I WILL MARRY YOU.
HIC!
HUH?! B-B-BUT...
WOULDN'T YOU CALL THAT A TRAP?
WELL...
...IT SEEMS THAT WAS HER WAY OF PRO-POSING TO ME.

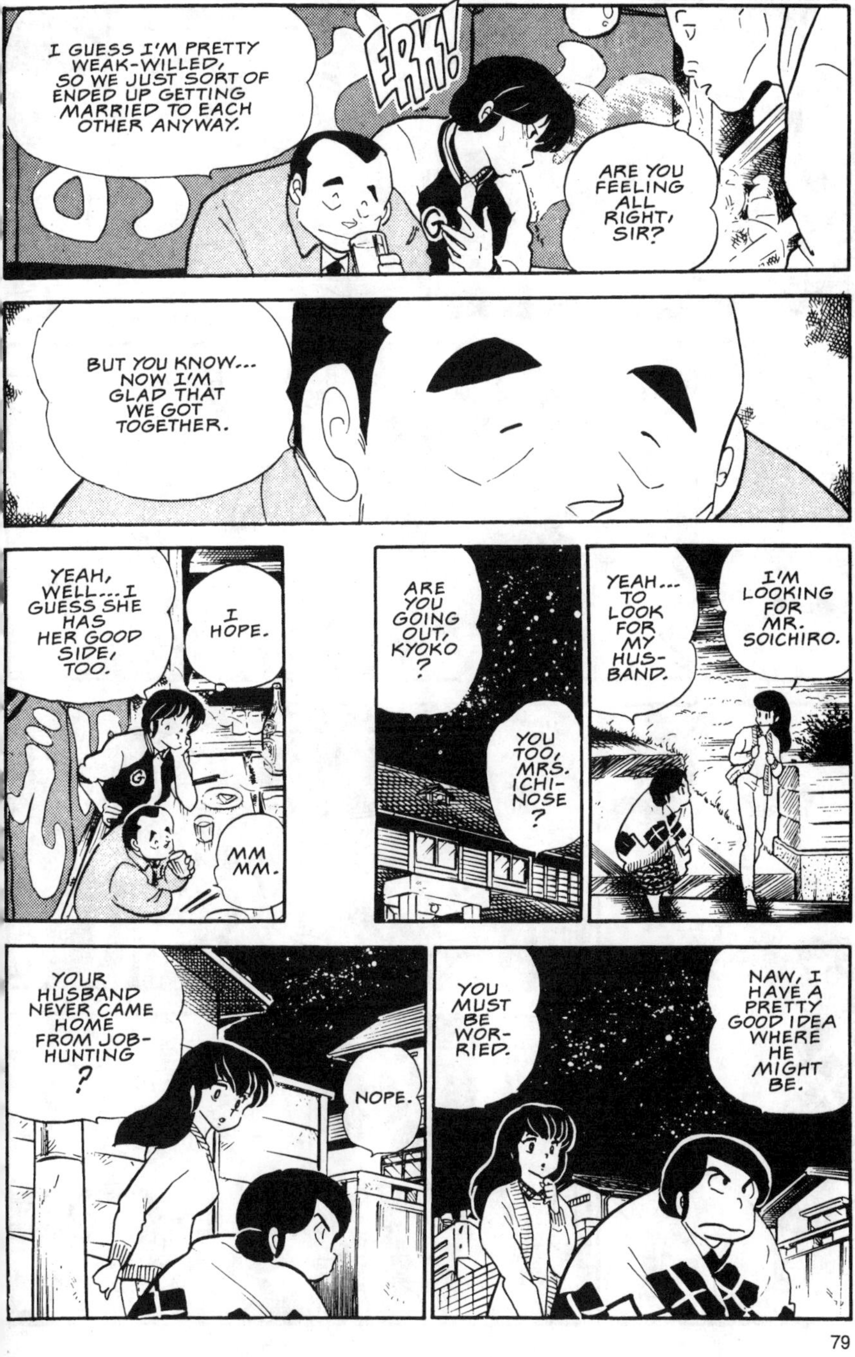
I GUESS I'M PRETTY WEAK-WILLED, SO WE JUST SORT OF ENDED UP GETTING MARRIED TO EACH OTHER ANYWAY.
ERK!
ARE YOU FEELING ALL RIGHT, SIR?
BUT YOU KNOW... NOW I'M GLAD THAT WE GOT TOGETHER.
YEAH, WELL... I GUESS SHE HAS HER GOOD SIDE, TOO.
I HOPE.
MM MM.
ARE YOU GOING OUT, KYOKO?
YOU TOO, MRS. ICHINOSE?
YEAH... TO LOOK FOR MY HUSBAND.
I'M LOOKING FOR MR. SOICHIRO.
YOUR HUSBAND NEVER CAME HOME FROM JOB-HUNTING?
NOPE.
YOU MUST BE WORRIED.
NAW, I HAVE A PRETTY GOOD IDEA WHERE HE MIGHT BE.

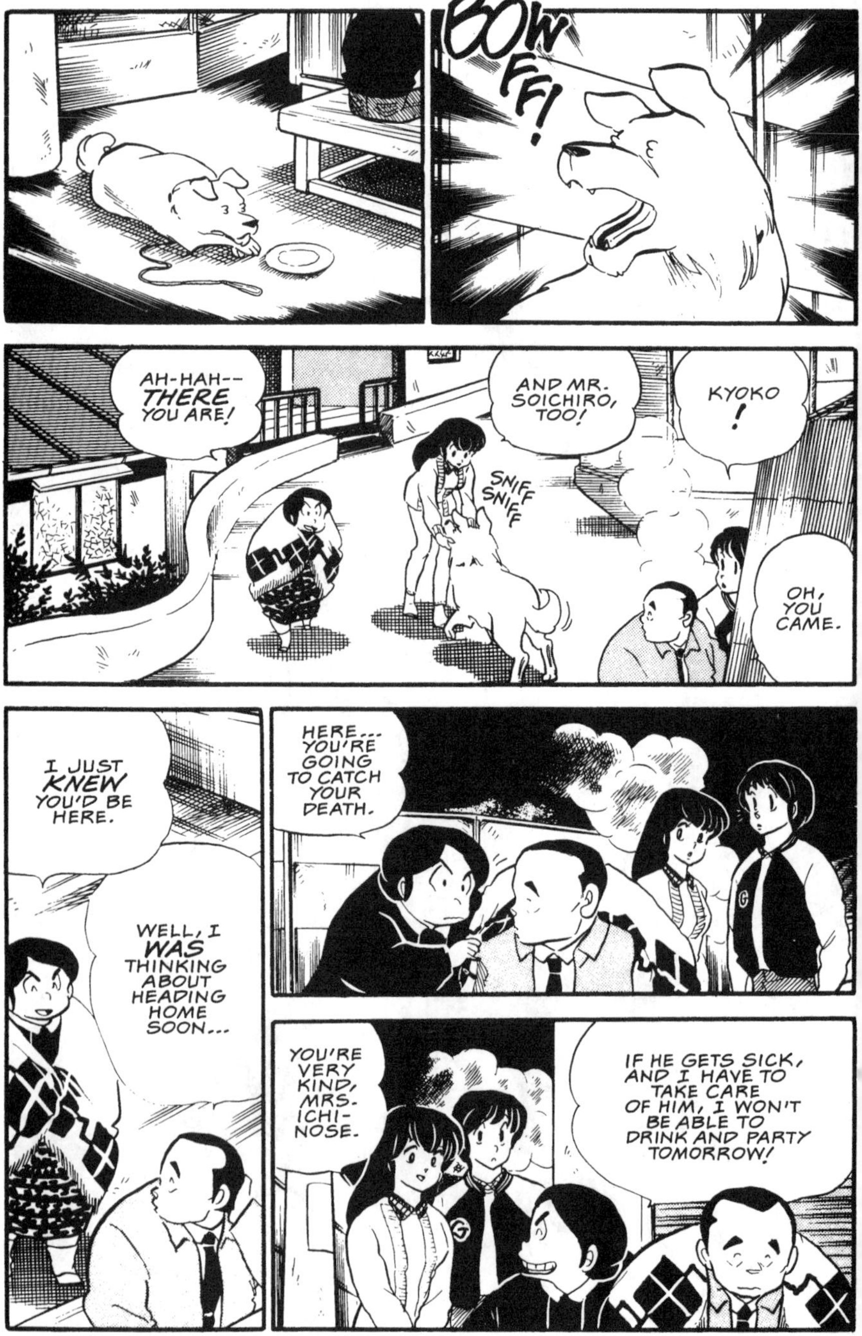
BOWFF!
AH-HAH-- THERE YOU ARE!
AND MR. SOICHIRO, TOO!
KYOKO!
SNIFF SNIFF
OH, YOU CAME.
I JUST KNEW YOU'D BE HERE.
WELL, I WAS THINKING ABOUT HEADING HOME SOON...
HERE... YOU'RE GOING TO CATCH YOUR DEATH.
YOU'RE VERY KIND, MRS. ICHI-NOSE.
IF HE GETS SICK, AND I HAVE TO TAKE CARE OF HIM, I WON'T BE ABLE TO DRINK AND PARTY TOMORROW!

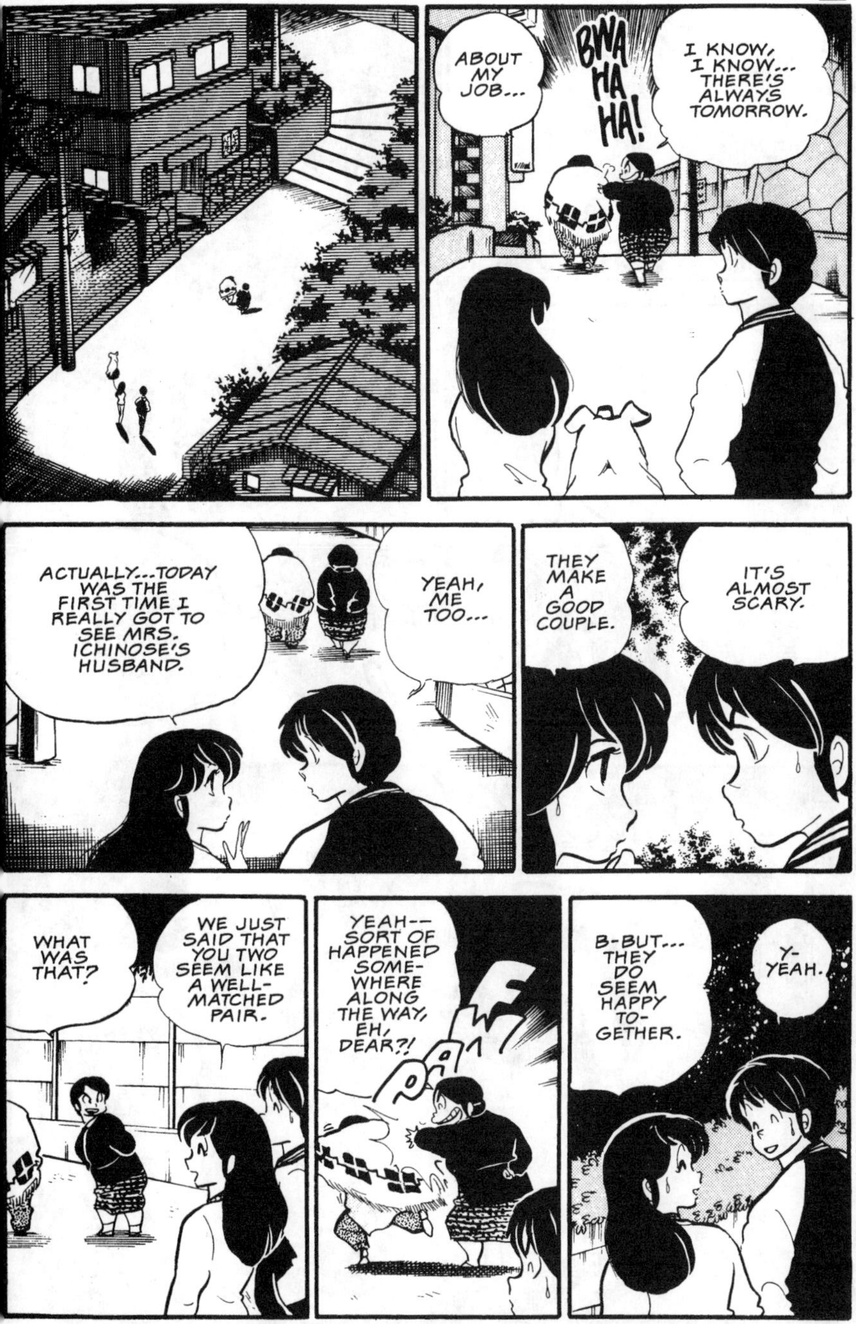
ABOUT MY JOB...
BWA HA HA!
I KNOW, I KNOW... THERE'S ALWAYS TOMORROW.
ACTUALLY...TODAY WAS THE FIRST TIME I REALLY GOT TO SEE MRS. ICHINOSE'S HUSBAND.
YEAH, ME TOO...
THEY MAKE A GOOD COUPLE.
IT'S ALMOST SCARY.
WHAT WAS THAT?
WE JUST SAID THAT YOU TWO SEEM LIKE A WELL-MATCHED PAIR.
YEAH-- SORT OF HAPPENED SOME-WHERE ALONG THE WAY, EH, DEAR?!
B-BUT... THEY DO SEEM HAPPY TO-GETHER.
Y-YEAH.

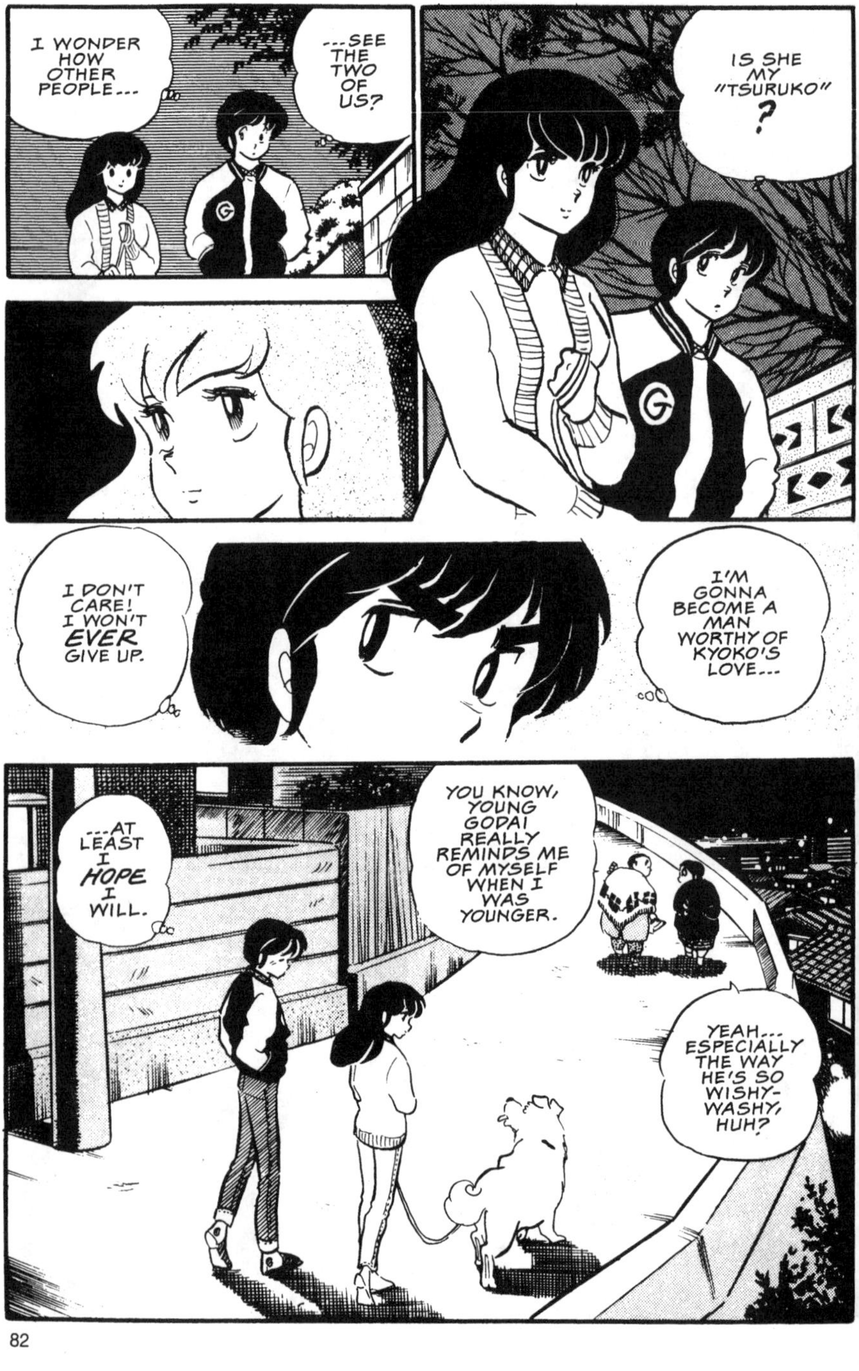

I WONDER HOW OTHER PEOPLE...
...SEE THE TWO OF US?
IS SHE MY "TSURUKO"?
I DON'T CARE! I WON'T EVER GIVE UP.
I'M GONNA BECOME A MAN WORTHY OF KYOKO'S LOVE...
...AT LEAST I HOPE I WILL.
YOU KNOW, YOUNG GODAI REALLY REMINDS ME OF MYSELF WHEN I WAS YOUNGER.
YEAH... ESPECIALLY THE WAY HE'S SO WISHY-WASHY, HUH?

PART FIVE

RUN, ICHINOSE, RUN!

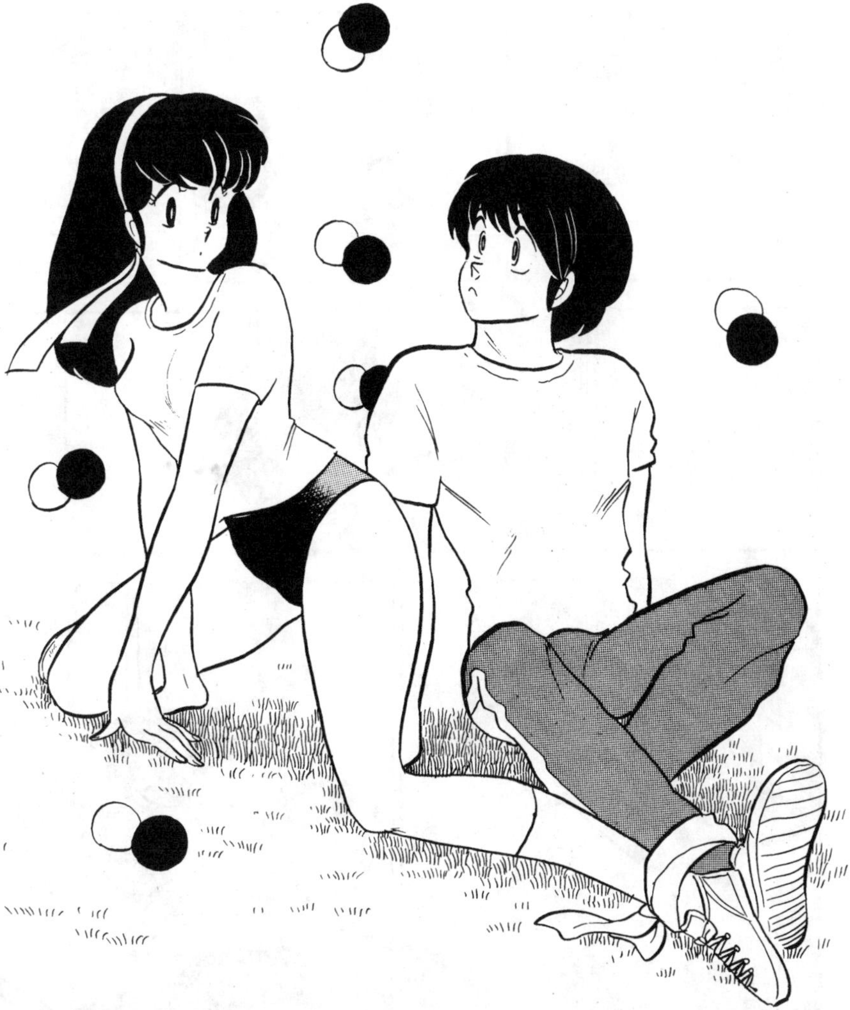

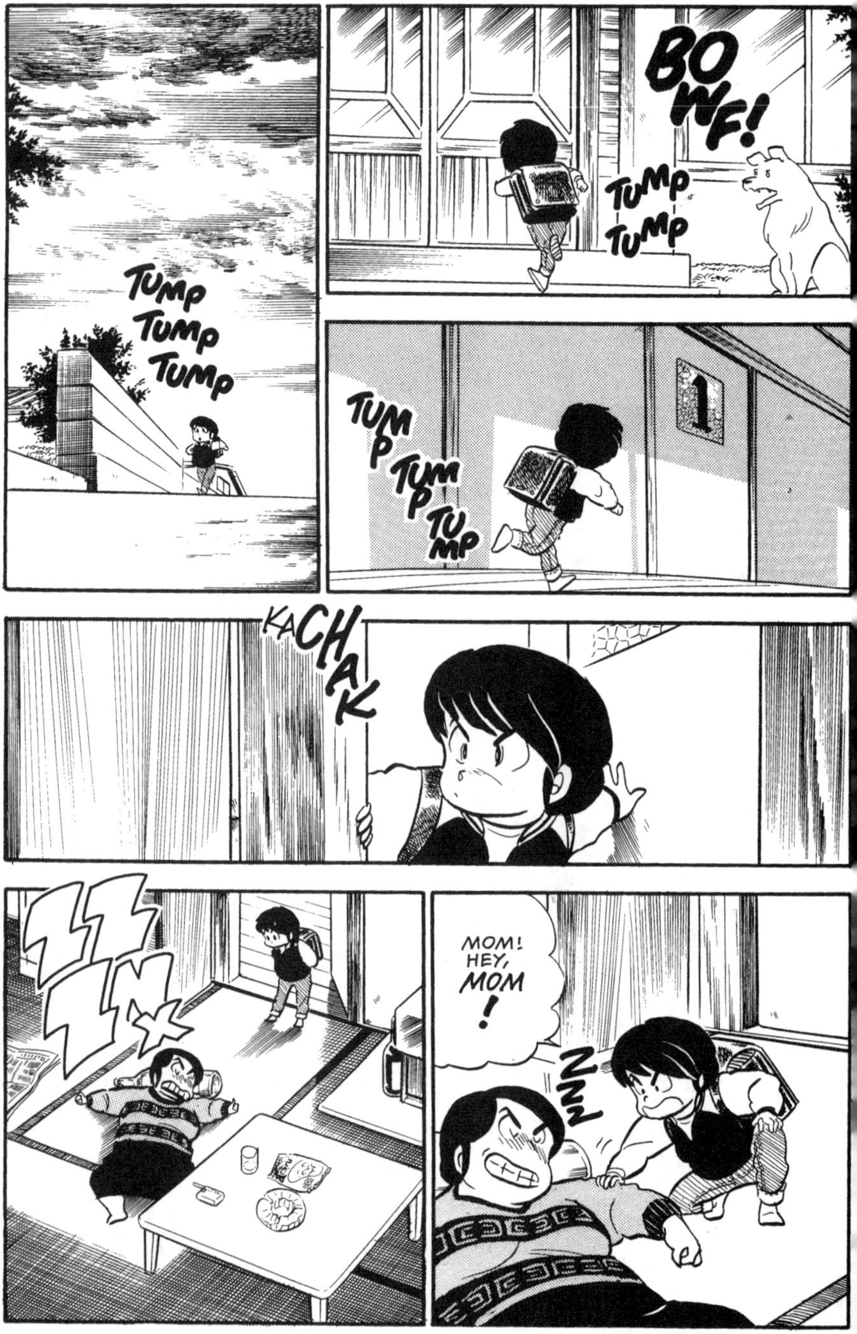
TUMP TUMP TUMP
BOWF!
TUMP TUMP
TUMP TUMP TUMP
KACHAK
ZZZNX
MOM! HEY, MOM!
NNN

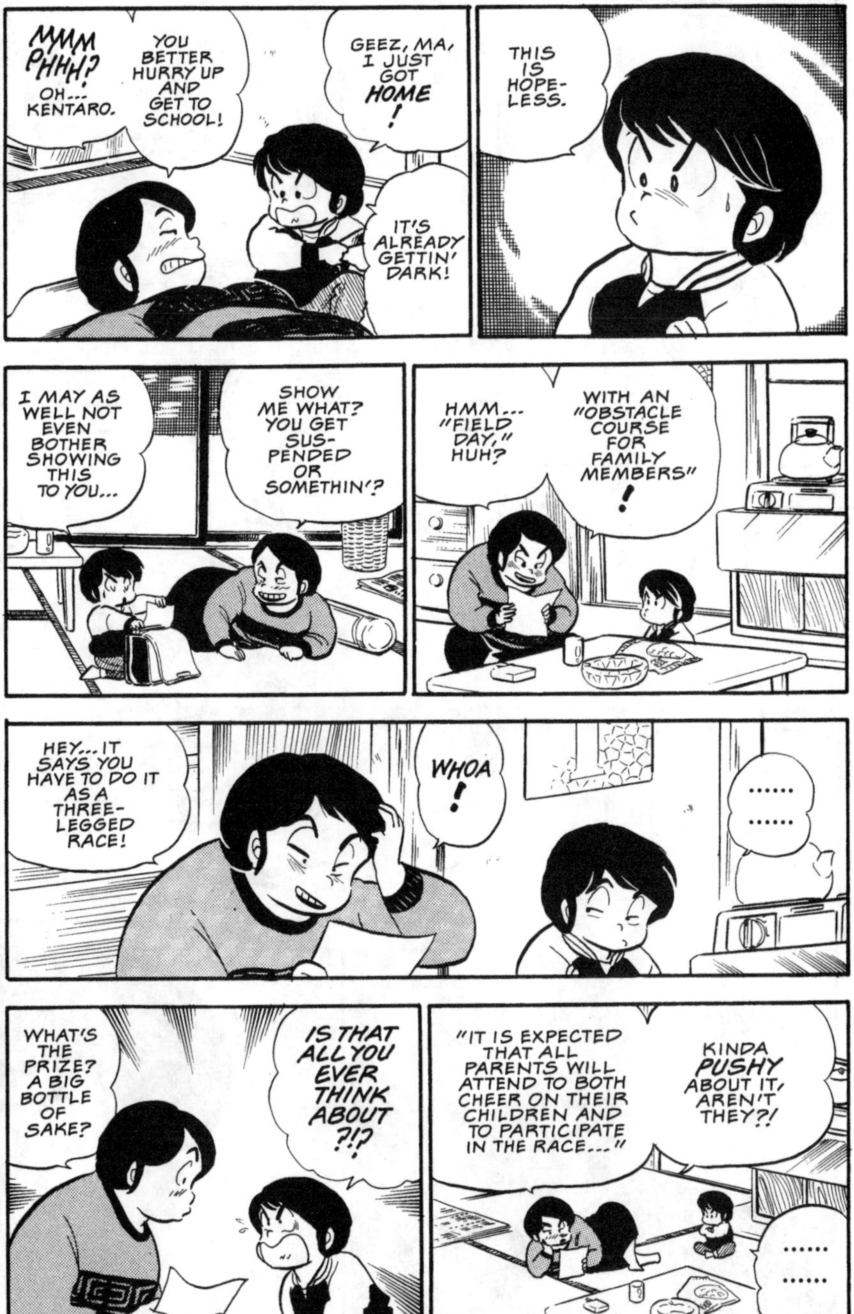
MMM PHHH?
OH... KENTARO.
YOU BETTER HURRY UP AND GET TO SCHOOL!
GEEZ, MA, I JUST GOT HOME!
IT'S ALREADY GETTIN' DARK!
THIS IS HOPE-LESS.
I MAY AS WELL NOT EVEN BOTHER SHOWING THIS TO YOU...
SHOW ME WHAT? YOU GET SUS-PENDED OR SOMETHIN'?
HMM... "FIELD DAY," HUH?
WITH AN "OBSTACLE COURSE FOR FAMILY MEMBERS"!
HEY... IT SAYS YOU HAVE TO DO IT AS A THREE-LEGGED RACE!
WHOA!
......
......
WHAT'S THE PRIZE? A BIG BOTTLE OF SAKE?
IS THAT ALL YOU EVER THINK ABOUT?!?
"IT IS EXPECTED THAT ALL PARENTS WILL ATTEND TO BOTH CHEER ON THEIR CHILDREN AND TO PARTICIPATE IN THE RACE..."
KINDA PUSHY ABOUT IT, AREN'T THEY?!
......
......

HMM? A FAMILY THREE-LEGGED RACE?

BUT, KENTARO... WHY ASK ME?

I MEAN, SURELY BOTH YOUR MOTHER AND FATHER WILL BE THERE TO CHEER YOU ON.

WELL, YEAH, BUT...

...YOU KNOW MOM.

BWAH HA HA HA!

SHE'LL JUST TURN THE WHOLE THING INTO A BIG OL' DRINKING PARTY.

SO WHEN THEY GO INTO THE RACE, ALL DRUNK AND STUFF...

WHISPER WHISPER WHISPER

...I COULD NEVER SHOW MY FACE AT SCHOOL AGAIN!

HEY, WHOSE PARENTS ARE THOSE?

KENTARO'S, I HEARD.

NO WAY!

THOSE DRUNKEN SLOBS?!

BUT... ARE YOU SURE IT'S OKAY?

I MEAN... FOR ME TO ENTER INSTEAD?

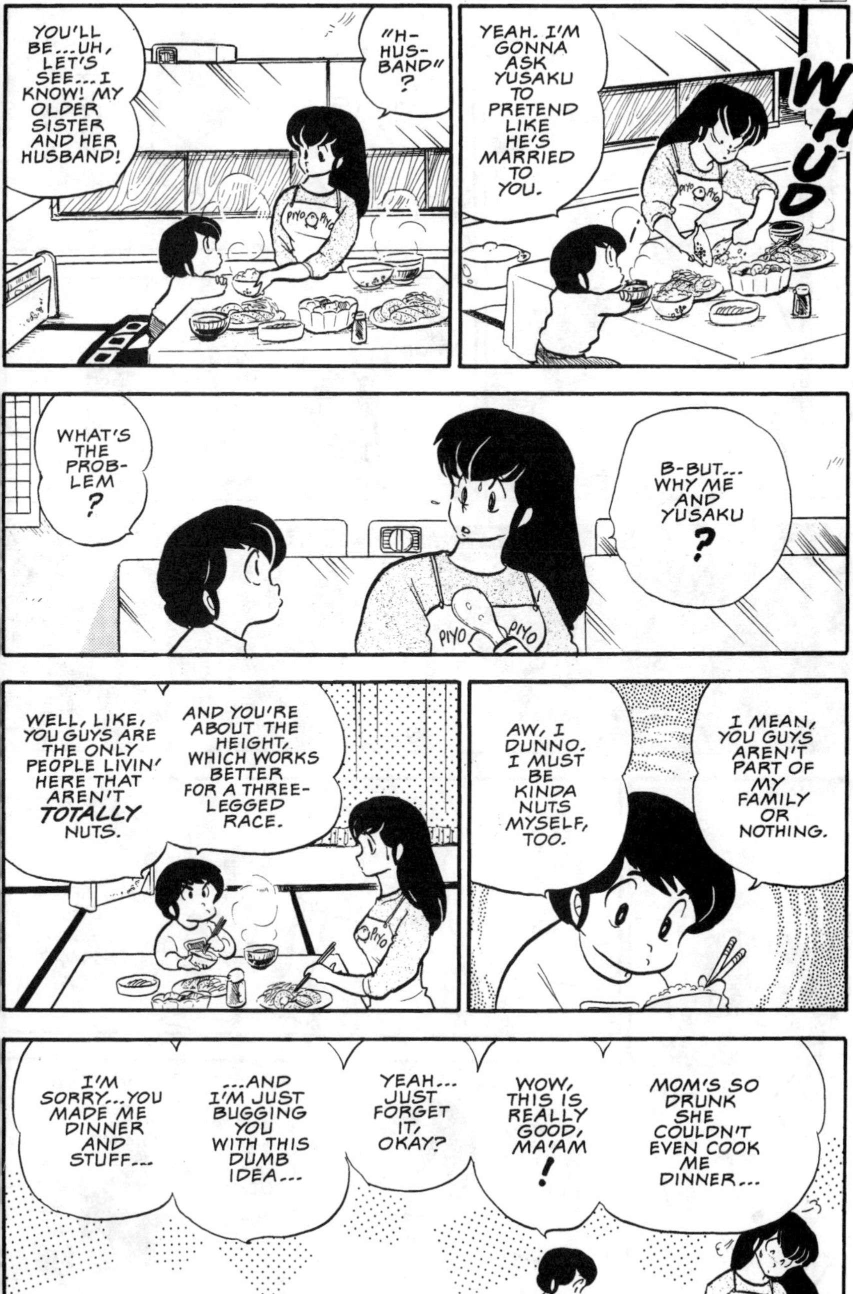
YOU'LL BE...UH, LET'S SEE...I KNOW! MY OLDER SISTER AND HER HUSBAND!
"H-HUS-BAND"?
YEAH. I'M GONNA ASK YUSAKU TO PRETEND LIKE HE'S MARRIED TO YOU.
WHUD
WHAT'S THE PROB-LEM?
B-BUT... WHY ME AND YUSAKU?
PIYO PIYO
WELL, LIKE, YOU GUYS ARE THE ONLY PEOPLE LIVIN' HERE THAT AREN'T TOTALLY NUTS.
AND YOU'RE ABOUT THE HEIGHT, WHICH WORKS BETTER FOR A THREE-LEGGED RACE.
AW, I DUNNO. I MUST BE KINDA NUTS MYSELF, TOO.
I MEAN, YOU GUYS AREN'T PART OF MY FAMILY OR NOTHING.
I'M SORRY...YOU MADE ME DINNER AND STUFF...
...AND I'M JUST BUGGING YOU WITH THIS DUMB IDEA...
YEAH... JUST FORGET IT, OKAY?
WOW, THIS IS REALLY GOOD, MA'AM!
MOM'S SO DRUNK SHE COULDN'T EVEN COOK ME DINNER...

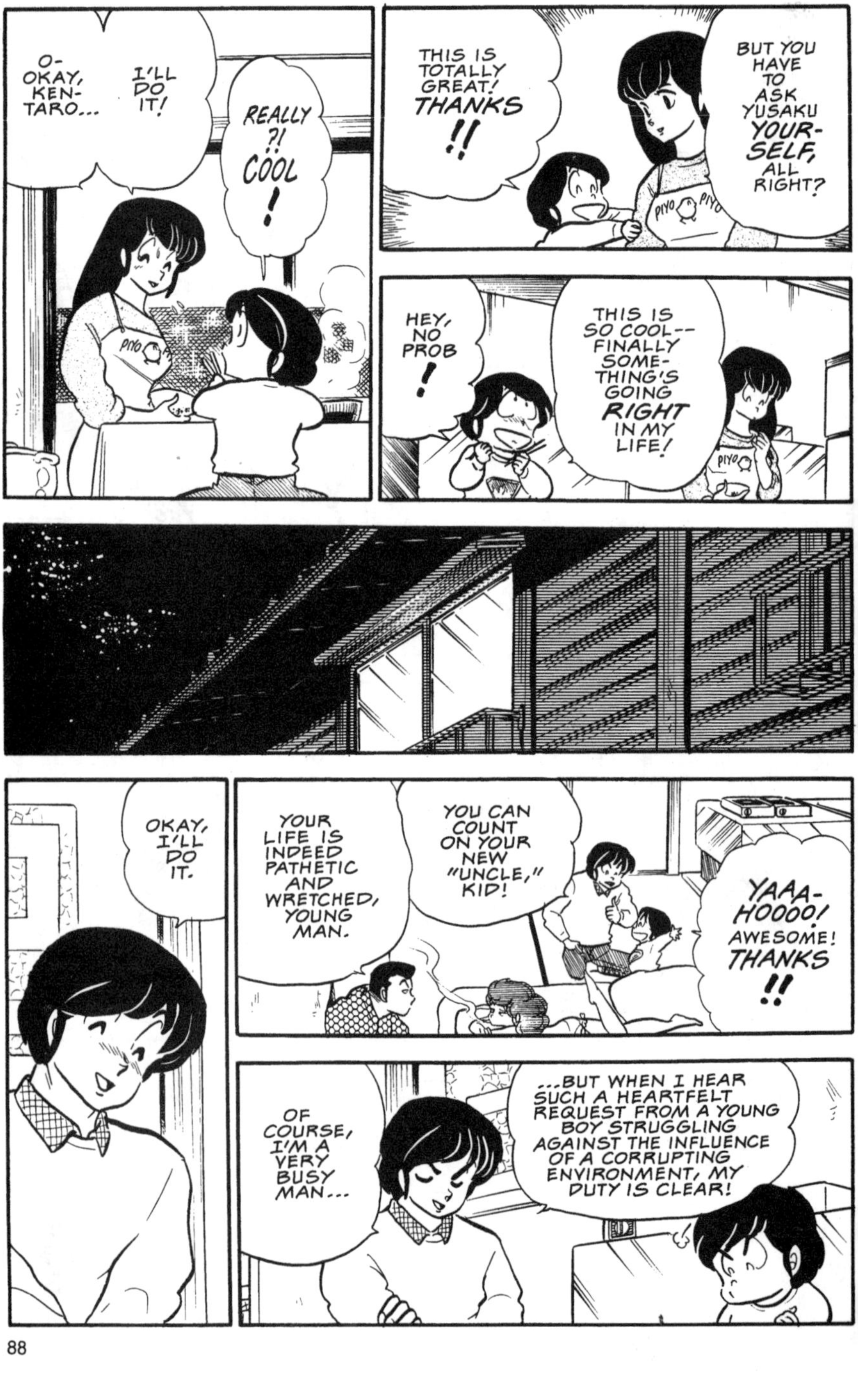
O-OKAY, KENTARO... I'LL DO IT!
REALLY ?! COOL !
THIS IS TOTALLY GREAT! THANKS !!
BUT YOU HAVE TO ASK YUSAKU YOURSELF, ALL RIGHT?
PIYO PIYO
HEY, NO PROB !
THIS IS SO COOL-- FINALLY SOMETHING'S GOING RIGHT IN MY LIFE!
OKAY, I'LL DO IT.
YOUR LIFE IS INDEED PATHETIC AND WRETCHED, YOUNG MAN.
YOU CAN COUNT ON YOUR NEW "UNCLE," KID!
YAAA-HOOOO! AWESOME! THANKS !!
OF COURSE, I'M A VERY BUSY MAN...
...BUT WHEN I HEAR SUCH A HEARTFELT REQUEST FROM A YOUNG BOY STRUGGLING AGAINST THE INFLUENCE OF A CORRUPTING ENVIRONMENT, MY DUTY IS CLEAR!

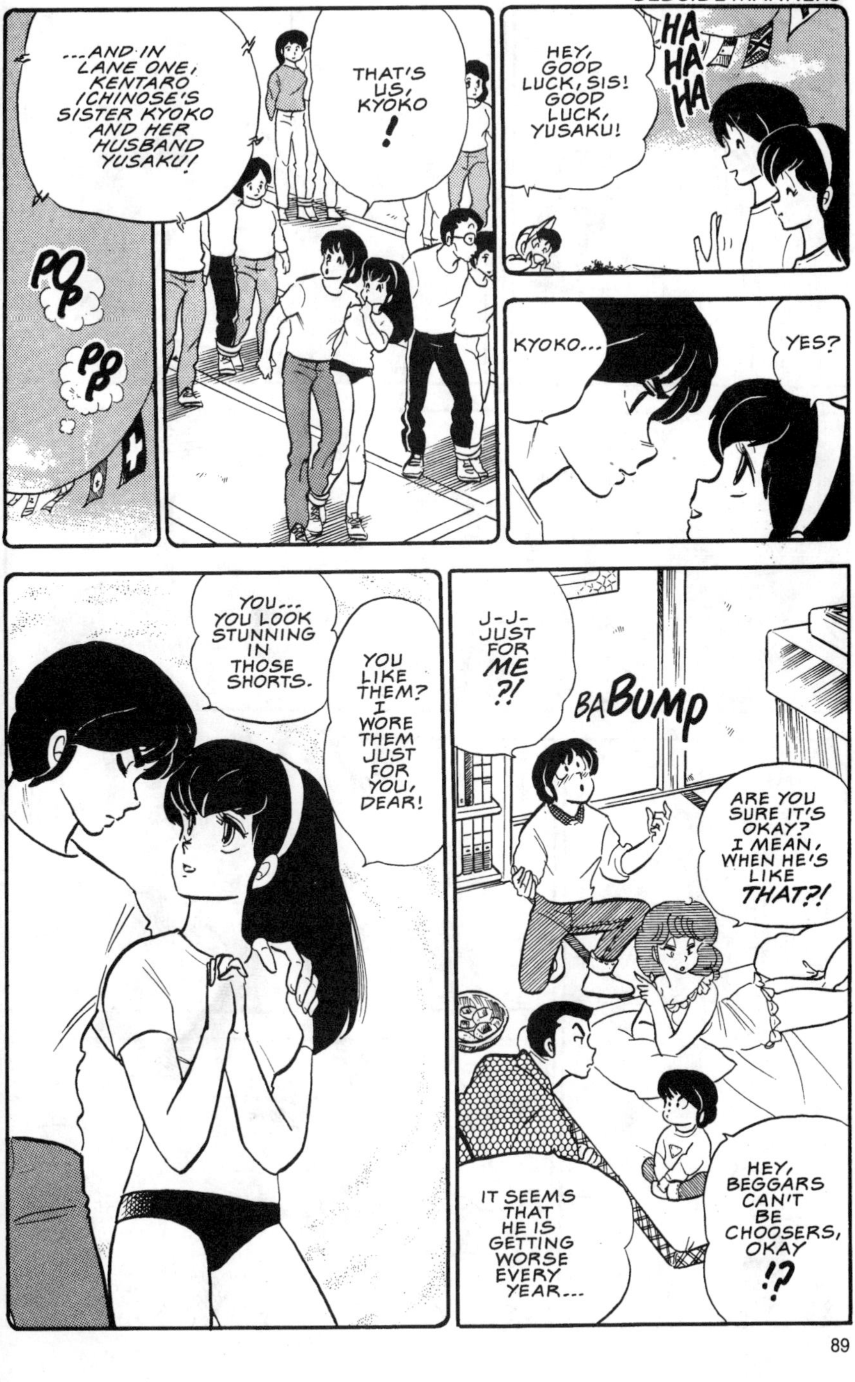
...AND IN LANE ONE, KENTARO ICHINOSE'S SISTER KYOKO AND HER HUSBAND YUSAKU!
POP
POP
THAT'S US, KYOKO!
HEY, GOOD LUCK, SIS! GOOD LUCK, YUSAKU!
HA HA HA
KYOKO...
YES?
YOU... YOU LOOK STUNNING IN THOSE SHORTS.
YOU LIKE THEM? I WORE THEM JUST FOR YOU, DEAR!
J-J-JUST FOR ME?!
BABUMP
ARE YOU SURE IT'S OKAY? I MEAN, WHEN HE'S LIKE THAT?!
IT SEEMS THAT HE IS GETTING WORSE EVERY YEAR...
HEY, BEGGARS CAN'T BE CHOOSERS, OKAY!?

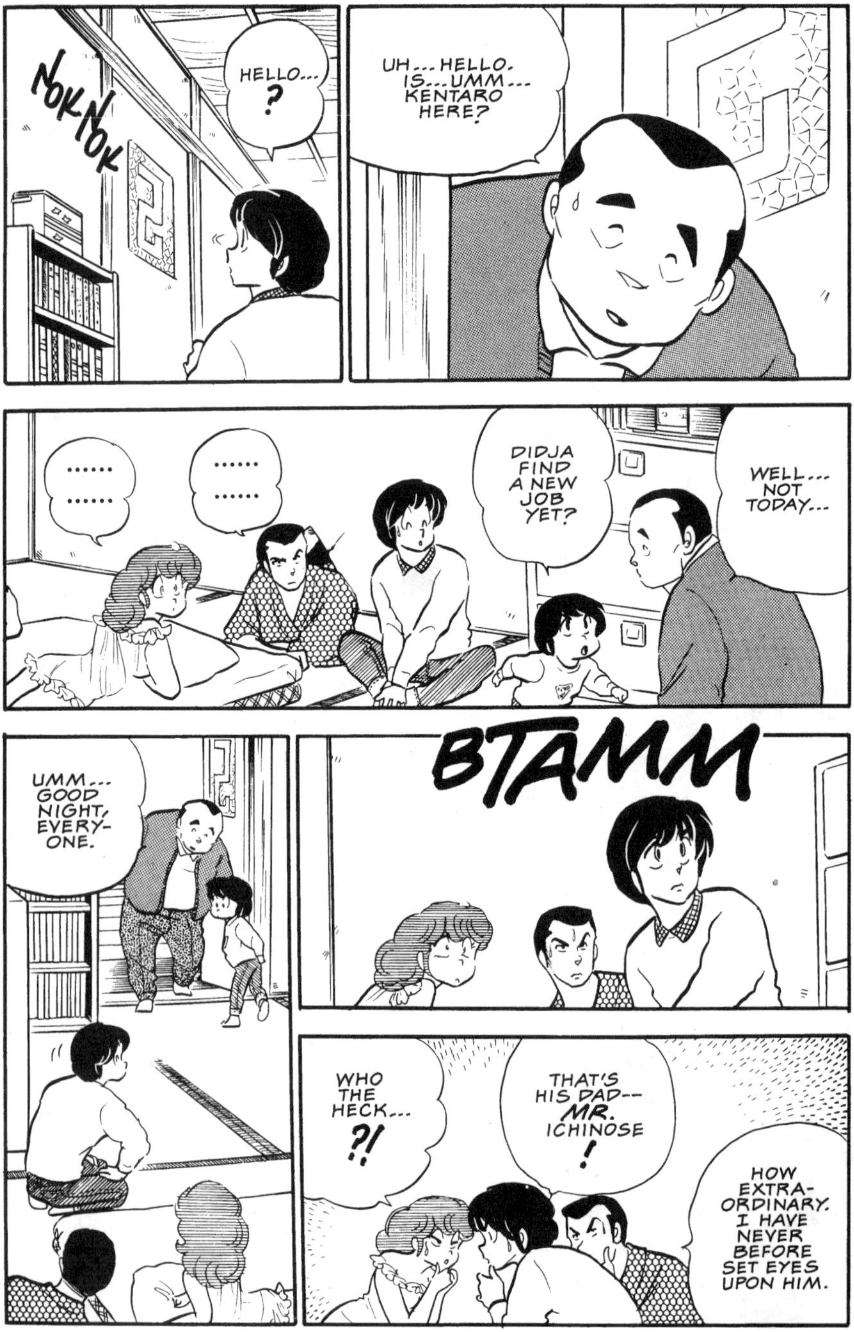
NOK NOK
HELLO... ?
UH... HELLO. IS... UMM... KENTARO HERE?
....
....
DIDJA FIND A NEW JOB YET?
WELL... NOT TODAY...
UMM... GOOD NIGHT, EVERY-ONE.
BTAMM
WHO THE HECK... ?!
THAT'S HIS DAD-- MR. ICHINOSE !
HOW EXTRA-ORDINARY. I HAVE NEVER BEFORE SET EYES UPON HIM.

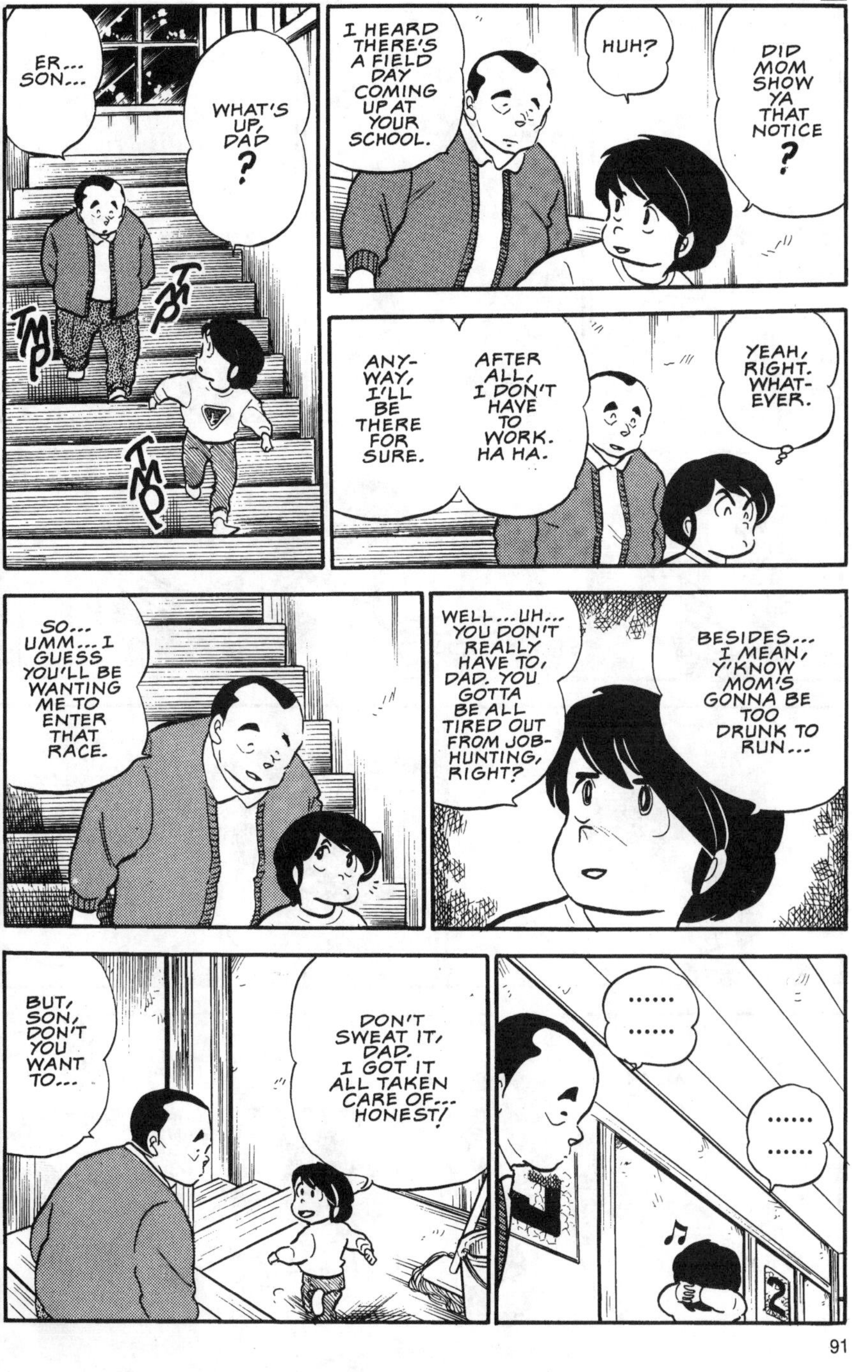
ER... SON...
WHAT'S UP, DAD?
TMP
TMP
TMP
I HEARD THERE'S A FIELD DAY COMING UP AT YOUR SCHOOL.
HUH?
DID MOM SHOW YA THAT NOTICE?
ANYWAY, I'LL BE THERE FOR SURE.
AFTER ALL, I DON'T HAVE TO WORK. HA HA.
YEAH, RIGHT. WHATEVER.
SO... UMM... I GUESS YOU'LL BE WANTING ME TO ENTER THAT RACE.
WELL... UH... YOU DON'T REALLY HAVE TO, DAD. YOU GOTTA BE ALL TIRED OUT FROM JOB-HUNTING, RIGHT?
BESIDES... I MEAN, Y'KNOW MOM'S GONNA BE TOO DRUNK TO RUN...
BUT, SON, DON'T YOU WANT TO...
DON'T SWEAT IT, DAD. I GOT IT ALL TAKEN CARE OF... HONEST!
....
....

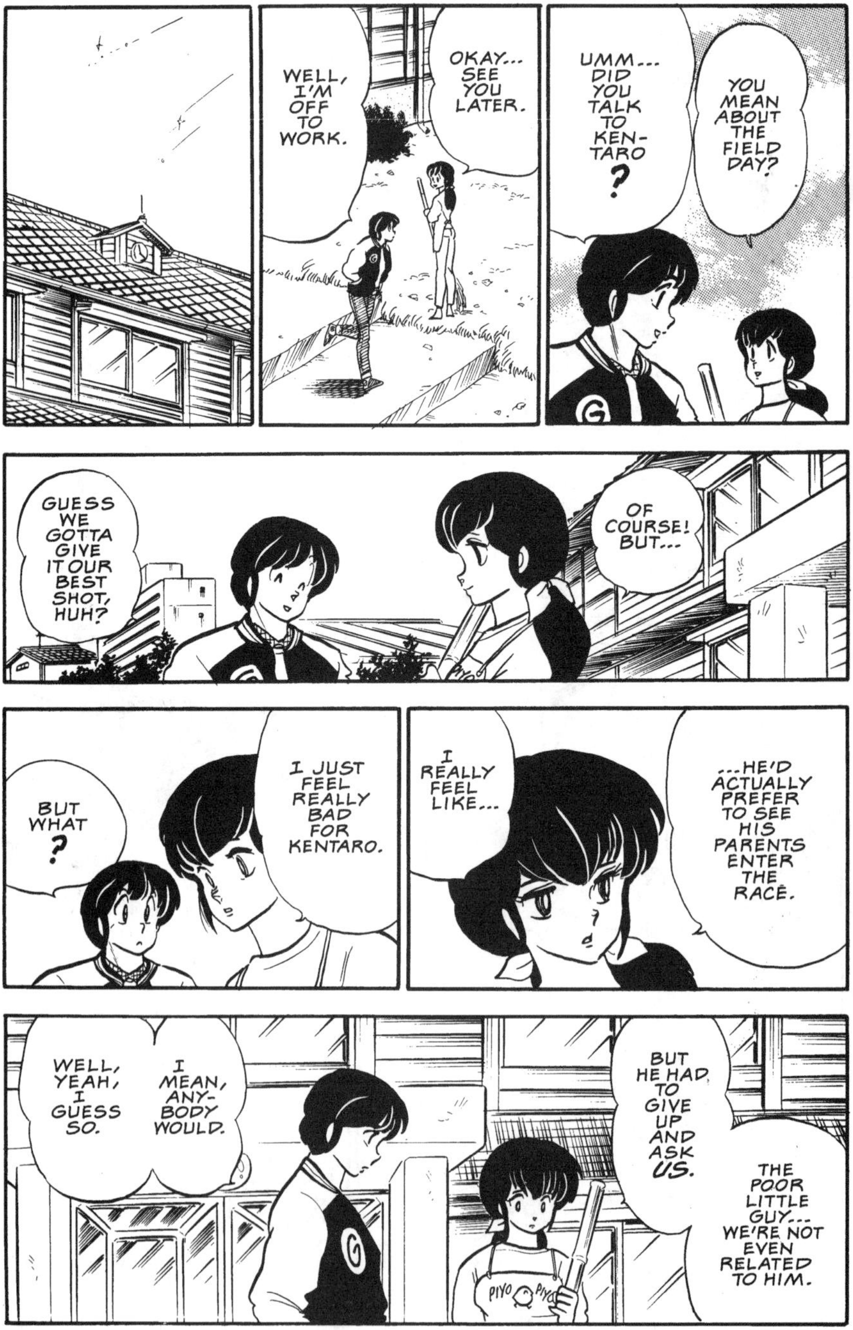
WELL, I'M OFF TO WORK.
OKAY... SEE YOU LATER.
UMM... DID YOU TALK TO KENTARO?
YOU MEAN ABOUT THE FIELD DAY?
GUESS WE GOTTA GIVE IT OUR BEST SHOT, HUH?
OF COURSE! BUT...
BUT WHAT?
I JUST FEEL REALLY BAD FOR KENTARO.
I REALLY FEEL LIKE...
...HE'D ACTUALLY PREFER TO SEE HIS PARENTS ENTER THE RACE.
WELL, YEAH, I GUESS SO.
I MEAN, ANYBODY WOULD.
BUT HE HAD TO GIVE UP AND ASK US.
THE POOR LITTLE GUY... WE'RE NOT EVEN RELATED TO HIM.
PIYO PIYO

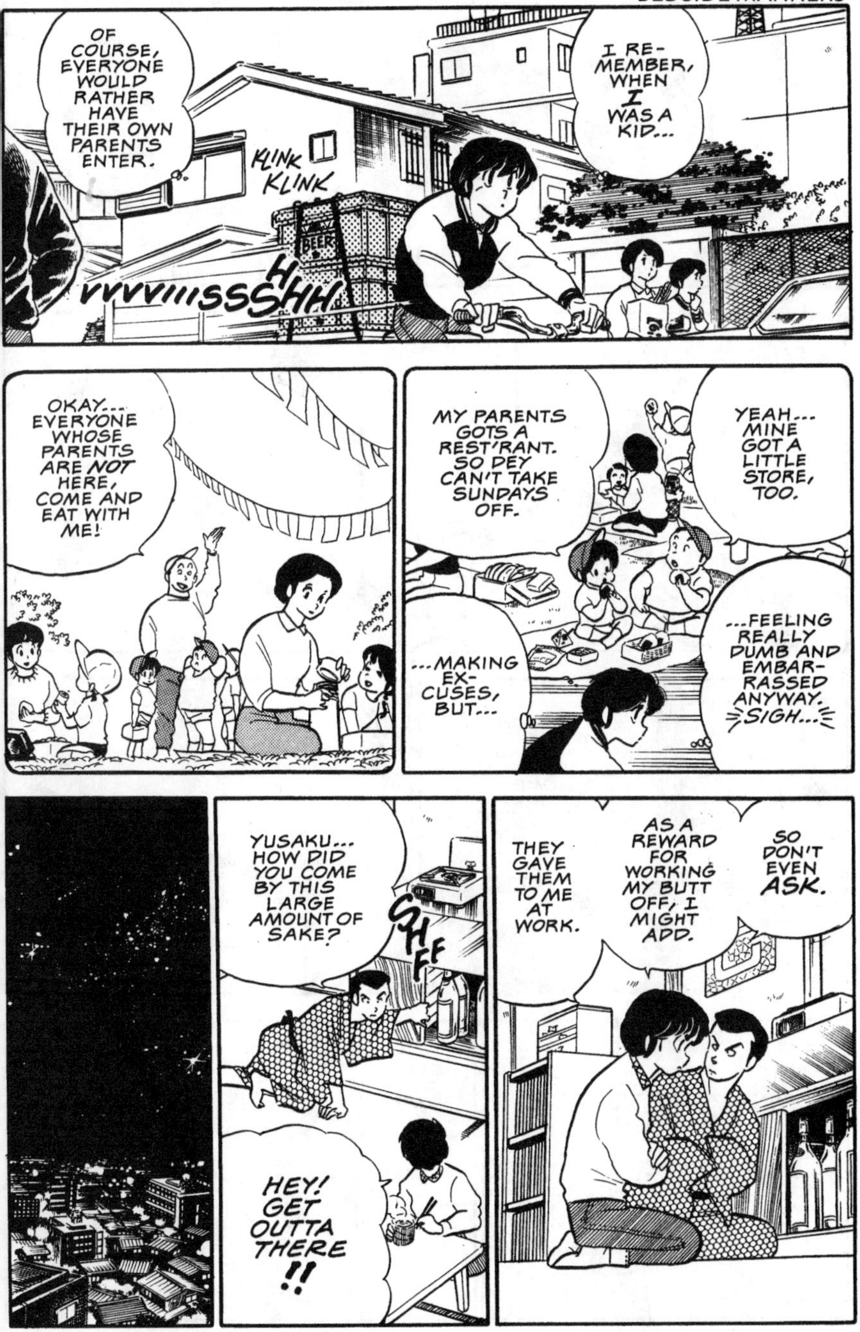
OF COURSE, EVERYONE WOULD RATHER HAVE THEIR OWN PARENTS ENTER.
KLINK KLINK
VVVVIIISSSHH
I REMEMBER, WHEN I WAS A KID...
OKAY... EVERYONE WHOSE PARENTS ARE NOT HERE, COME AND EAT WITH ME!
MY PARENTS GOTS A REST'RANT. SO DEY CAN'T TAKE SUNDAYS OFF.
YEAH... MINE GOT A LITTLE STORE, TOO.
...MAKING EX-CUSES, BUT...
...FEELING REALLY DUMB AND EMBAR-RASSED ANYWAY. SIGH...
YUSAKU... HOW DID YOU COME BY THIS LARGE AMOUNT OF SAKE?
SHFF
HEY! GET OUTTA THERE!!
THEY GAVE THEM TO ME AT WORK.
AS A REWARD FOR WORKING MY BUTT OFF, I MIGHT ADD.
SO DON'T EVEN ASK.

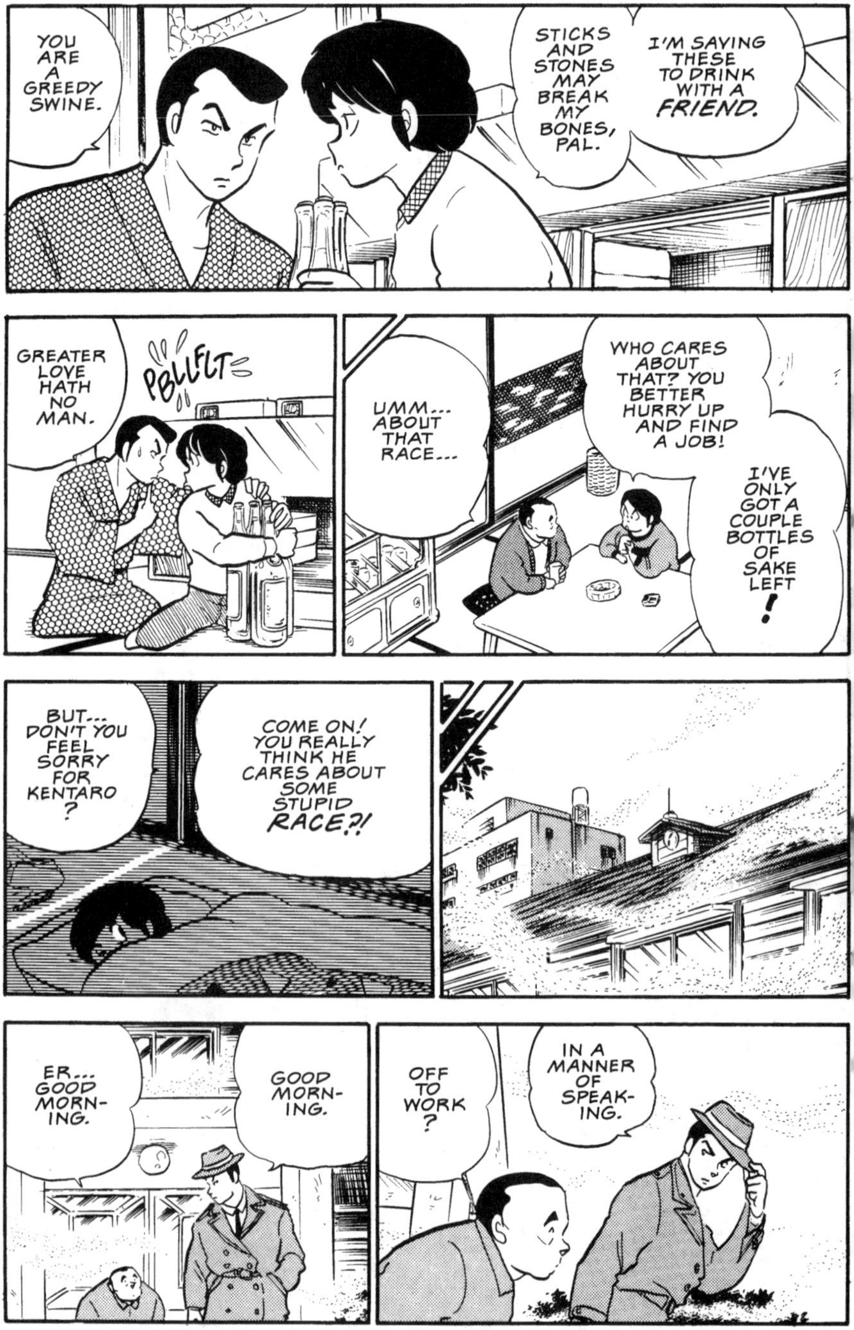
YOU ARE A GREEDY SWINE.
STICKS AND STONES MAY BREAK MY BONES, PAL.
I'M SAVING THESE TO DRINK WITH A FRIEND.
GREATER LOVE HATH NO MAN.
PBLLFLT
UMM... ABOUT THAT RACE...
WHO CARES ABOUT THAT? YOU BETTER HURRY UP AND FIND A JOB!
I'VE ONLY GOT A COUPLE BOTTLES OF SAKE LEFT!
BUT... DON'T YOU FEEL SORRY FOR KENTARO?
COME ON! YOU REALLY THINK HE CARES ABOUT SOME STUPID RACE?!
ER... GOOD MORN-ING.
GOOD MORN-ING.
OFF TO WORK?
IN A MANNER OF SPEAK-ING.

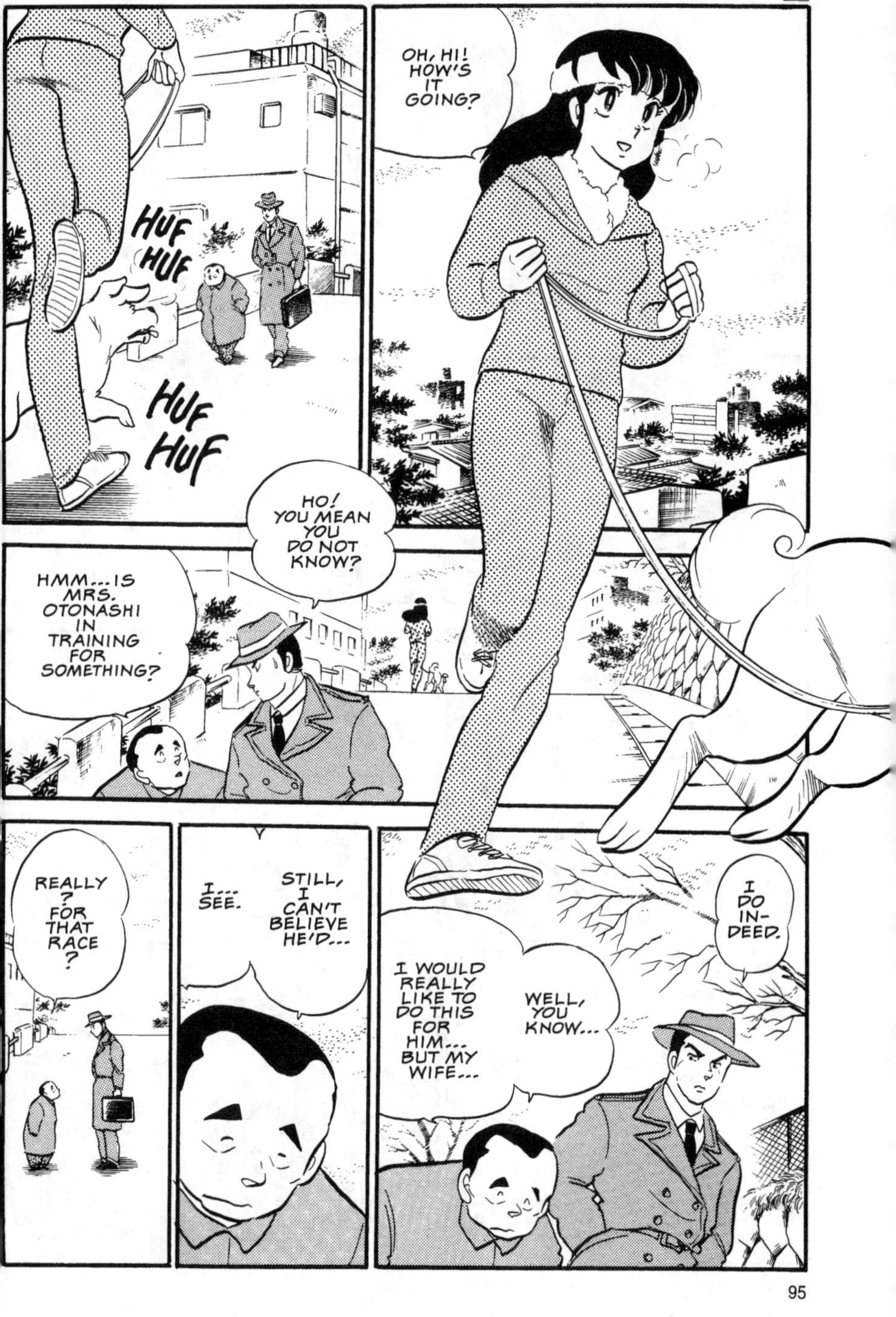
HUF
HUF
HUF
HUF
OH, HI! HOW'S IT GOING?
HMM...IS MRS. OTONASHI IN TRAINING FOR SOMETHING?
HO! YOU MEAN YOU DO NOT KNOW?
REALLY? FOR THAT RACE?
I... SEE.
STILL, I CAN'T BELIEVE HE'D...
I DO IN-DEED.
I WOULD REALLY LIKE TO DO THIS FOR HIM... BUT MY WIFE...
WELL, YOU KNOW...

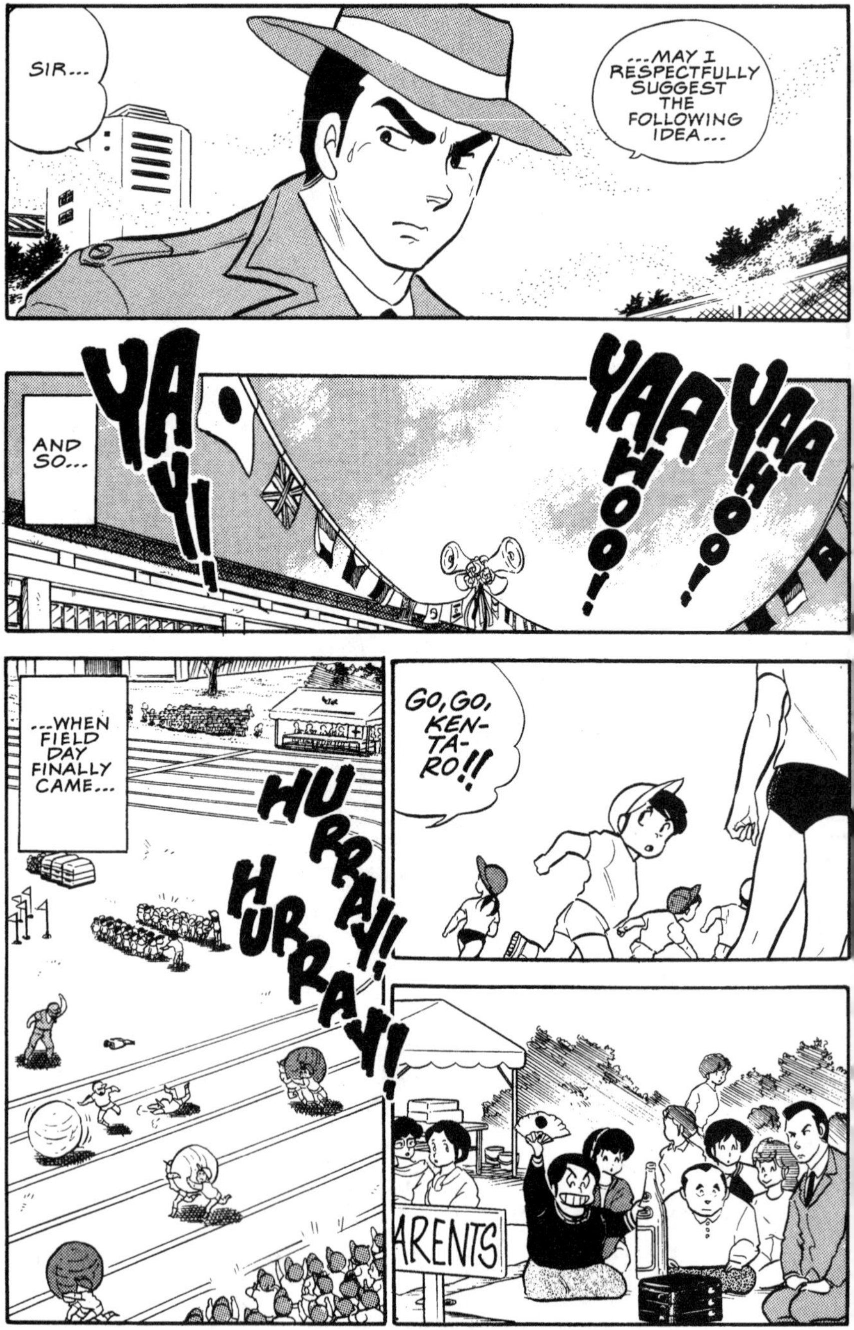
SIR...
...MAY I RESPECTFULLY SUGGEST THE FOLLOWING IDEA...
AND SO...
YAY!!
YAAHOO!
YAAHOO!
...WHEN FIELD DAY FINALLY CAME...
HURRAY!
HURRAY!
GO, GO, KEN-TA-RO!!
ARENTS

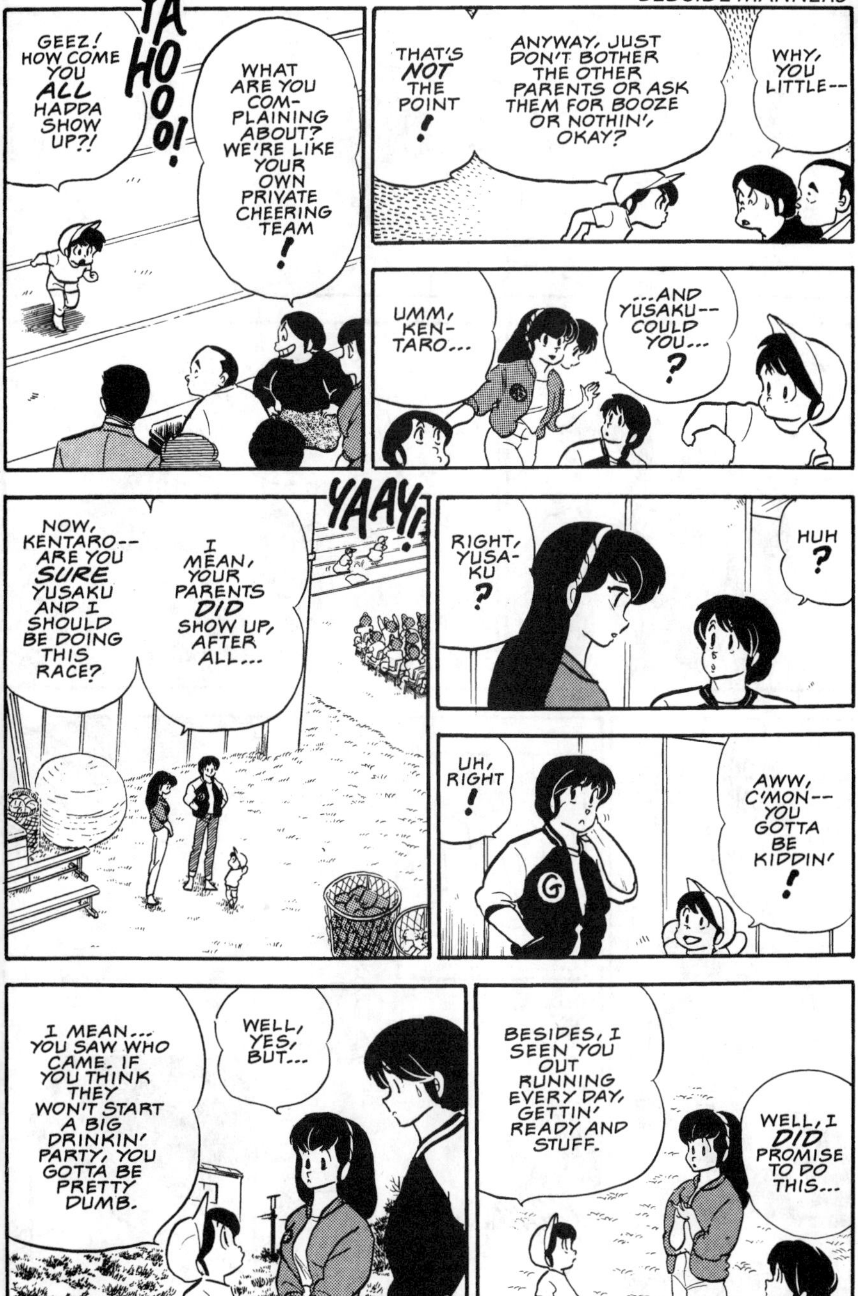
GEEZ! HOW COME YOU ALL HADDA SHOW UP?!
YAHOOO!
WHAT ARE YOU COMPLAINING ABOUT? WE'RE LIKE YOUR OWN PRIVATE CHEERING TEAM!
THAT'S NOT THE POINT!
ANYWAY, JUST DON'T BOTHER THE OTHER PARENTS OR ASK THEM FOR BOOZE OR NOTHIN', OKAY?
WHY, YOU LITTLE--
UMM, KENTARO...
...AND YUSAKU--COULD YOU...?
YAAY!
NOW, KENTARO--ARE YOU SURE YUSAKU AND I SHOULD BE DOING THIS RACE?
I MEAN, YOUR PARENTS DID SHOW UP, AFTER ALL...
RIGHT, YUSAKU?
HUH?
UH, RIGHT!
AWW, C'MON--YOU GOTTA BE KIDDIN'!
I MEAN... YOU SAW WHO CAME. IF YOU THINK THEY WON'T START A BIG DRINKIN' PARTY, YOU GOTTA BE PRETTY DUMB.
WELL, YES, BUT...
BESIDES, I SEEN YOU OUT RUNNING EVERY DAY, GETTIN' READY AND STUFF.
WELL, I DID PROMISE TO DO THIS...

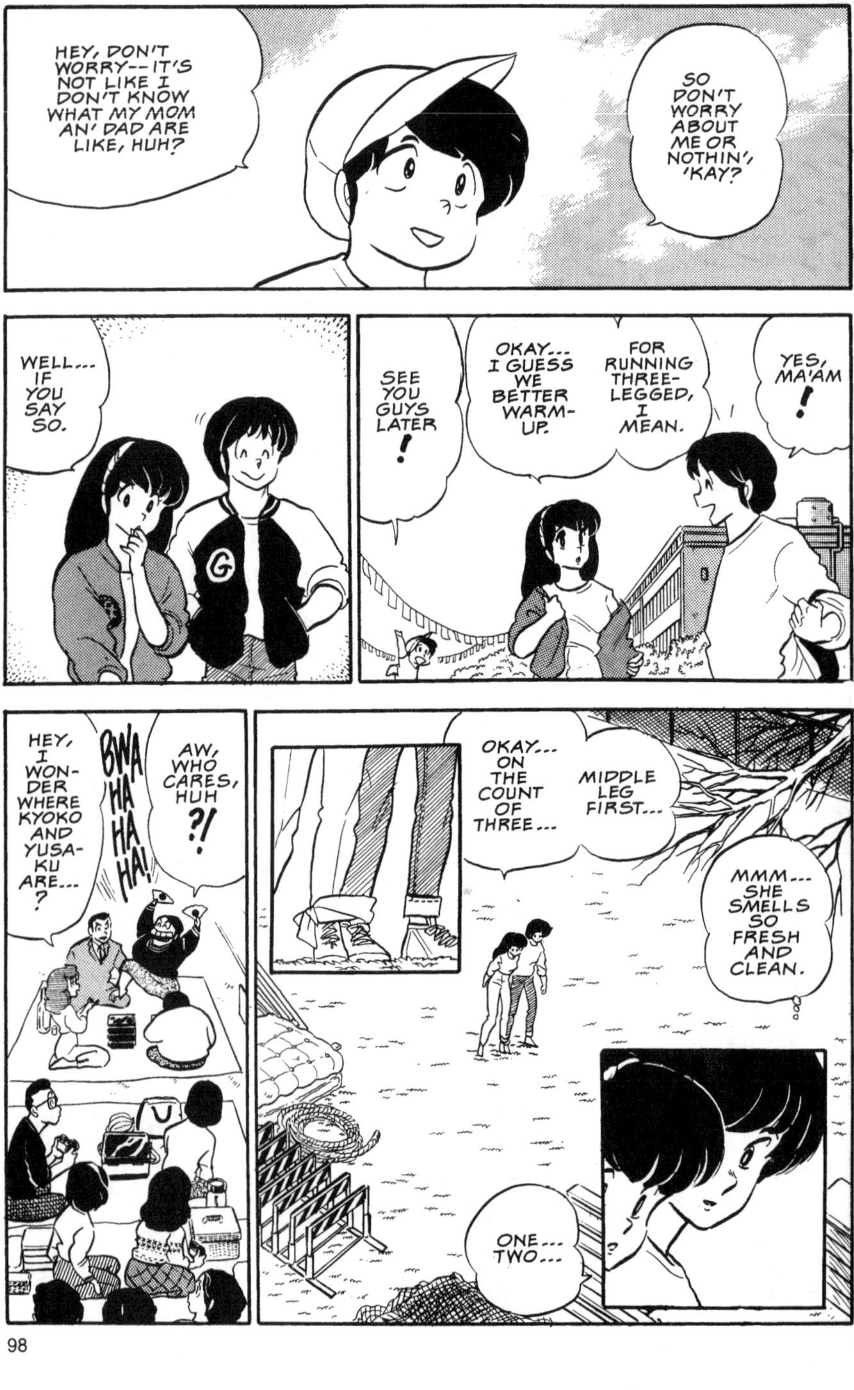
HEY, DON'T WORRY-- IT'S NOT LIKE I DON'T KNOW WHAT MY MOM AN' DAD ARE LIKE, HUH?
SO DON'T WORRY ABOUT ME OR NOTHIN', 'KAY?
WELL... IF YOU SAY SO.
SEE YOU GUYS LATER!
OKAY... I GUESS WE BETTER WARM-UP.
FOR RUNNING THREE-LEGGED, I MEAN.
YES, MA'AM!
HEY, I WONDER WHERE KYOKO AND YUSAKU ARE...?
BWA HA HA HA HA!
AW, WHO CARES, HUH?!
OKAY... ON THE COUNT OF THREE...
MIDDLE LEG FIRST...
MMM... SHE SMELLS SO FRESH AND CLEAN.
ONE... TWO...

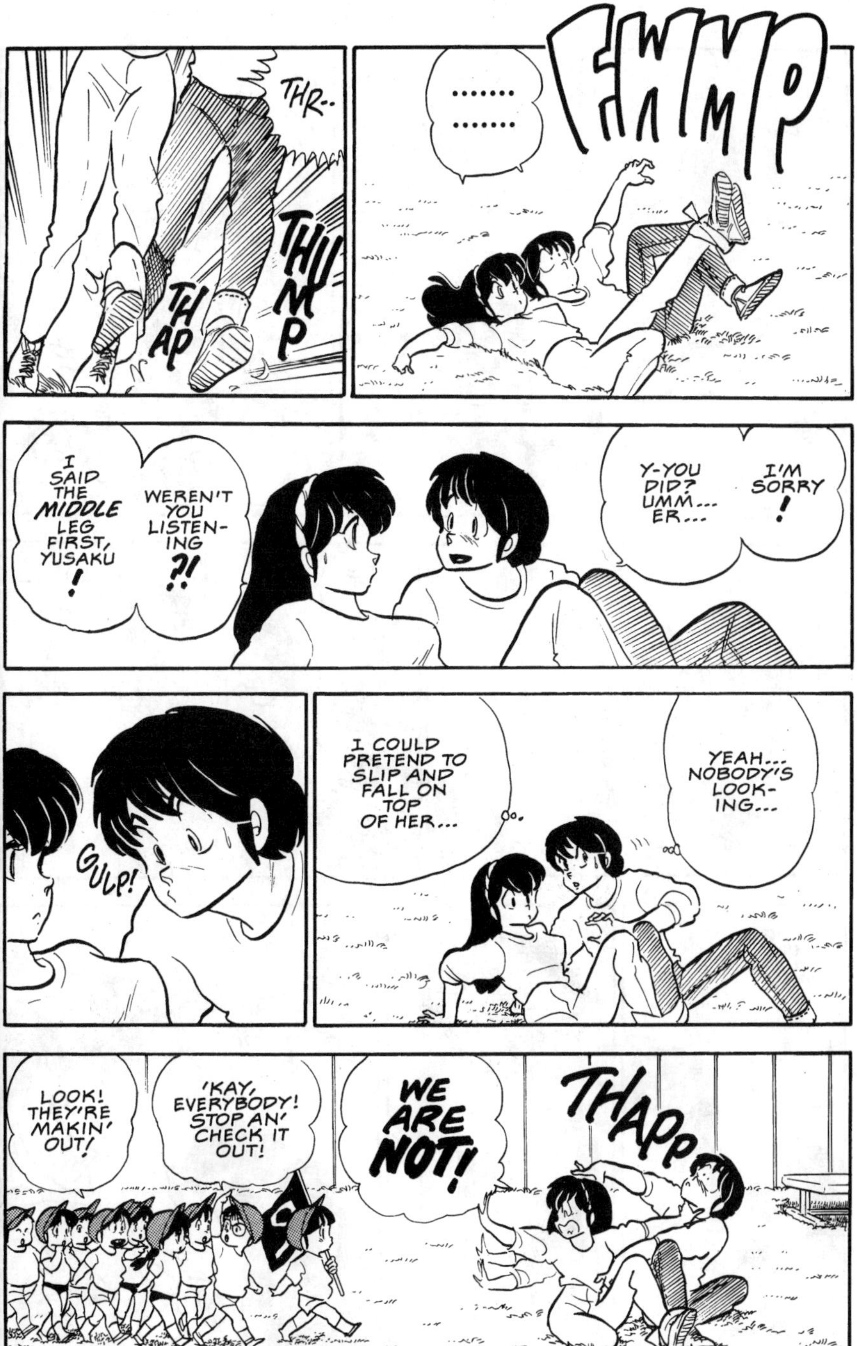
THR--
THAP
THUMP
....
FWUMP
I SAID THE MIDDLE LEG FIRST, YUSAKU!
WEREN'T YOU LISTENING ?!
Y-YOU DID? UMMM... ER...
I'M SORRY!
GULP!
I COULD PRETEND TO SLIP AND FALL ON TOP OF HER...
YEAH... NOBODY'S LOOKING...
LOOK! THEY'RE MAKIN' OUT!
'KAY, EVERYBODY! STOP AN' CHECK IT OUT!
WE ARE NOT!
THAPP

LUNCH BREAK!

EVENTS WILL RESUME AT ONE O'CLOCK!

WHAT THE HECK *IS* THIS, ANYWAY?! THEY DON'T LET KIDS EAT WITH THEIR PARENTS ANYMORE? WHY, WHEN *I* WAS A KID...

SLRP

GEE, I SURE WISH I COULD EAT WITH MY MA...

THANK GOD I DON'T HAVE TO!

SAY, KYOKO... AREN'T YOU GETTING HUNGRY?

HUF HUF HUF HUF HUF

YES...BUT WE STILL HAVEN'T BEEN ABLE TO GO MORE THAN TEN STEPS WITHOUT FALLING DOWN!

LET'S GIVE IT ONE MORE TRY BE- FORE--

WOBBLE

UMM... LOOK, KYOKO... THIS IS JUST AN IDEA...

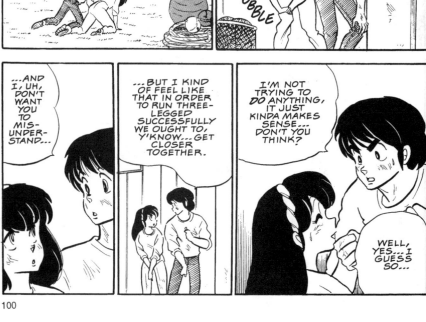

...AND I, UH, DON'T WANT YOU TO MIS- UNDER- STAND...

...BUT I KIND OF FEEL LIKE THAT IN ORDER TO RUN THREE- LEGGED SUCCESSFULLY WE OUGHT TO, Y'KNOW.... GET CLOSER TOGETHER.

I'M NOT TRYING TO *DO* ANYTHING, IT JUST KINDA MAKES SENSE... DON'T YOU THINK?

WELL, YES... I GUESS SO...

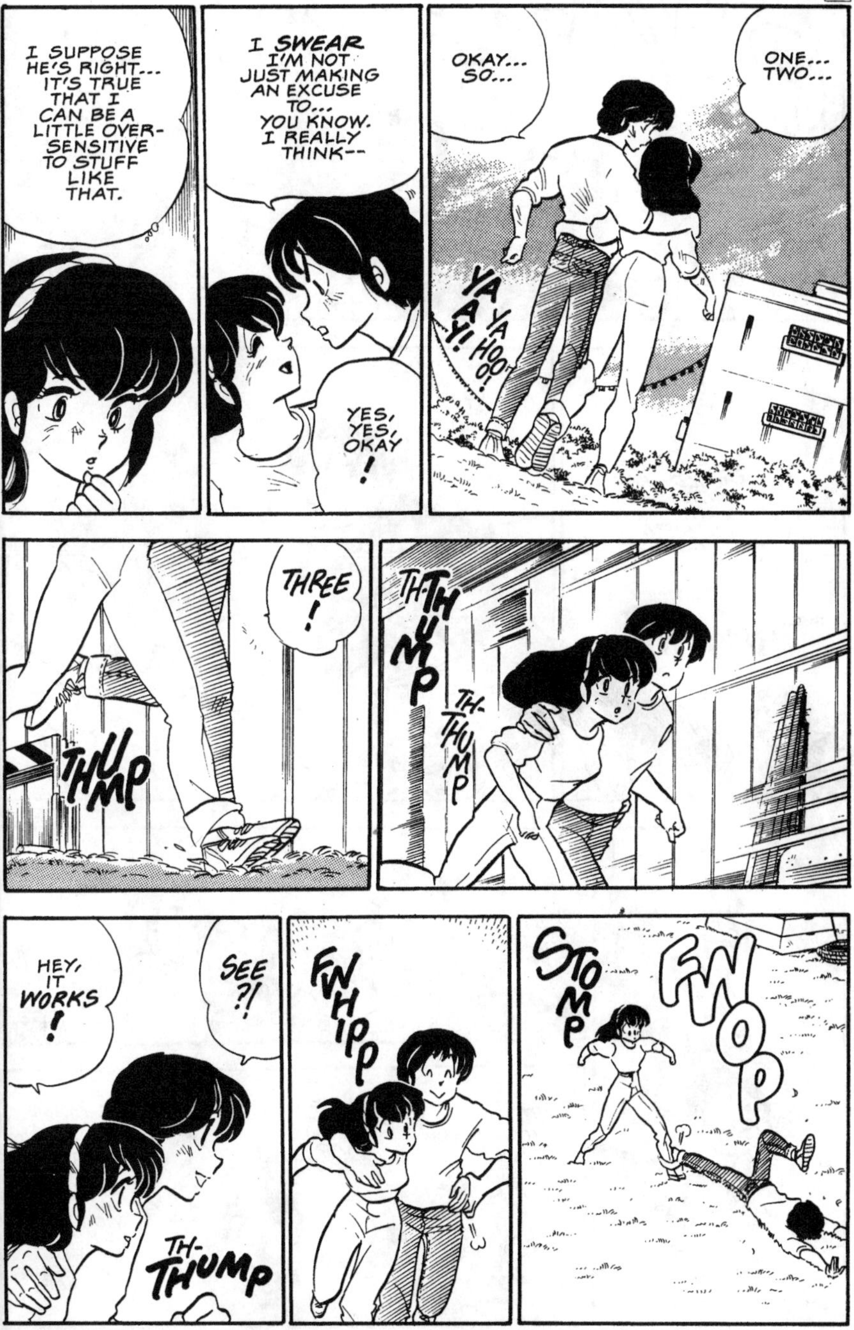
I SUPPOSE HE'S RIGHT... IT'S TRUE THAT I CAN BE A LITTLE OVER-SENSITIVE TO STUFF LIKE THAT.
I SWEAR I'M NOT JUST MAKING AN EXCUSE TO... YOU KNOW. I REALLY THINK--
YES, YES, OKAY!
OKAY... SO...
ONE... TWO...
YA YA YA HOO! YI!
THREE!
THUMP
TH-THUMP
TH-THUMP
HEY, IT WORKS!
SEE?!
TH-THUMP
FWHIPP
STOMP
FWOP

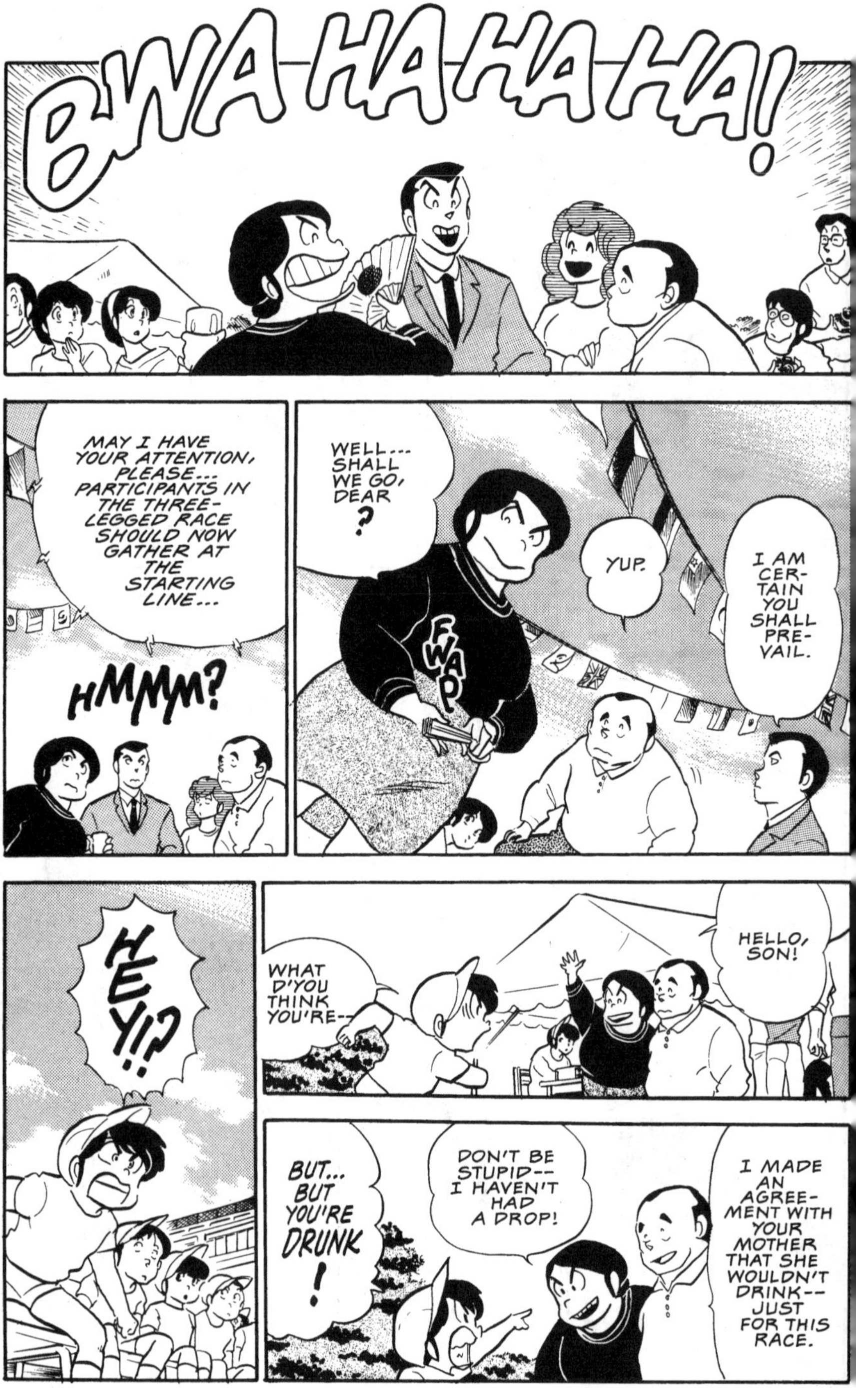
BWA HA HA HA HA!
MAY I HAVE YOUR ATTENTION, PLEASE... PARTICIPANTS IN THE THREE-LEGGED RACE SHOULD NOW GATHER AT THE STARTING LINE...
HMMM?
WELL... SHALL WE GO, DEAR?
FWAP!
YUP.
I AM CERTAIN YOU SHALL PREVAIL.
HEY!!?
WHAT D'YOU THINK YOU'RE--
HELLO, SON!
BUT... BUT YOU'RE DRUNK!
DON'T BE STUPID-- I HAVEN'T HAD A DROP!
I MADE AN AGREEMENT WITH YOUR MOTHER THAT SHE WOULDN'T DRINK-- JUST FOR THIS RACE.

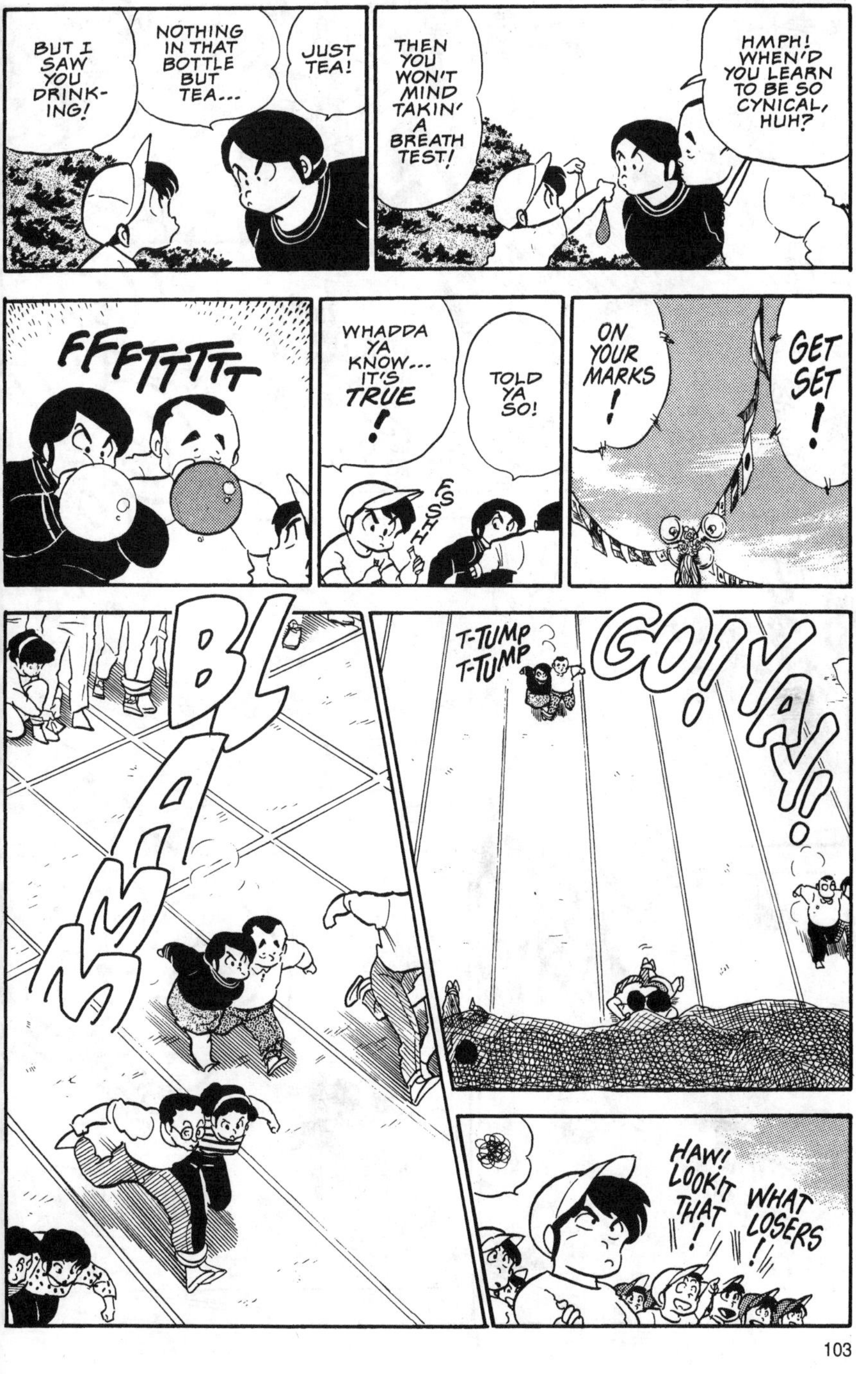
BUT I SAW YOU DRINK-ING!
NOTHING IN THAT BOTTLE BUT TEA...
JUST TEA!
THEN YOU WON'T MIND TAKIN' A BREATH TEST!
HMPH! WHEN'D YOU LEARN TO BE SO CYNICAL, HUH?
FFFTTTTT
WHADDA YA KNOW... IT'S TRUE!
TOLD YA SO!
FSSHH
ON YOUR MARKS!
GET SET!
BLAMMM
T-TUMP T-TUMP
GO!
YAY!
HAW! LOOKIT THAT!
WHAT LOSERS!

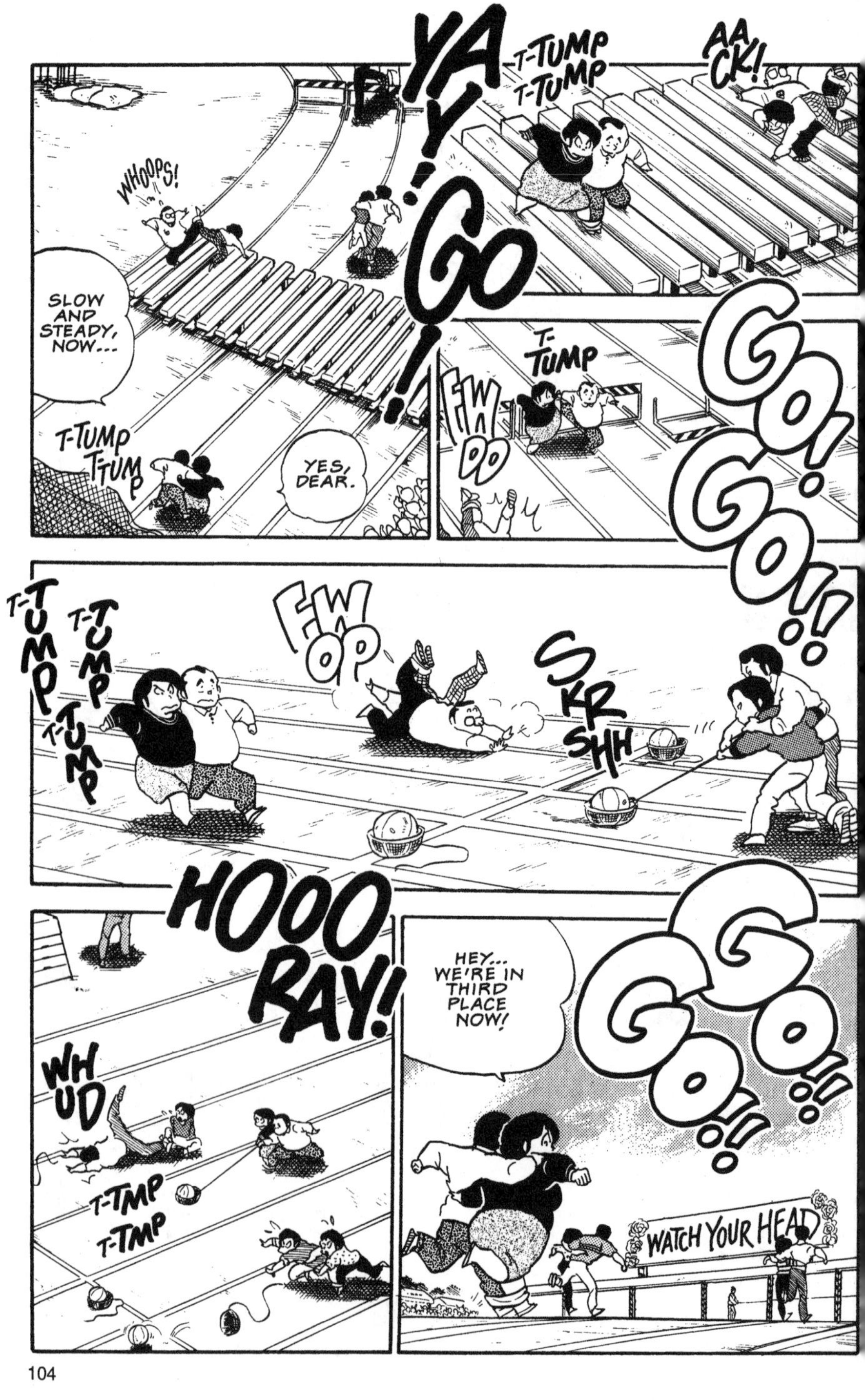
WHOOPS!
SLOW AND STEADY, NOW...
T-TUMP T-TUMP
YES, DEAR.
YAY! GO!
T-TUMP T-TUMP
AACK!
FWDD
T-TUMP
GO! GO! GO!!
T-TUMP T-TUMP T-TUMP
FWOP
SKRSHH
HOOORAY!
WHUD
T-TMP T-TMP
HEY... WE'RE IN THIRD PLACE NOW!
GO GO!! GO!!
WATCH YOUR HEAD

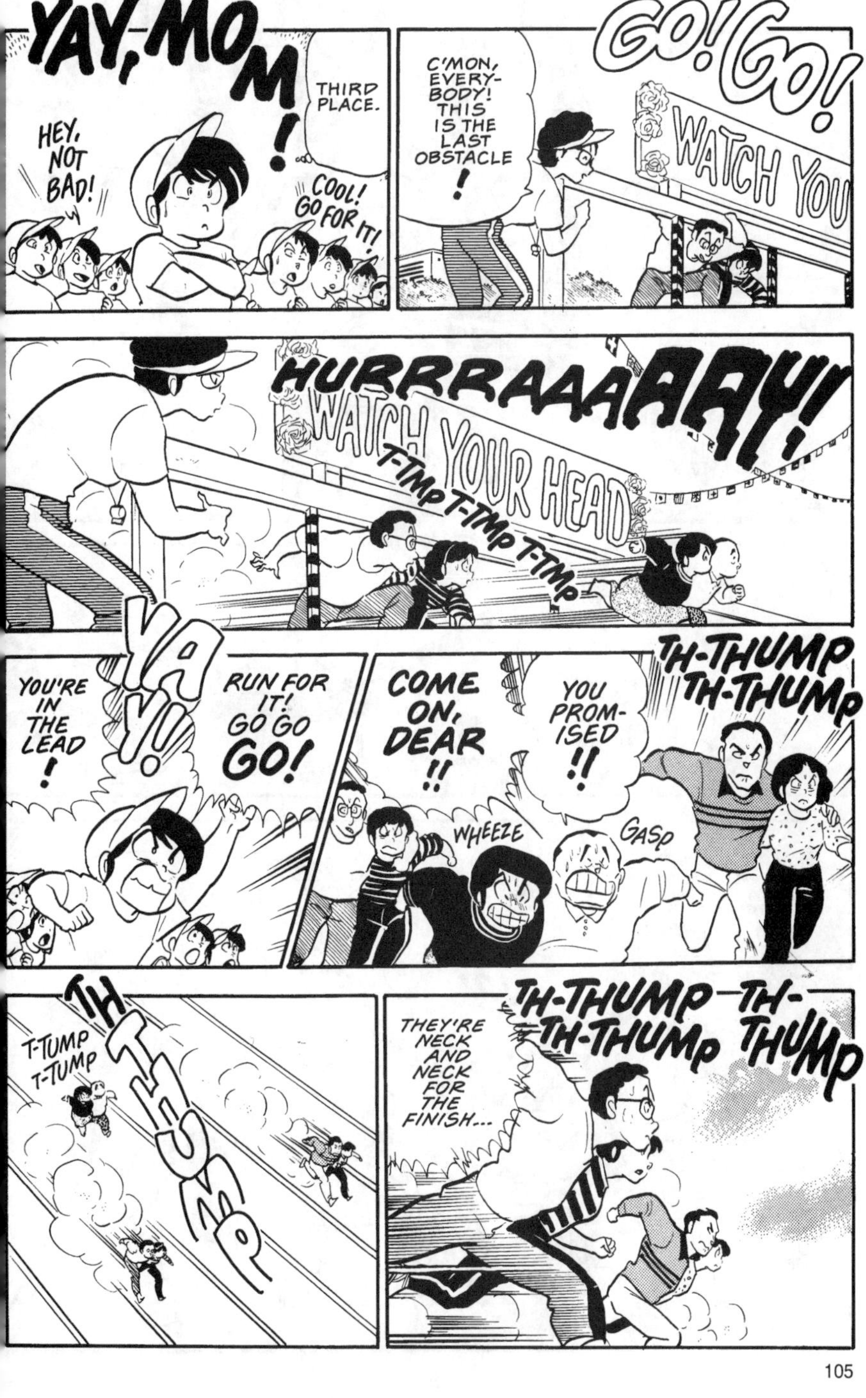
YAY, MOM!
HEY, NOT BAD!
THIRD PLACE.
COOL! GO FOR IT!
C'MON, EVERY-BODY! THIS IS THE LAST OBSTACLE!
GO! GO!
WATCH YOU
HURRRAAAAAAY!
WATCH YOUR HEAD
T-TMP T-TMP T-TMP
YOU'RE IN THE LEAD!
YAY!!
RUN FOR IT! GO GO GO!
COME ON, DEAR!!
YOU PROMISED!!
TH-THUMP TH-THUMP
WHEEZE
GASP
T-TUMP T-TUMP
THTHUMP
THEY'RE NECK AND NECK FOR THE FINISH...
TH-THUMP TH-THUMP TH-THUMP

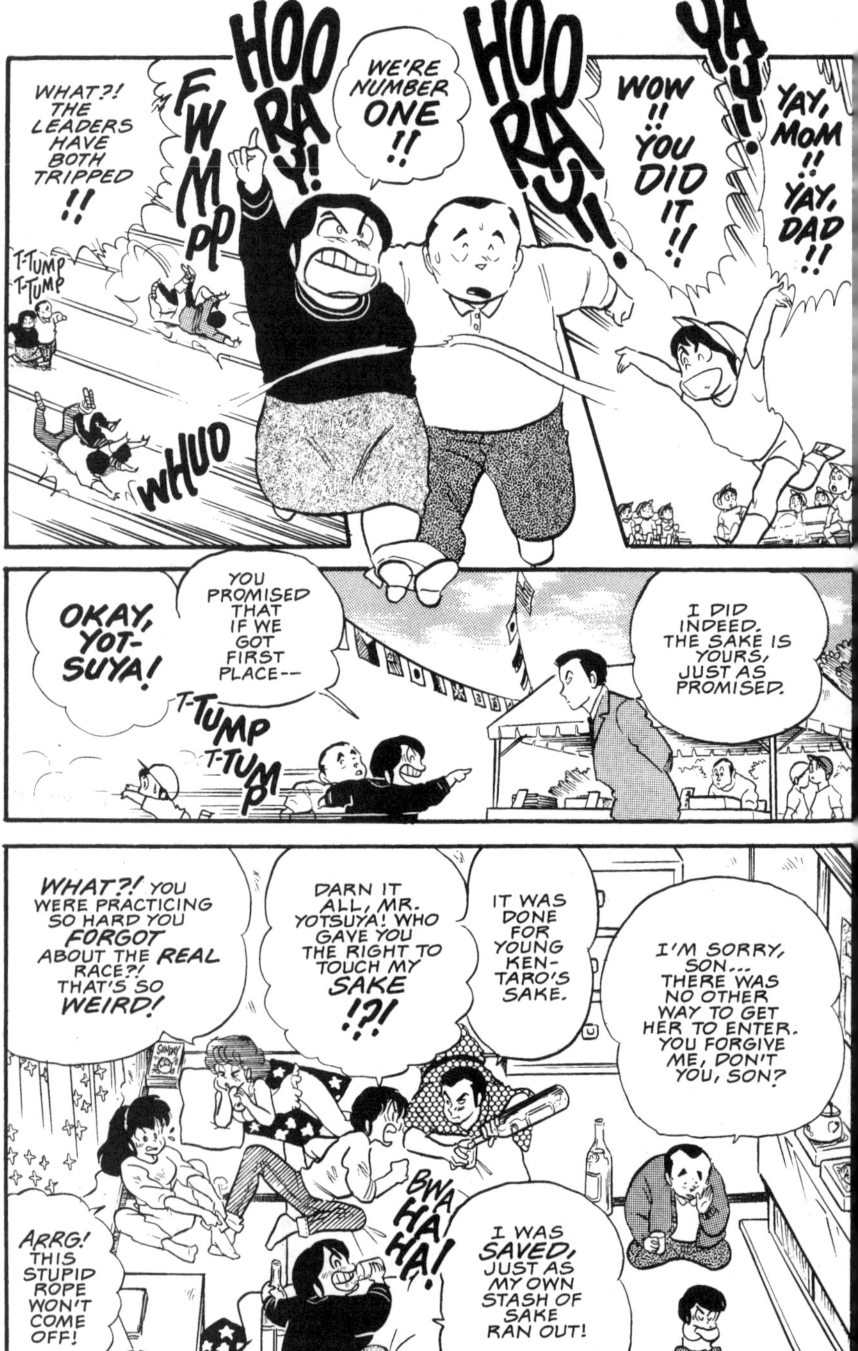
WHAT?! THE LEADERS HAVE BOTH TRIPPED !!
T-TUMP T-TUMP
FWMPP
HOORAY!
WE'RE NUMBER ONE !!
HOORAY!!
WHUD
WOW !! YOU DID IT !!
YAY!!
YAY, MOM !! YAY, DAD !!
OKAY, YOT-SUYA!
YOU PROMISED THAT IF WE GOT FIRST PLACE--
T-TUMP T-TUMP
I DID INDEED. THE SAKE IS YOURS, JUST AS PROMISED.
WHAT?! YOU WERE PRACTICING SO HARD YOU FORGOT ABOUT THE REAL RACE?! THAT'S SO WEIRD!
DARN IT ALL, MR. YOTSUYA! WHO GAVE YOU THE RIGHT TO TOUCH MY SAKE !?!
IT WAS DONE FOR YOUNG KEN-TARO'S SAKE.
I'M SORRY, SON... THERE WAS NO OTHER WAY TO GET HER TO ENTER. YOU FORGIVE ME, DON'T YOU, SON?
ARRG! THIS STUPID ROPE WON'T COME OFF!
BWAHAHA!
I WAS SAVED, JUST AS MY OWN STASH OF SAKE RAN OUT!

PART SIX

FALLING FOR YOU

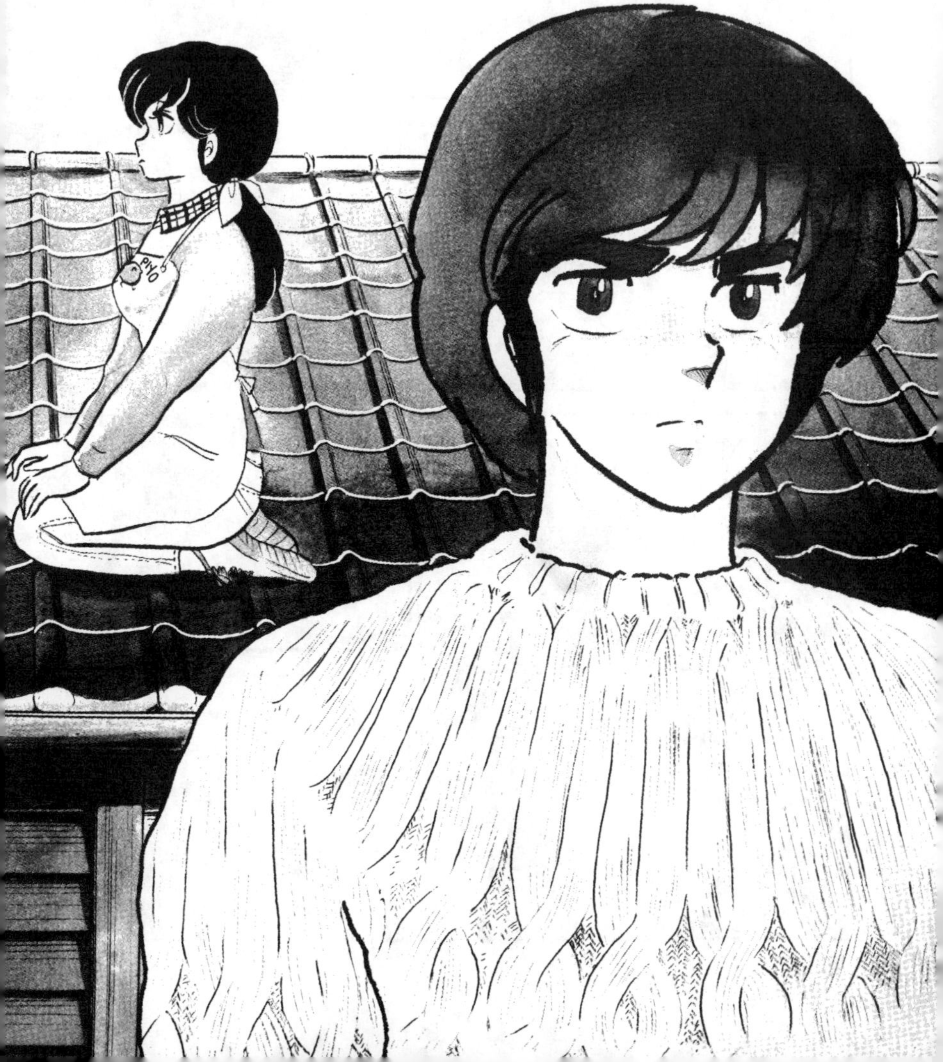

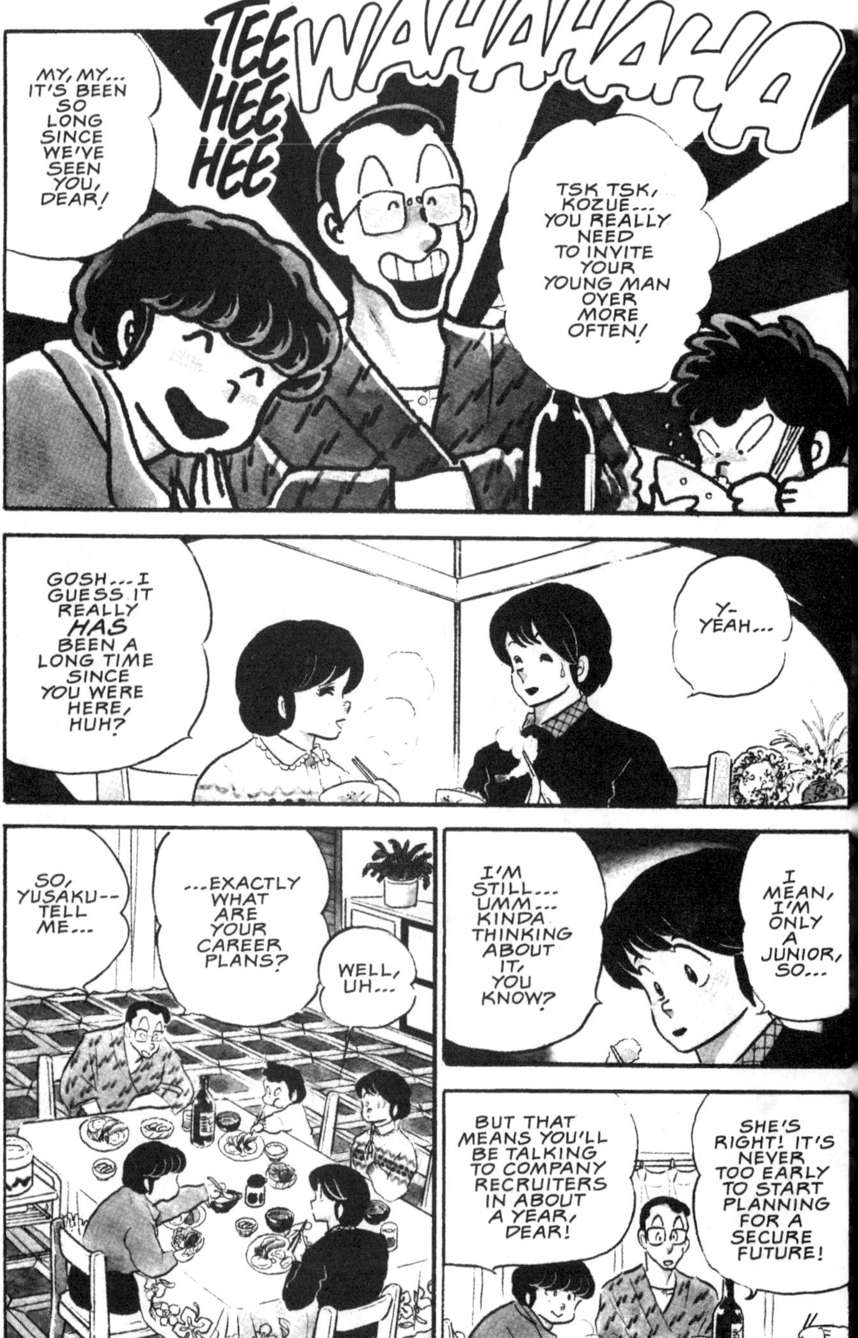
TEE HEE HEE
WAHAHAHAHA
MY, MY... IT'S BEEN SO LONG SINCE WE'VE SEEN YOU, DEAR!
TSK TSK, KOZUE... YOU REALLY NEED TO INVITE YOUR YOUNG MAN OVER MORE OFTEN!
GOSH... I GUESS IT REALLY HAS BEEN A LONG TIME SINCE YOU WERE HERE, HUH?
Y-YEAH...
SO, YUSAKU--TELL ME...
...EXACTLY WHAT ARE YOUR CAREER PLANS?
WELL, UH...
I'M STILL... UMM... KINDA THINKING ABOUT IT, YOU KNOW?
I MEAN, I'M ONLY A JUNIOR, SO...
BUT THAT MEANS YOU'LL BE TALKING TO COMPANY RECRUITERS IN ABOUT A YEAR, DEAR!
SHE'S RIGHT! IT'S NEVER TOO EARLY TO START PLANNING FOR A SECURE FUTURE!

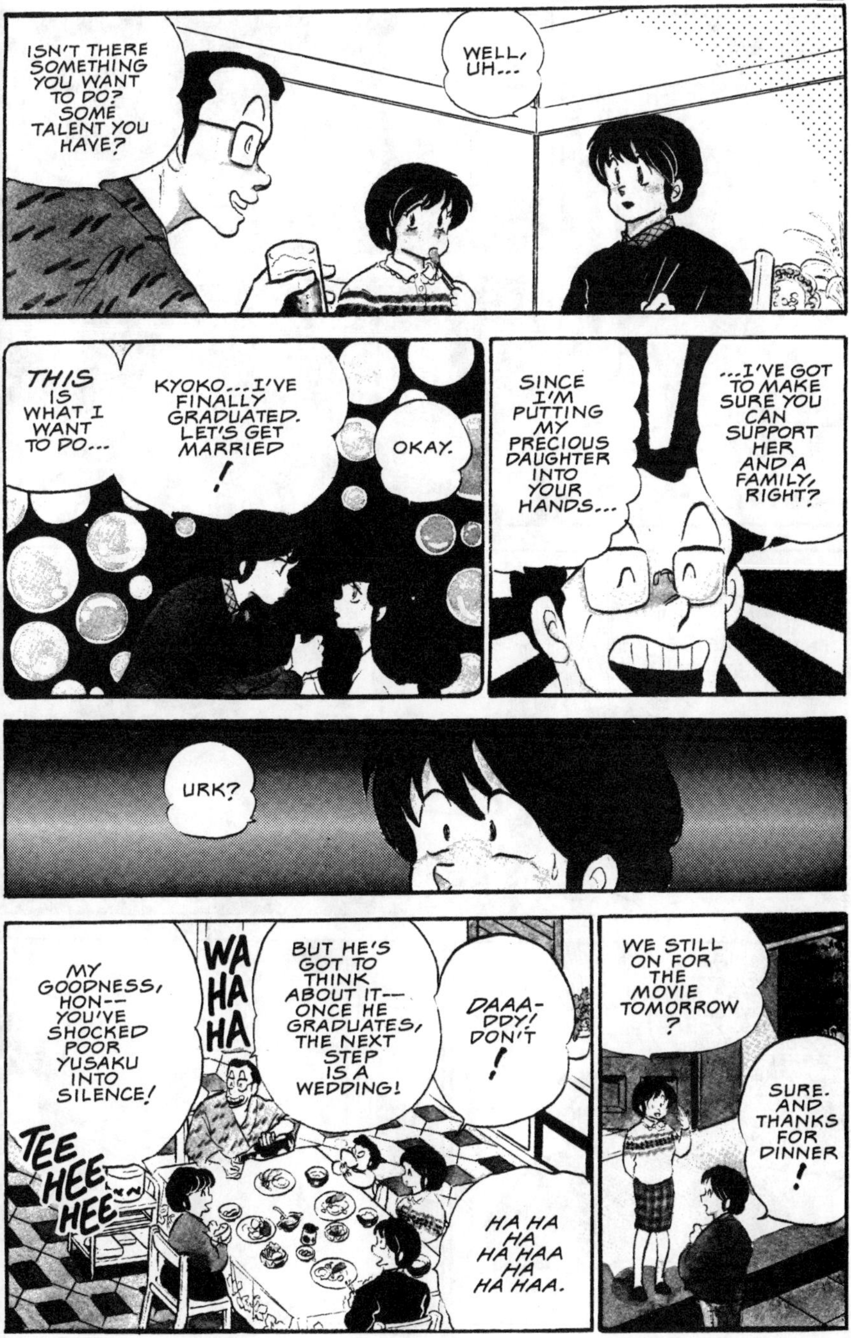
ISN'T THERE SOMETHING YOU WANT TO DO? SOME TALENT YOU HAVE?
WELL, UH...
THIS IS WHAT I WANT TO DO...
KYOKO...I'VE FINALLY GRADUATED. LET'S GET MARRIED!
OKAY.
SINCE I'M PUTTING MY PRECIOUS DAUGHTER INTO YOUR HANDS...
...I'VE GOT TO MAKE SURE YOU CAN SUPPORT HER AND A FAMILY, RIGHT?
URK?
MY GOODNESS, HON--YOU'VE SHOCKED POOR YUSAKU INTO SILENCE!
WA HA HA
BUT HE'S GOT TO THINK ABOUT IT--ONCE HE GRADUATES, THE NEXT STEP IS A WEDDING!
DAAA-DDY! DON'T!
TEE HEE HEE
HA HA HA HA HAA HA HA HAA.
WE STILL ON FOR THE MOVIE TOMORROW?
SURE. AND THANKS FOR DINNER!

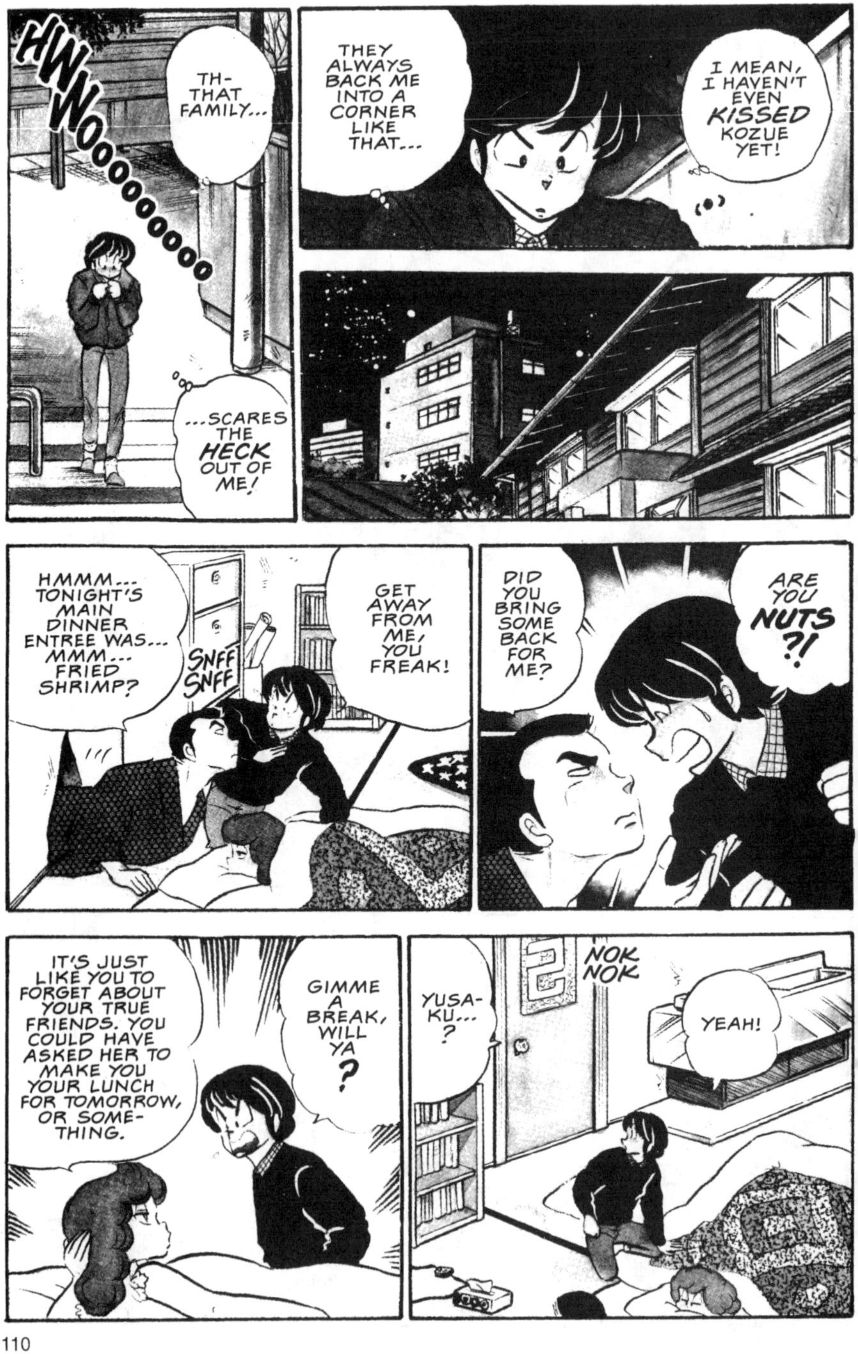
HWWOOOOOOOOOOOOO
TH- THAT FAMILY...
...SCARES THE HECK OUT OF ME!
THEY ALWAYS BACK ME INTO A CORNER LIKE THAT...
I MEAN, I HAVEN'T EVEN KISSED KOZUE YET!
HMMM... TONIGHT'S MAIN DINNER ENTREE WAS... MMM... FRIED SHRIMP?
SNFF SNFF
GET AWAY FROM ME, YOU FREAK!
DID YOU BRING SOME BACK FOR ME?
ARE YOU NUTS ?!
IT'S JUST LIKE YOU TO FORGET ABOUT YOUR TRUE FRIENDS. YOU COULD HAVE ASKED HER TO MAKE YOU YOUR LUNCH FOR TOMORROW, OR SOME- THING.
GIMME A BREAK, WILL YA ?
YUSA- KU... ?
NOK NOK
YEAH!

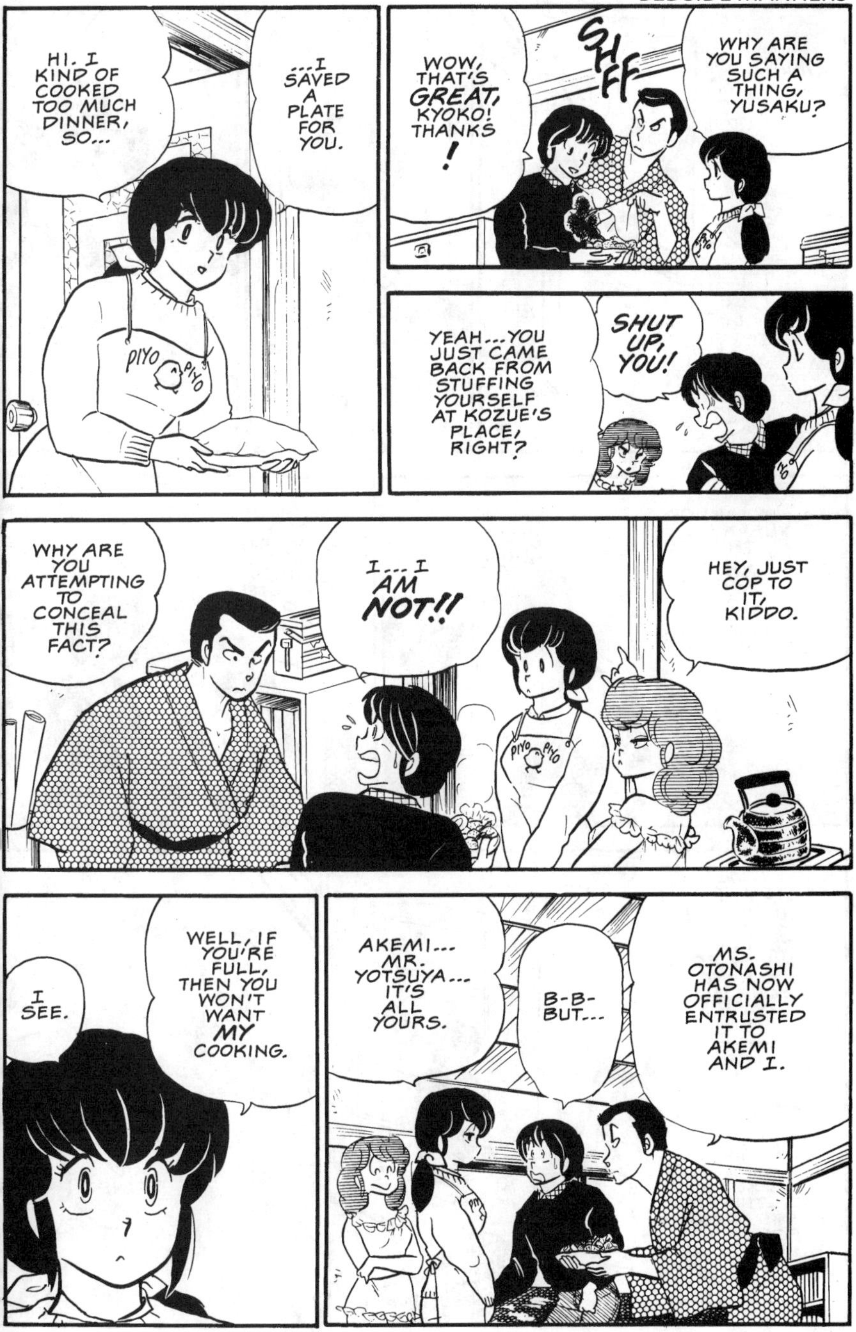
HI. I KIND OF COOKED TOO MUCH DINNER, SO...
...I SAVED A PLATE FOR YOU.
WOW, THAT'S GREAT, KYOKO! THANKS!
SHFF
WHY ARE YOU SAYING SUCH A THING, YUSAKU?
YEAH...YOU JUST CAME BACK FROM STUFFING YOURSELF AT KOZUE'S PLACE, RIGHT?
SHUT UP, YOU!
WHY ARE YOU ATTEMPTING TO CONCEAL THIS FACT?
I...I AM NOT!!
HEY, JUST COP TO IT, KIDDO.
I SEE.
WELL, IF YOU'RE FULL, THEN YOU WON'T WANT MY COOKING.
AKEMI... MR. YOTSUYA... IT'S ALL YOURS.
B-B-BUT...
MS. OTONASHI HAS NOW OFFICIALLY ENTRUSTED IT TO AKEMI AND I.

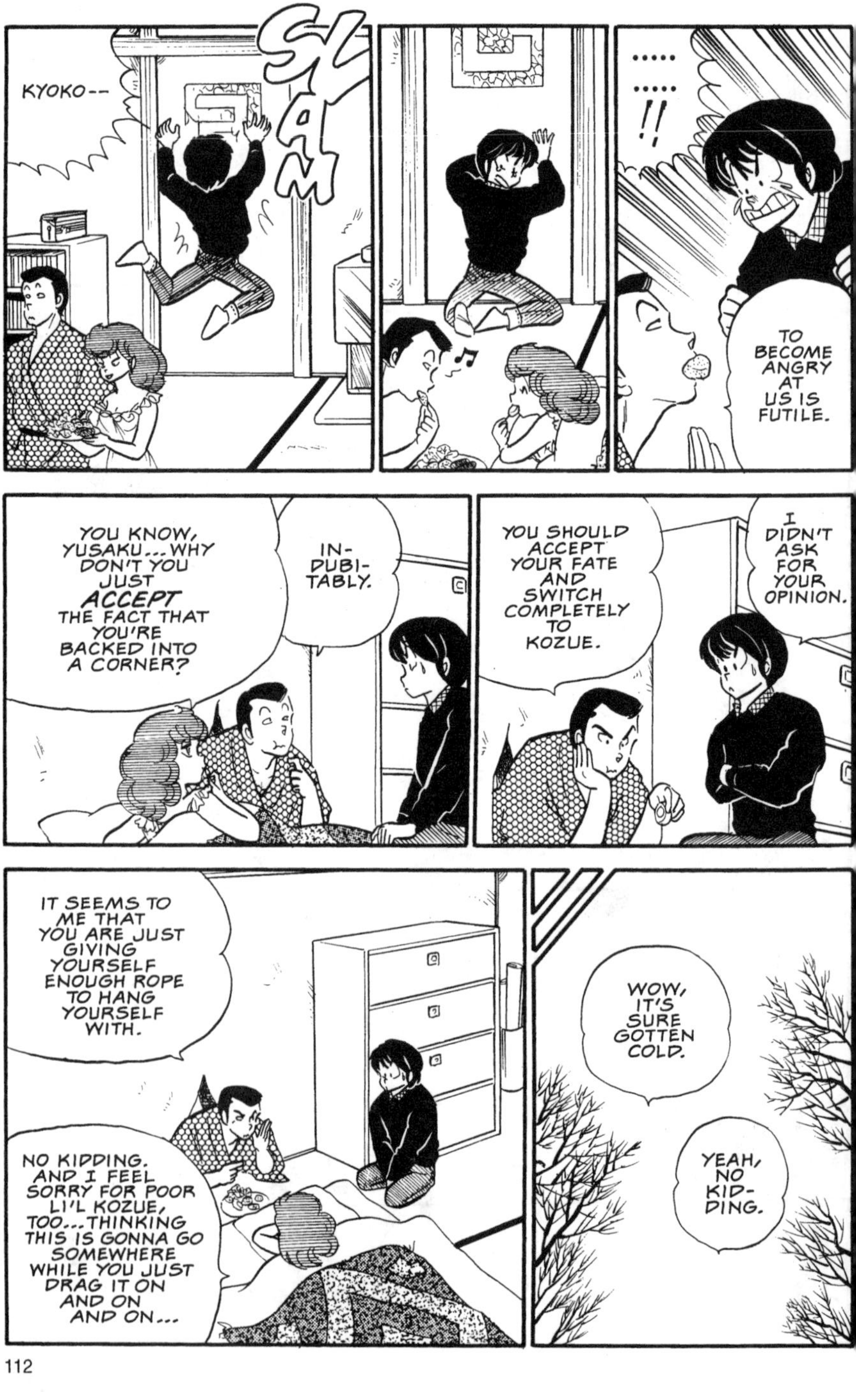
KYOKO--
SLAM
......
......
!!
TO BECOME ANGRY AT US IS FUTILE.
YOU KNOW, YUSAKU...WHY DON'T YOU JUST ACCEPT THE FACT THAT YOU'RE BACKED INTO A CORNER?
IN-DUBI-TABLY.
YOU SHOULD ACCEPT YOUR FATE AND SWITCH COMPLETELY TO KOZUE.
I DIDN'T ASK FOR YOUR OPINION.
IT SEEMS TO ME THAT YOU ARE JUST GIVING YOURSELF ENOUGH ROPE TO HANG YOURSELF WITH.
NO KIDDING. AND I FEEL SORRY FOR POOR LI'L KOZUE, TOO...THINKING THIS IS GONNA GO SOMEWHERE WHILE YOU JUST DRAG IT ON AND ON AND ON...
WOW, IT'S SURE GOTTEN COLD.
YEAH, NO KID-DING.

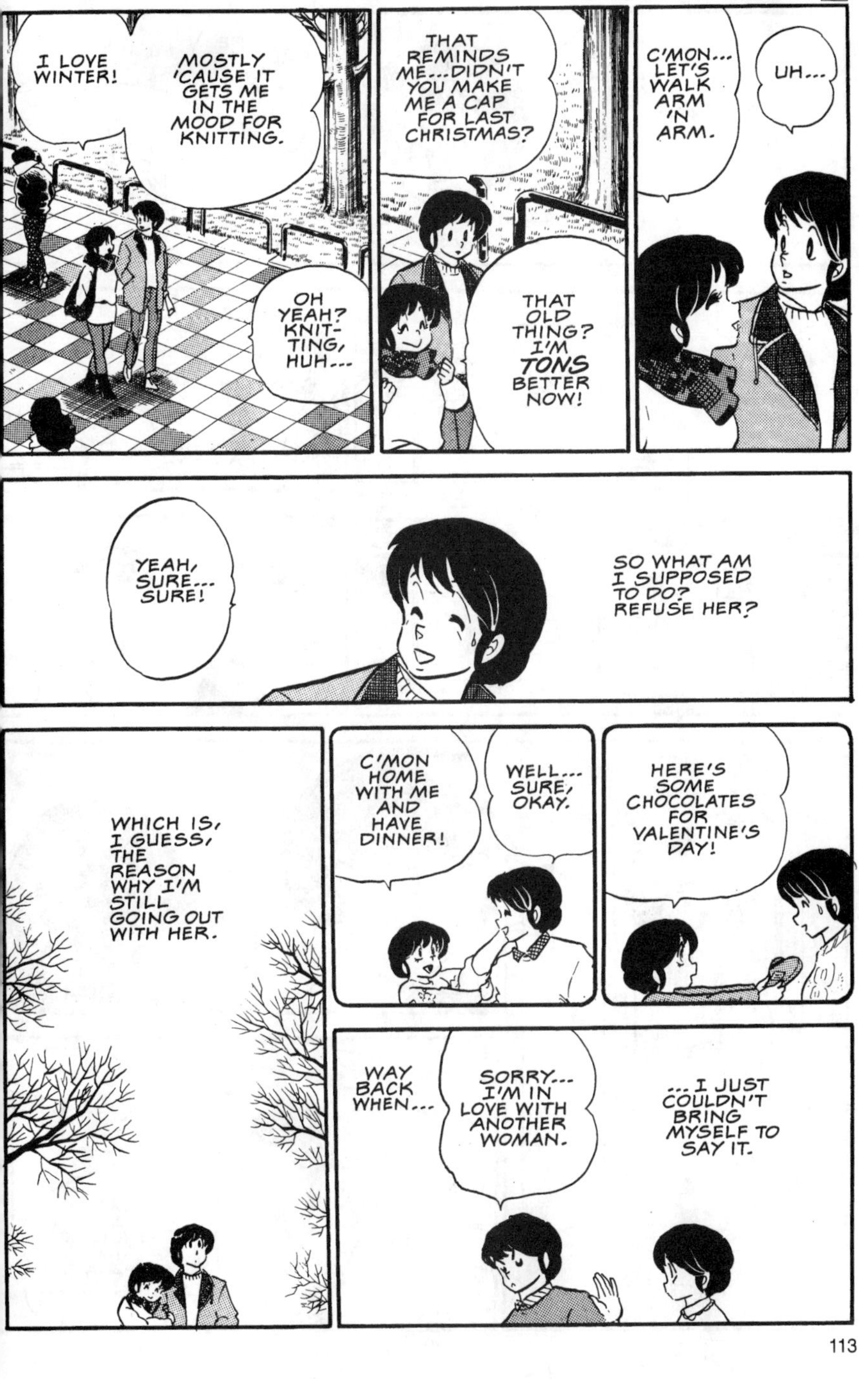
I LOVE WINTER!
MOSTLY 'CAUSE IT GETS ME IN THE MOOD FOR KNITTING.
OH YEAH? KNIT-TING, HUH...
THAT REMINDS ME...DIDN'T YOU MAKE ME A CAP FOR LAST CHRISTMAS?
THAT OLD THING? I'M TONS BETTER NOW!
C'MON... LET'S WALK ARM 'N ARM.
UH...
YEAH, SURE... SURE!
SO WHAT AM I SUPPOSED TO DO? REFUSE HER?
WHICH IS, I GUESS, THE REASON WHY I'M STILL GOING OUT WITH HER.
C'MON HOME WITH ME AND HAVE DINNER!
WELL... SURE, OKAY.
HERE'S SOME CHOCOLATES FOR VALENTINE'S DAY!
WAY BACK WHEN...
SORRY... I'M IN LOVE WITH ANOTHER WOMAN.
...I JUST COULDN'T BRING MYSELF TO SAY IT.

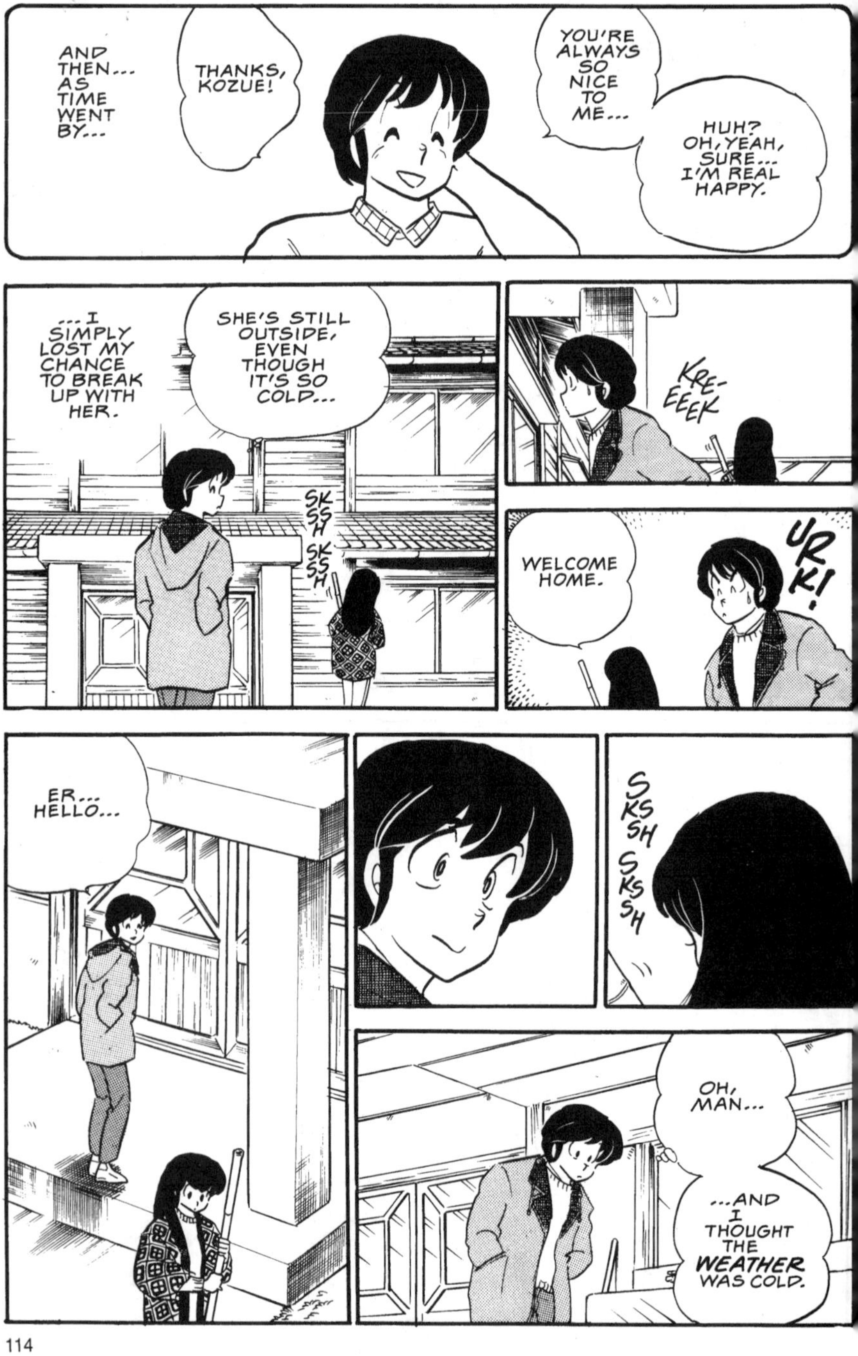
AND THEN... AS TIME WENT BY...
THANKS, KOZUE!
YOU'RE ALWAYS SO NICE TO ME...
HUH? OH, YEAH, SURE... I'M REAL HAPPY.
...I SIMPLY LOST MY CHANCE TO BREAK UP WITH HER.
SHE'S STILL OUTSIDE, EVEN THOUGH IT'S SO COLD...
SKSSH SKSSH
KREEEEK
WELCOME HOME.
URK!
ER... HELLO...
SKSSH SKSSH
OH, MAN...
...AND I THOUGHT THE WEATHER WAS COLD.

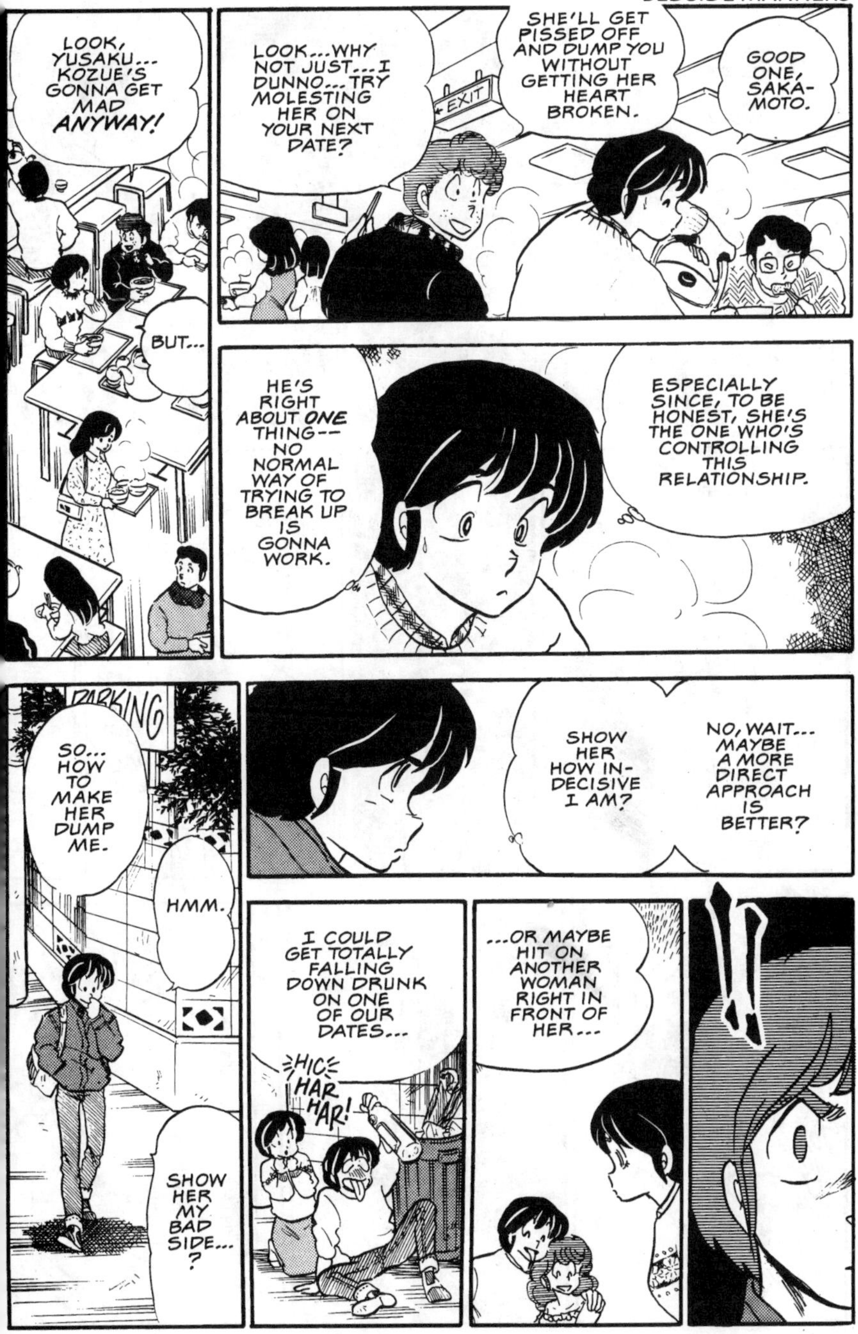
LOOK, YUSAKU... KOZUE'S GONNA GET MAD *ANYWAY!*
BUT...
LOOK...WHY NOT JUST...I DUNNO...TRY MOLESTING HER ON YOUR NEXT DATE?
EXIT
SHE'LL GET PISSED OFF AND DUMP YOU WITHOUT GETTING HER HEART BROKEN.
GOOD ONE, SAKAMOTO.
HE'S RIGHT ABOUT *ONE* THING--NO NORMAL WAY OF TRYING TO BREAK UP IS GONNA WORK.
ESPECIALLY SINCE, TO BE HONEST, SHE'S THE ONE WHO'S CONTROLLING THIS RELATIONSHIP.
PARKING
SO... HOW TO MAKE HER DUMP ME.
HMM.
SHOW HER MY BAD SIDE...?
SHOW HER HOW INDECISIVE I AM?
NO, WAIT... MAYBE A MORE DIRECT APPROACH IS BETTER?
I COULD GET TOTALLY FALLING DOWN DRUNK ON ONE OF OUR DATES...
HIC
HAR HAR!
...OR MAYBE HIT ON ANOTHER WOMAN RIGHT IN FRONT OF HER...

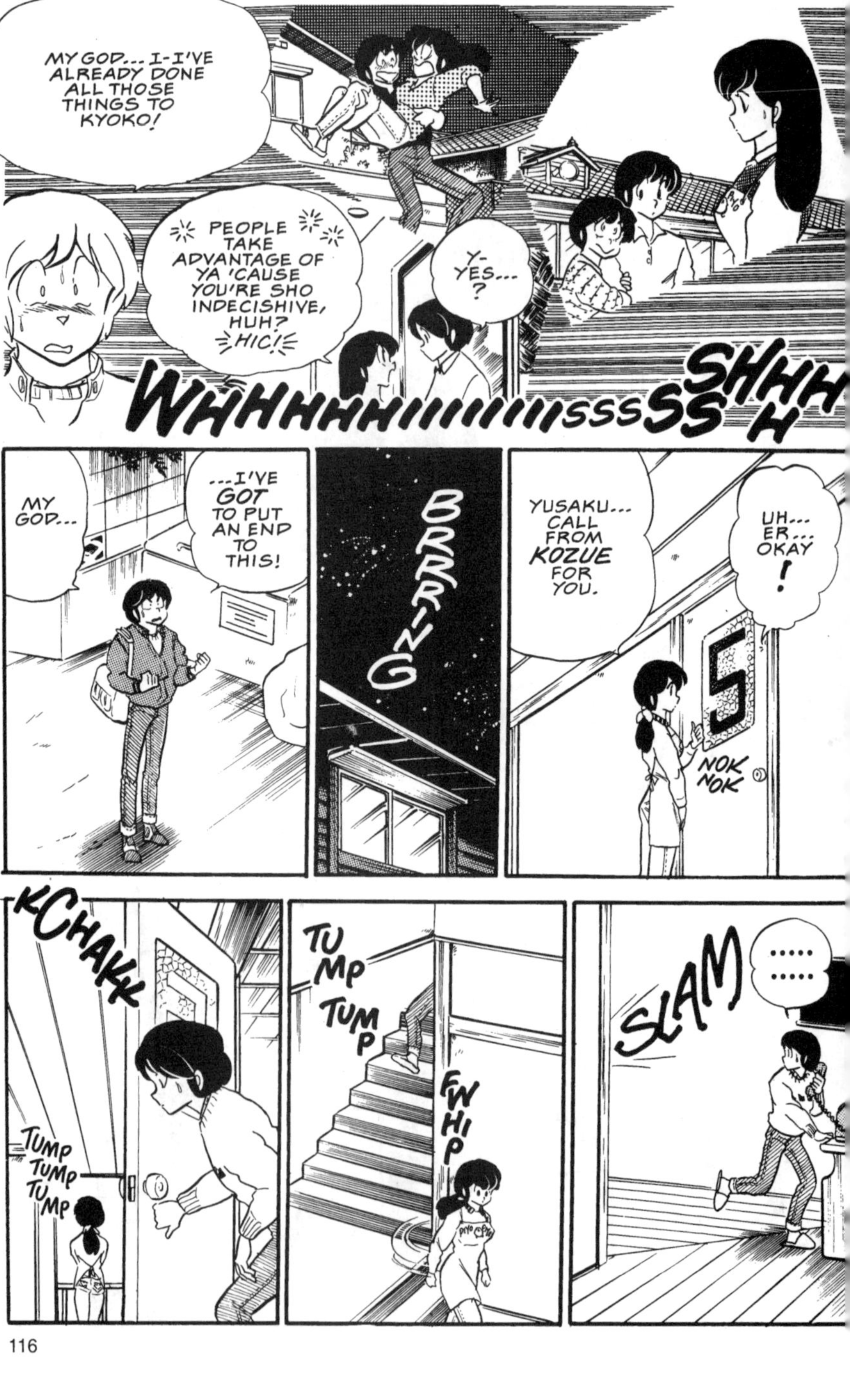
MY GOD... I-I'VE ALREADY DONE ALL THOSE THINGS TO KYOKO!
PEOPLE TAKE ADVANTAGE OF YA 'CAUSE YOU'RE SHO INDECISHIVE, HUH? HIC!
Y-YES...?
WHHHHHIIIIIIIISSSSSSHHHH
MY GOD...
...I'VE GOT TO PUT AN END TO THIS!
BRRRING
YUSAKU... CALL FROM KOZUE FOR YOU.
UH... ER... OKAY!
NOK NOK
KCHAKK
TUMP TUMP TUMP
TUMP TUMP
FWHIP
SLAM
....

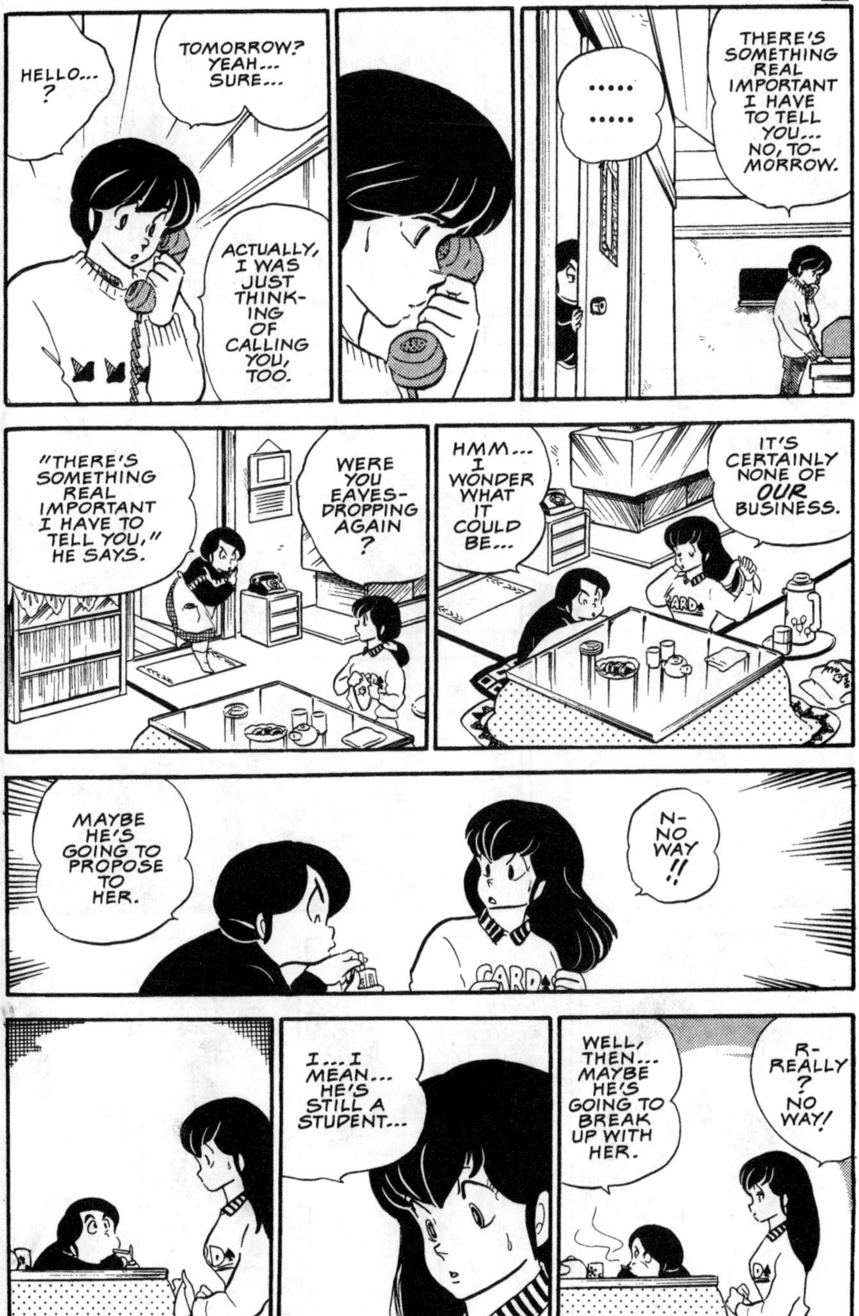
HELLO... ?
TOMORROW? YEAH... SURE...
ACTUALLY, I WAS JUST THINKING OF CALLING YOU, TOO.
.....
.....
THERE'S SOMETHING REAL IMPORTANT I HAVE TO TELL YOU... NO, TOMORROW.
"THERE'S SOMETHING REAL IMPORTANT I HAVE TO TELL YOU," HE SAYS.
WERE YOU EAVESDROPPING AGAIN ?
HMM... I WONDER WHAT IT COULD BE...
IT'S CERTAINLY NONE OF OUR BUSINESS.
MAYBE HE'S GOING TO PROPOSE TO HER.
N-NO WAY !!
I... I MEAN... HE'S STILL A STUDENT...
WELL, THEN... MAYBE HE'S GOING TO BREAK UP WITH HER.
R-REALLY ? NO WAY!

WELL, YOU'VE CERTAINLY BEEN GIVING HIM THE COLD SHOULDER LATELY.

......

AND EVEN IF HE *DOES* BREAK UP WITH KOZUE, THAT DOESN'T MEAN HE'LL GET ANYWHERE WITH *YOU.*

WE DON'T KNOW HE'S BREAKING UP WITH HER YET, DO WE?!

POOR GUY...

SORRY TO BOTHER YOU, BUT THE ROOF IN MY ROOM'S LEAKING AGAIN.

NO PROBLEM. I'LL GET ON IT THIS AFTERNOON.

UMM... I'M OFF.

OKAY... SEE YOU LATER.

WOW... HE SEEMS PRETTY DEPRESSED.

IS HE REALLY GOING TO BREAK UP WITH HER?

BECAUSE OF ME?

OKAY... FIRST OF ALL, DON'T LET THE ATMOSPHERE GET TOO CHEERFUL.

DON'T FORGET YOU'RE THERE TO BREAK UP!

I GOTTA BE REALLY CAREFUL.... HER MOODS ARE SO DAMN INFECTIOUS.

SO WATCH IT!

PNCH

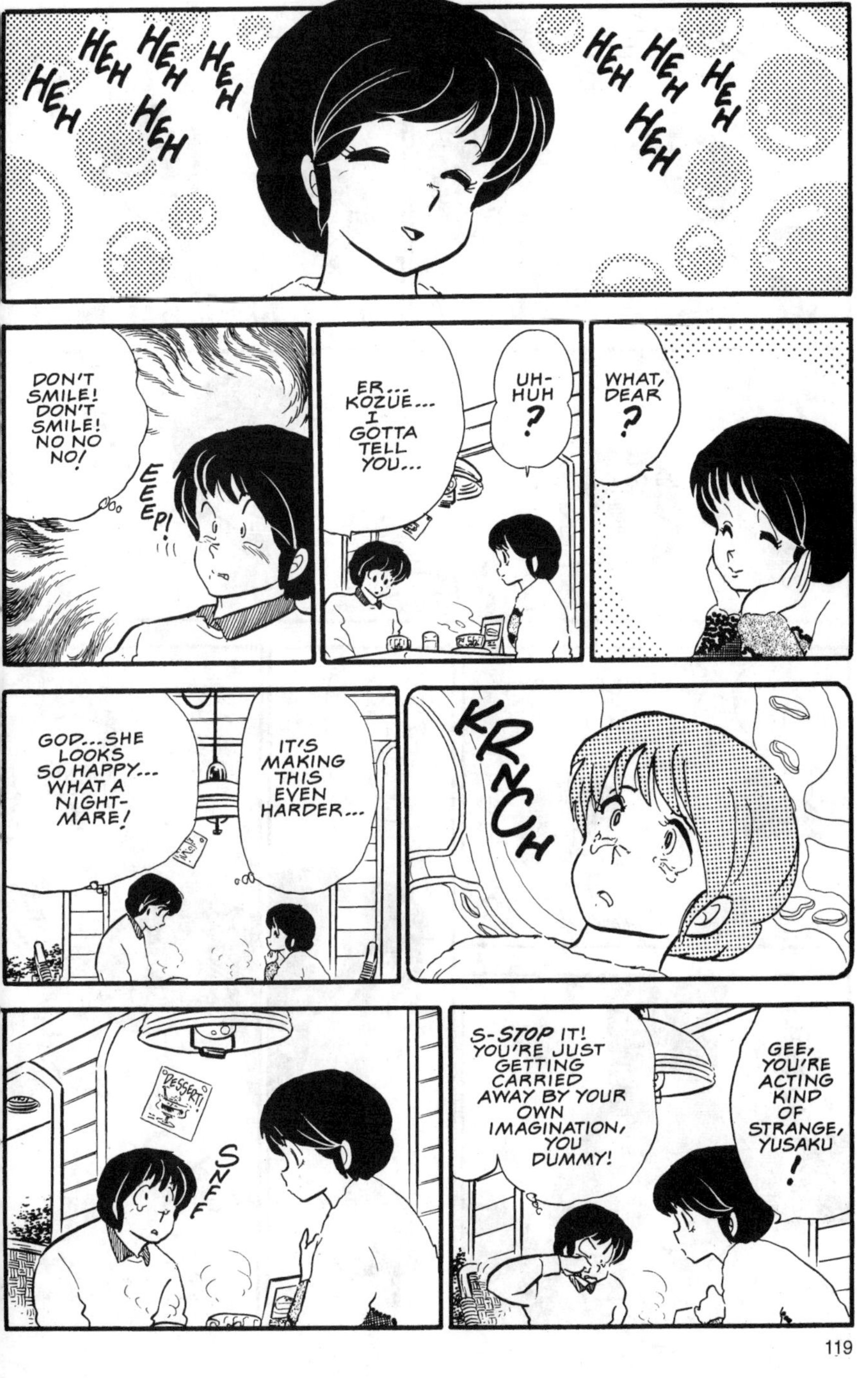
HEH HEH HEH HEH HEH
HEH HEH HEH HEH
DON'T SMILE! DON'T SMILE! NO NO NO!
EEEP!
ER... KOZUE... I GOTTA TELL YOU...
UH-HUH?
WHAT, DEAR?
GOD...SHE LOOKS SO HAPPY... WHAT A NIGHT-MARE!
IT'S MAKING THIS EVEN HARDER...
KRNCH
DESSERT!
SNFF
S-STOP IT! YOU'RE JUST GETTING CARRIED AWAY BY YOUR OWN IMAGINATION, YOU DUMMY!
GEE, YOU'RE ACTING KIND OF STRANGE, YUSAKU!

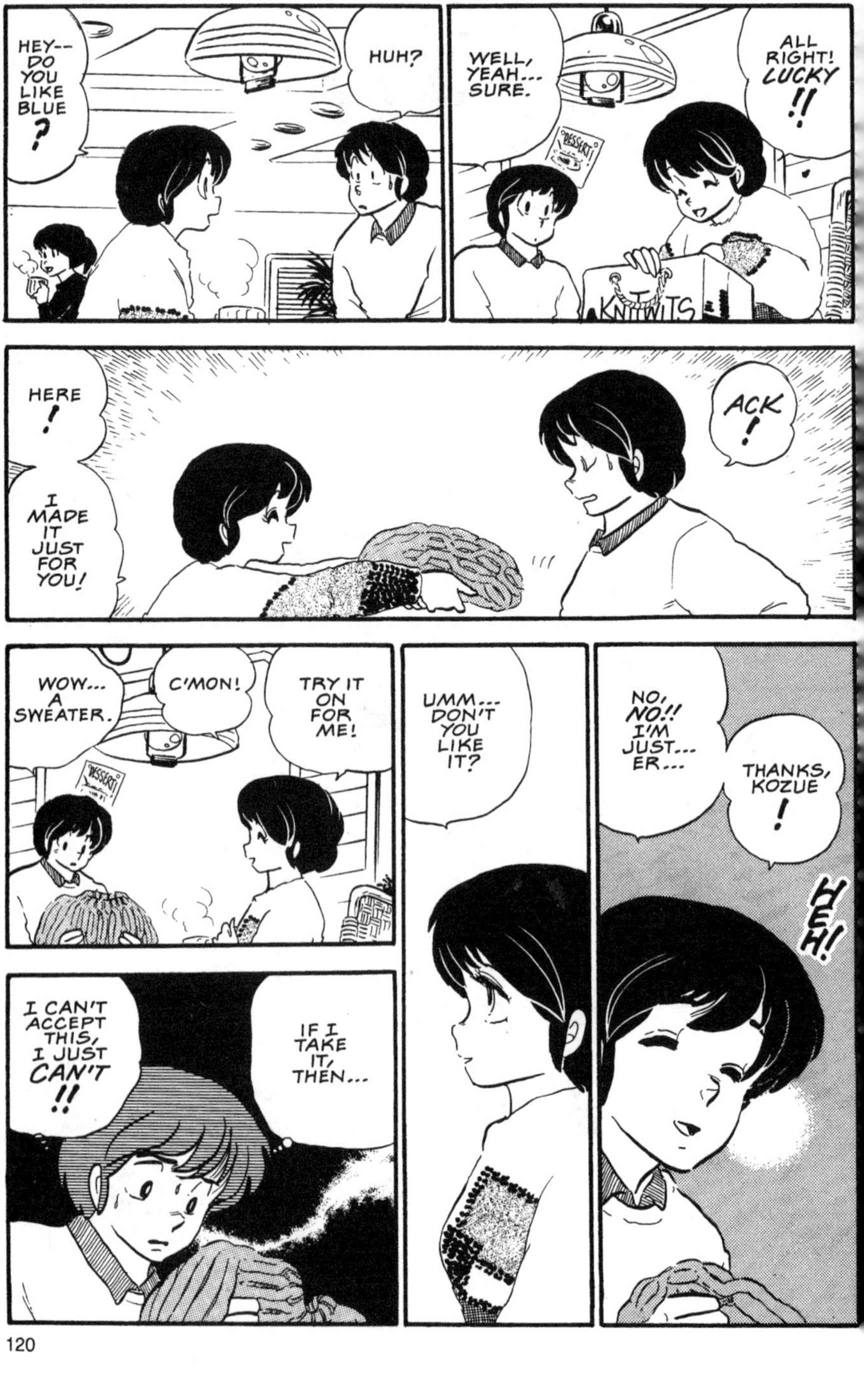

HEY-- DO YOU LIKE BLUE ?
HUH?
WELL, YEAH... SURE.
ALL RIGHT! LUCKY !!
KNITWITS
HERE !
I MADE IT JUST FOR YOU!
ACK !
WOW... A SWEATER.
C'MON!
TRY IT ON FOR ME!
DESSERT
I CAN'T ACCEPT THIS, I JUST CAN'T !!
IF I TAKE IT, THEN...
UMM... DON'T YOU LIKE IT?
NO, NO!! I'M JUST... ER...
THANKS, KOZUE !
HEH!

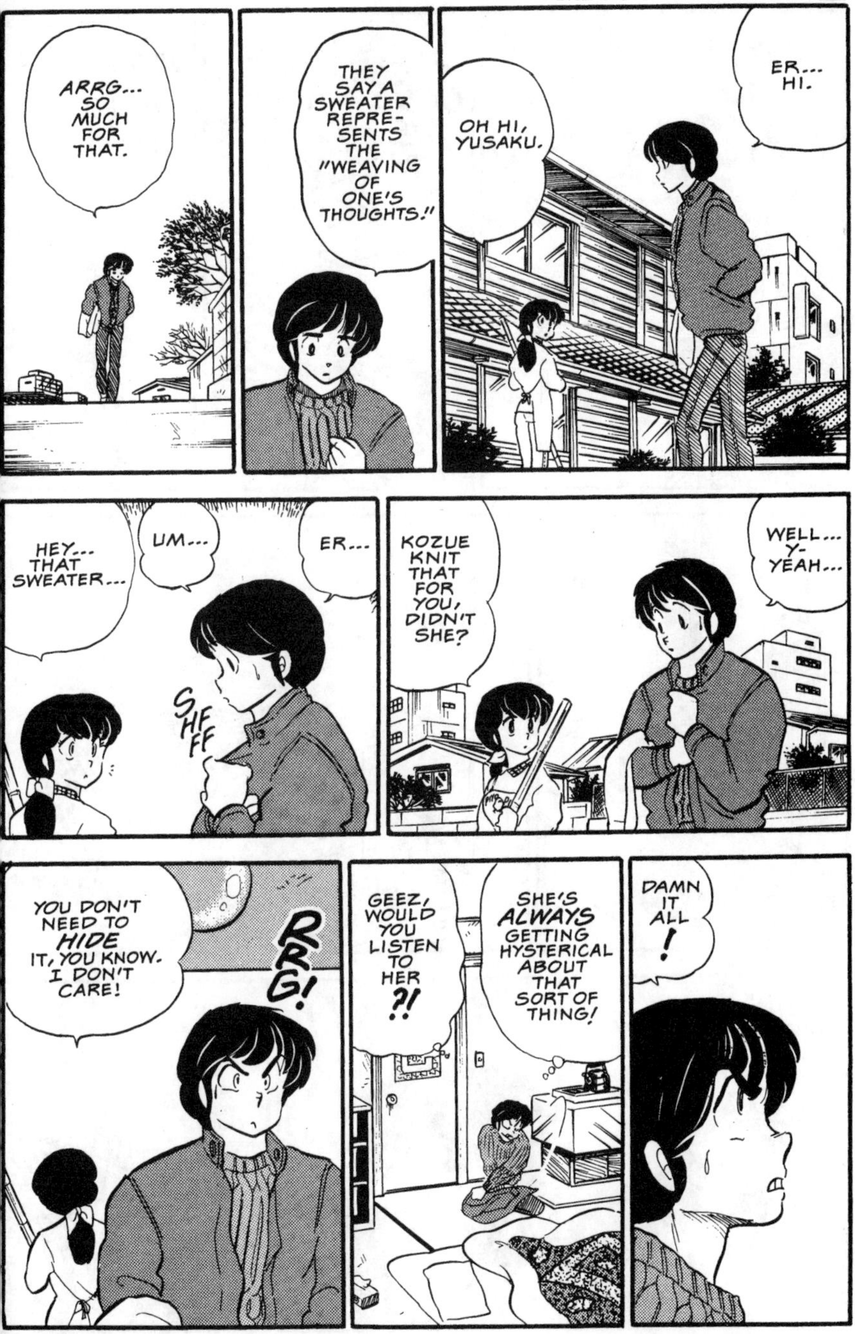
ARRG... SO MUCH FOR THAT.
THEY SAY A SWEATER REPRE-SENTS THE "WEAVING OF ONE'S THOUGHTS."
OH HI, YUSAKU.
ER... HI.
HEY... THAT SWEATER...
UM...
SHFF
ER...
KOZUE KNIT THAT FOR YOU, DIDN'T SHE?
WELL... Y-YEAH...
YOU DON'T NEED TO HIDE IT, YOU KNOW. I DON'T CARE!
RRG!
GEEZ, WOULD YOU LISTEN TO HER ?!
SHE'S ALWAYS GETTING HYSTERICAL ABOUT THAT SORT OF THING!
DAMN IT ALL !

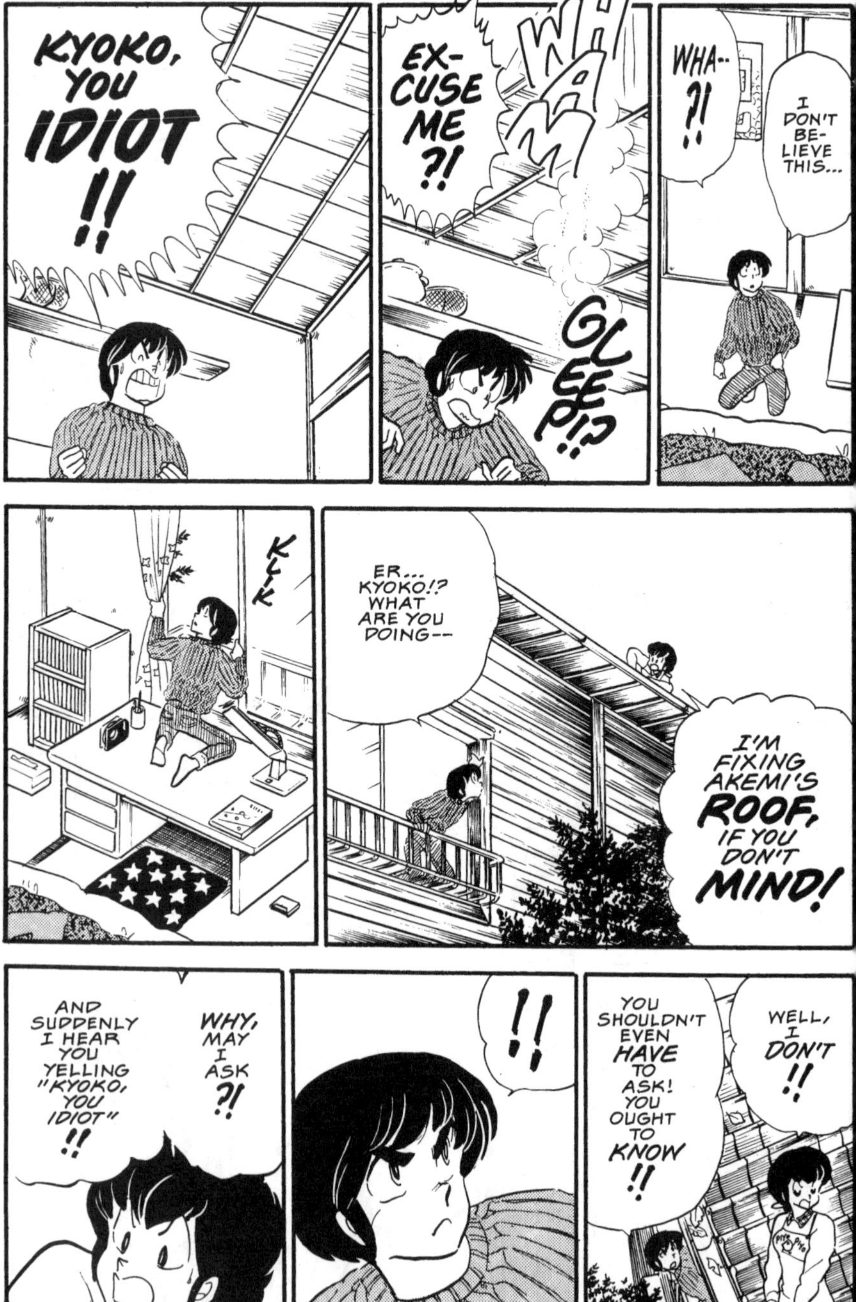
KYOKO, YOU IDIOT !!
EX-CUSE ME ?!
WHAM
GLEEP!!?
WHA-- ?!
I DON'T BE-LIEVE THIS...
KLIK
ER... KYOKO!? WHAT ARE YOU DOING--
I'M FIXING AKEMI'S ROOF, IF YOU DON'T MIND!
AND SUDDENLY I HEAR YOU YELLING "KYOKO, YOU IDIOT" !!
WHY, MAY I ASK ?!
!!
YOU SHOULDN'T EVEN HAVE TO ASK! YOU OUGHT TO KNOW !!
WELL, I DON'T !!

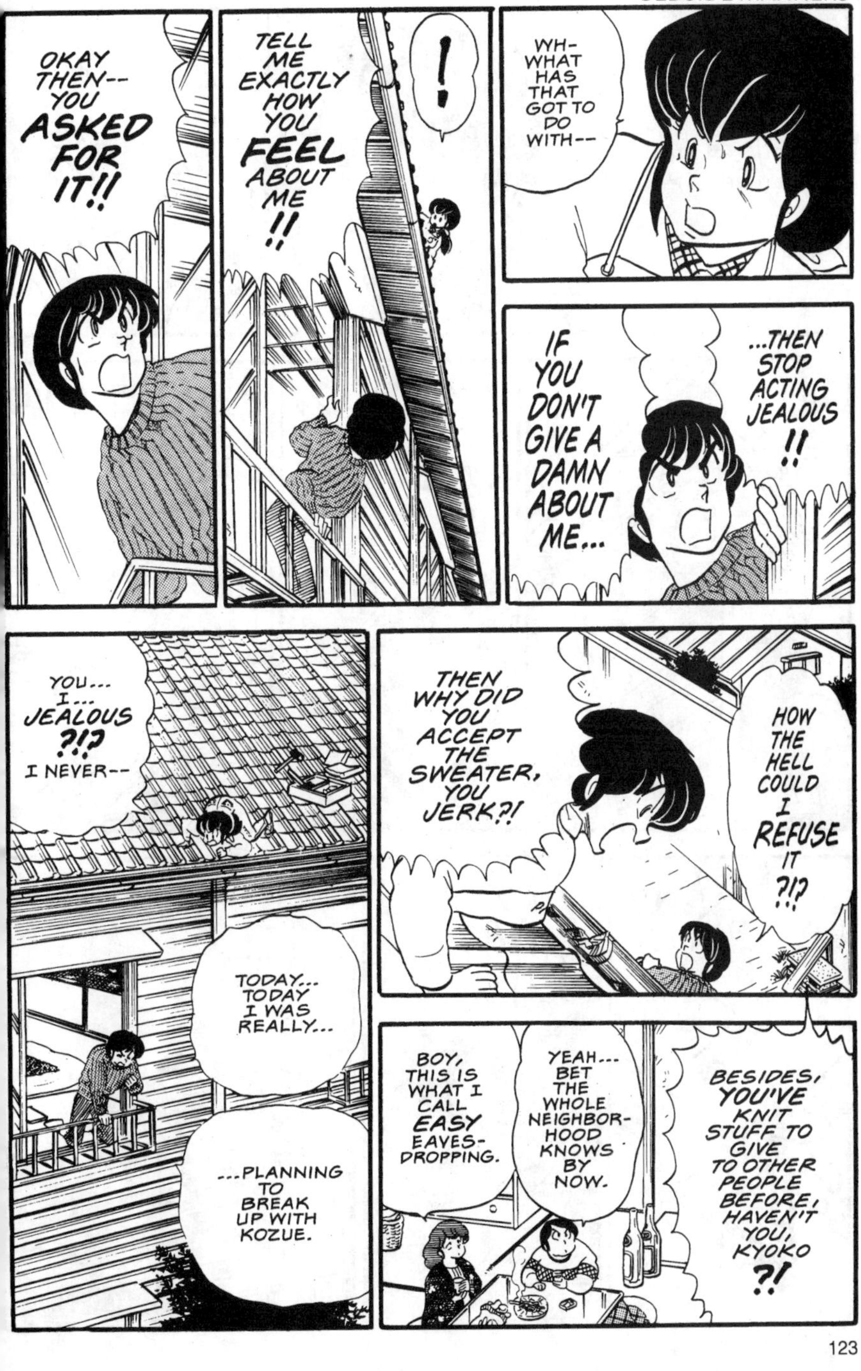
OKAY THEN-- YOU ASKED FOR IT!!
TELL ME EXACTLY HOW YOU FEEL ABOUT ME!!
!
WH-WHAT HAS THAT GOT TO DO WITH--
IF YOU DON'T GIVE A DAMN ABOUT ME...
...THEN STOP ACTING JEALOUS!!
YOU... I... JEALOUS?!? I NEVER--
TODAY... TODAY I WAS REALLY...
...PLANNING TO BREAK UP WITH KOZUE.
THEN WHY DID YOU ACCEPT THE SWEATER, YOU JERK?!
HOW THE HELL COULD I REFUSE IT?!?
BOY, THIS IS WHAT I CALL EASY EAVES-DROPPING.
YEAH... BET THE WHOLE NEIGHBOR-HOOD KNOWS BY NOW.
BESIDES, YOU'VE KNIT STUFF TO GIVE TO OTHER PEOPLE BEFORE, HAVEN'T YOU, KYOKO?!

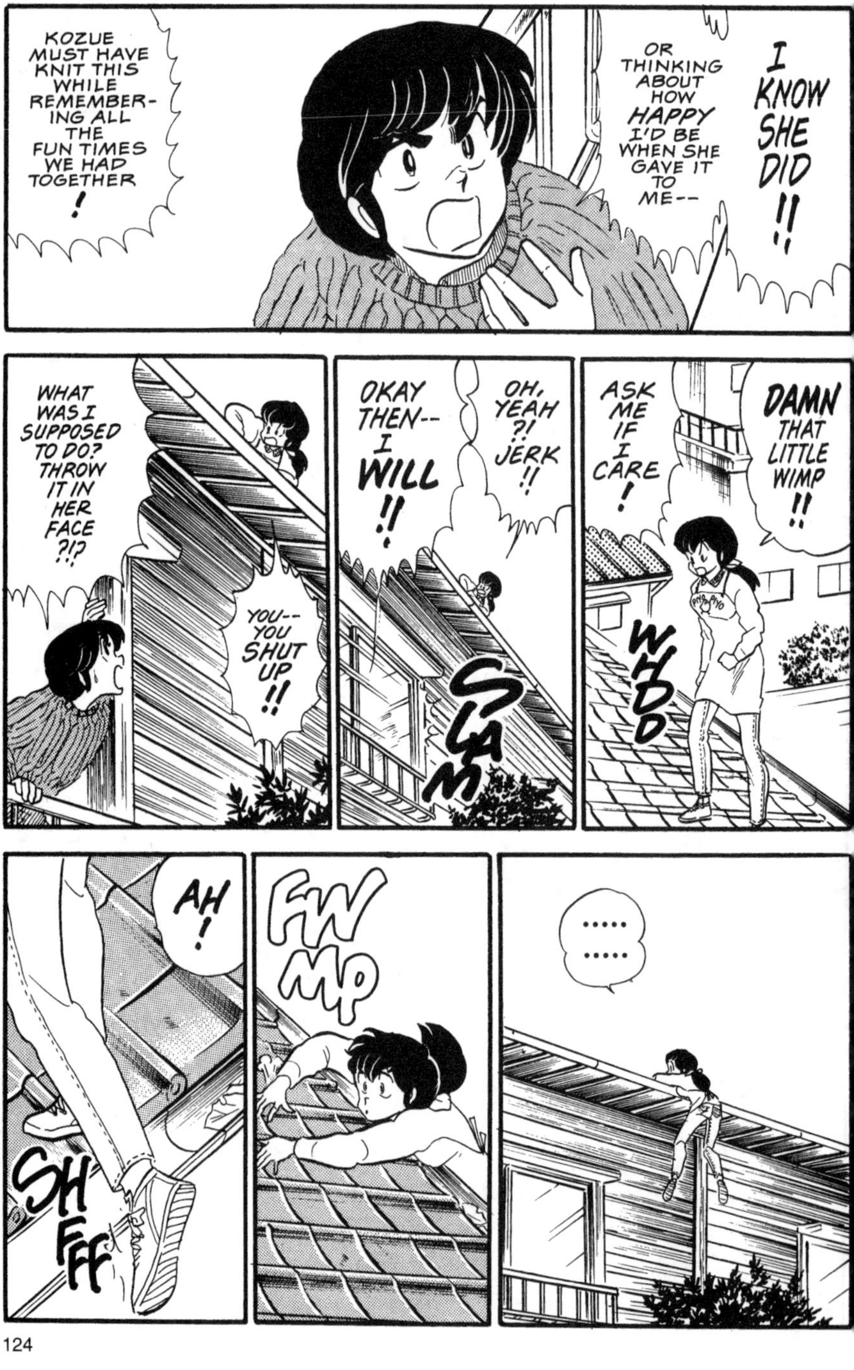
KOZUE MUST HAVE KNIT THIS WHILE REMEMBERING ALL THE FUN TIMES WE HAD TOGETHER!
OR THINKING ABOUT HOW HAPPY I'D BE WHEN SHE GAVE IT TO ME--
I KNOW SHE DID!!
WHAT WAS I SUPPOSED TO DO? THROW IT IN HER FACE?!?
YOU-- YOU SHUT UP!!
OKAY THEN-- I WILL!!
OH, YEAH?! JERK!!
SLAM
ASK ME IF I CARE!
DAMN THAT LITTLE WIMP!!
WHOD
AH!
SHFFF
FWMP
....

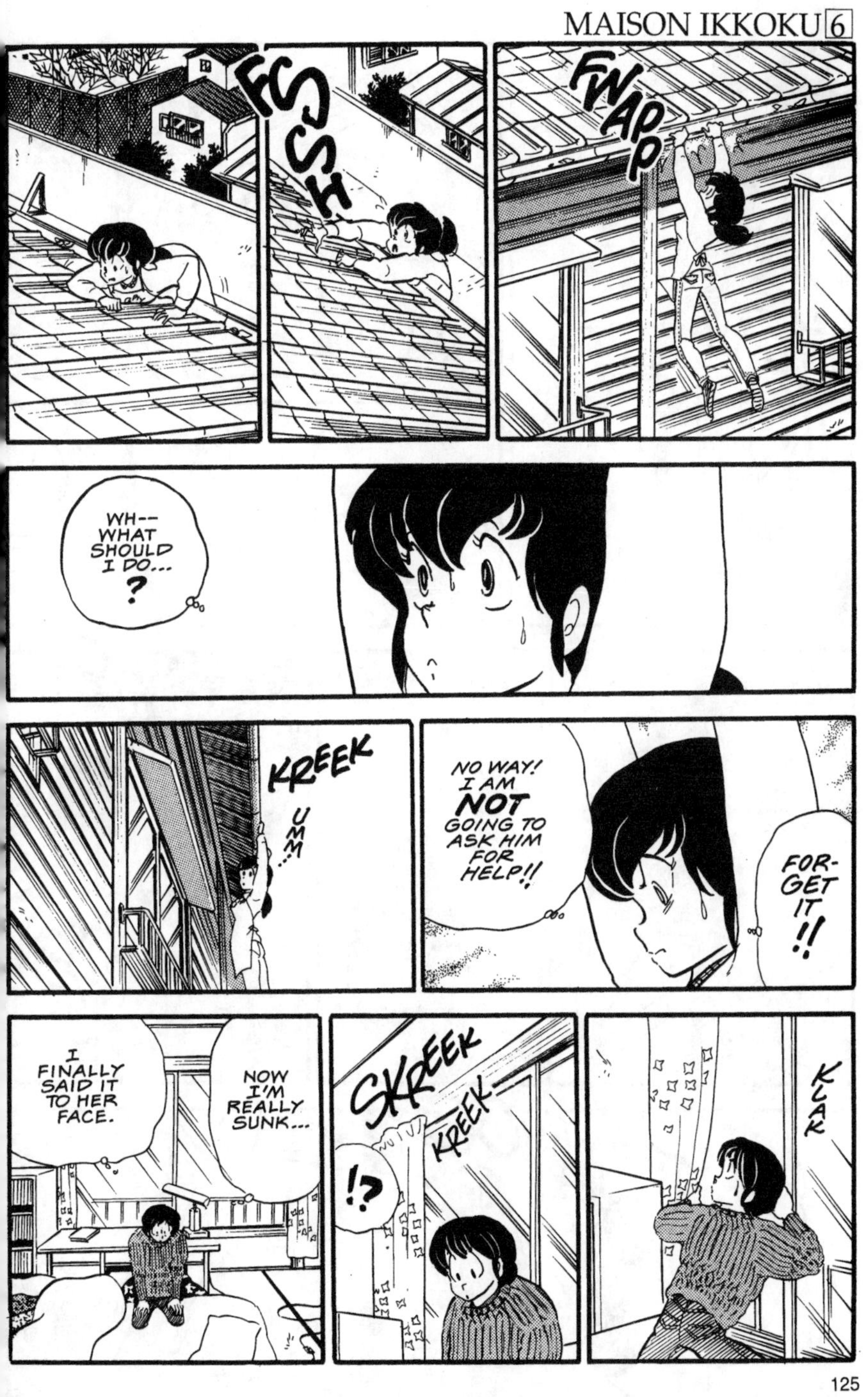
FCSSH
FWAP
WH-- WHAT SHOULD I DO...?
KREEK
UMM...
NO WAY! I AM NOT GOING TO ASK HIM FOR HELP!!
FOR-GET IT!!
I FINALLY SAID IT TO HER FACE.
NOW I'M REALLY SUNK...
SKREEK
KREEK
!?
KLAK

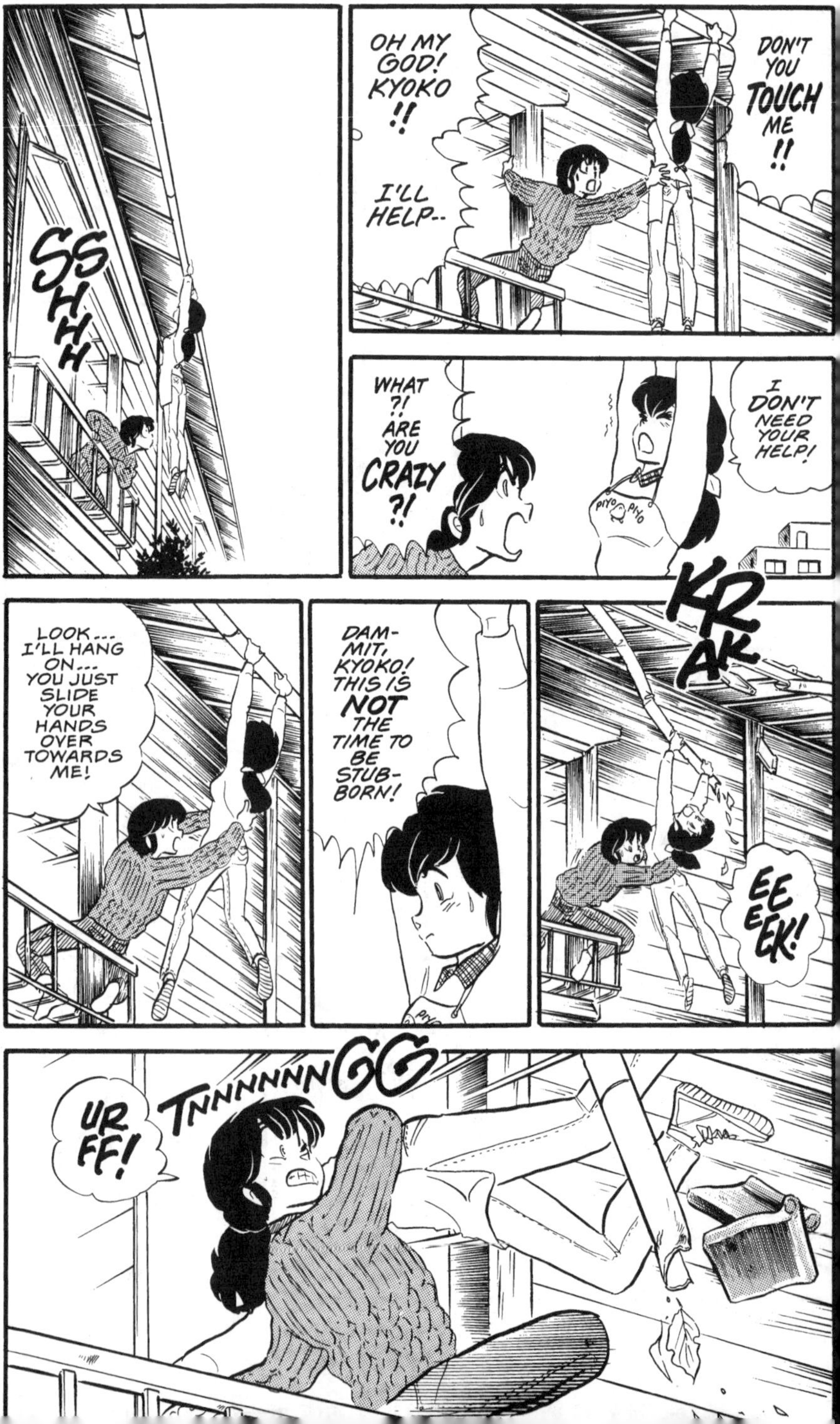
SSHHHH
OH MY GOD! KYOKO!!
I'LL HELP..
DON'T YOU TOUCH ME!!
WHAT?! ARE YOU CRAZY?!
I DON'T NEED YOUR HELP!
PIYO PIYO
LOOK... I'LL HANG ON... YOU JUST SLIDE YOUR HANDS OVER TOWARDS ME!
DAMMIT, KYOKO! THIS IS NOT THE TIME TO BE STUBBORN!
KRAK
EEEEK!
URFF!
TNNNNNNGG

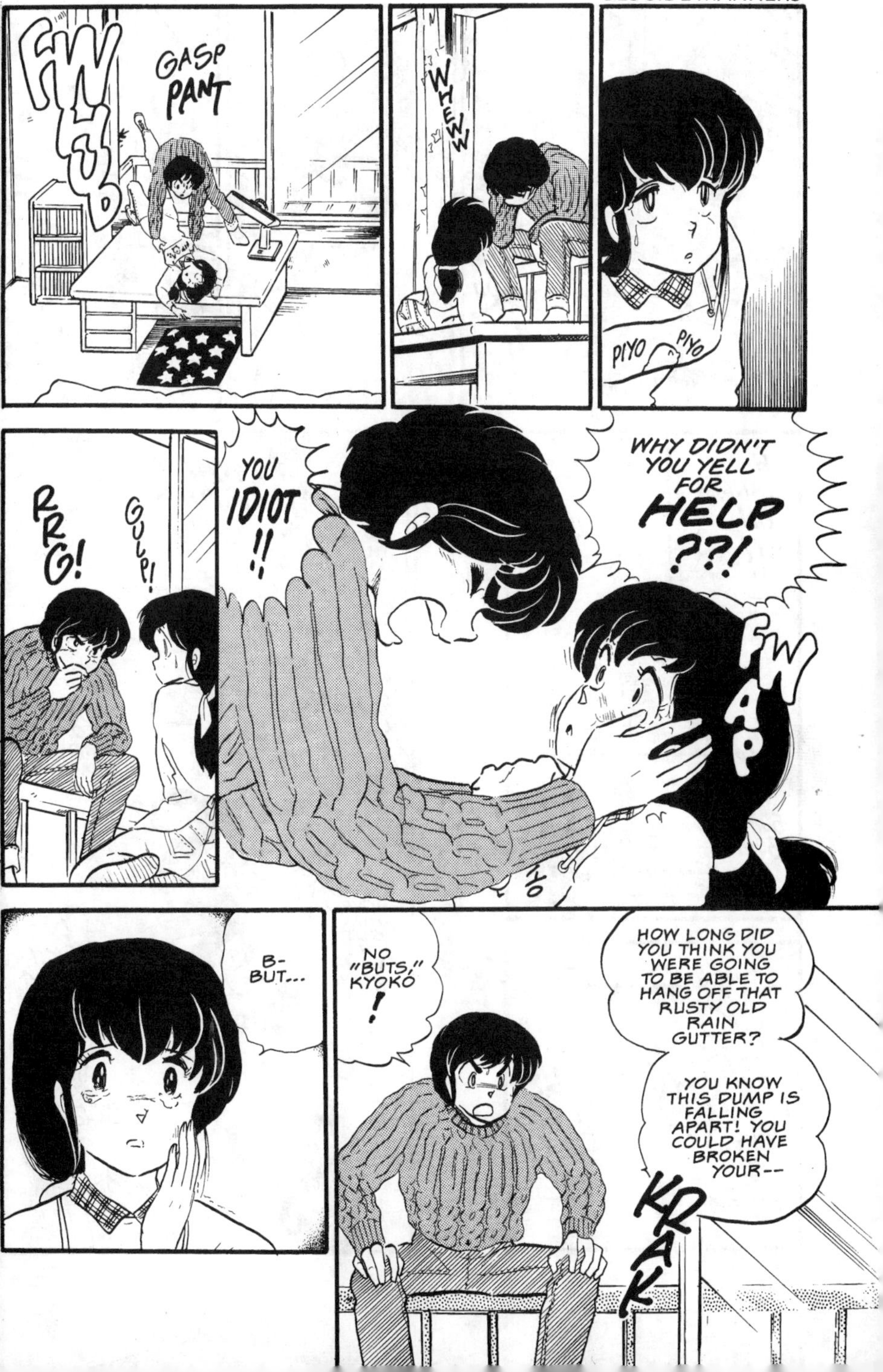
FWUMP
GASP
PANT
WHEWW
PIYO PIYO
RRG!
GULP!
YOU IDIOT!!
WHY DIDN'T YOU YELL FOR HELP??!
FWAP
B- BUT...
NO "BUTS," KYOKO!
HOW LONG DID YOU THINK YOU WERE GOING TO BE ABLE TO HANG OFF THAT RUSTY OLD RAIN GUTTER?
YOU KNOW THIS DUMP IS FALLING APART! YOU COULD HAVE BROKEN YOUR--
KRAK

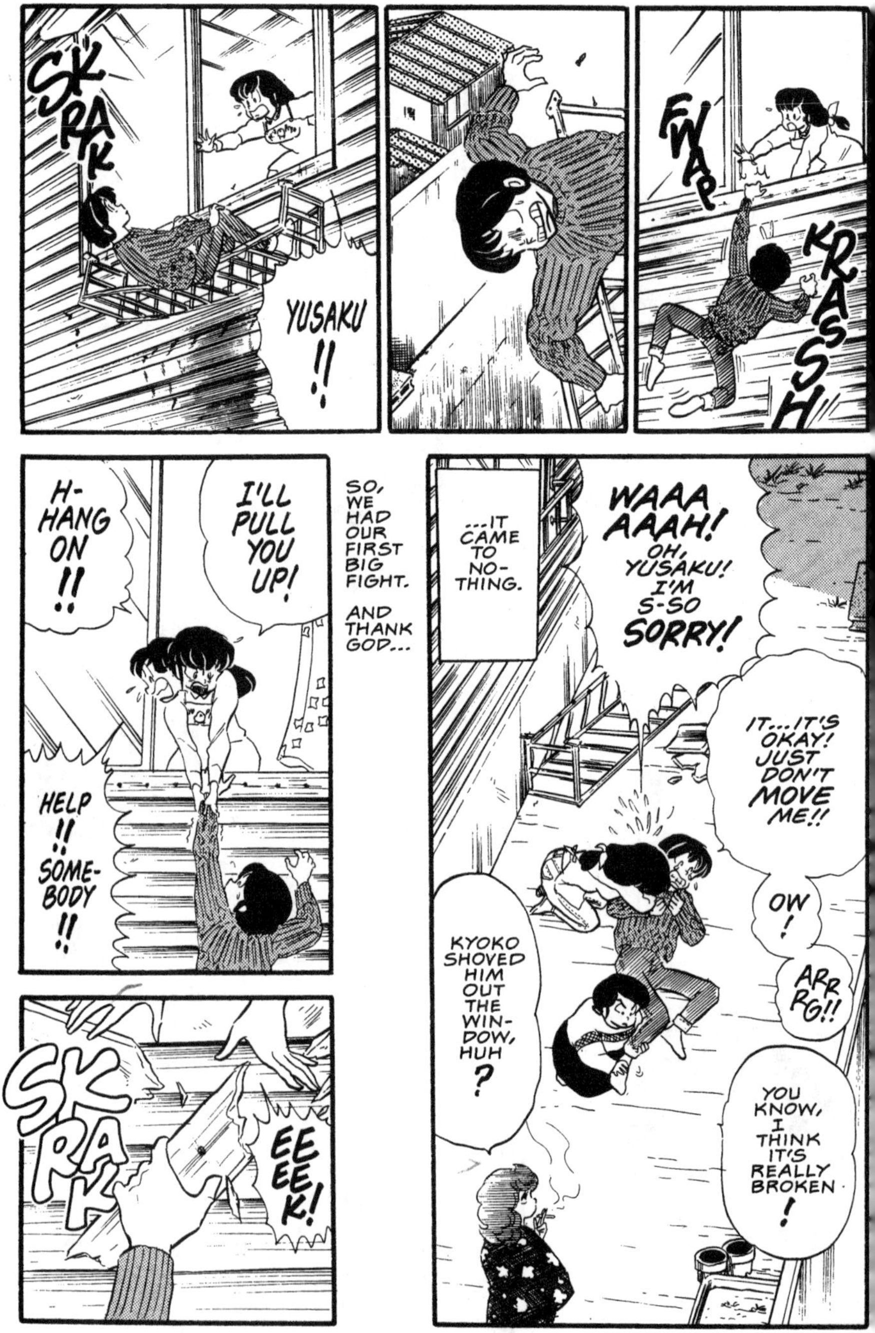
SKRAK
YUSAKU!!
FWAP
KRASSH
H-HANG ON!!
I'LL PULL YOU UP!
HELP!! SOMEBODY!!
SKRAK
EEEEK!
SO, WE HAD OUR FIRST BIG FIGHT.
AND THANK GOD...
...IT CAME TO NOTHING.
WAAAAAAH! OH, YUSAKU! I'M S-SO SORRY!
IT...IT'S OKAY! JUST DON'T MOVE ME!!
KYOKO SHOVED HIM OUT THE WINDOW, HUH?
OW!
ARRRG!!
YOU KNOW, I THINK IT'S REALLY BROKEN!

PART SEVEN

NO VISITORS. PLEASE!

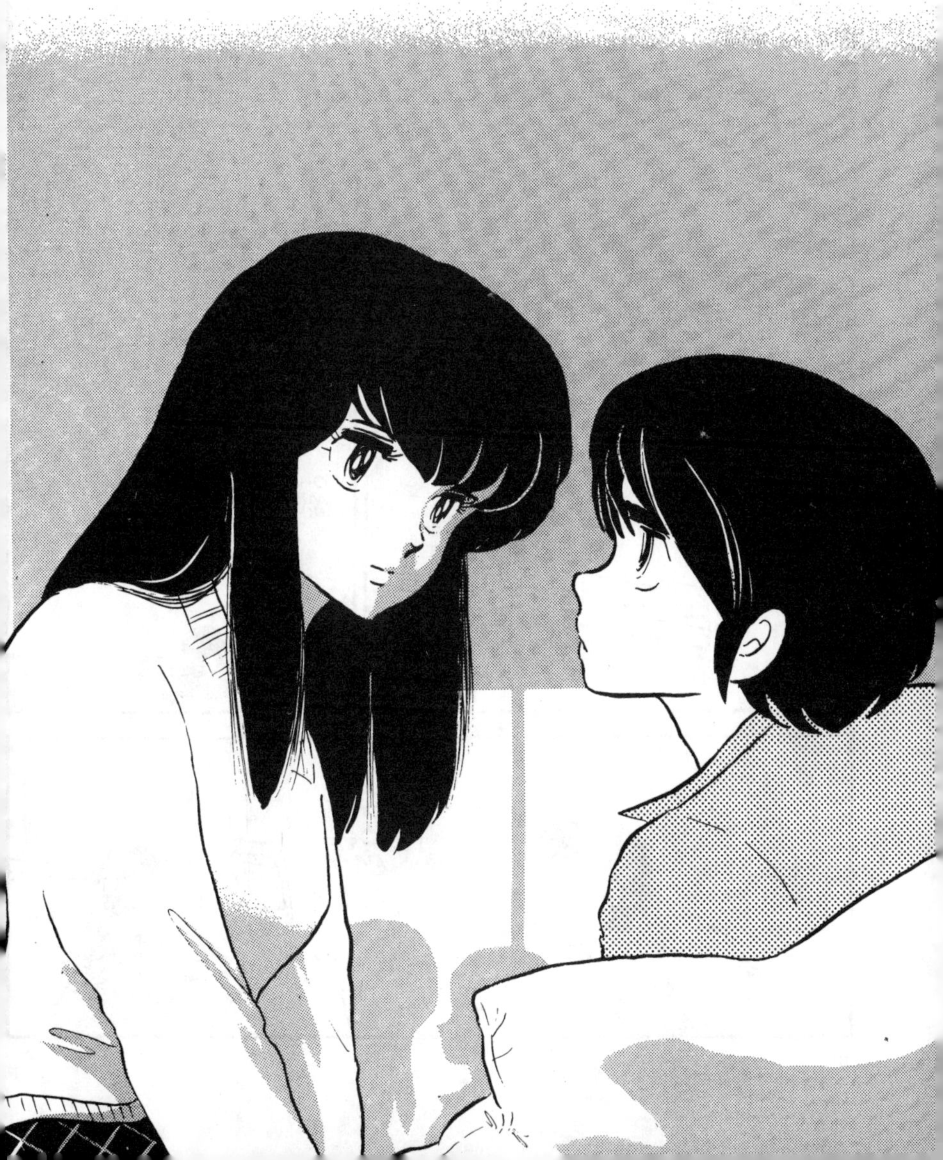

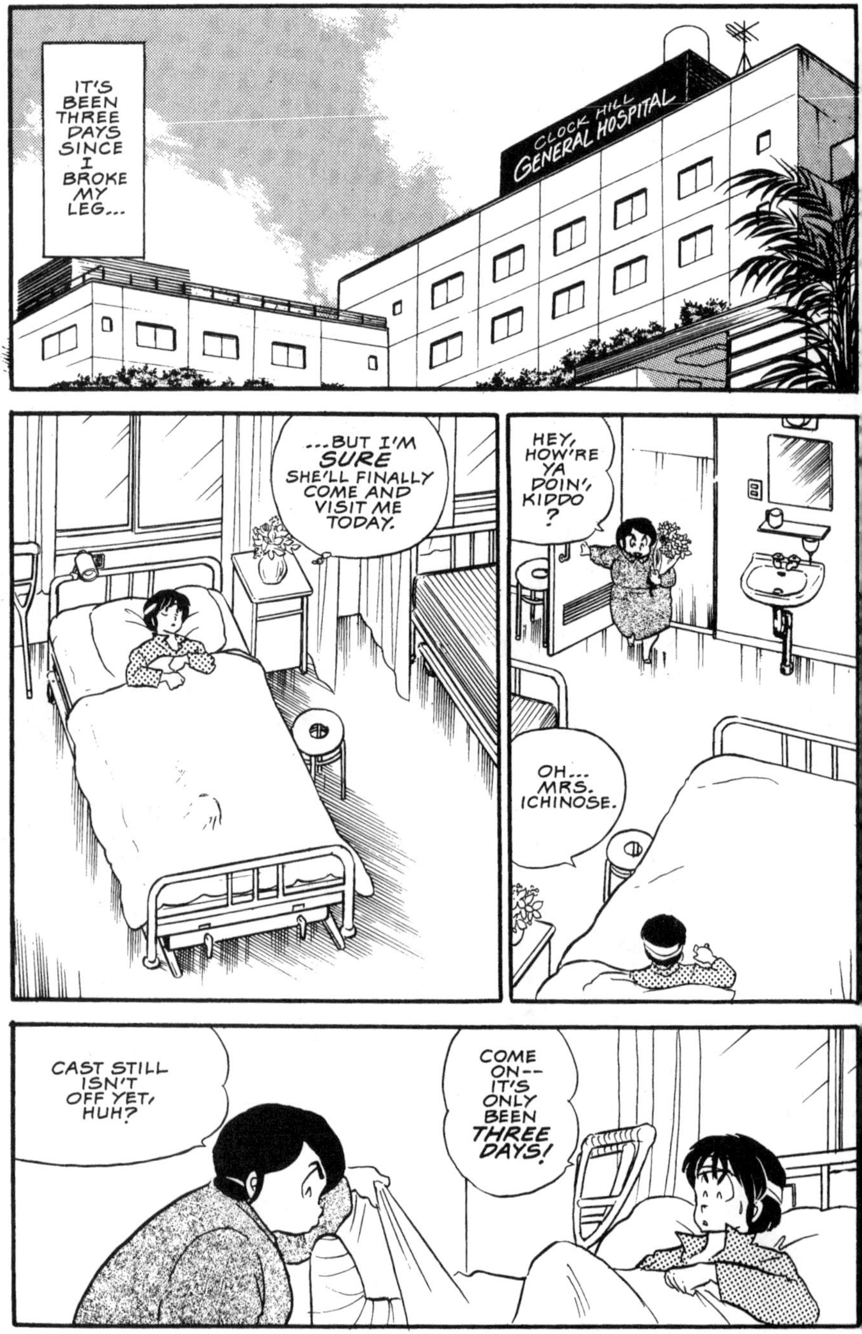

IT'S BEEN THREE DAYS SINCE I BROKE MY LEG...
CLOCK HILL GENERAL HOSPITAL
...BUT I'M SURE SHE'LL FINALLY COME AND VISIT ME TODAY.
HEY, HOW'RE YA DOIN', KIDDO?
OH... MRS. ICHINOSE.
CAST STILL ISN'T OFF YET, HUH?
COME ON-- IT'S ONLY BEEN THREE DAYS!

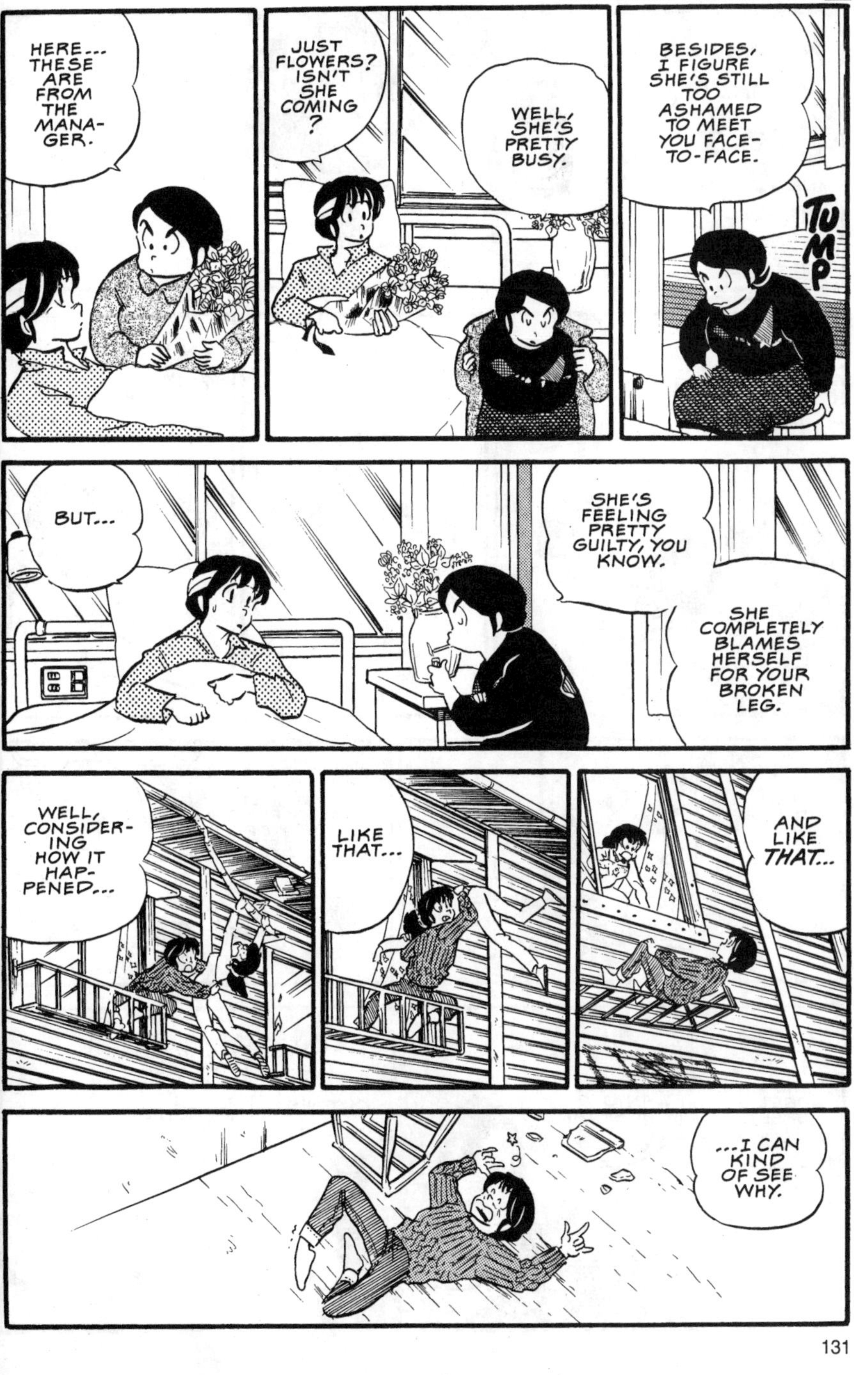
HERE... THESE ARE FROM THE MANAGER.
JUST FLOWERS? ISN'T SHE COMING?
WELL, SHE'S PRETTY BUSY.
BESIDES, I FIGURE SHE'S STILL TOO ASHAMED TO MEET YOU FACE-TO-FACE.
TUMP
BUT...
SHE'S FEELING PRETTY GUILTY, YOU KNOW.
SHE COMPLETELY BLAMES HERSELF FOR YOUR BROKEN LEG.
WELL, CONSIDERING HOW IT HAPPENED...
LIKE THAT...
AND LIKE *THAT*...
...I CAN KIND OF SEE WHY.

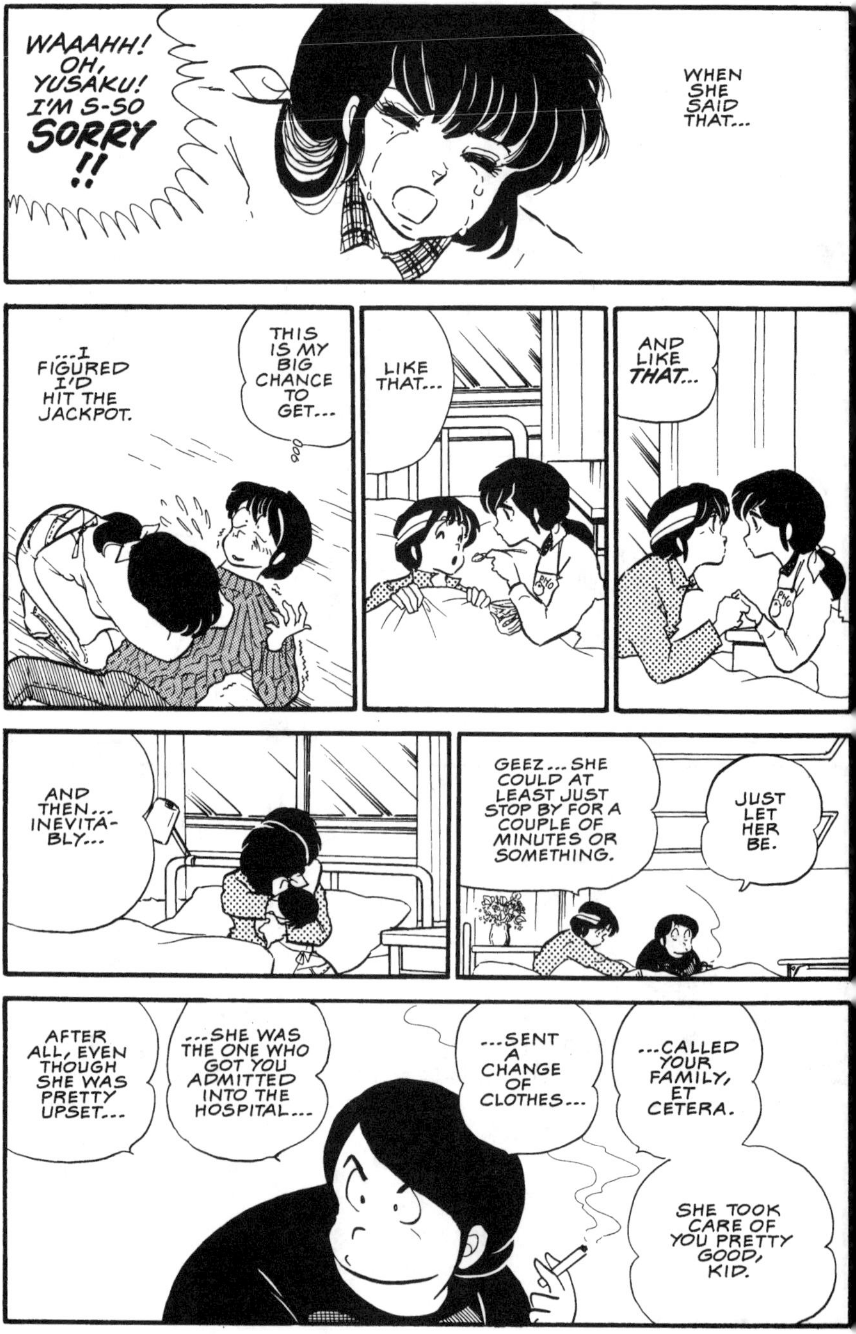

WAAAHH! OH, YUSAKU! I'M S-SO SORRY!!
WHEN SHE SAID THAT...
...I FIGURED I'D HIT THE JACKPOT.
THIS IS MY BIG CHANCE TO GET...
LIKE THAT...
AND LIKE THAT...
AND THEN... INEVITABLY...
GEEZ... SHE COULD AT LEAST JUST STOP BY FOR A COUPLE OF MINUTES OR SOMETHING.
JUST LET HER BE.
AFTER ALL, EVEN THOUGH SHE WAS PRETTY UPSET...
...SHE WAS THE ONE WHO GOT YOU ADMITTED INTO THE HOSPITAL...
...SENT A CHANGE OF CLOTHES...
...CALLED YOUR FAMILY, ET CETERA.
SHE TOOK CARE OF YOU PRETTY GOOD, KID.

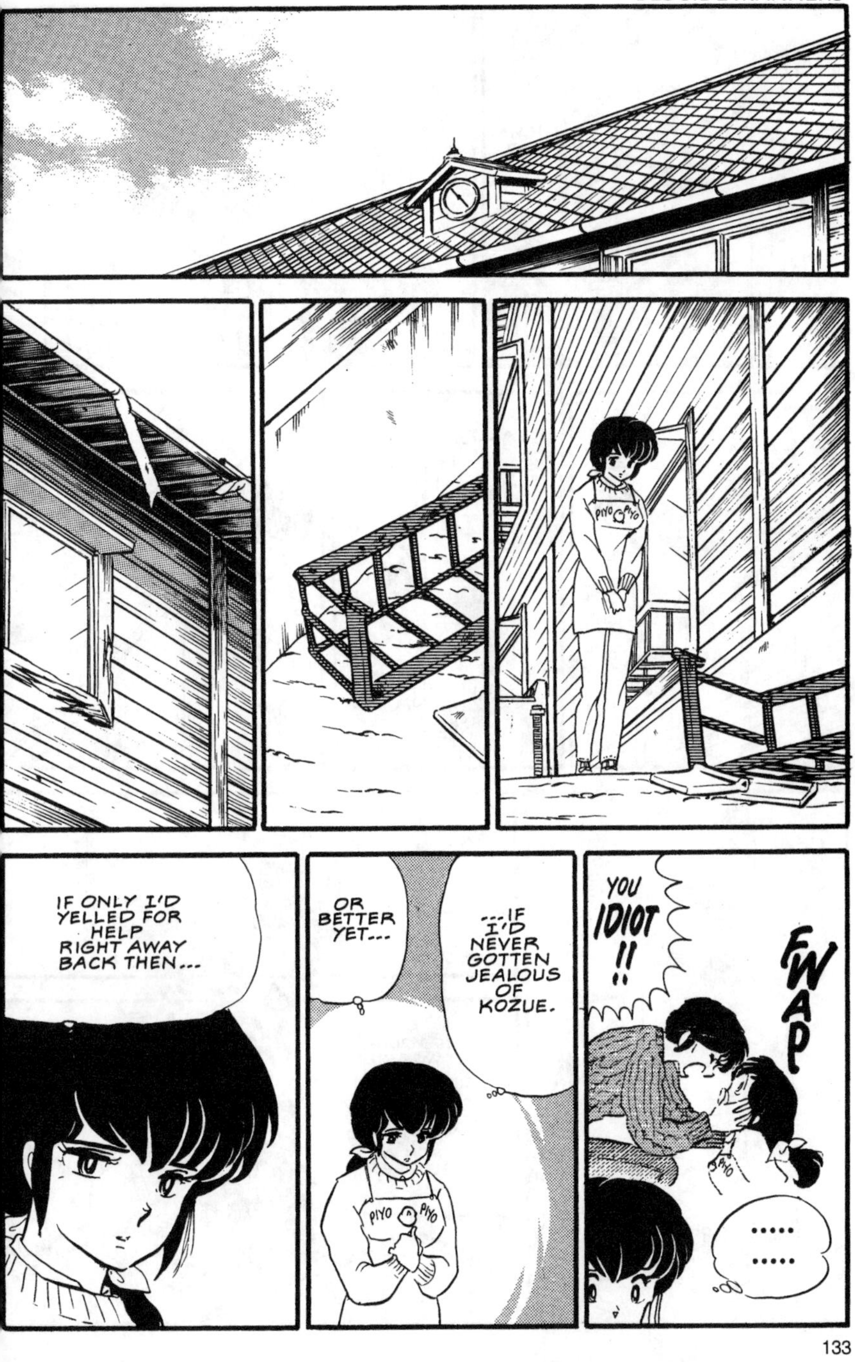
PIYO PIYO
IF ONLY I'D YELLED FOR HELP RIGHT AWAY BACK THEN...
OR BETTER YET...
...IF I'D NEVER GOTTEN JEALOUS OF KOZUE.
PIYO PIYO
YOU IDIOT !!
FWAP!
PIYO
....

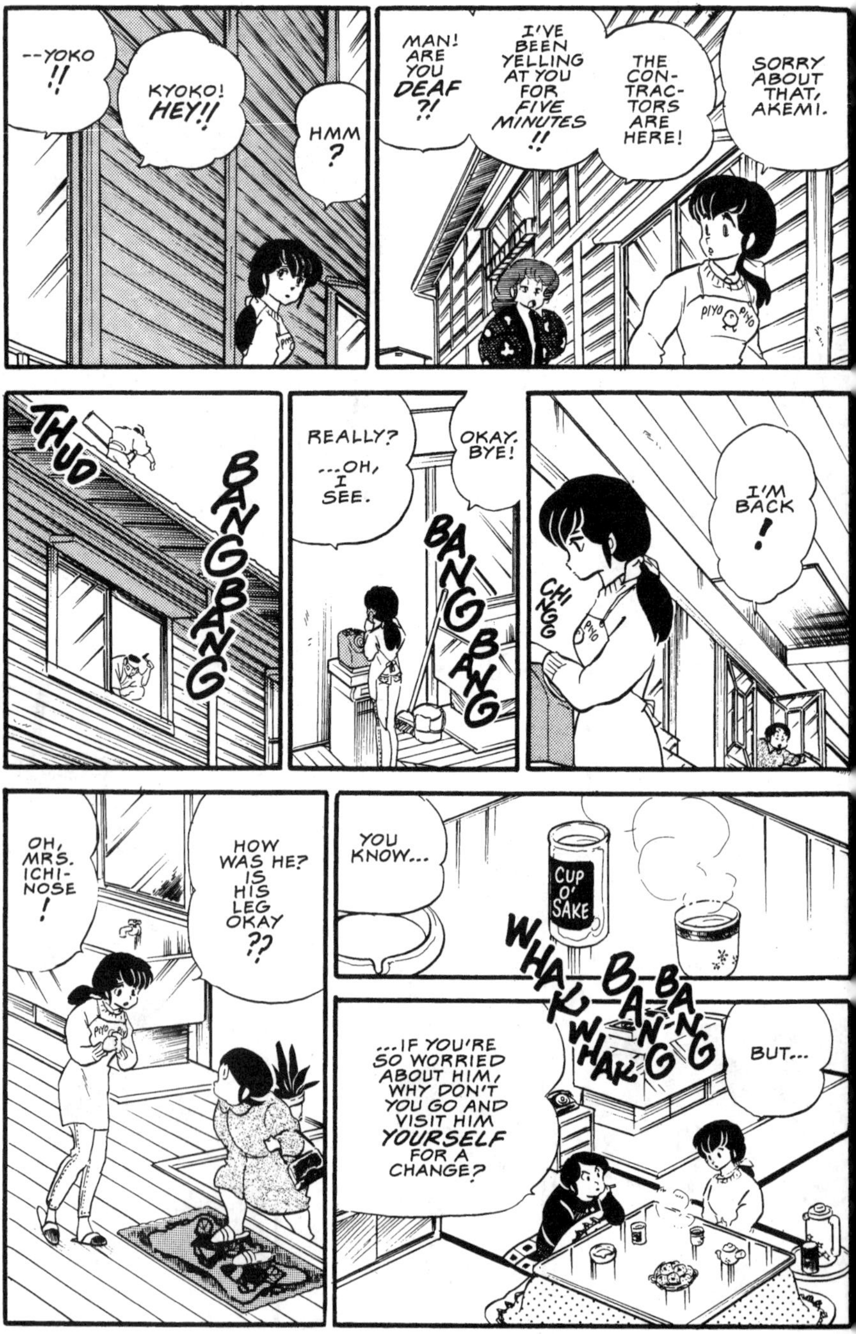
--YOKO !!
KYOKO! HEY!!
HMM ?
MAN! ARE YOU DEAF ?!
I'VE BEEN YELLING AT YOU FOR FIVE MINUTES !!
THE CONTRACTORS ARE HERE!
SORRY ABOUT THAT, AKEMI.
PIYO PIYO
THUD
BANG BANG BANG
REALLY?
...OH, I SEE.
OKAY. BYE!
BANG BANG BANG
I'M BACK!
CHINGG
OH, MRS. ICHINOSE!
HOW WAS HE? IS HIS LEG OKAY??
YOU KNOW...
CUP O' SAKE
WHAK WHAK WHAK
B-BANG B-BANG
...IF YOU'RE SO WORRIED ABOUT HIM, WHY DON'T YOU GO AND VISIT HIM YOURSELF FOR A CHANGE?
BUT...

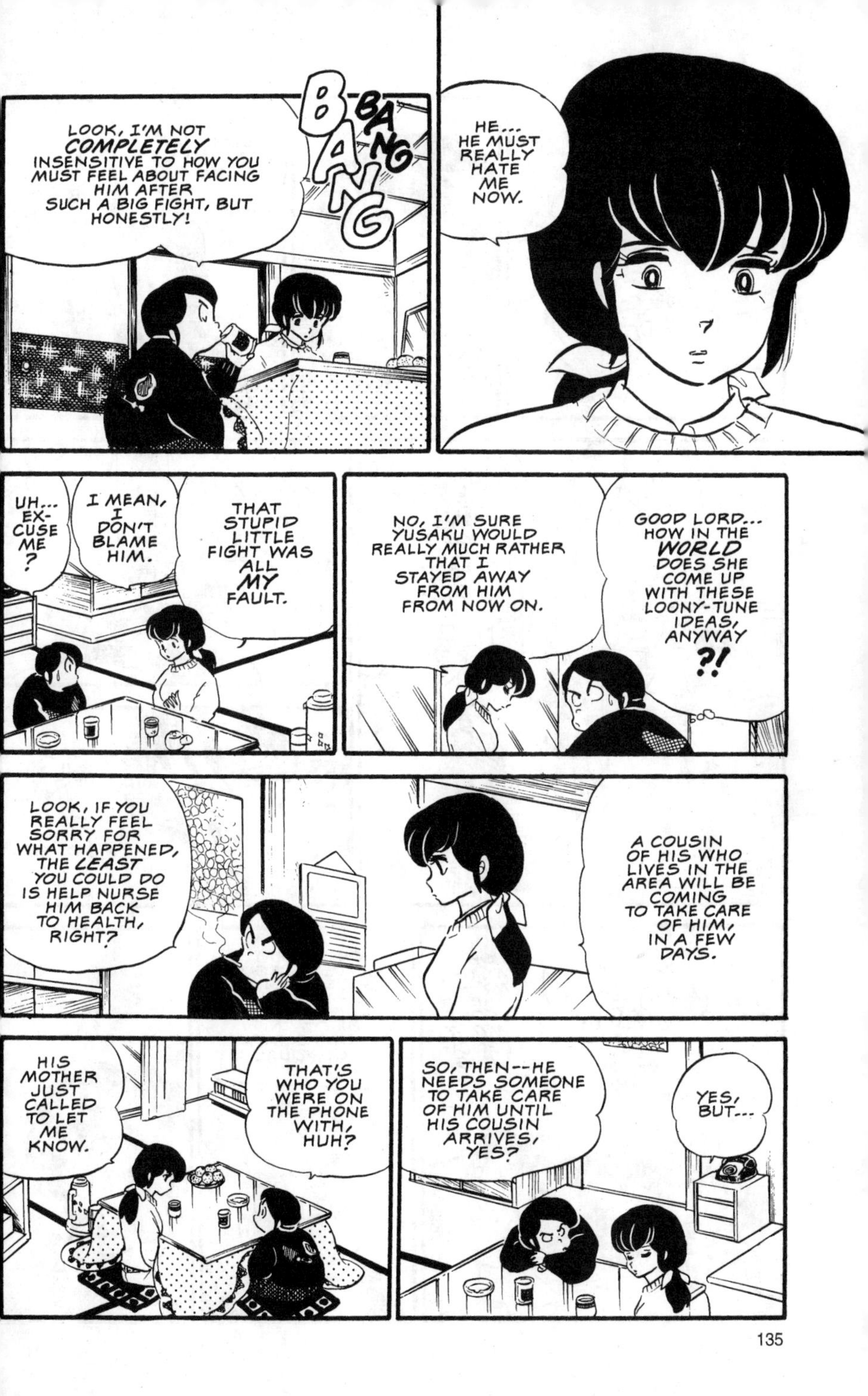

LOOK, I'M NOT COMPLETELY INSENSITIVE TO HOW YOU MUST FEEL ABOUT FACING HIM AFTER SUCH A BIG FIGHT, BUT HONESTLY!
BBANG BANG
HE... HE MUST REALLY HATE ME NOW.
UH... EX-CUSE ME?
I MEAN, I DON'T BLAME HIM.
THAT STUPID LITTLE FIGHT WAS ALL MY FAULT.
NO, I'M SURE YUSAKU WOULD REALLY MUCH RATHER THAT I STAYED AWAY FROM HIM FROM NOW ON.
GOOD LORD... HOW IN THE WORLD DOES SHE COME UP WITH THESE LOONY-TUNE IDEAS, ANYWAY ?!
LOOK, IF YOU REALLY FEEL SORRY FOR WHAT HAPPENED, THE LEAST YOU COULD DO IS HELP NURSE HIM BACK TO HEALTH, RIGHT?
A COUSIN OF HIS WHO LIVES IN THE AREA WILL BE COMING TO TAKE CARE OF HIM, IN A FEW DAYS.
HIS MOTHER JUST CALLED TO LET ME KNOW.
THAT'S WHO YOU WERE ON THE PHONE WITH, HUH?
SO, THEN--HE NEEDS SOMEONE TO TAKE CARE OF HIM UNTIL HIS COUSIN ARRIVES, YES?
YES, BUT...

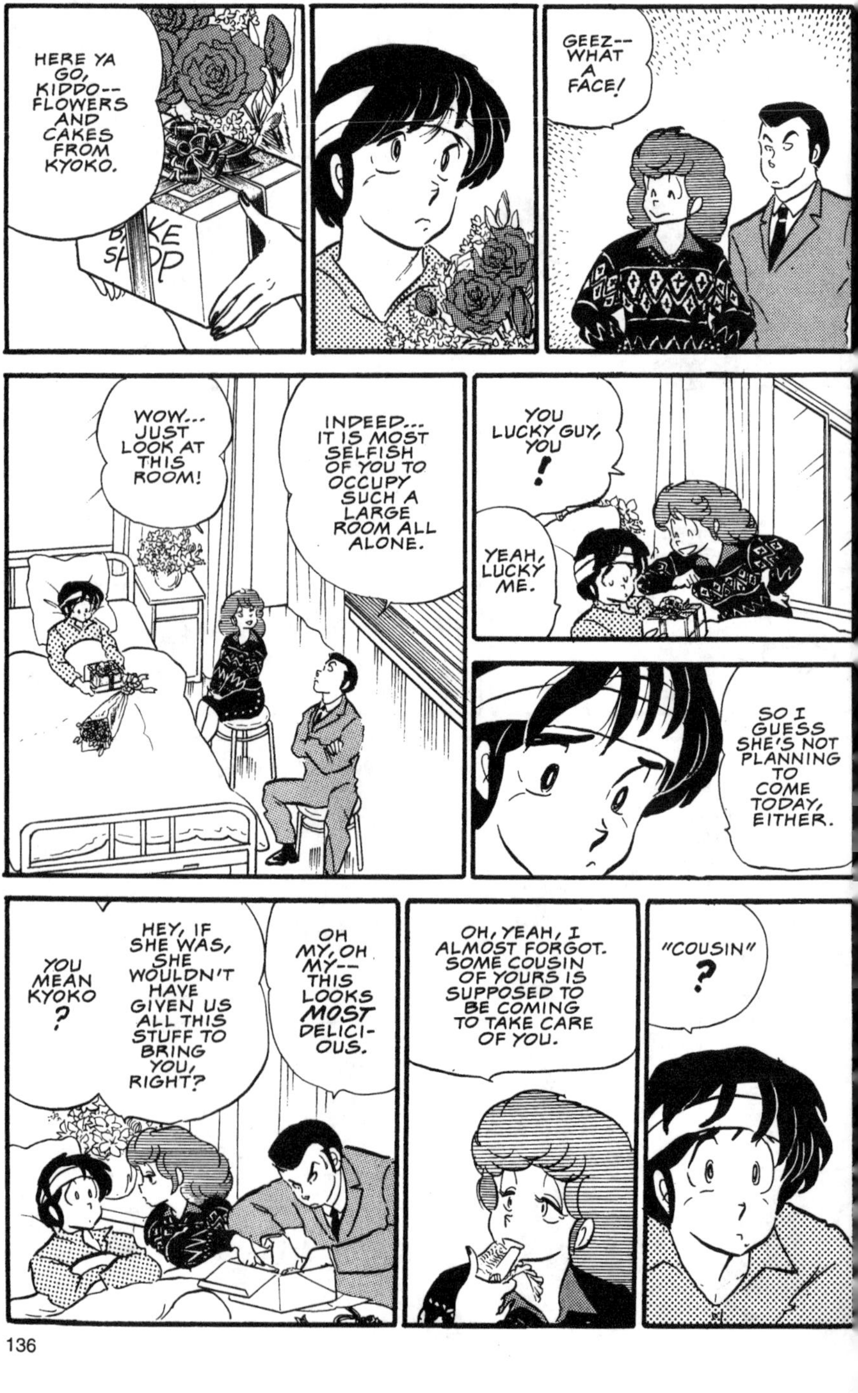
HERE YA GO, KIDDO-- FLOWERS AND CAKES FROM KYOKO.
BAKE SHOP
GEEZ-- WHAT A FACE!
WOW... JUST LOOK AT THIS ROOM!
INDEED... IT IS MOST SELFISH OF YOU TO OCCUPY SUCH A LARGE ROOM ALL ALONE.
YOU LUCKY GUY, YOU!
YEAH, LUCKY ME.
SO I GUESS SHE'S NOT PLANNING TO COME TODAY, EITHER.
YOU MEAN KYOKO?
HEY, IF SHE WAS, SHE WOULDN'T HAVE GIVEN US ALL THIS STUFF TO BRING YOU, RIGHT?
OH MY, OH MY-- THIS LOOKS MOST DELICIOUS.
OH, YEAH, I ALMOST FORGOT. SOME COUSIN OF YOURS IS SUPPOSED TO BE COMING TO TAKE CARE OF YOU.
"COUSIN"?

IF IT'S A COUSIN FROM THE TOKYO AREA...

...IT'S GOTTA BE AKIRA.

HEY, THAT BLUEBERRY STRUDEL'S MY FAVORITE! GET YOUR GRUBBY MEATHOOKS OFFA IT!

SUCH HARSH WORDS FROM THE ONE WHO HAS CONSUMED ALL OF MY FAVORITE, THE CHEESECAKE!

I REMEMBER HER... A SKINNY LITTLE MUNCHKIN.

OF COURSE, I HAVEN'T SEEN HER FOR TEN YEARS...

NYA HA HA HA!

HOW ABOUT A PIECE FOR ME?

HUH?

YOU WISHED TO INDULGE? HOW UNFORTUNATE.

I'M TELLING YA, KYOKO, YOU'VE GOTTA GO VISIT.

BUT...

HE SEEMS PRETTY DEPRESSED AND STUFF, Y'KNOW.

HE DID NOT CONSUME SO MUCH AS A SINGLE ONE OF THE FINE PASTRIES YOU SENT.

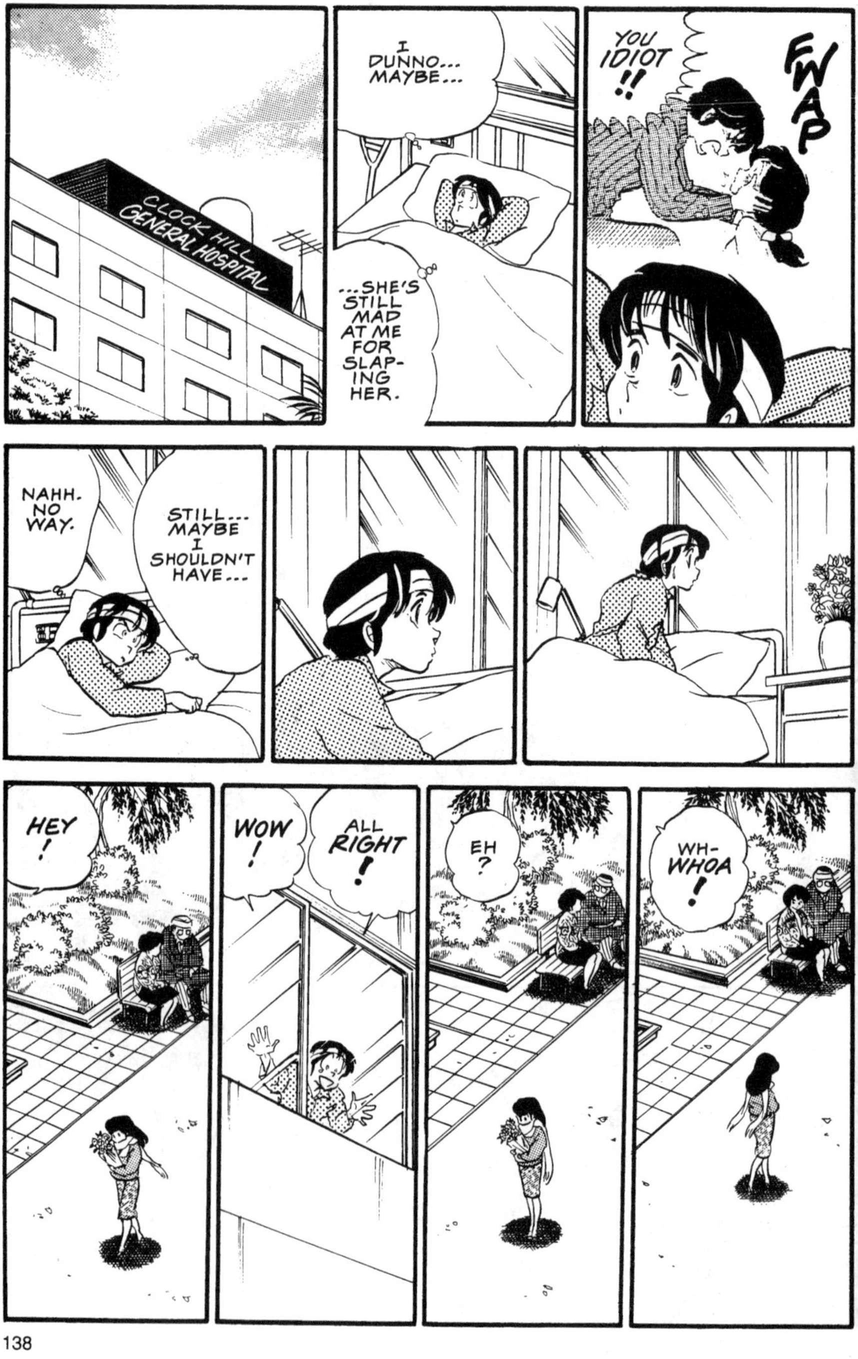
CLOCK HILL GENERAL HOSPITAL
I DUNNO... MAYBE...
...SHE'S STILL MAD AT ME FOR SLAPPING HER.
YOU IDIOT !!
FWAP
NAHH. NO WAY.
STILL... MAYBE I SHOULDN'T HAVE...
HEY!
WOW!
ALL RIGHT!
EH?
WH-WHOA!

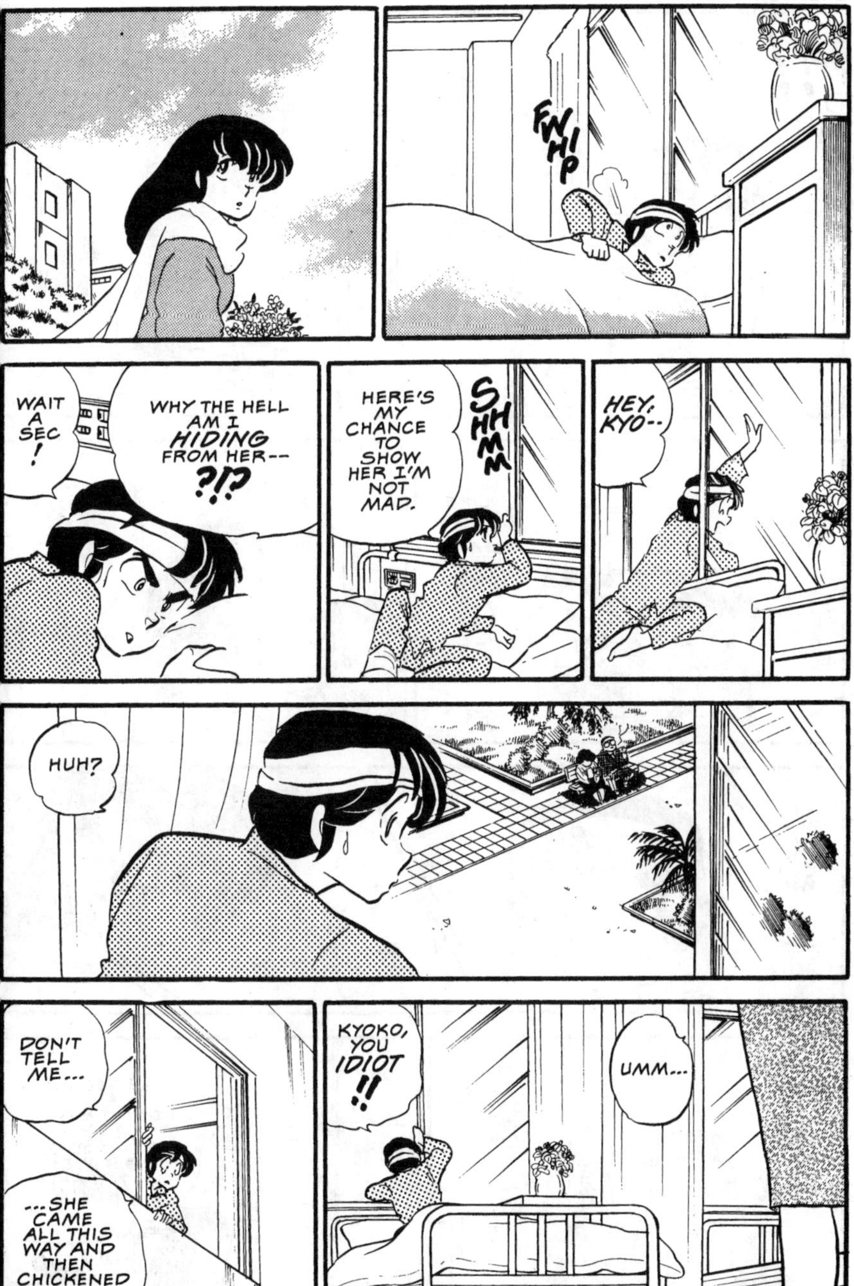
FWHIP
WAIT A SEC!
WHY THE HELL AM I HIDING FROM HER--?!?
HERE'S MY CHANCE TO SHOW HER I'M NOT MAD.
SHHMM
HEY, KYO--
HUH?
DON'T TELL ME...
...SHE CAME ALL THIS WAY AND THEN CHICKENED OUT?!
KYOKO, YOU IDIOT!!
UMM...

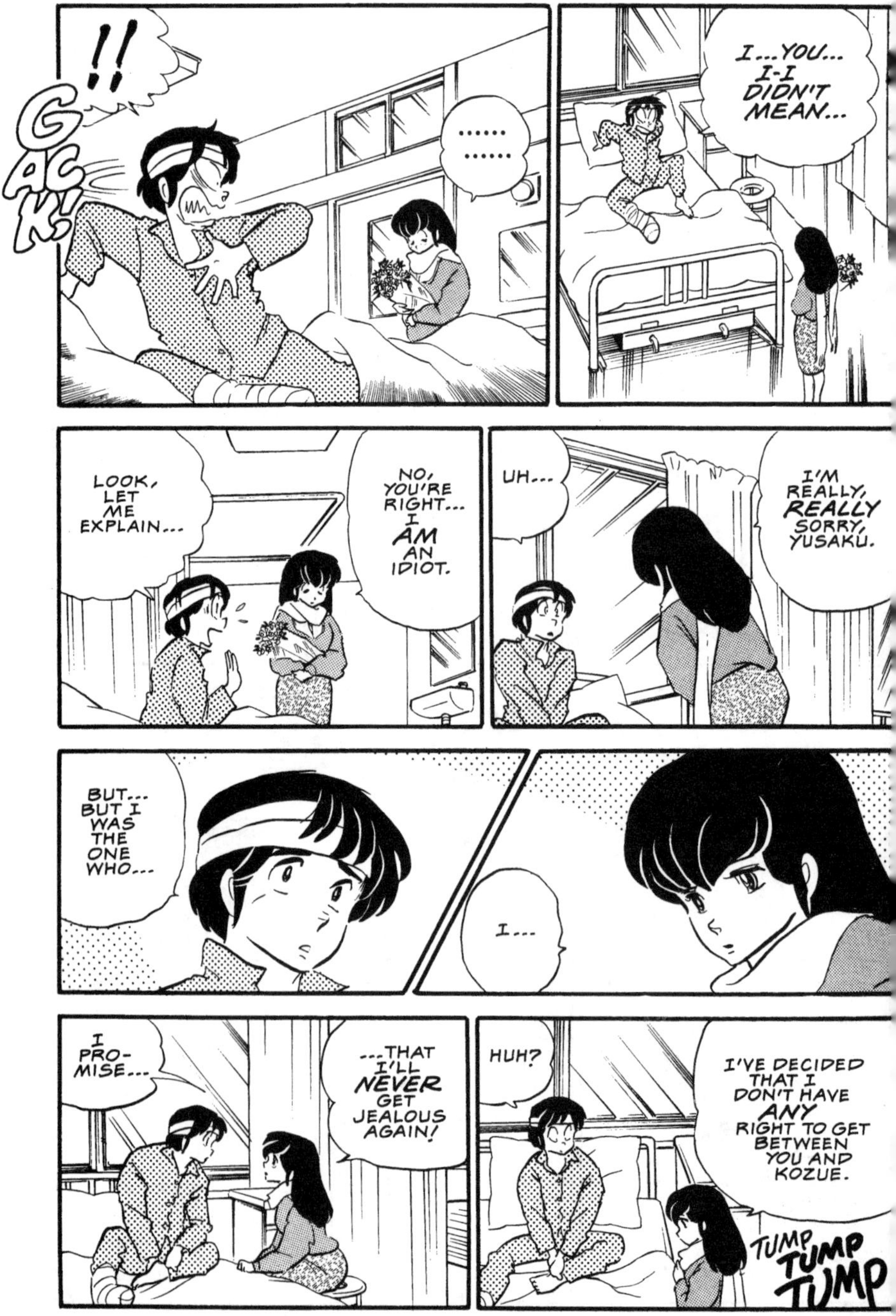
!!
GACK!
......
......
I...YOU... I-I DIDN'T MEAN...
LOOK, LET ME EXPLAIN...
NO, YOU'RE RIGHT... I AM AN IDIOT.
UH...
I'M REALLY, REALLY SORRY, YUSAKU.
BUT... BUT I WAS THE ONE WHO...
I...
I PRO-MISE...
...THAT I'LL NEVER GET JEALOUS AGAIN!
HUH?
I'VE DECIDED THAT I DON'T HAVE ANY RIGHT TO GET BETWEEN YOU AND KOZUE.
TUMP TUMP TUMP

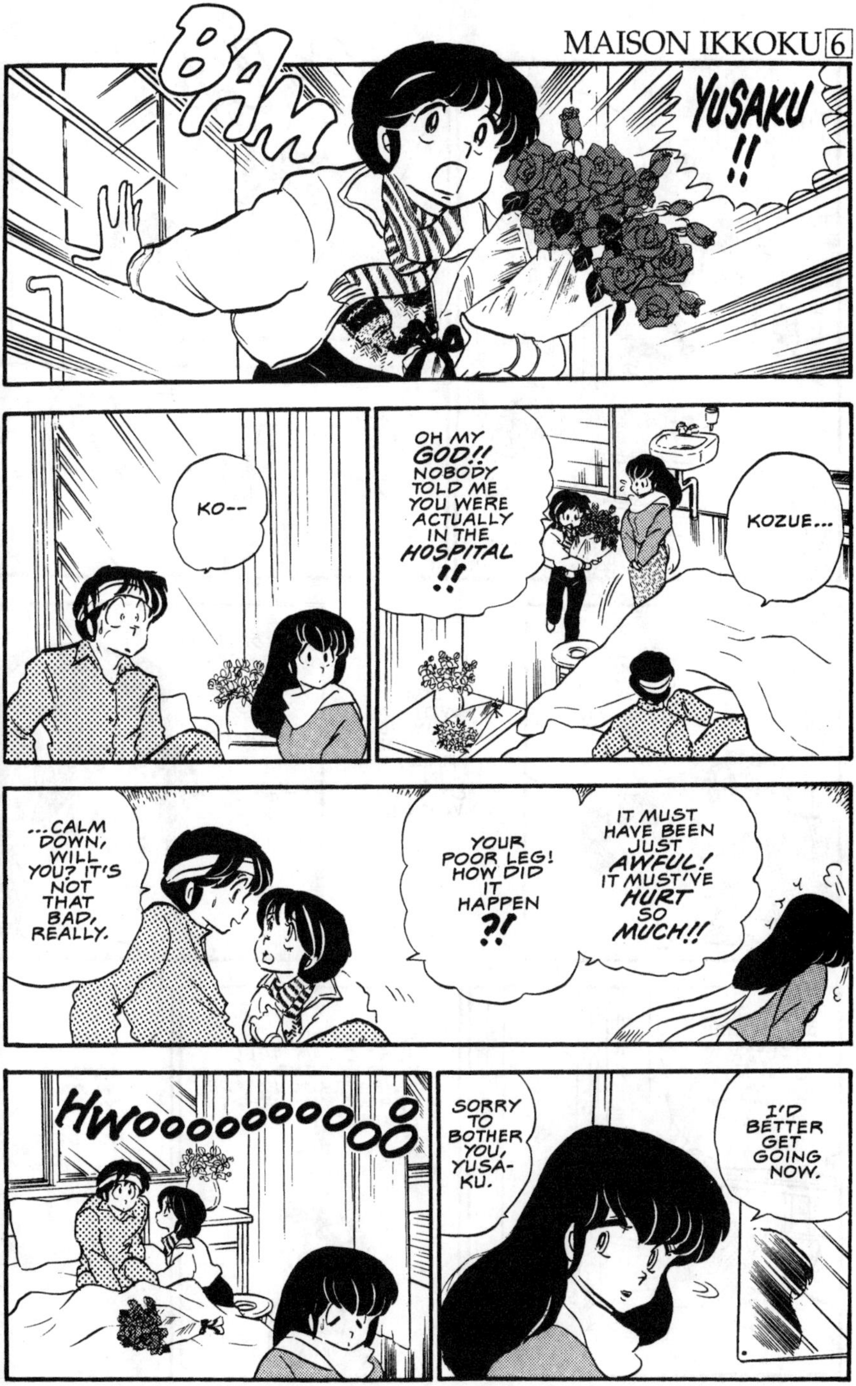
BAM
YUSAKU !!
KO--
OH MY GOD!! NOBODY TOLD ME YOU WERE ACTUALLY IN THE HOSPITAL !!
KOZUE...
...CALM DOWN, WILL YOU? IT'S NOT THAT BAD, REALLY.
YOUR POOR LEG! HOW DID IT HAPPEN ?!
IT MUST HAVE BEEN JUST AWFUL! IT MUST'VE HURT SO MUCH!!
HWOOOOOOOOOO
SORRY TO BOTHER YOU, YUSA-KU.
I'D BETTER GET GOING NOW.

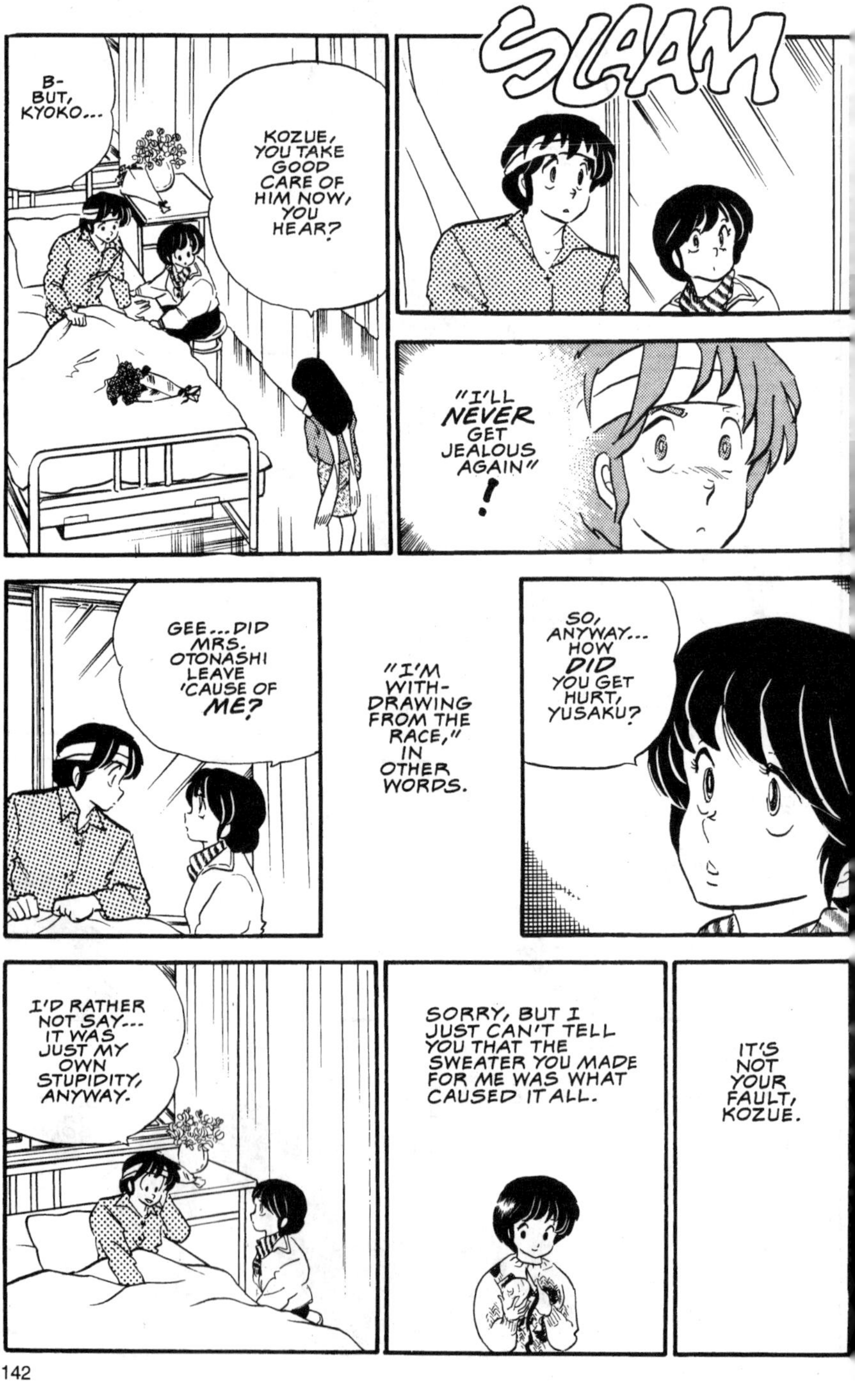
B-BUT, KYOKO...
KOZUE, YOU TAKE GOOD CARE OF HIM NOW, YOU HEAR?
SLAAM
"I'LL NEVER GET JEALOUS AGAIN" !
GEE...DID MRS. OTONASHI LEAVE 'CAUSE OF ME?
"I'M WITH-DRAWING FROM THE RACE," IN OTHER WORDS.
SO, ANYWAY... HOW DID YOU GET HURT, YUSAKU?
I'D RATHER NOT SAY... IT WAS JUST MY OWN STUPIDITY, ANYWAY.
SORRY, BUT I JUST CAN'T TELL YOU THAT THE SWEATER YOU MADE FOR ME WAS WHAT CAUSED IT ALL.
IT'S NOT YOUR FAULT, KOZUE.

"I'LL *NEVER* GET JEALOUS AGAIN"!

SAY "AHH-HHH"!

WAIT A SEC...!

SEE YA LATER, 'KAY?

SLAAM

KYOKO *COULDN'T* HAVE MEANT *THAT!*

UNLESS... EVEN *KNOWING* HOW I FEEL ABOUT HER...

WAAAAH! SHE *DOESN'T* CARE ABOUT ME, AFTER ALL!!

BWA HA HA HA

AW, COME ON, DON'T BE SUCH A BIG BABY!

I FEAR FOR OUR FUTURE.

WILL YOU *PLEASE* SHUT UP IN HERE?!

143

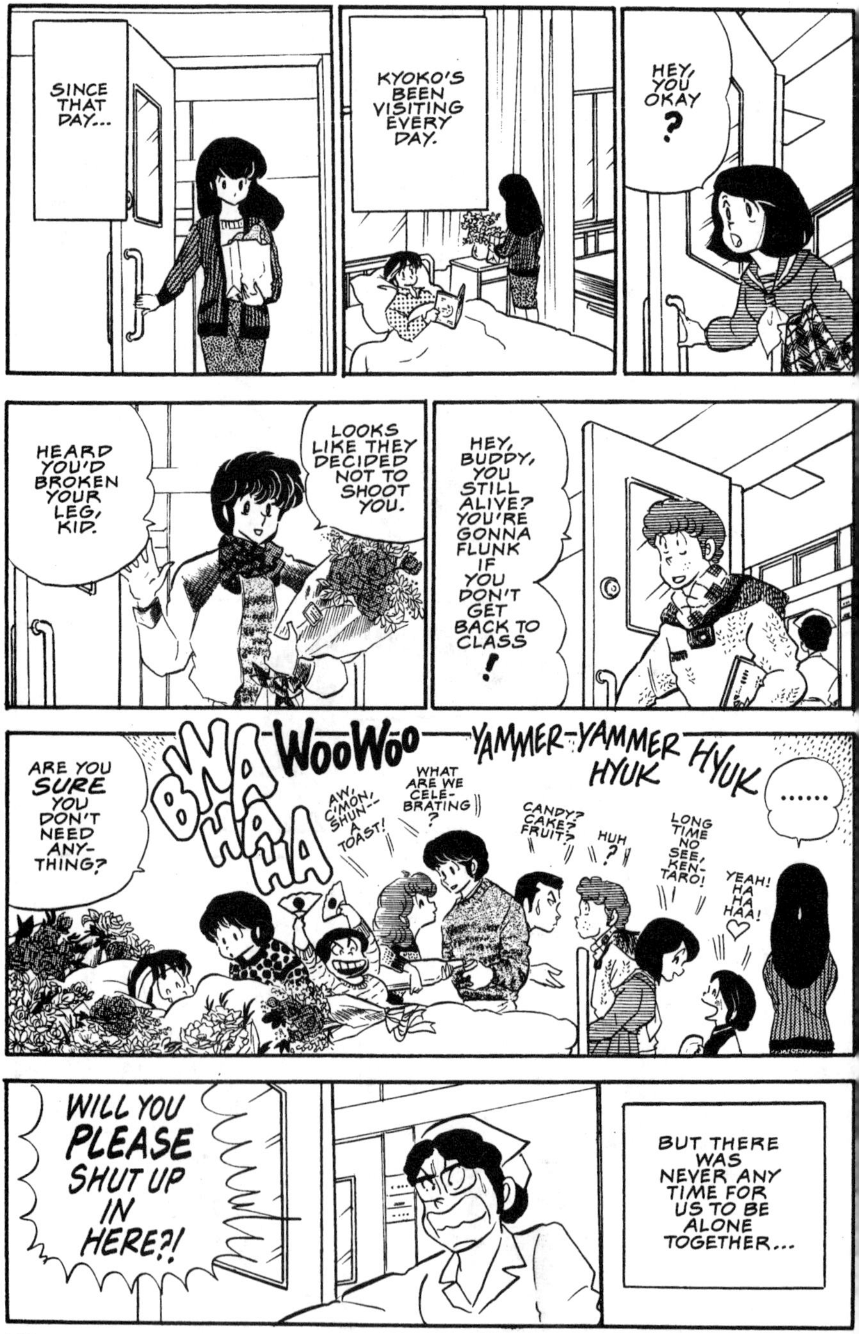
SINCE THAT DAY...
KYOKO'S BEEN VISITING EVERY DAY.
HEY, YOU OKAY?
HEARD YOU'D BROKEN YOUR LEG, KID.
LOOKS LIKE THEY DECIDED NOT TO SHOOT YOU.
HEY, BUDDY, YOU STILL ALIVE? YOU'RE GONNA FLUNK IF YOU DON'T GET BACK TO CLASS!
ARE YOU SURE YOU DON'T NEED ANYTHING?
BWAHAHAHA
WooWoo
YAMMER-YAMMER
HYUK HYUK
AW, C'MON, SHUN-- A TOAST!
WHAT ARE WE CELEBRATING?
CANDY? CAKE? FRUIT?
HUH?
LONG TIME NO SEE, KENTARO!
YEAH! HA HA HAA!
......
WILL YOU PLEASE SHUT UP IN HERE?!
BUT THERE WAS NEVER ANY TIME FOR US TO BE ALONE TOGETHER...

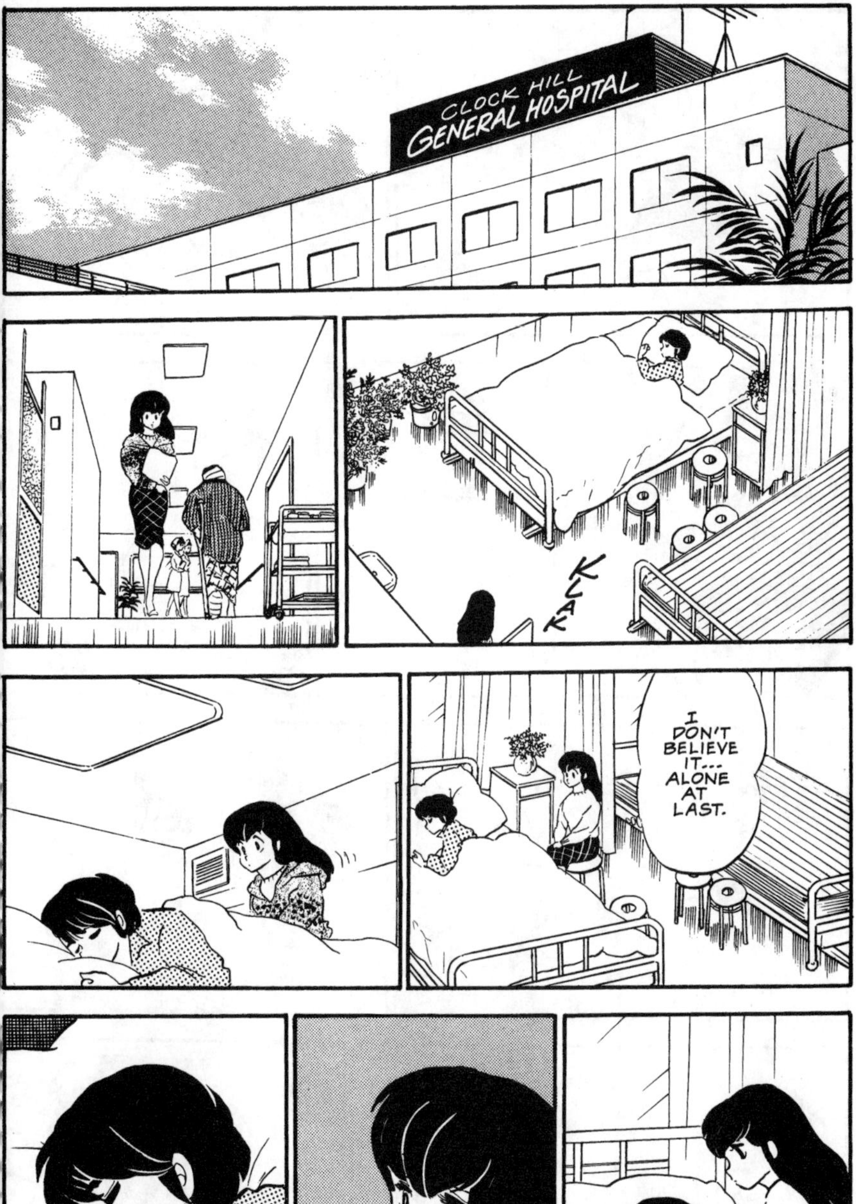
CLOCK HILL
GENERAL HOSPITAL
KLAK
I DON'T BELIEVE IT... ALONE AT LAST.

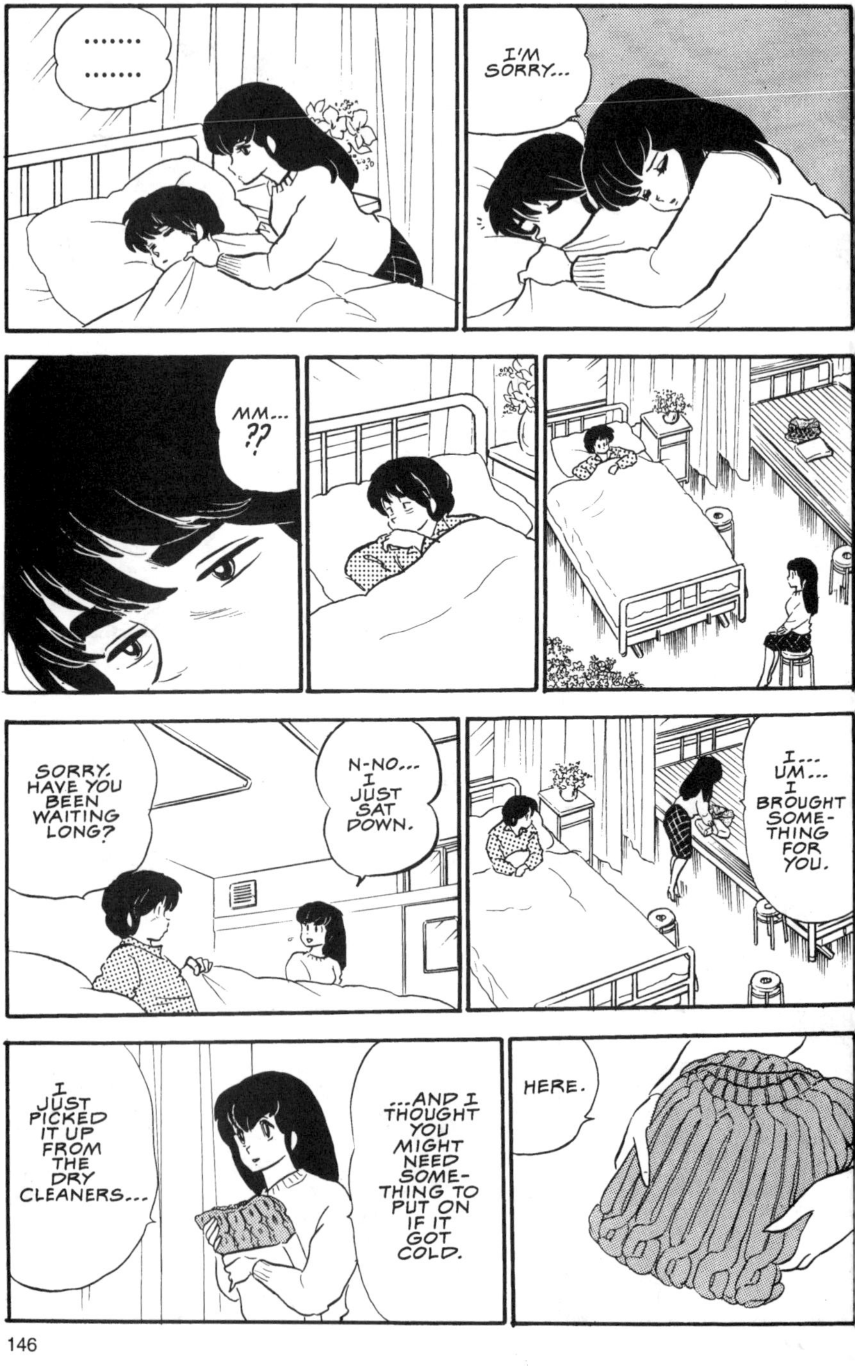

....
....
I'M SORRY...
MM... ??
SORRY. HAVE YOU BEEN WAITING LONG?
N-NO... I JUST SAT DOWN.
I... UM... I BROUGHT SOME-THING FOR YOU.
I JUST PICKED IT UP FROM THE DRY CLEANERS...
...AND I THOUGHT YOU MIGHT NEED SOME-THING TO PUT ON IF IT GOT COLD.
HERE.

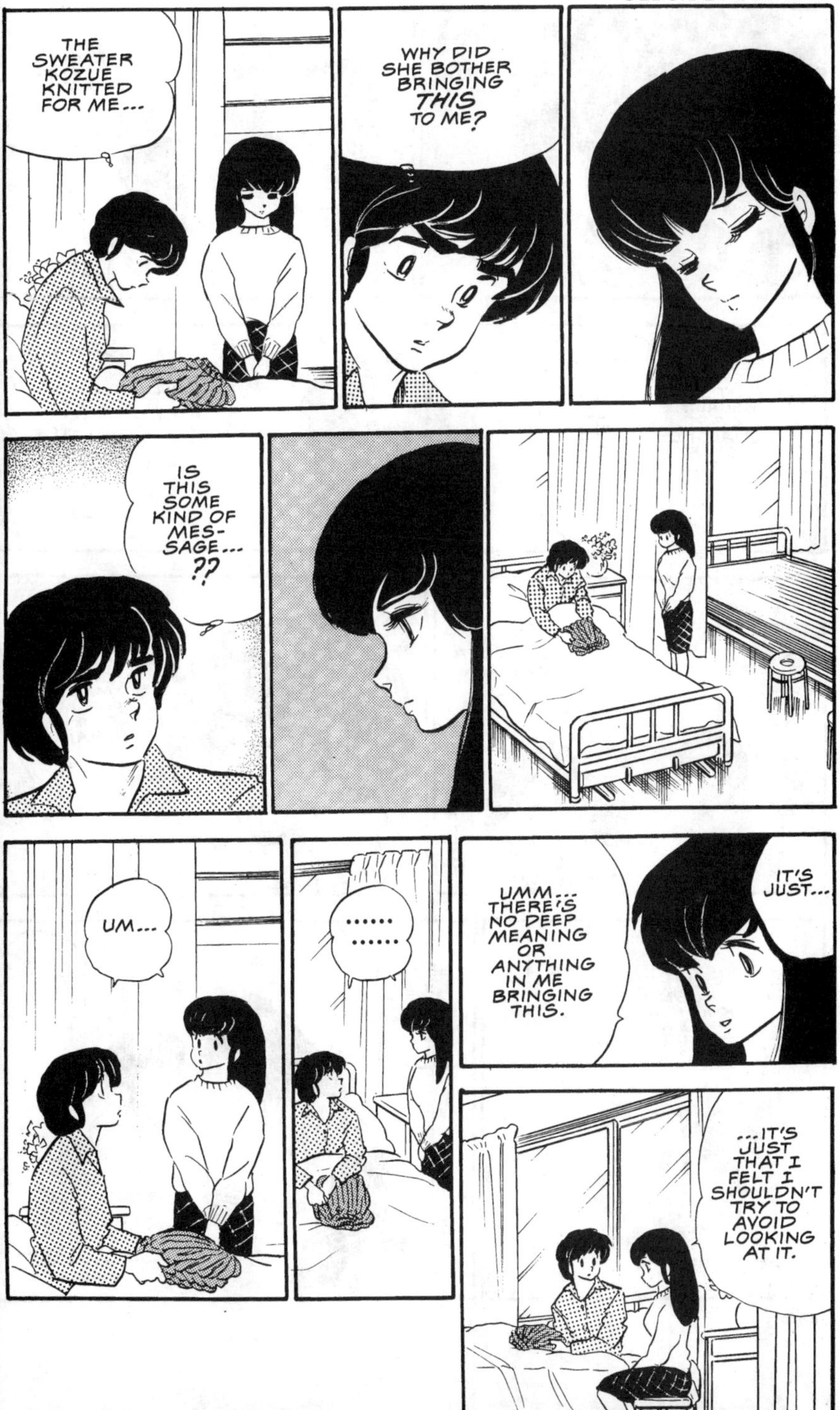
THE SWEATER KOZUE KNITTED FOR ME...
WHY DID SHE BOTHER BRINGING THIS TO ME?
IS THIS SOME KIND OF MES-SAGE...??
UM...
....
....
UMM... THERE'S NO DEEP MEANING OR ANYTHING IN ME BRINGING THIS.
IT'S JUST...
...IT'S JUST THAT I FELT I SHOULDN'T TRY TO AVOID LOOKING AT IT.

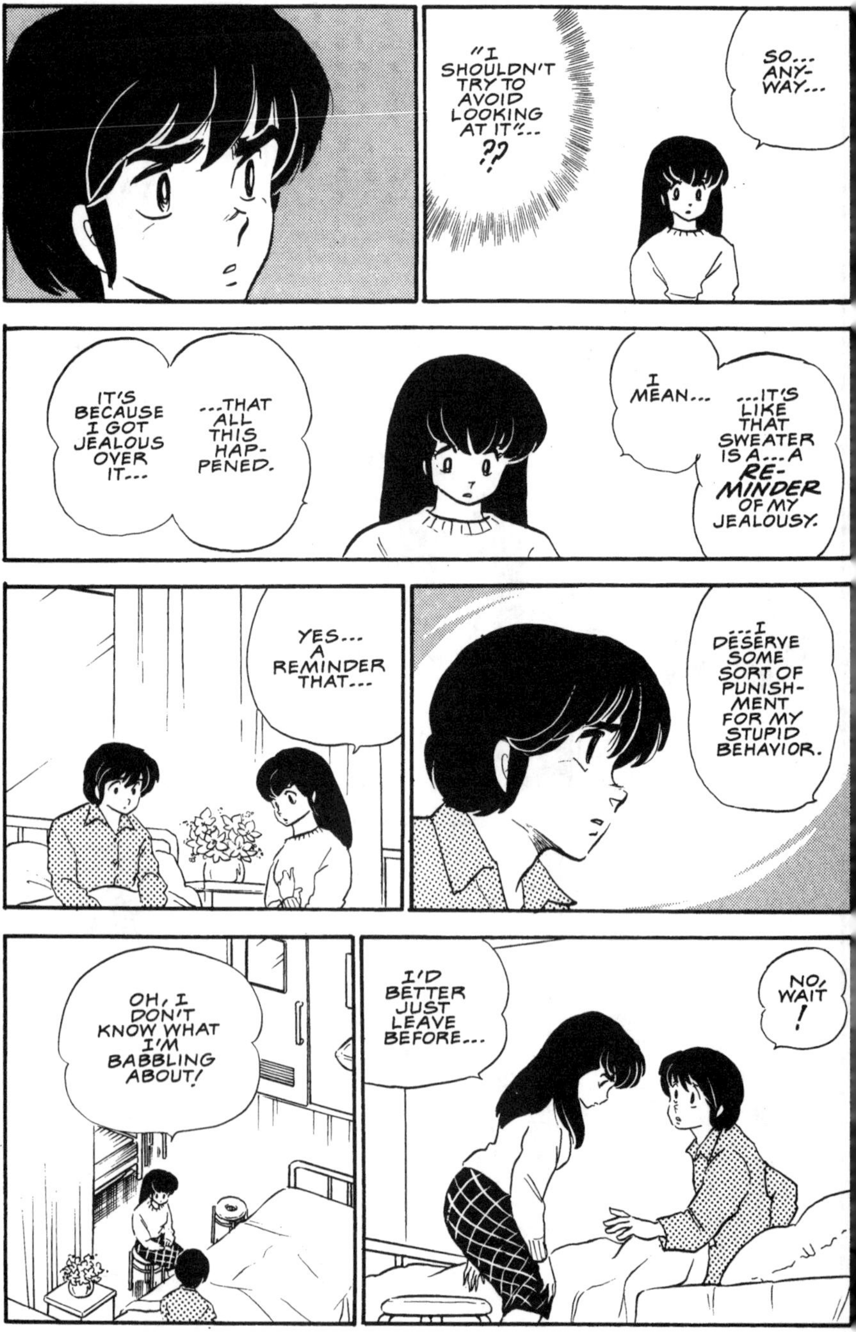
"I SHOULDN'T TRY TO AVOID LOOKING AT IT"...
??
SO... ANYWAY...
IT'S BECAUSE I GOT JEALOUS OVER IT...
...THAT ALL THIS HAPPENED.
I MEAN...
...IT'S LIKE THAT SWEATER IS A... A REMINDER OF MY JEALOUSY.
YES... A REMINDER THAT...
...I DESERVE SOME SORT OF PUNISHMENT FOR MY STUPID BEHAVIOR.
OH, I DON'T KNOW WHAT I'M BABBLING ABOUT!
I'D BETTER JUST LEAVE BEFORE...
NO, WAIT!

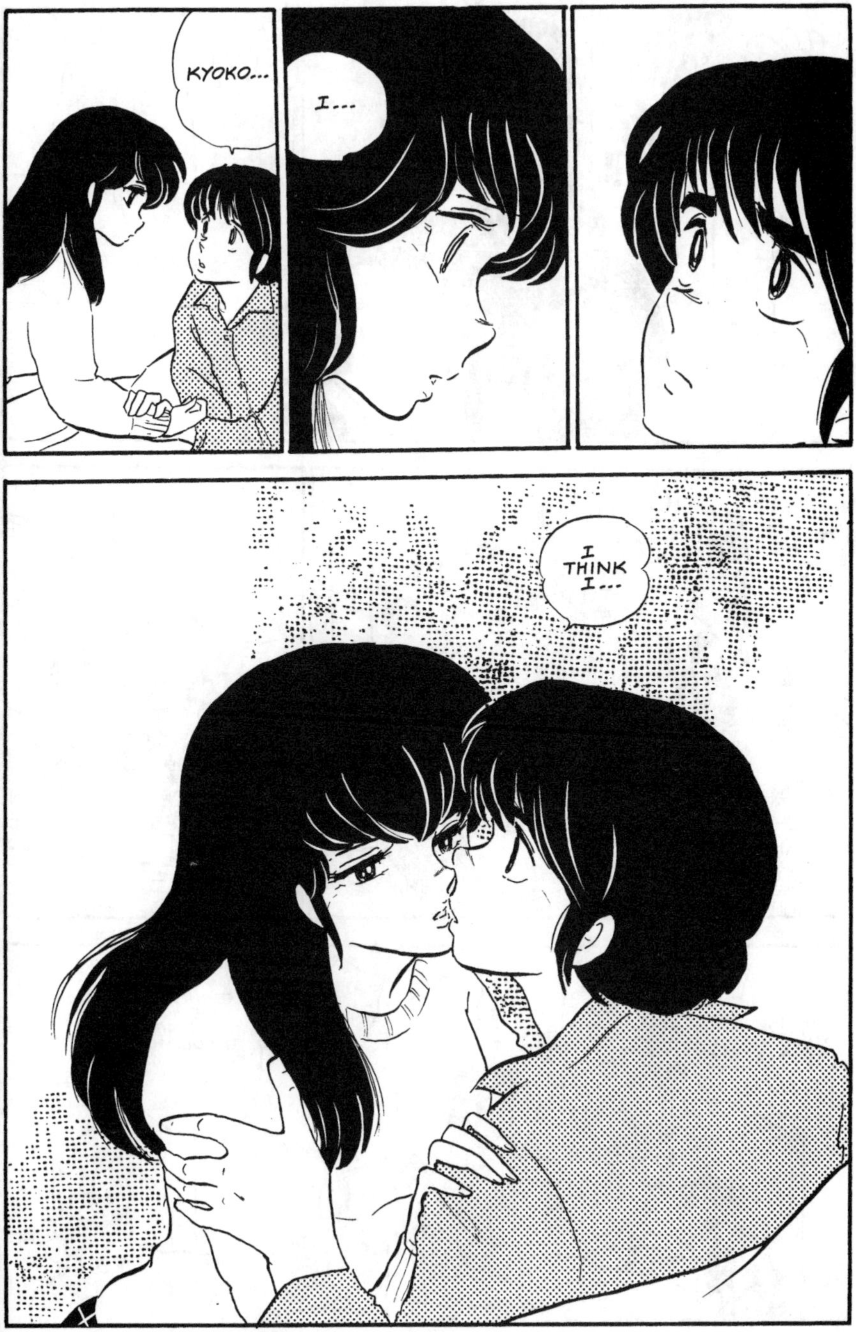
KYOKO...
I...
I THINK I...

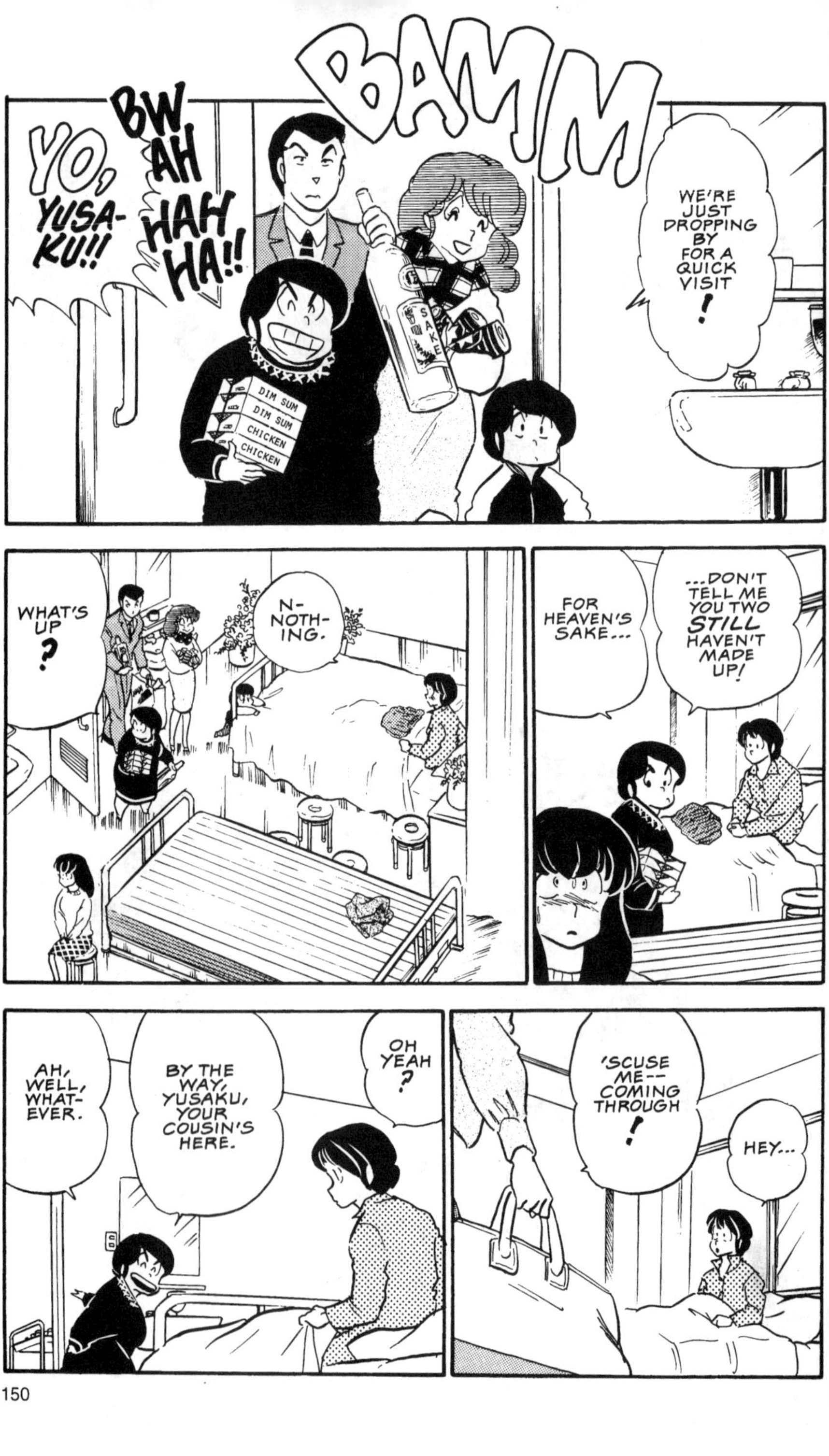
BAMM
YO, YUSAKU!!
BWAH HAH HAH HA!!
WE'RE JUST DROPPING BY FOR A QUICK VISIT!
DIM SUM
DIM SUM
CHICKEN
CHICKEN
SAKE
WHAT'S UP?
N-NOTHING.
FOR HEAVEN'S SAKE...
...DON'T TELL ME YOU TWO STILL HAVEN'T MADE UP!
AH, WELL, WHATEVER.
BY THE WAY, YUSAKU, YOUR COUSIN'S HERE.
OH YEAH?
'SCUSE ME-- COMING THROUGH!
HEY...

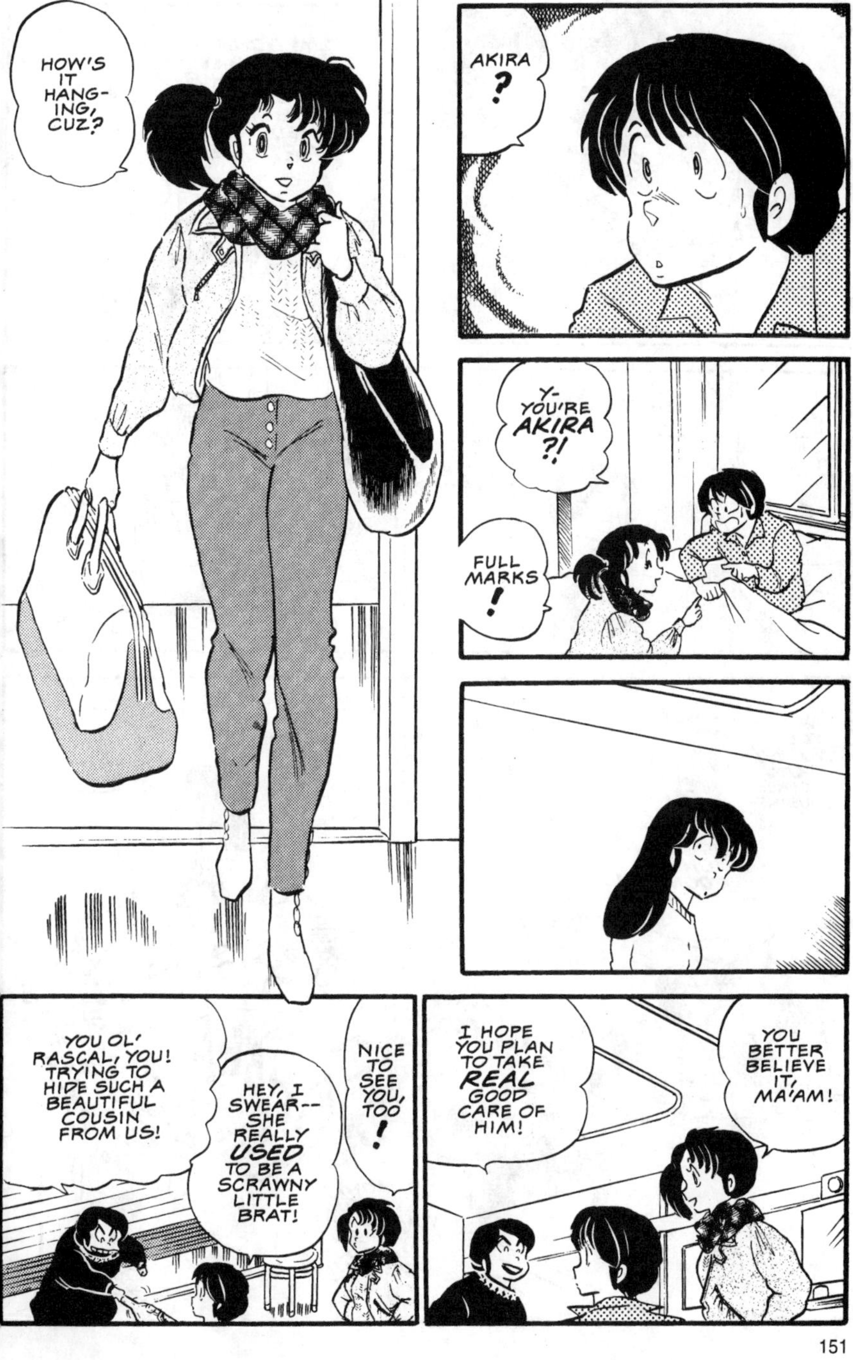
HOW'S IT HANGING, CUZ?
AKIRA?
Y-YOU'RE AKIRA?!
FULL MARKS!
YOU OL' RASCAL, YOU! TRYING TO HIDE SUCH A BEAUTIFUL COUSIN FROM US!
HEY, I SWEAR-- SHE REALLY USED TO BE A SCRAWNY LITTLE BRAT!
NICE TO SEE YOU, TOO!
I HOPE YOU PLAN TO TAKE REAL GOOD CARE OF HIM!
YOU BETTER BELIEVE IT, MA'AM!

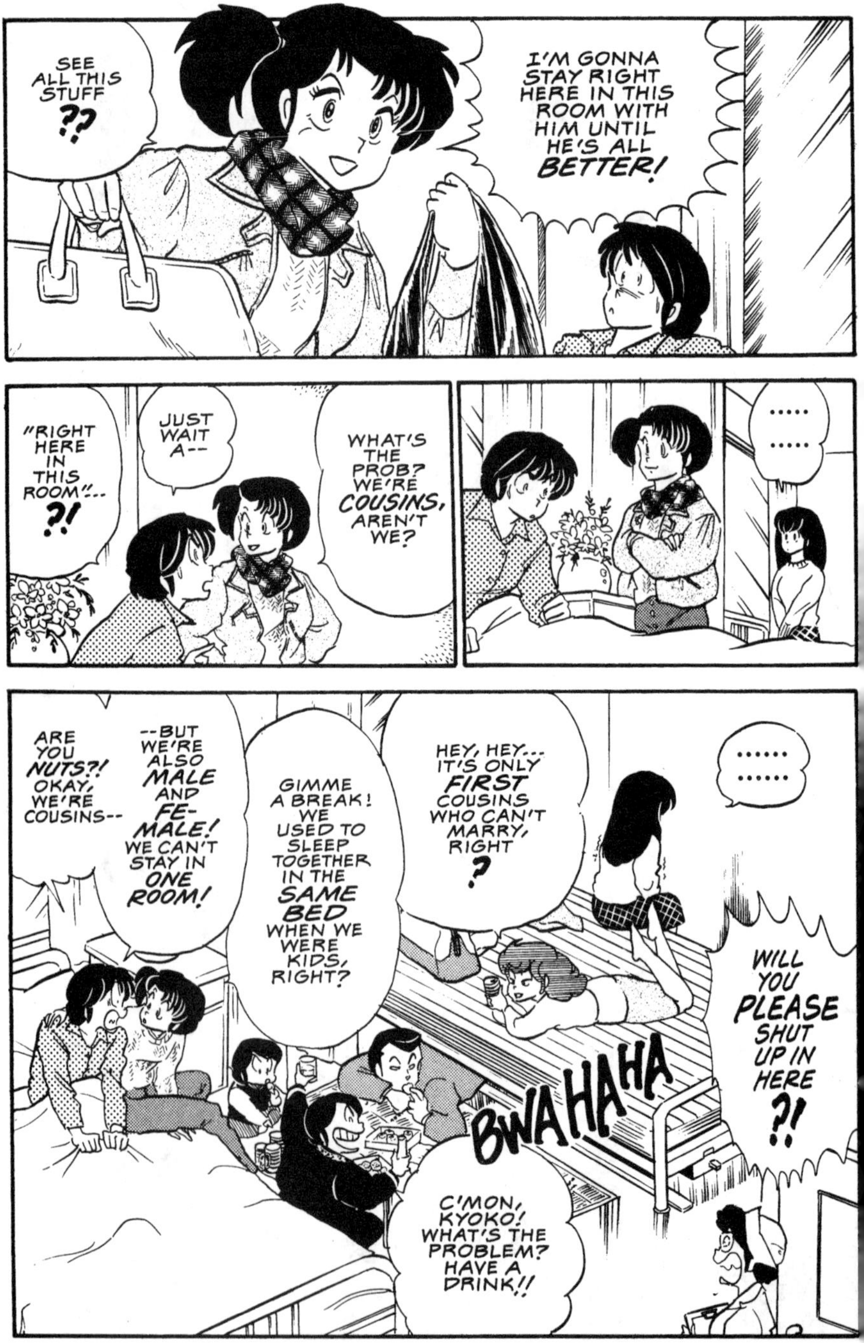
SEE ALL THIS STUFF ??
I'M GONNA STAY RIGHT HERE IN THIS ROOM WITH HIM UNTIL HE'S ALL BETTER!
"RIGHT HERE IN THIS ROOM"!... ?!
JUST WAIT A--
WHAT'S THE PROB? WE'RE COUSINS, AREN'T WE?
....
ARE YOU NUTS?! OKAY, WE'RE COUSINS--
--BUT WE'RE ALSO MALE AND FE-MALE! WE CAN'T STAY IN ONE ROOM!
GIMME A BREAK! WE USED TO SLEEP TOGETHER IN THE SAME BED WHEN WE WERE KIDS, RIGHT?
HEY, HEY... IT'S ONLY FIRST COUSINS WHO CAN'T MARRY, RIGHT ?
....
WILL YOU PLEASE SHUT UP IN HERE ?!
BWAHAHA
C'MON, KYOKO! WHAT'S THE PROBLEM? HAVE A DRINK!!

PART EIGHT

MISSION IMPOSSIBLE: THE PARTY CRACKER CAPER

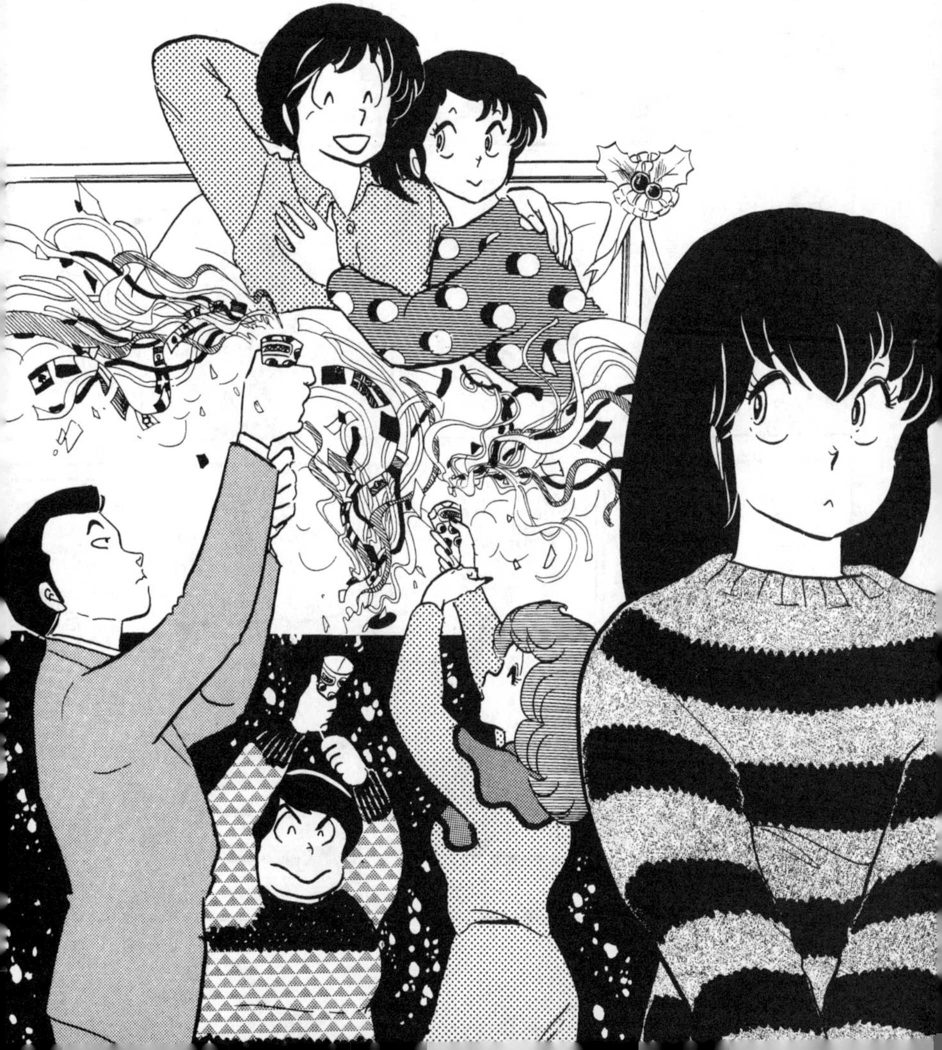

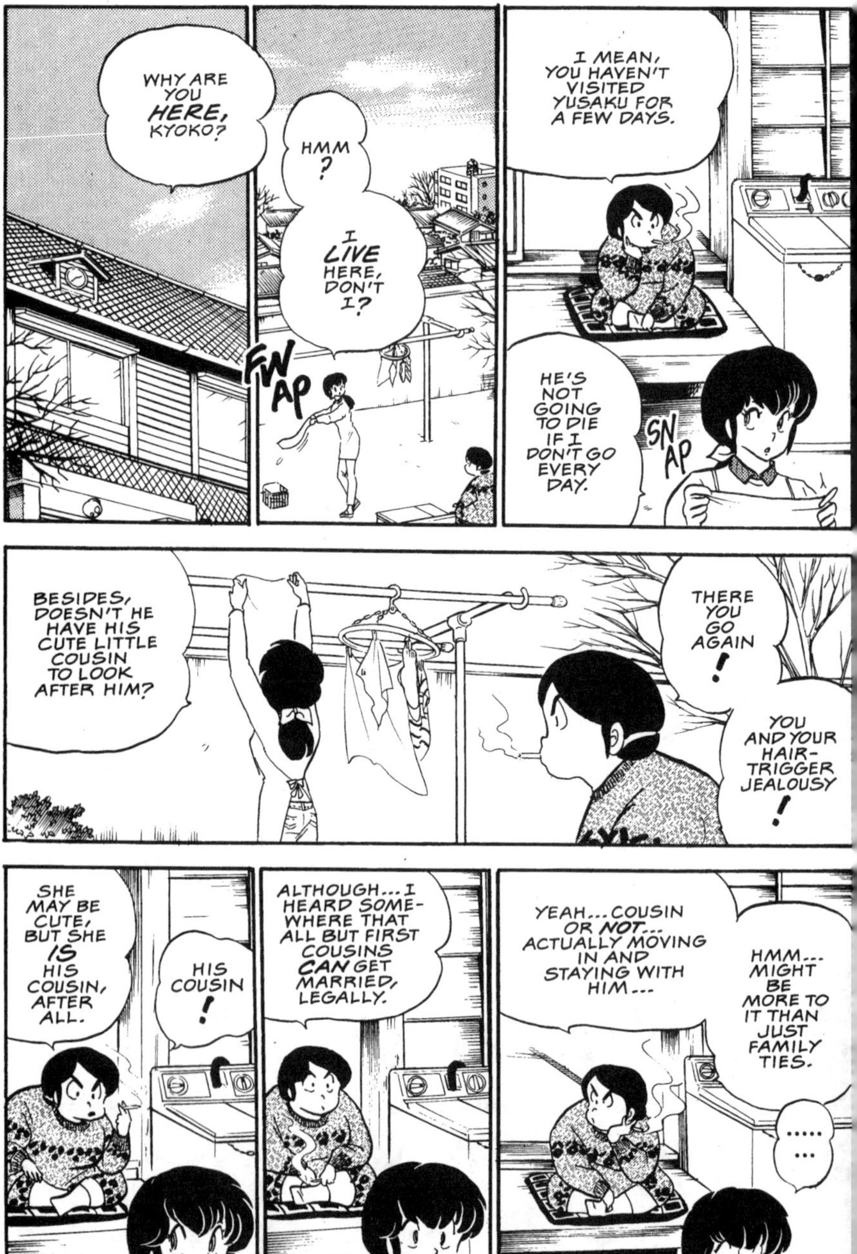
WHY ARE YOU HERE, KYOKO?
HMM?
I LIVE HERE, DON'T I?
FWAP
I MEAN, YOU HAVEN'T VISITED YUSAKU FOR A FEW DAYS.
HE'S NOT GOING TO DIE IF I DON'T GO EVERY DAY.
SNAP
BESIDES, DOESN'T HE HAVE HIS CUTE LITTLE COUSIN TO LOOK AFTER HIM?
THERE YOU GO AGAIN!
YOU AND YOUR HAIR-TRIGGER JEALOUSY!
SHE MAY BE CUTE, BUT SHE IS HIS COUSIN, AFTER ALL.
HIS COUSIN!
ALTHOUGH... I HEARD SOME-WHERE THAT ALL BUT FIRST COUSINS CAN GET MARRIED, LEGALLY.
YEAH... COUSIN OR NOT... ACTUALLY MOVING IN AND STAYING WITH HIM...
HMM... MIGHT BE MORE TO IT THAN JUST FAMILY TIES.
....

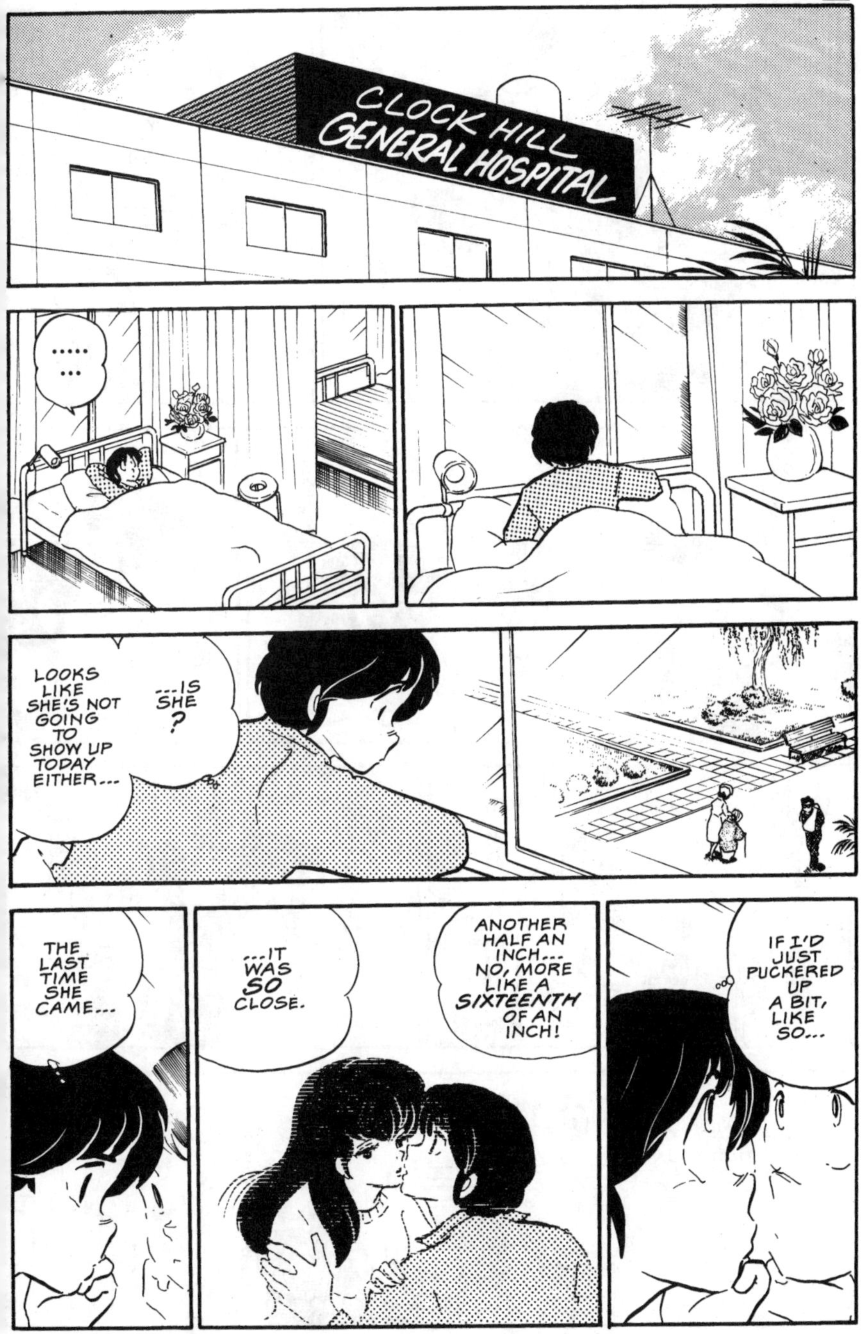
CLOCK HILL GENERAL HOSPITAL
....
LOOKS LIKE SHE'S NOT GOING TO SHOW UP TODAY EITHER...
...IS SHE ?
THE LAST TIME SHE CAME...
...IT WAS SO CLOSE.
ANOTHER HALF AN INCH... NO, MORE LIKE A SIXTEENTH OF AN INCH!
IF I'D JUST PUCKERED UP A BIT, LIKE SO...

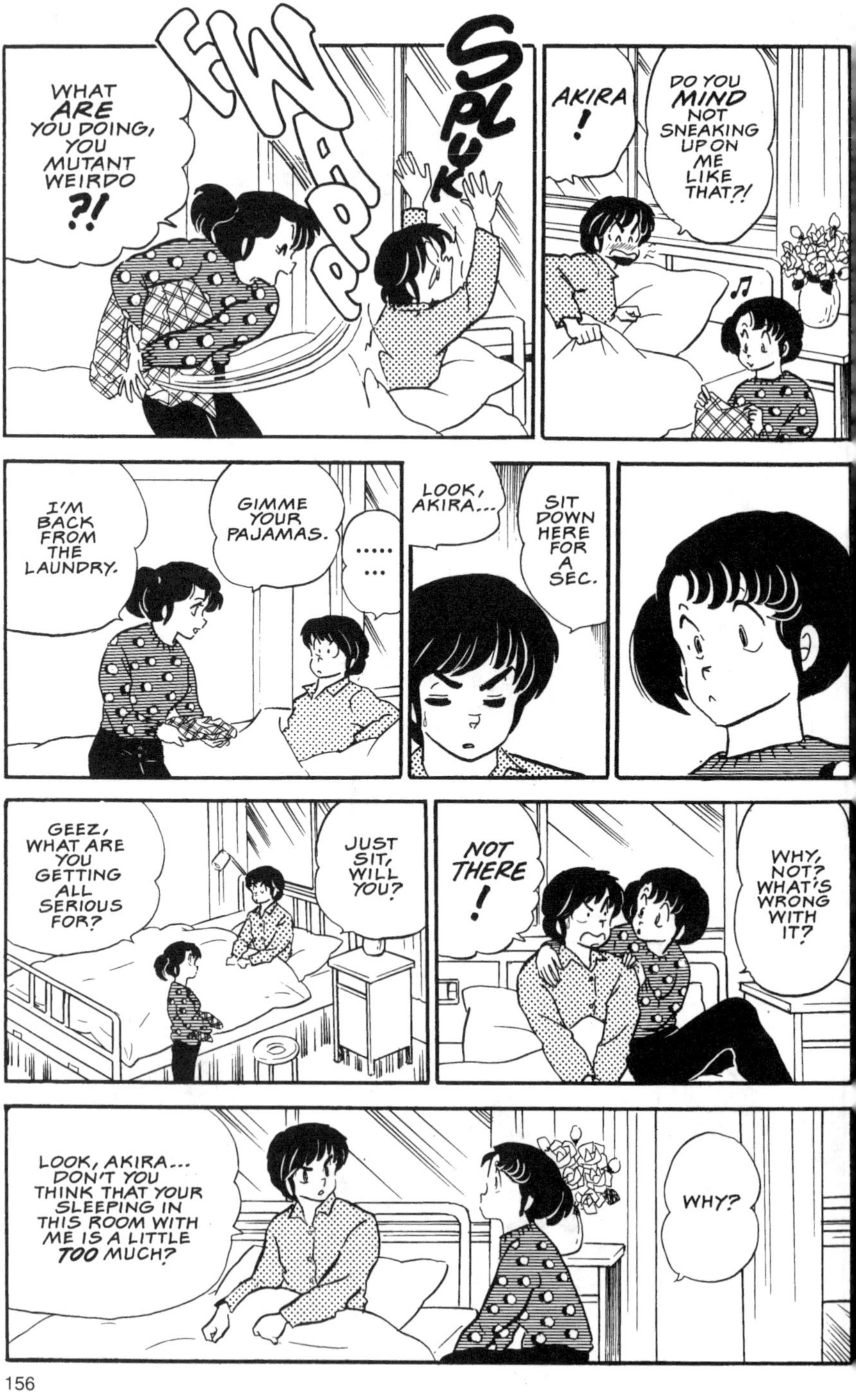
WHAT ARE YOU DOING, YOU MUTANT WEIRDO ?!
FWAPP
SPLUK
AKIRA!
DO YOU MIND NOT SNEAKING UP ON ME LIKE THAT?!
I'M BACK FROM THE LAUNDRY.
GIMME YOUR PAJAMAS.
....
LOOK, AKIRA...
SIT DOWN HERE FOR A SEC.
GEEZ, WHAT ARE YOU GETTING ALL SERIOUS FOR?
JUST SIT, WILL YOU?
NOT THERE!
WHY, NOT? WHAT'S WRONG WITH IT?
LOOK, AKIRA... DON'T YOU THINK THAT YOUR SLEEPING IN THIS ROOM WITH ME IS A LITTLE TOO MUCH?
WHY?

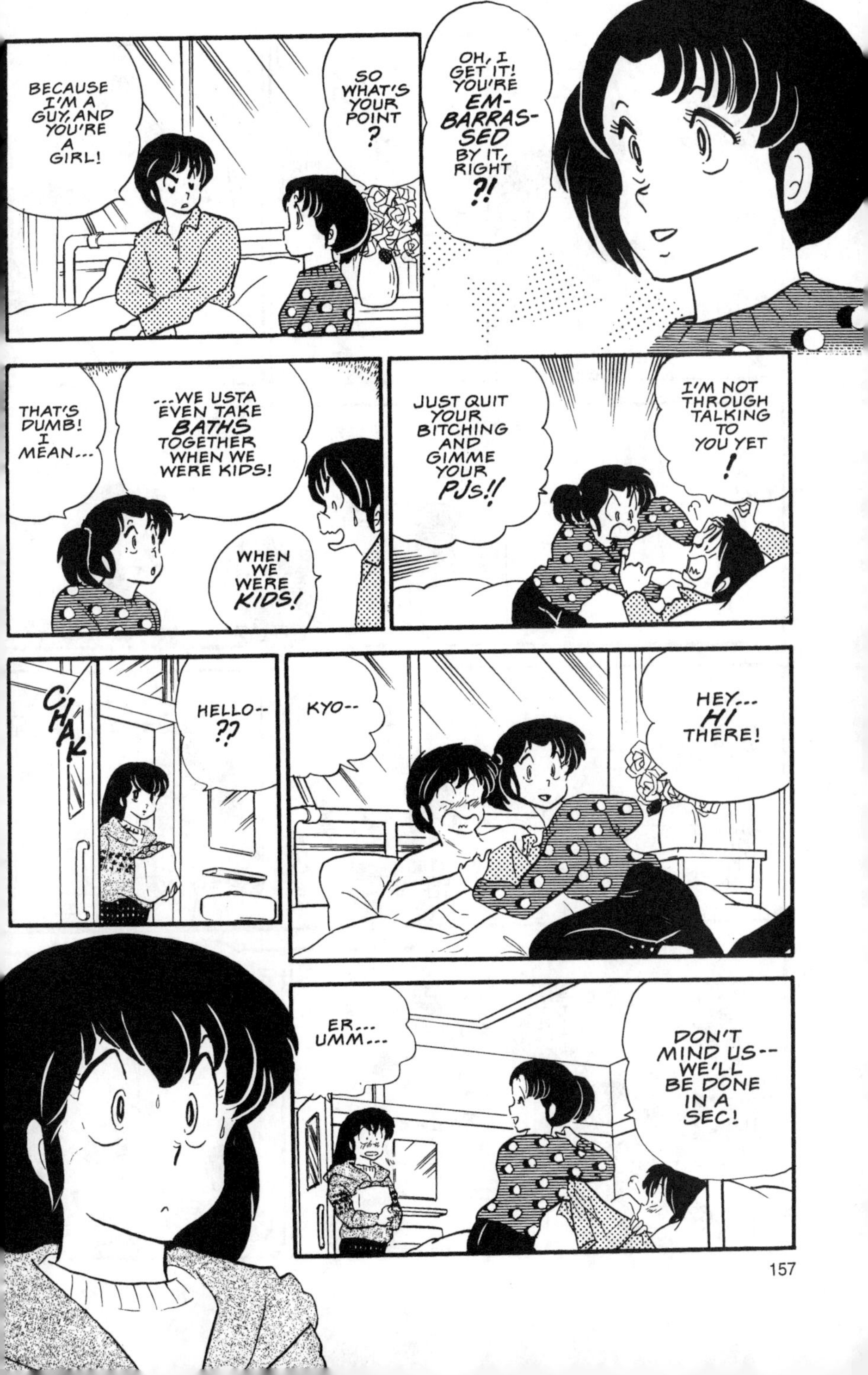
BECAUSE I'M A GUY, AND YOU'RE A GIRL!
SO WHAT'S YOUR POINT ?
OH, I GET IT! YOU'RE EM-BARRAS-SED BY IT, RIGHT ?!
THAT'S DUMB! I MEAN...
...WE USTA EVEN TAKE BATHS TOGETHER WHEN WE WERE KIDS!
WHEN WE WERE KIDS!
JUST QUIT YOUR BITCHING AND GIMME YOUR PJs!!
I'M NOT THROUGH TALKING TO YOU YET !
CHAK
HELLO-- ??
KYO--
HEY... HI THERE!
ER... UMM...
DON'T MIND US-- WE'LL BE DONE IN A SEC!

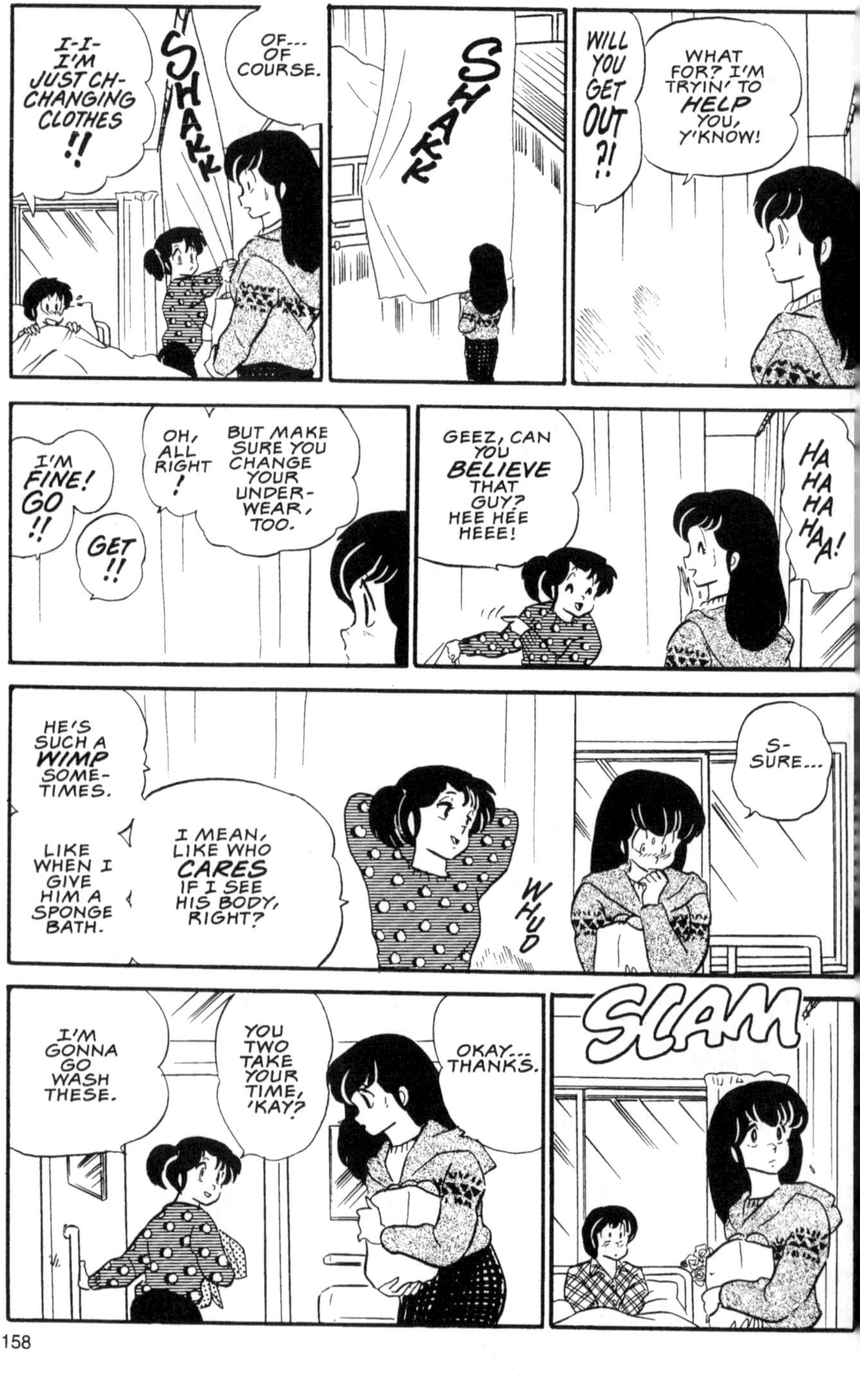
I-I-I'M JUST CH-CHANGING CLOTHES!!
SHAKK
OF--- OF COURSE.
SHAKK
WILL YOU GET OUT?!
WHAT FOR? I'M TRYIN' TO HELP YOU, Y'KNOW!
I'M FINE! GO!!
GET!!
OH, ALL RIGHT!
BUT MAKE SURE YOU CHANGE YOUR UNDER-WEAR, TOO.
GEEZ, CAN YOU BELIEVE THAT GUY? HEE HEE HEEE!
HA HA HA HAA!
HE'S SUCH A WIMP SOME-TIMES.
LIKE WHEN I GIVE HIM A SPONGE BATH.
I MEAN, LIKE WHO CARES IF I SEE HIS BODY, RIGHT?
WHUD
S-SURE...
I'M GONNA GO WASH THESE.
YOU TWO TAKE YOUR TIME, 'KAY?
OKAY... THANKS.
SLAM

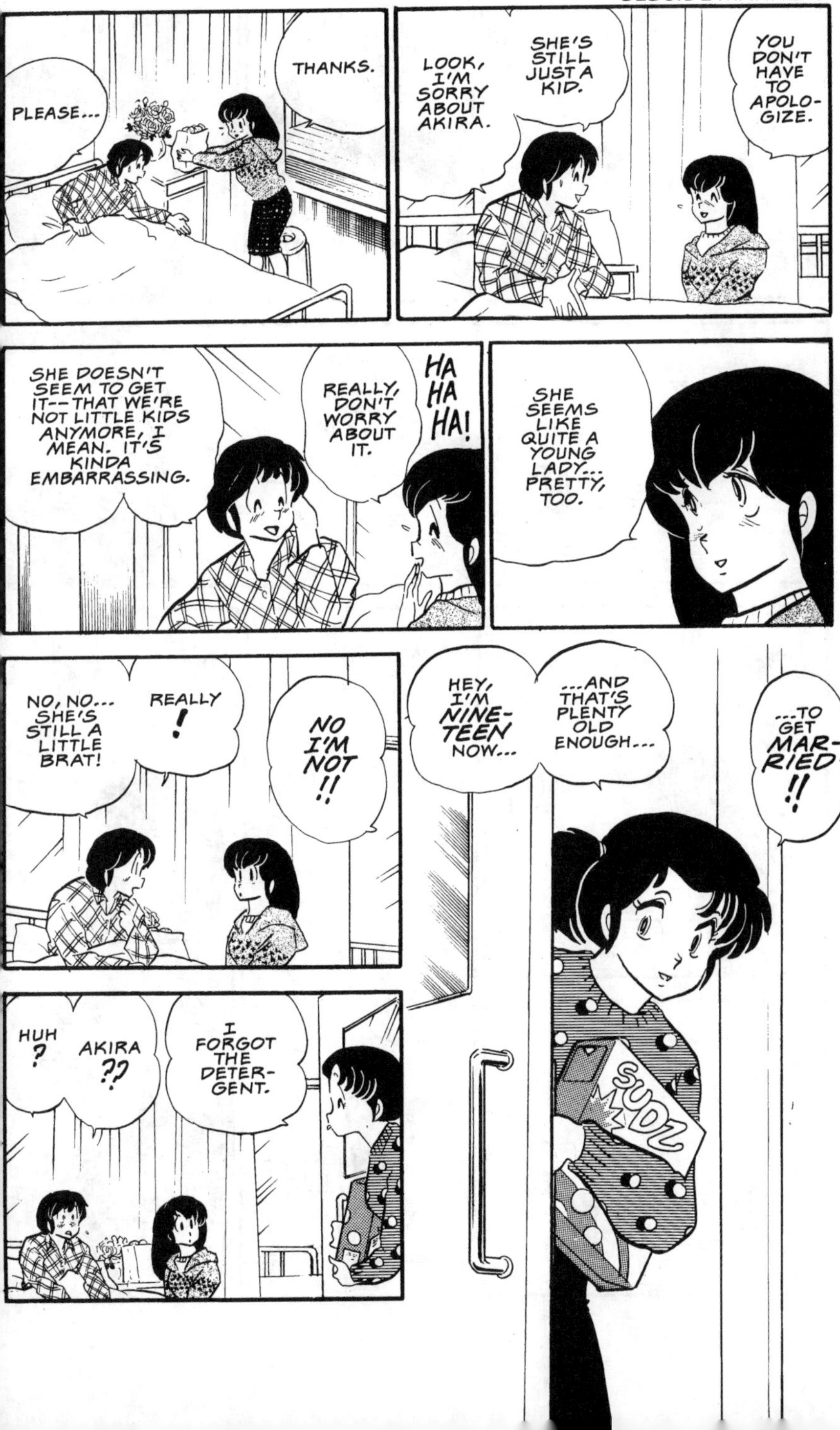
PLEASE...
THANKS.
LOOK, I'M SORRY ABOUT AKIRA.
SHE'S STILL JUST A KID.
YOU DON'T HAVE TO APOLOGIZE.
SHE DOESN'T SEEM TO GET IT--THAT WE'RE NOT LITTLE KIDS ANYMORE, I MEAN. IT'S KINDA EMBARRASSING.
REALLY, DON'T WORRY ABOUT IT.
HA HA HA!
SHE SEEMS LIKE QUITE A YOUNG LADY... PRETTY, TOO.
NO, NO... SHE'S STILL A LITTLE BRAT!
REALLY!
NO I'M NOT!!
HUH?
AKIRA??
I FORGOT THE DETERGENT.
HEY, I'M NINETEEN NOW...
...AND THAT'S PLENTY OLD ENOUGH...
...TO GET MARRIED!!
SUDZ

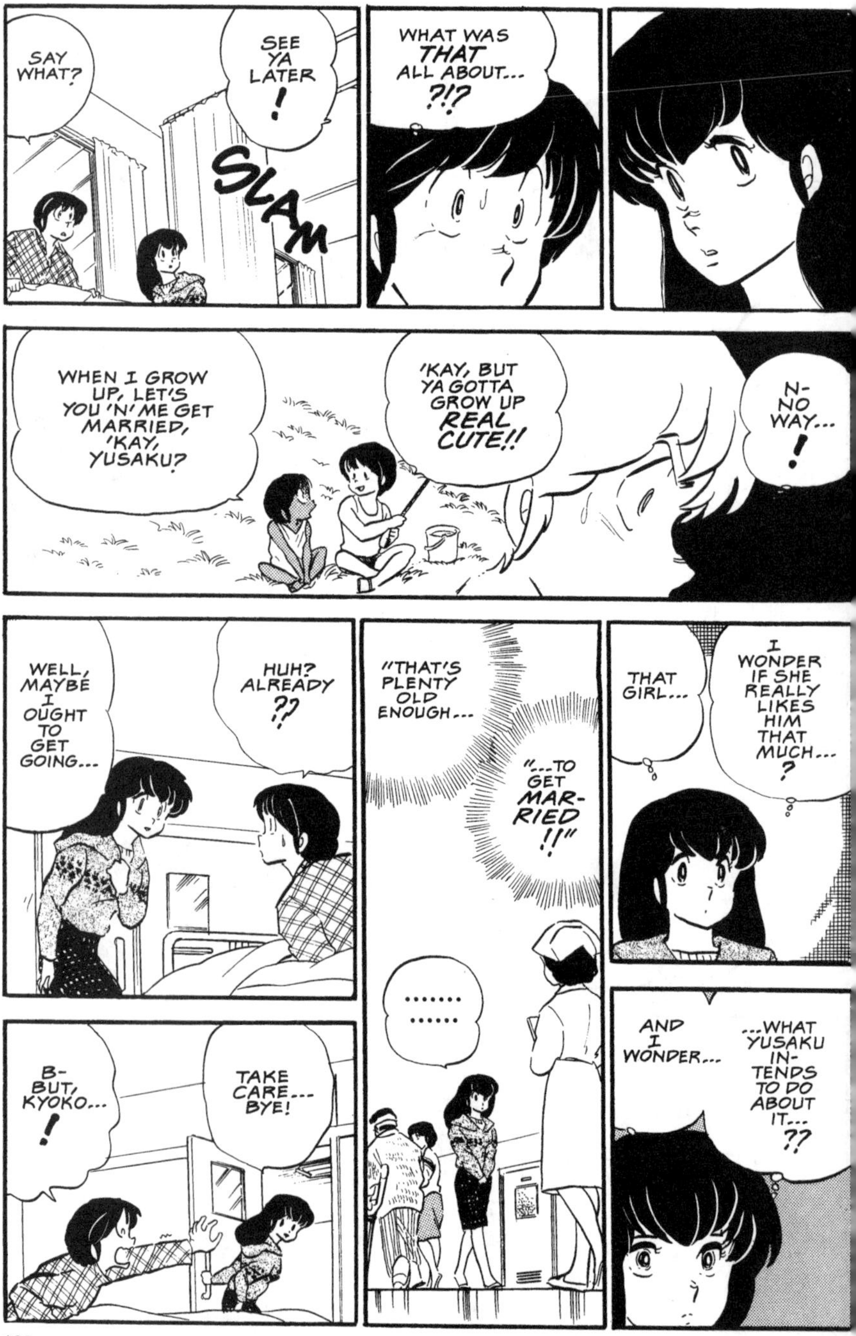

SAY WHAT?
SEE YA LATER !
SLAM
WHAT WAS THAT ALL ABOUT... ?!?
WHEN I GROW UP, LET'S YOU 'N' ME GET MARRIED, 'KAY, YUSAKU?
'KAY, BUT YA GOTTA GROW UP REAL CUTE!!
N-NO WAY... !
WELL, MAYBE I OUGHT TO GET GOING...
HUH? ALREADY ??
"THAT'S PLENTY OLD ENOUGH...
"...TO GET MAR-RIED !!"
THAT GIRL...
I WONDER IF SHE REALLY LIKES HIM THAT MUCH... ?
B-BUT, KYOKO... !
TAKE CARE... BYE!
....
....
AND I WONDER...
...WHAT YUSAKU IN-TENDS TO DO ABOUT IT... ??

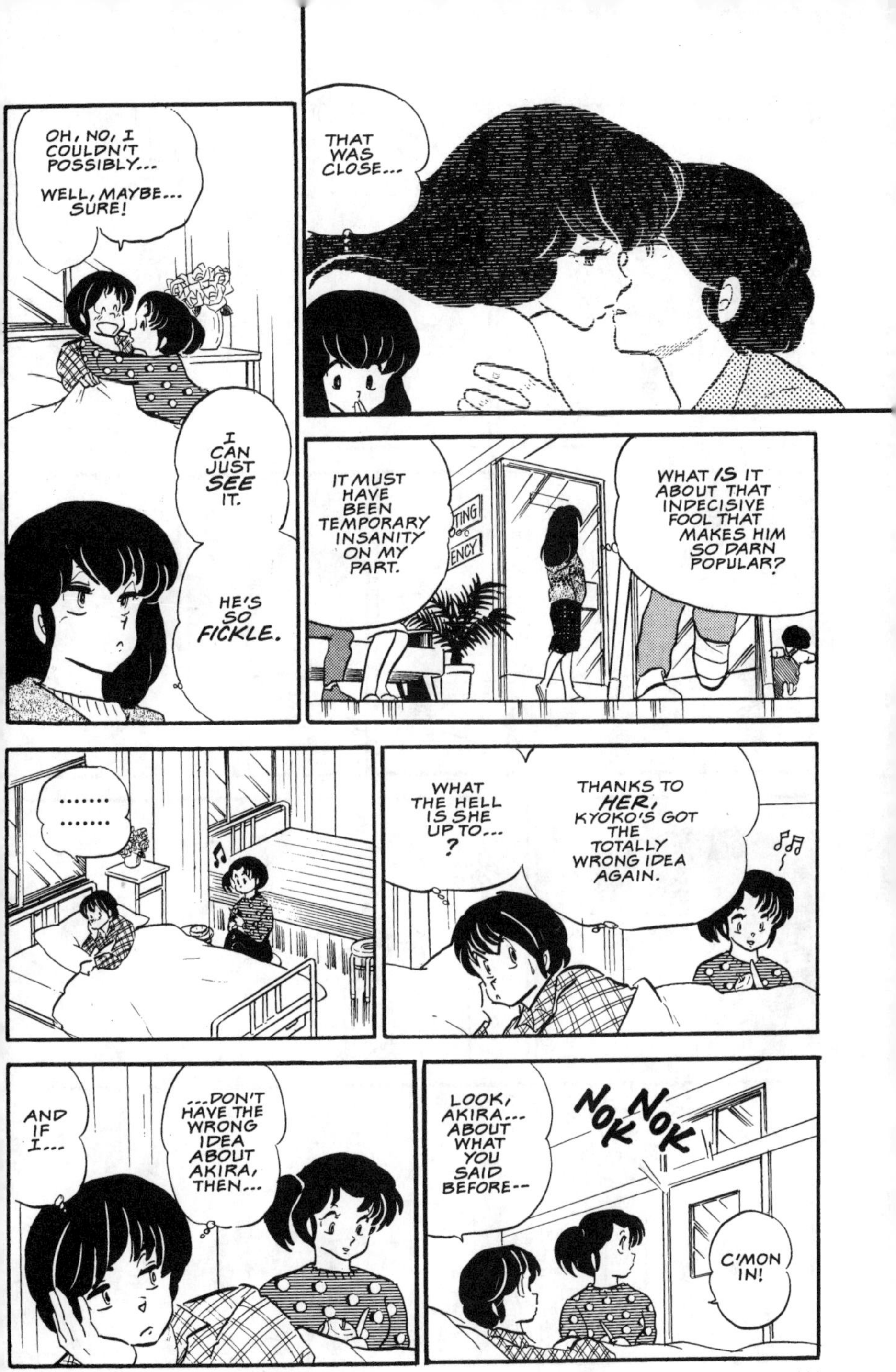
OH, NO, I COULDN'T POSSIBLY...
WELL, MAYBE... SURE!
I CAN JUST SEE IT.
HE'S SO FICKLE.
THAT WAS CLOSE...
IT MUST HAVE BEEN TEMPORARY INSANITY ON MY PART.
WHAT IS IT ABOUT THAT INDECISIVE FOOL THAT MAKES HIM SO DARN POPULAR?
....
....
WHAT THE HELL IS SHE UP TO...?
THANKS TO HER, KYOKO'S GOT THE TOTALLY WRONG IDEA AGAIN.
AND IF I...
...DON'T HAVE THE WRONG IDEA ABOUT AKIRA, THEN...
LOOK, AKIRA... ABOUT WHAT YOU SAID BEFORE--
NOK NOK
C'MON IN!

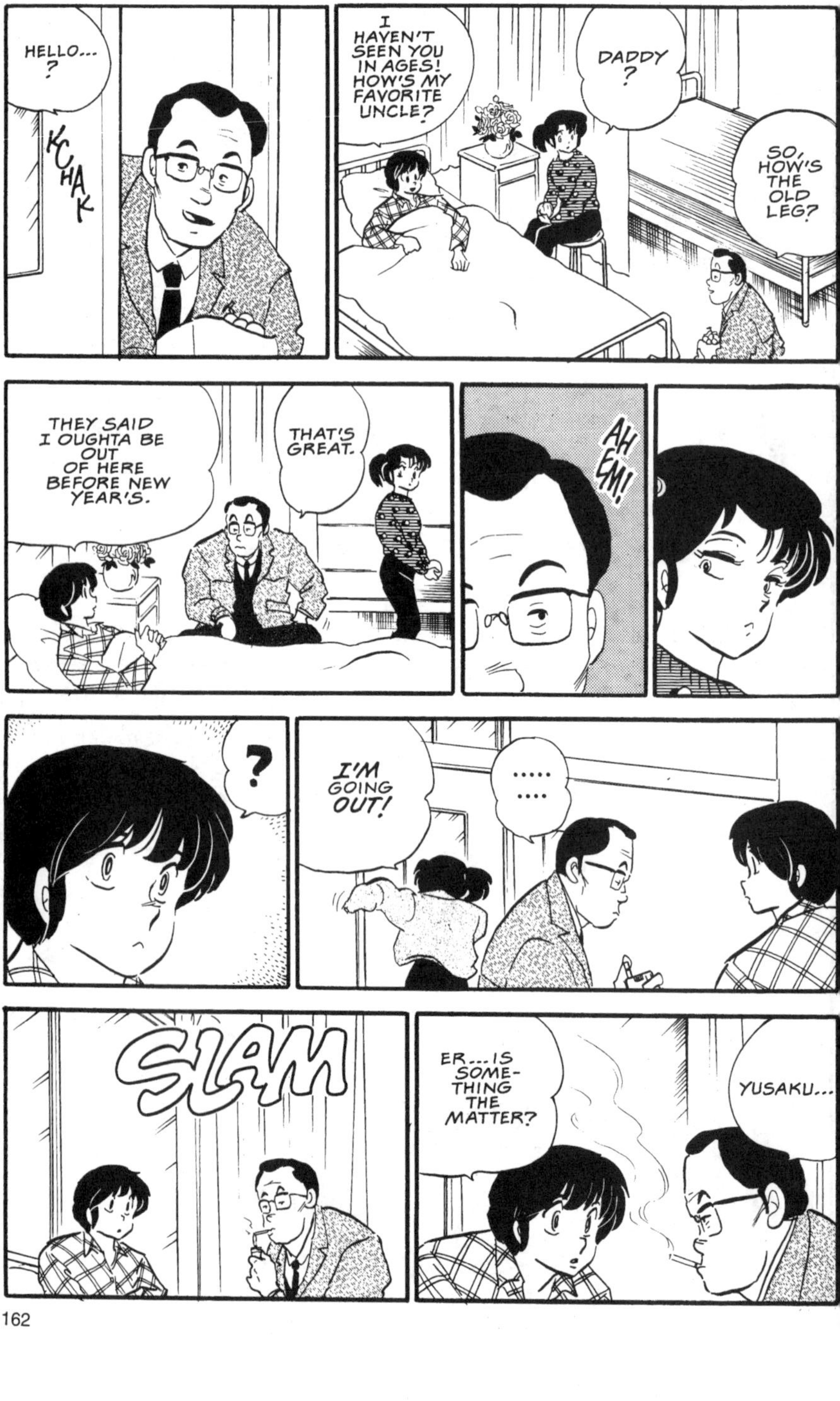
HELLO...?
KCHAK
I HAVEN'T SEEN YOU IN AGES! HOW'S MY FAVORITE UNCLE?
DADDY?
SO, HOW'S THE OLD LEG?
THEY SAID I OUGHTA BE OUT OF HERE BEFORE NEW YEAR'S.
THAT'S GREAT.
AHEM!
?
I'M GOING OUT!
.....
....
SLAM
ER...IS SOMETHING THE MATTER?
YUSAKU...

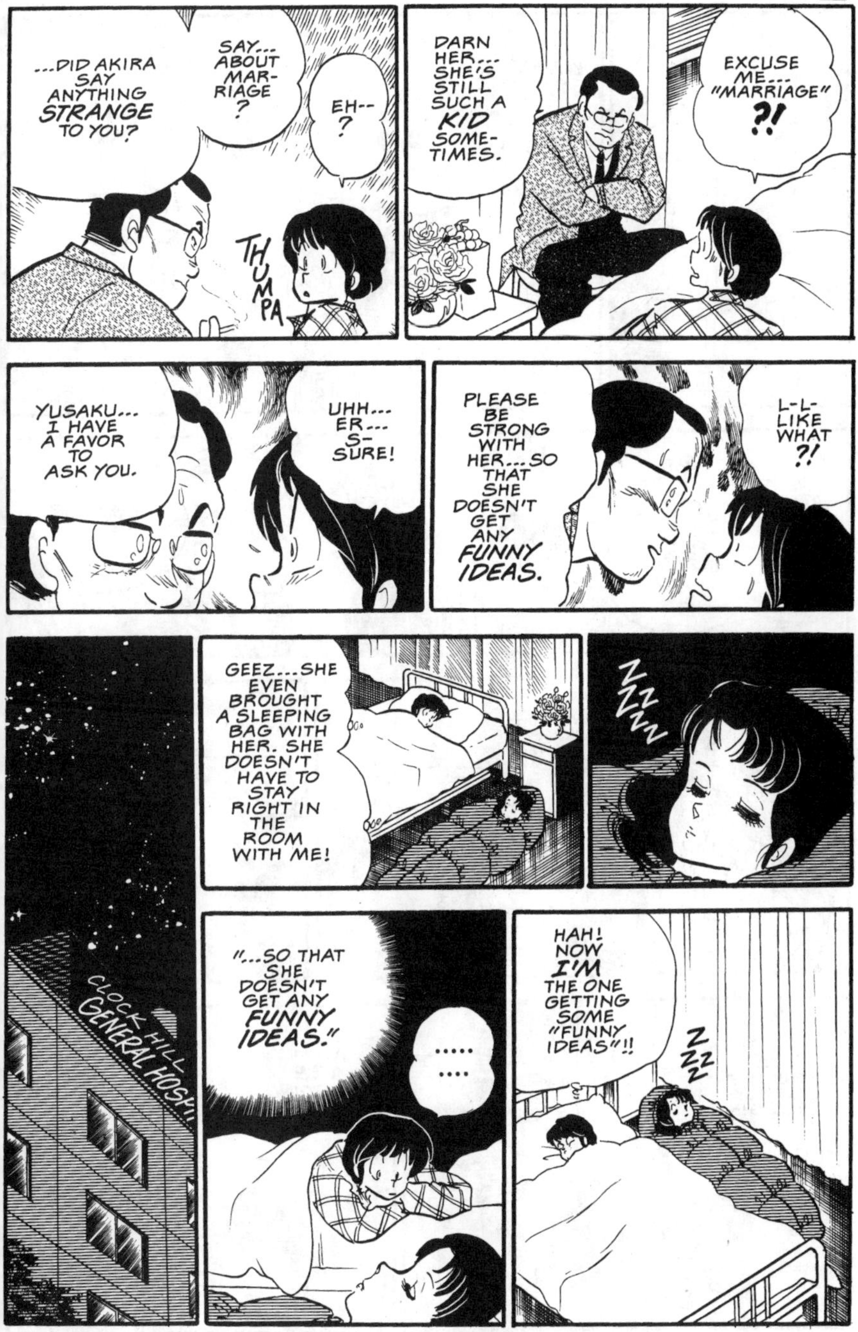
...DID AKIRA SAY ANYTHING STRANGE TO YOU?
SAY... ABOUT MARRIAGE ?
EH-- ?
THUMPA
DARN HER... SHE'S STILL SUCH A KID SOMETIMES.
EXCUSE ME... "MARRIAGE" ?!
YUSAKU... I HAVE A FAVOR TO ASK YOU.
UHH... ER... S-SURE!
PLEASE BE STRONG WITH HER... SO THAT SHE DOESN'T GET ANY FUNNY IDEAS.
L-L-LIKE WHAT ?!
CLOCK HILL GENERAL HOSP
GEEZ... SHE EVEN BROUGHT A SLEEPING BAG WITH HER. SHE DOESN'T HAVE TO STAY RIGHT IN THE ROOM WITH ME!
ZZZZ
"...SO THAT SHE DOESN'T GET ANY FUNNY IDEAS."
....
HAH! NOW I'M THE ONE GETTING SOME "FUNNY IDEAS"!!
ZZZ

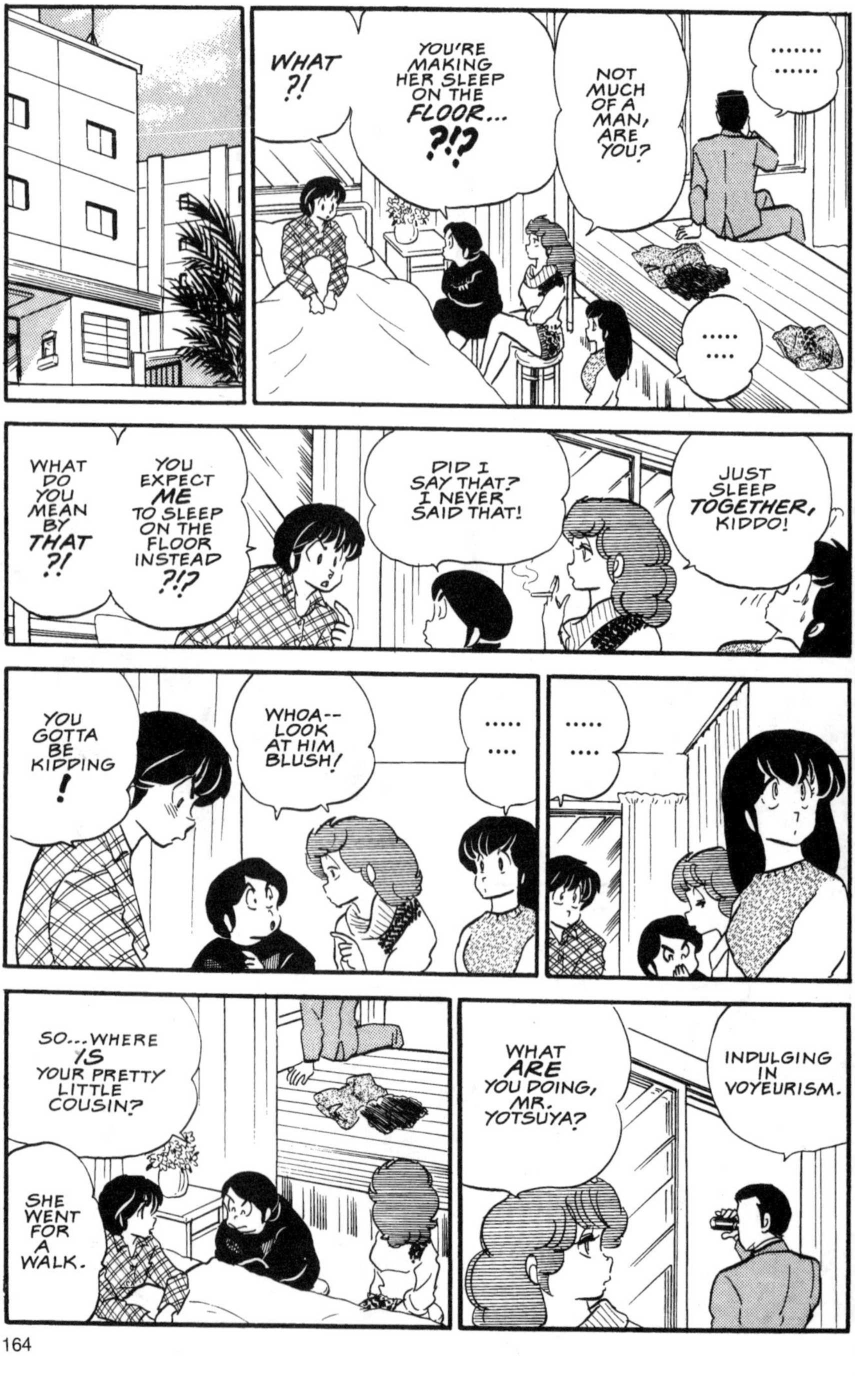
WHAT ?!
YOU'RE MAKING HER SLEEP ON THE FLOOR...?!?
NOT MUCH OF A MAN, ARE YOU?
....
....
.....
....
WHAT DO YOU MEAN BY THAT ?!
YOU EXPECT ME TO SLEEP ON THE FLOOR INSTEAD ?!?
DID I SAY THAT? I NEVER SAID THAT!
JUST SLEEP TOGETHER, KIDDO!
YOU GOTTA BE KIDDING!
WHOA-- LOOK AT HIM BLUSH!
.....
....
.....
....
SO...WHERE IS YOUR PRETTY LITTLE COUSIN?
SHE WENT FOR A WALK.
WHAT ARE YOU DOING, MR. YOTSUYA?
INDULGING IN VOYEURISM.

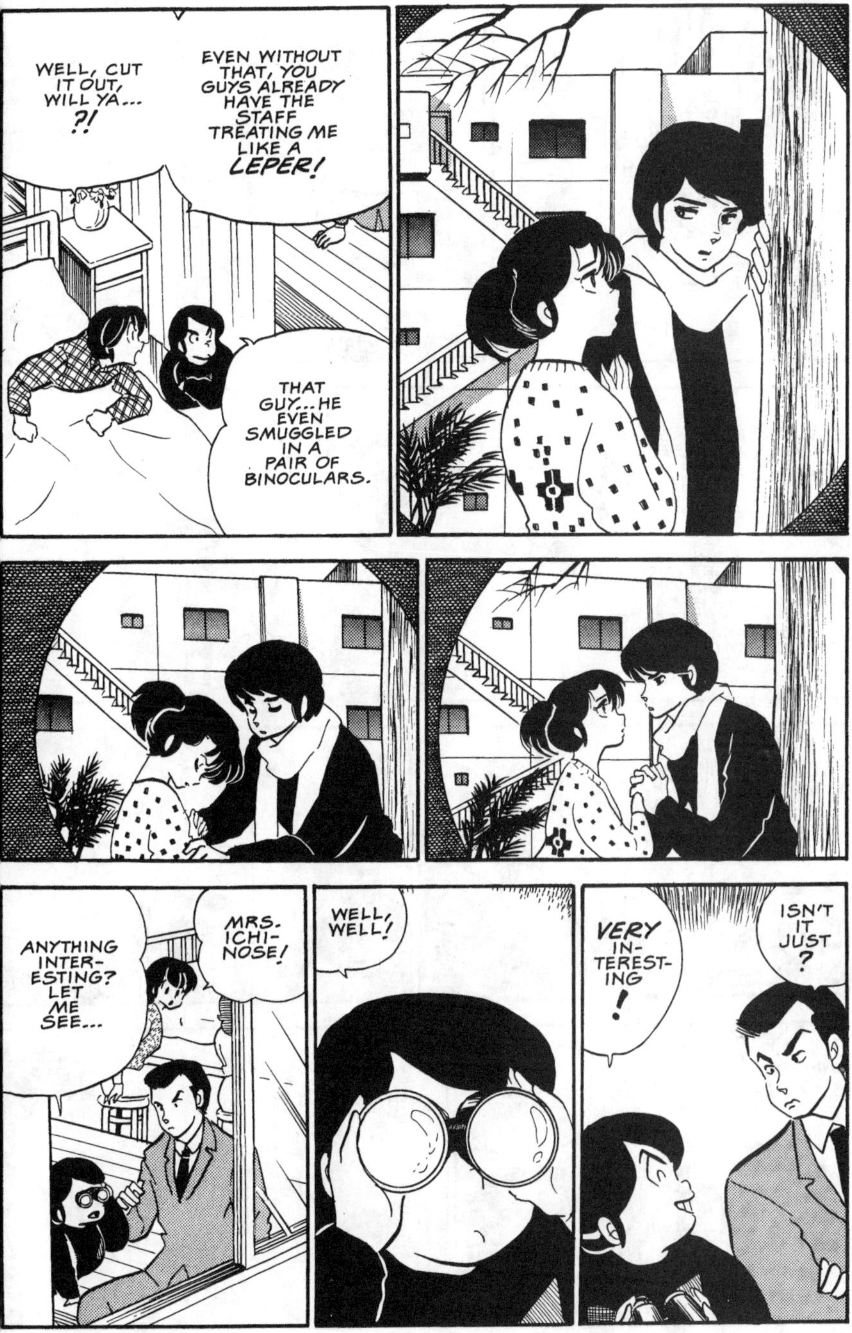
WELL, CUT IT OUT, WILL YA... ?!
EVEN WITHOUT THAT, YOU GUYS ALREADY HAVE THE STAFF TREATING ME LIKE A LEPER!
THAT GUY... HE EVEN SMUGGLED IN A PAIR OF BINOCULARS.
ANYTHING INTERESTING? LET ME SEE...
MRS. ICHINOSE!
WELL, WELL!
VERY INTERESTING!
ISN'T IT JUST?

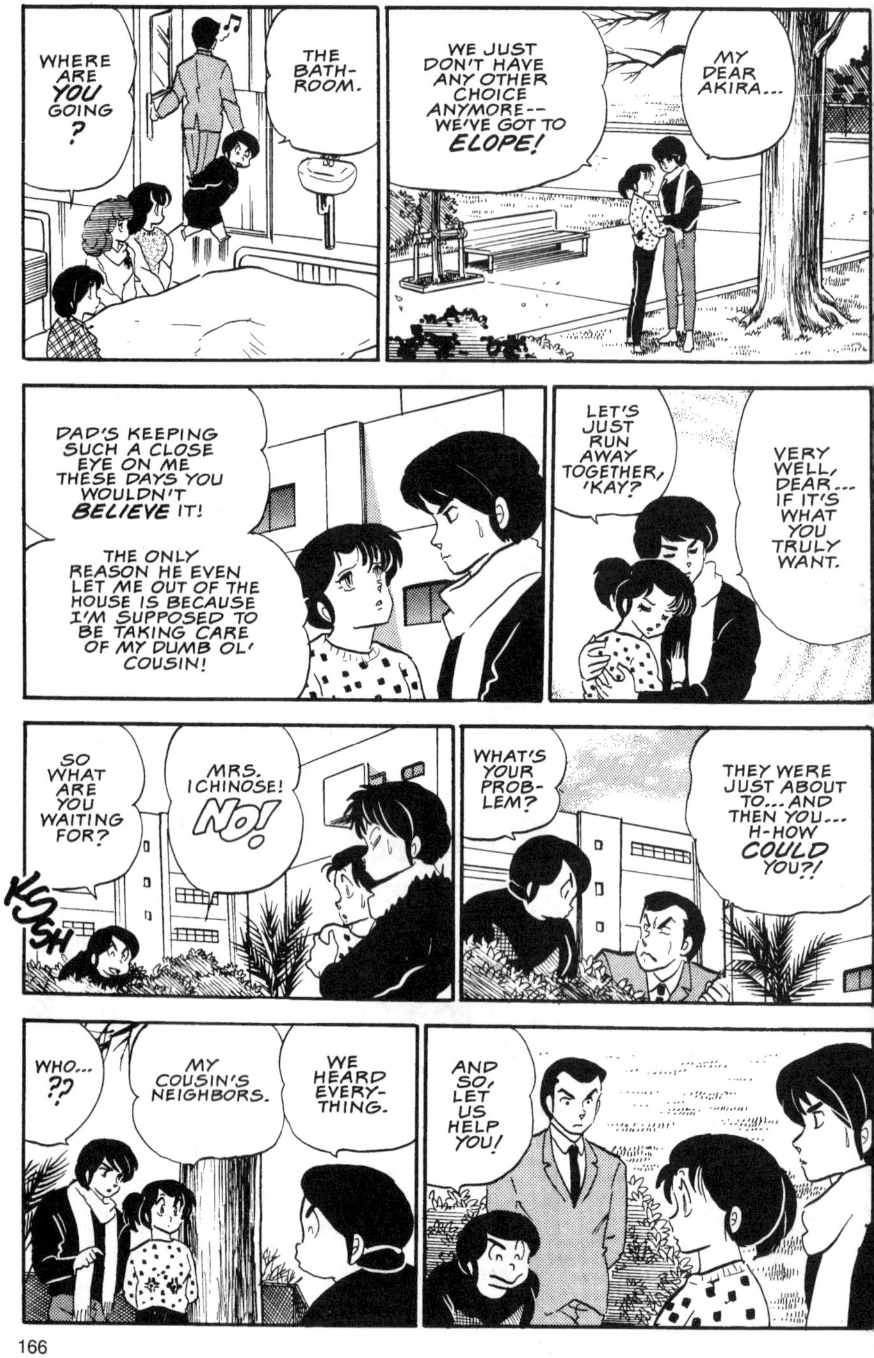
WHERE ARE YOU GOING?
THE BATHROOM.
WE JUST DON'T HAVE ANY OTHER CHOICE ANYMORE-- WE'VE GOT TO ELOPE!
MY DEAR AKIRA...
DAD'S KEEPING SUCH A CLOSE EYE ON ME THESE DAYS YOU WOULDN'T BELIEVE IT!
THE ONLY REASON HE EVEN LET ME OUT OF THE HOUSE IS BECAUSE I'M SUPPOSED TO BE TAKING CARE OF MY DUMB OL' COUSIN!
LET'S JUST RUN AWAY TOGETHER, 'KAY?
VERY WELL, DEAR... IF IT'S WHAT YOU TRULY WANT.
SO WHAT ARE YOU WAITING FOR?
KSSH
MRS. ICHINOSE!
NO!
WHAT'S YOUR PROBLEM?
THEY WERE JUST ABOUT TO... AND THEN YOU... H-HOW COULD YOU?!
WHO...??
MY COUSIN'S NEIGHBORS.
WE HEARD EVERYTHING.
AND SO, LET US HELP YOU!

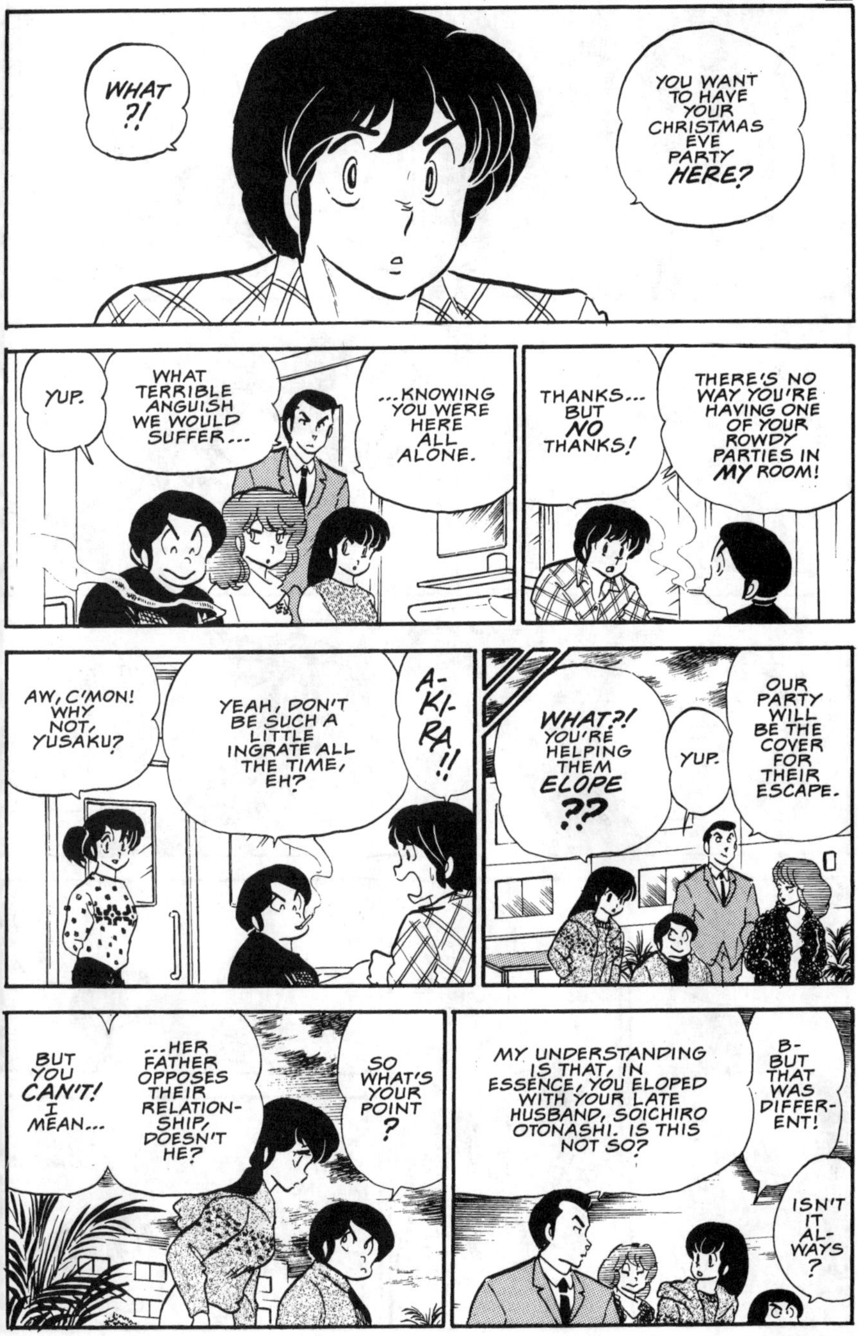
WHAT ?!
YOU WANT TO HAVE YOUR CHRISTMAS EVE PARTY HERE?
YUP.
WHAT TERRIBLE ANGUISH WE WOULD SUFFER...
...KNOWING YOU WERE HERE ALL ALONE.
THANKS... BUT NO THANKS!
THERE'S NO WAY YOU'RE HAVING ONE OF YOUR ROWDY PARTIES IN MY ROOM!
AW, C'MON! WHY NOT, YUSAKU?
YEAH, DON'T BE SUCH A LITTLE INGRATE ALL THE TIME, EH?
A-KI-RA!!
WHAT?! YOU'RE HELPING THEM ELOPE??
YUP.
OUR PARTY WILL BE THE COVER FOR THEIR ESCAPE.
BUT YOU CAN'T! I MEAN...
...HER FATHER OPPOSES THEIR RELATION-SHIP, DOESN'T HE?
SO WHAT'S YOUR POINT ?
MY UNDERSTANDING IS THAT, IN ESSENCE, YOU ELOPED WITH YOUR LATE HUSBAND, SOICHIRO OTONASHI. IS THIS NOT SO?
B-BUT THAT WAS DIFFER-ENT!
ISN'T IT AL-WAYS ?

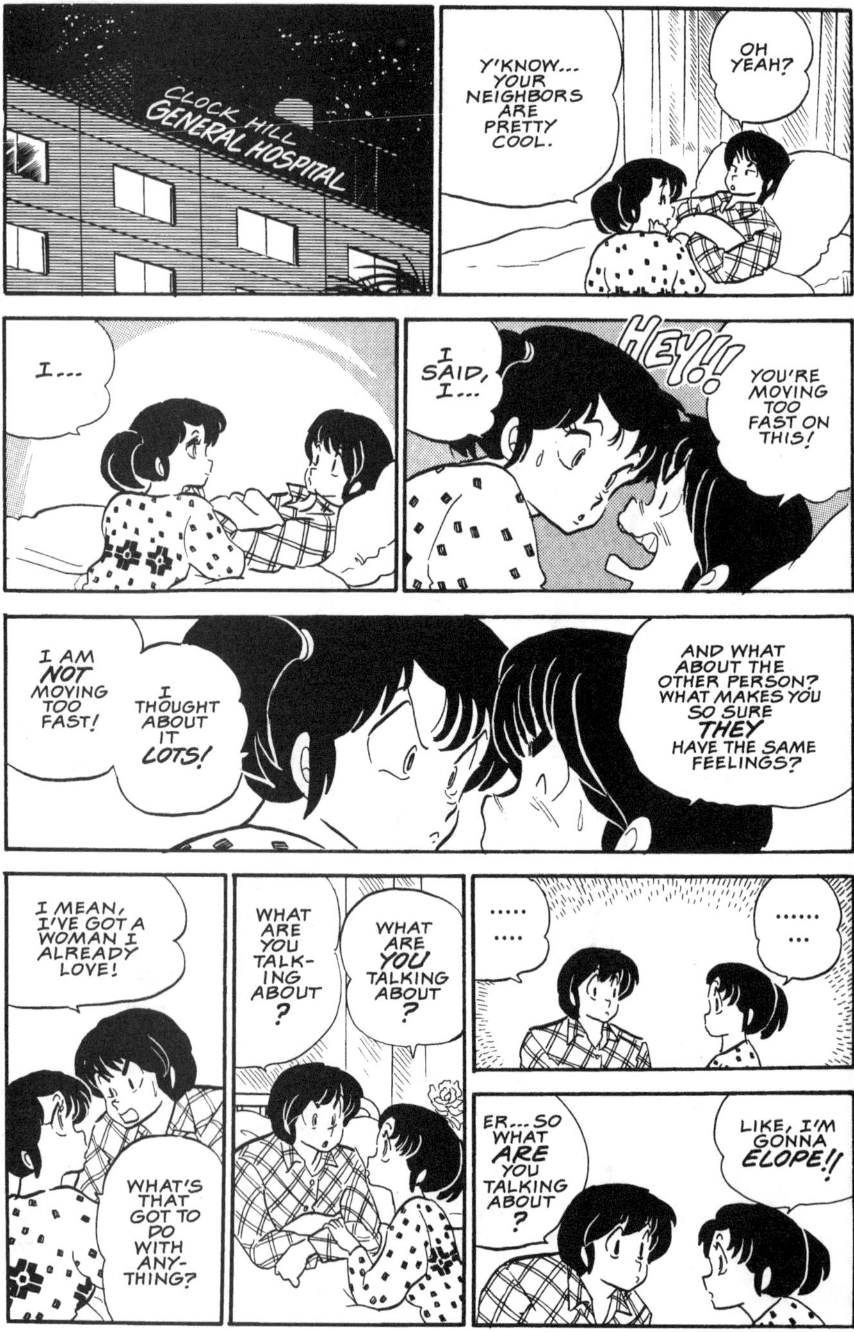
CLOCK HILL
GENERAL HOSPITAL
Y'KNOW... YOUR NEIGHBORS ARE PRETTY COOL.
OH YEAH?
I...
I SAID, I...
HEY!!
YOU'RE MOVING TOO FAST ON THIS!
I AM NOT MOVING TOO FAST!
I THOUGHT ABOUT IT LOTS!
AND WHAT ABOUT THE OTHER PERSON? WHAT MAKES YOU SO SURE THEY HAVE THE SAME FEELINGS?
I MEAN, I'VE GOT A WOMAN I ALREADY LOVE!
WHAT'S THAT GOT TO DO WITH ANY-THING?
WHAT ARE YOU TALK-ING ABOUT?
WHAT ARE YOU TALKING ABOUT?
....
....
ER... SO WHAT ARE YOU TALKING ABOUT?
LIKE, I'M GONNA ELOPE!!

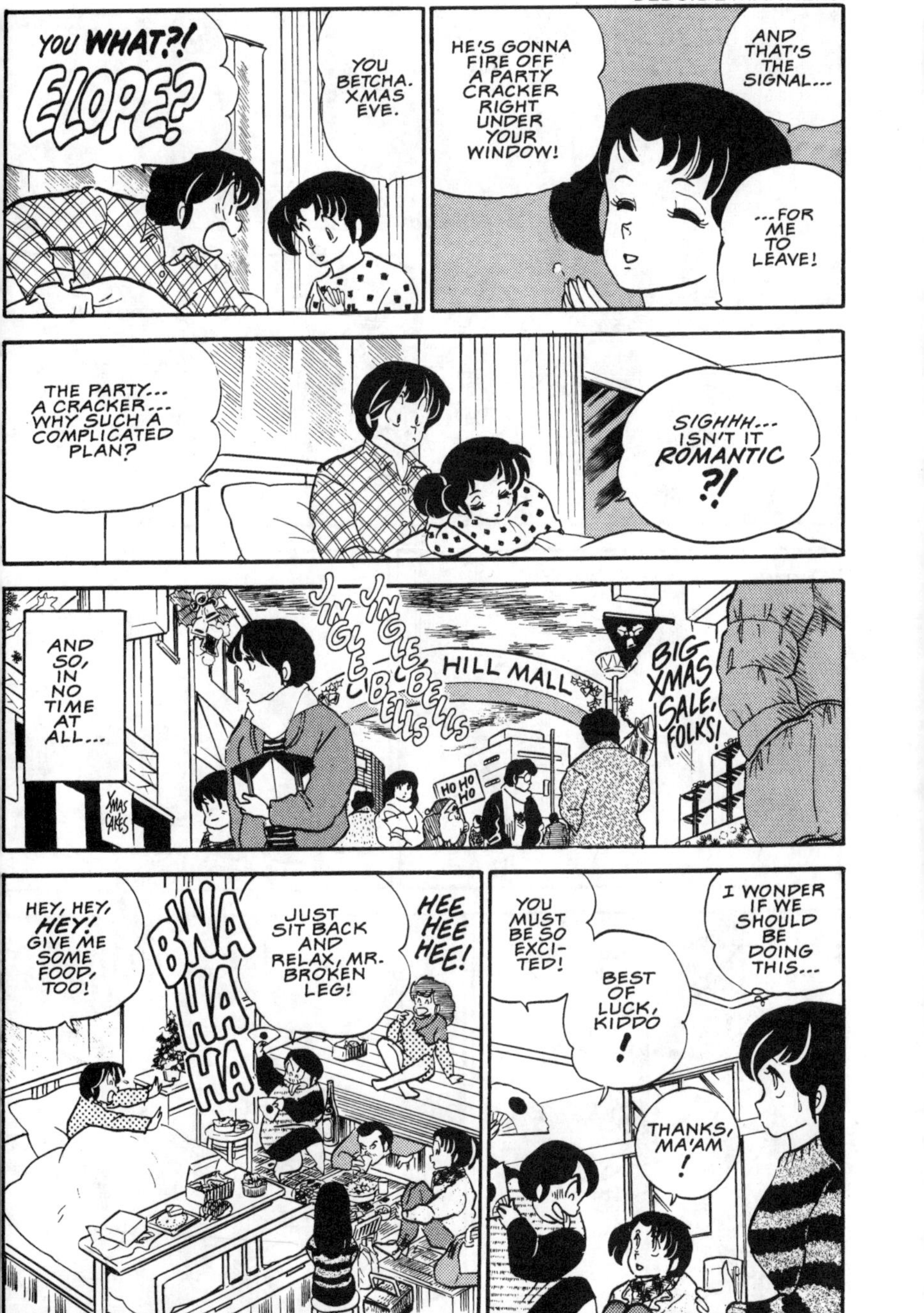
YOU WHAT?! ELOPE?
YOU BETCHA. XMAS EVE.
HE'S GONNA FIRE OFF A PARTY CRACKER RIGHT UNDER YOUR WINDOW!
AND THAT'S THE SIGNAL...
...FOR ME TO LEAVE!
THE PARTY... A CRACKER... WHY SUCH A COMPLICATED PLAN?
SIGHHH... ISN'T IT ROMANTIC ?!
AND SO, IN NO TIME AT ALL...
JINGLE BELLS JINGLE BELLS
HILL MALL
BIG XMAS SALE, FOLKS!
HO HO HO
XMAS CAKES
HEY, HEY, HEY! GIVE ME SOME FOOD, TOO!
BWAHAHAHA
JUST SIT BACK AND RELAX, MR. BROKEN LEG!
HEE HEE HEE!
YOU MUST BE SO EXCI-TED!
BEST OF LUCK, KIDDO!
I WONDER IF WE SHOULD BE DOING THIS...
THANKS, MA'AM!

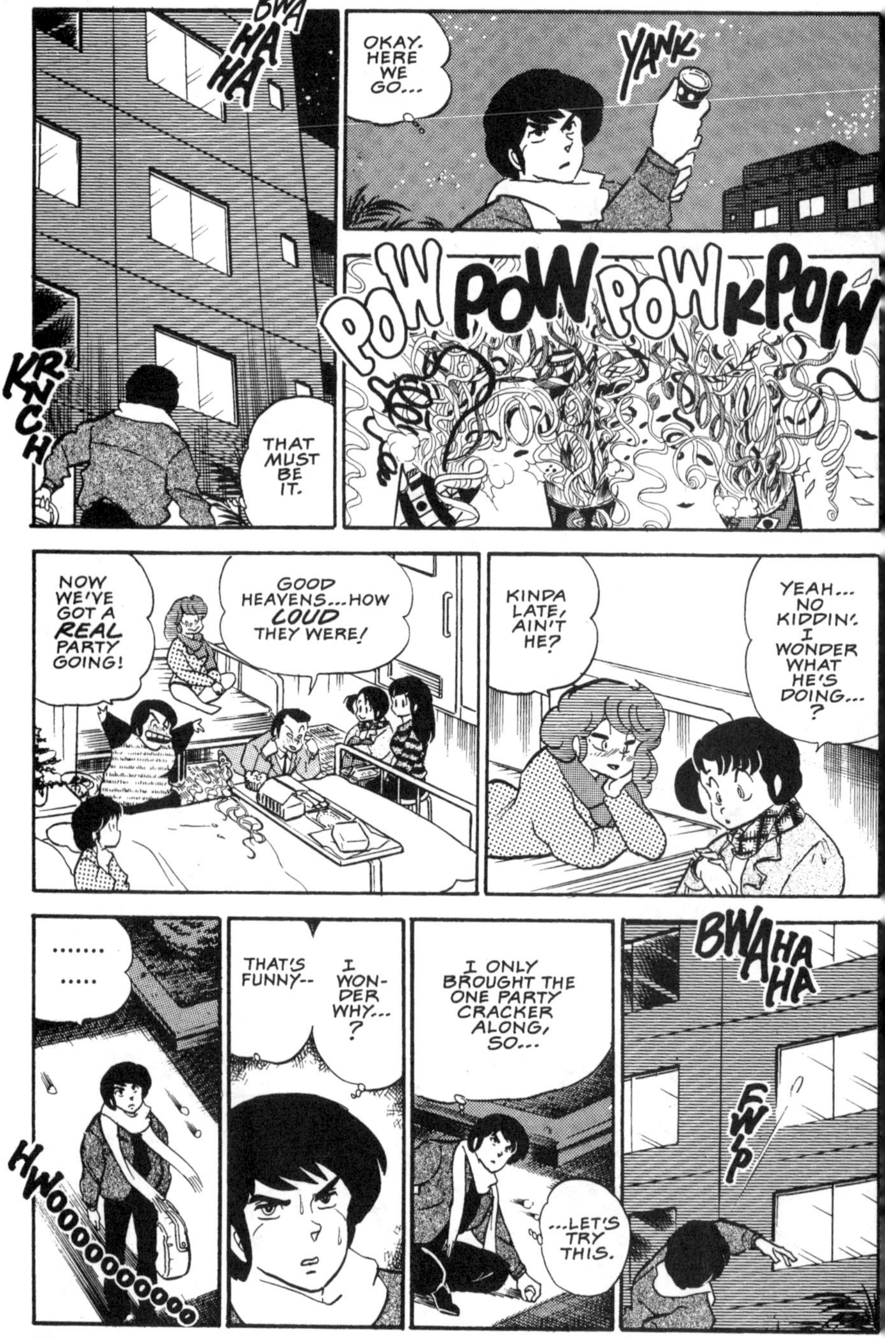
BWA HA HA
KRNCH
THAT MUST BE IT.
OKAY. HERE WE GO...
YANK
POW POW POW KPOW
NOW WE'VE GOT A REAL PARTY GOING!
GOOD HEAVENS...HOW LOUD THEY WERE!
KINDA LATE, AIN'T HE?
YEAH... NO KIDDIN'. I WONDER WHAT HE'S DOING...?
....
.....
HWOOOOOOOOOOO
THAT'S FUNNY--
I WONDER WHY...?
I ONLY BROUGHT THE ONE PARTY CRACKER ALONG, SO...
...LET'S TRY THIS.
BWAHAHA
FWIP

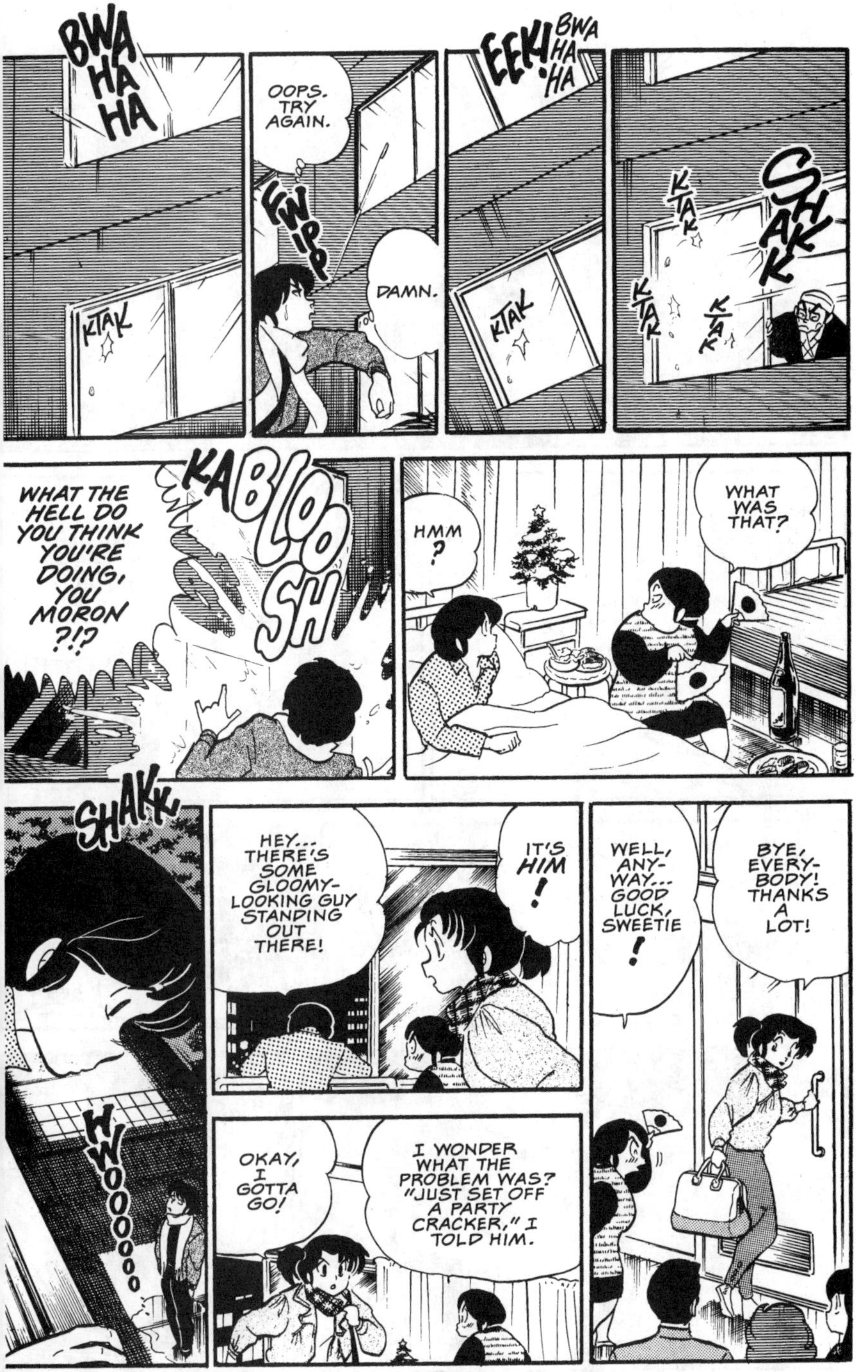
BWA HA HA HA
KTAK
OOPS. TRY AGAIN.
FWIPP
DAMN.
EEK!
BWA HA HA
KTAK
KTAK
SHAKK
KTAK
KTAK
WHAT THE HELL DO YOU THINK YOU'RE DOING, YOU MORON ?!?
KABLOOSH
HMM ?
WHAT WAS THAT?
SHAKK
HWOOOOOO
HEY... THERE'S SOME GLOOMY-LOOKING GUY STANDING OUT THERE!
IT'S HIM !
OKAY, I GOTTA GO!
I WONDER WHAT THE PROBLEM WAS? "JUST SET OFF A PARTY CRACKER," I TOLD HIM.
WELL, ANYWAY... GOOD LUCK, SWEETIE !
BYE, EVERYBODY! THANKS A LOT!

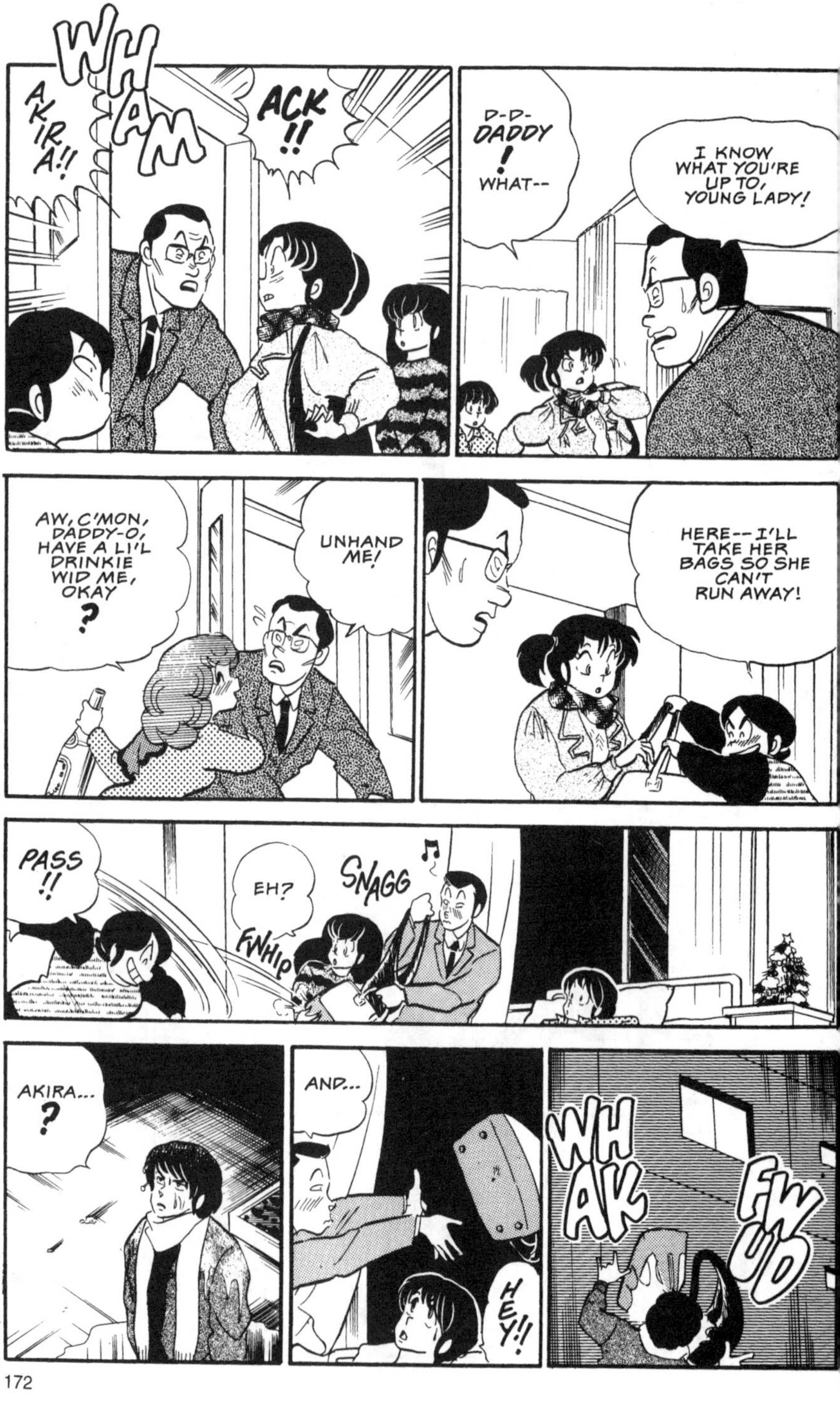
WHAM
AKIRA!!
ACK!!
D-D-DADDY! WHAT--
I KNOW WHAT YOU'RE UP TO, YOUNG LADY!
AW, C'MON, DADDY-O, HAVE A LI'L DRINKIE WID ME, OKAY?
UNHAND ME!
HERE--I'LL TAKE HER BAGS SO SHE CAN'T RUN AWAY!
PASS!!
EH?
SNAGG
FWHIP
AKIRA...?
AND...
HEY!!
WHAK
FWUD

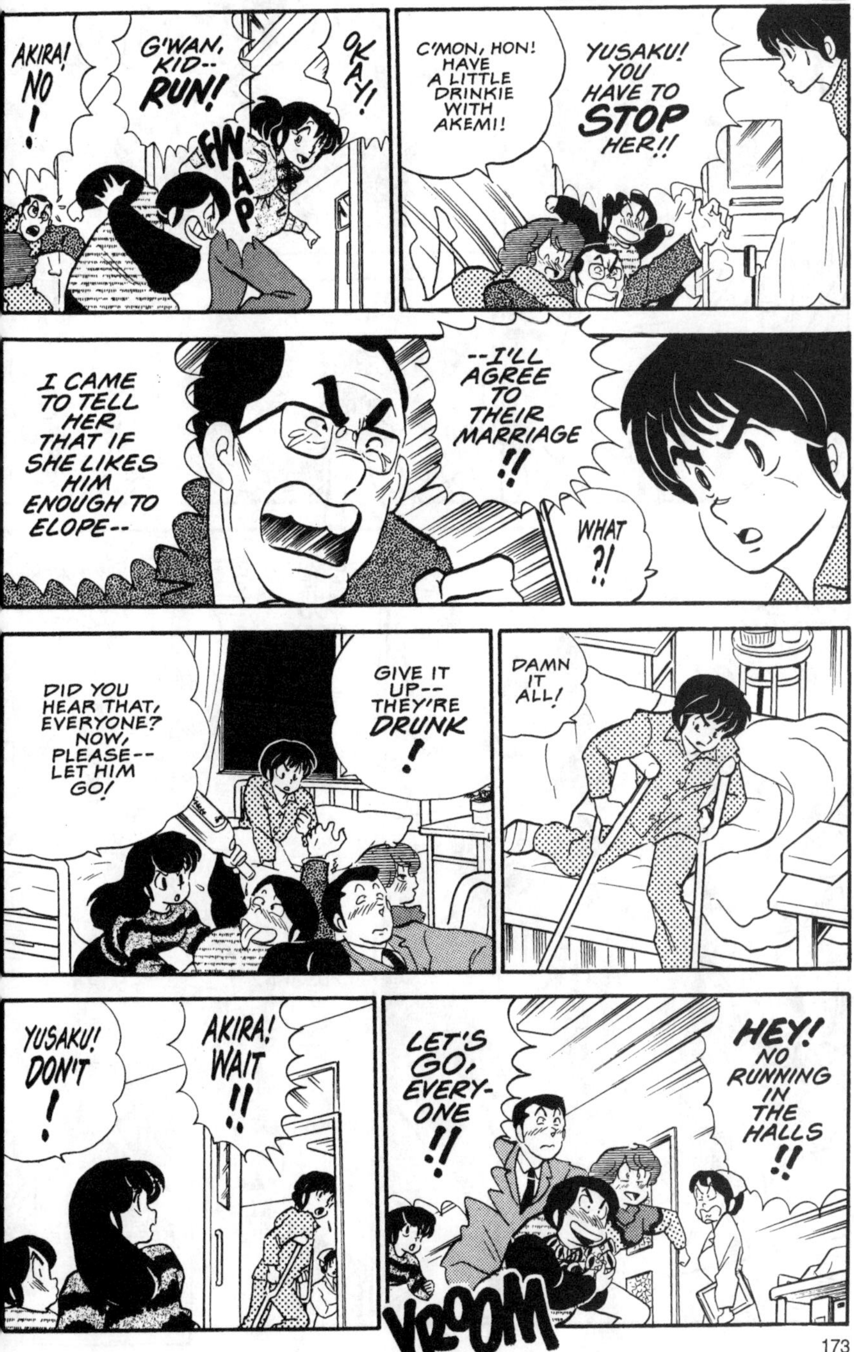
AKIRA! NO!
G'WAN, KID-- RUN!
OKAY!
FWAP
C'MON, HON! HAVE A LITTLE DRINKIE WITH AKEMI!
YUSAKU! YOU HAVE TO STOP HER!!
I CAME TO TELL HER THAT IF SHE LIKES HIM ENOUGH TO ELOPE--
--I'LL AGREE TO THEIR MARRIAGE!!
WHAT?!
DID YOU HEAR THAT, EVERYONE? NOW, PLEASE-- LET HIM GO!
GIVE IT UP-- THEY'RE DRUNK!
DAMN IT ALL!
YUSAKU! DON'T!
AKIRA! WAIT!!
LET'S GO, EVERY-ONE!!
HEY! NO RUNNING IN THE HALLS!!
VROOM

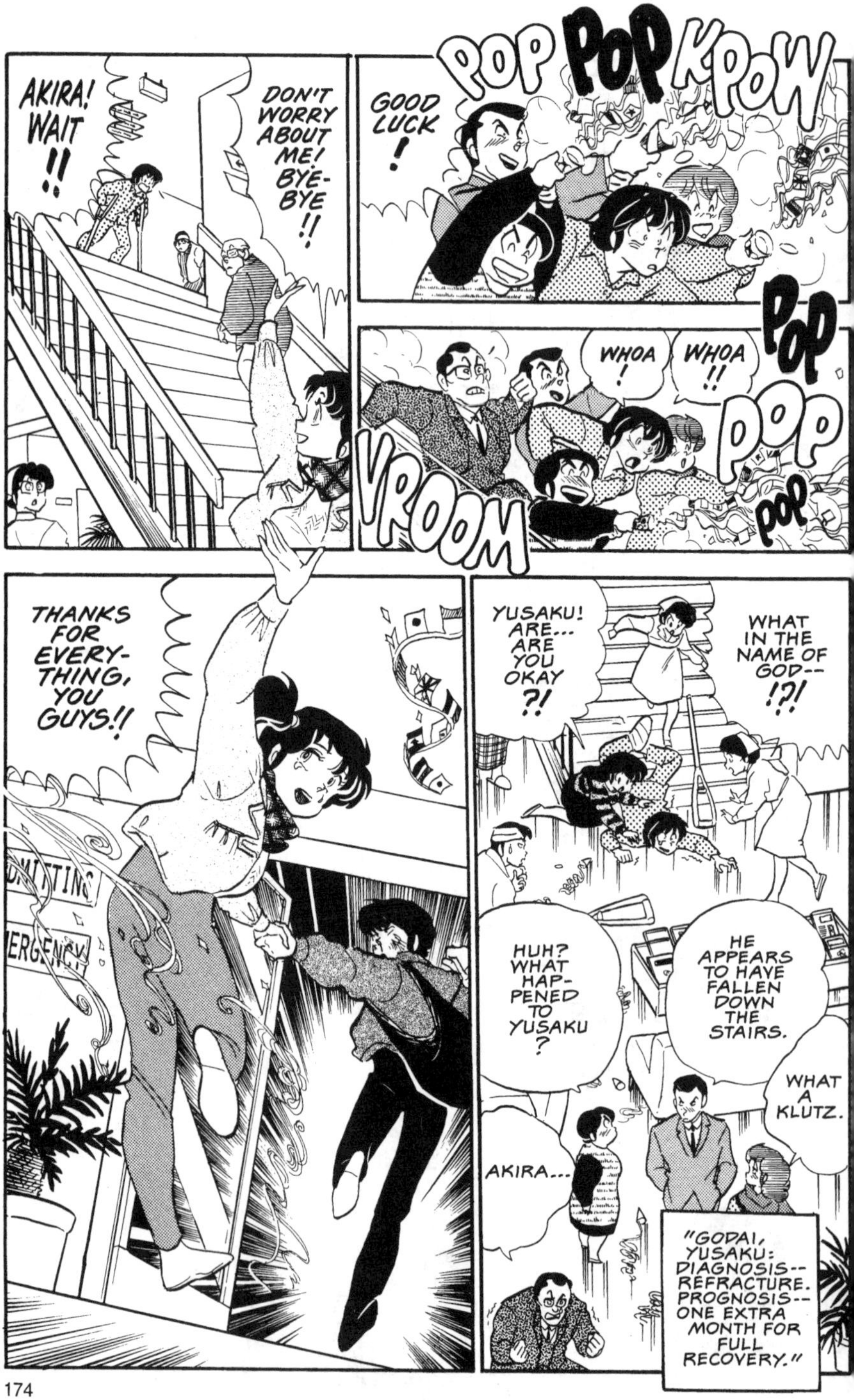
AKIRA! WAIT !!
DON'T WORRY ABOUT ME! BYE-BYE !!
GOOD LUCK !
POP POP KPOW
WHOA !
WHOA !!
POP
POP
POP
POP
VROOM
THANKS FOR EVERY-THING, YOU GUYS!!
YUSAKU! ARE... ARE YOU OKAY ?!
WHAT IN THE NAME OF GOD-- !?!
HUH? WHAT HAP-PENED TO YUSAKU ?
HE APPEARS TO HAVE FALLEN DOWN THE STAIRS.
WHAT A KLUTZ.
AKIRA...
"GODAI, YUSAKU: DIAGNOSIS--REFRACTURE. PROGNOSIS--ONE EXTRA MONTH FOR FULL RECOVERY."

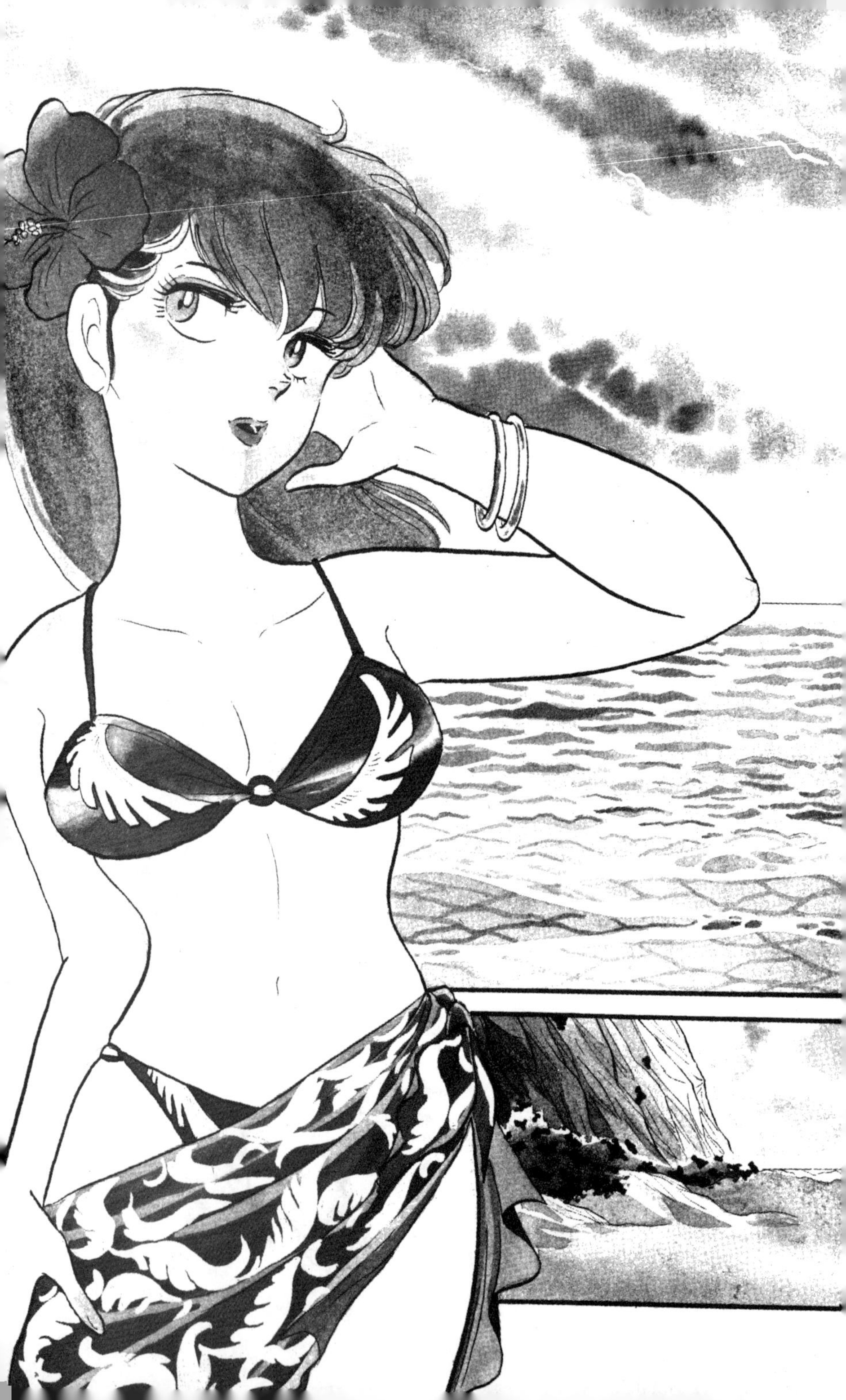

THE LOST EPISODE
YUSAKU'S ISLAND

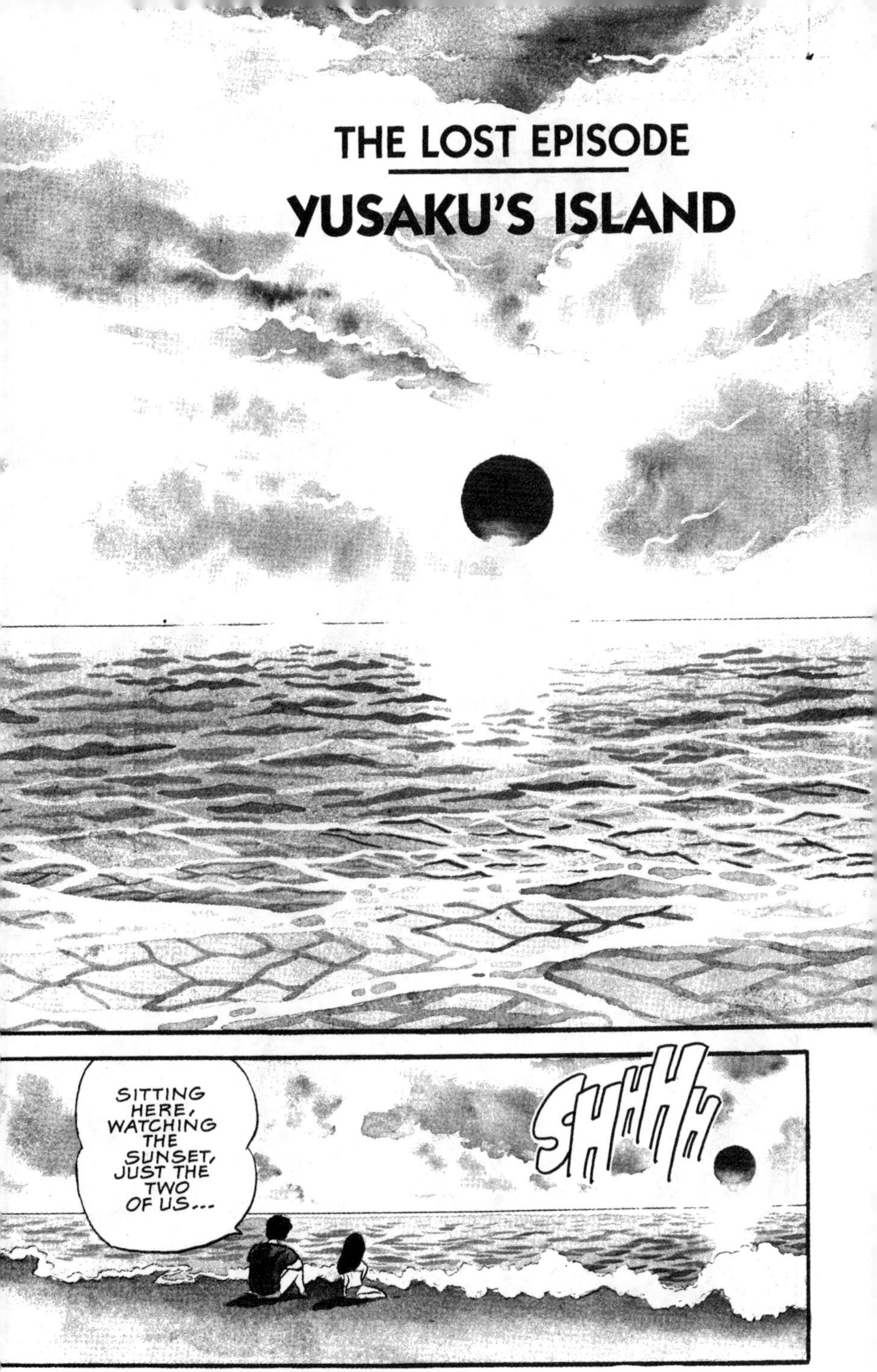
SITTING HERE, WATCHING THE SUNSET, JUST THE TWO OF US...
SHHHH

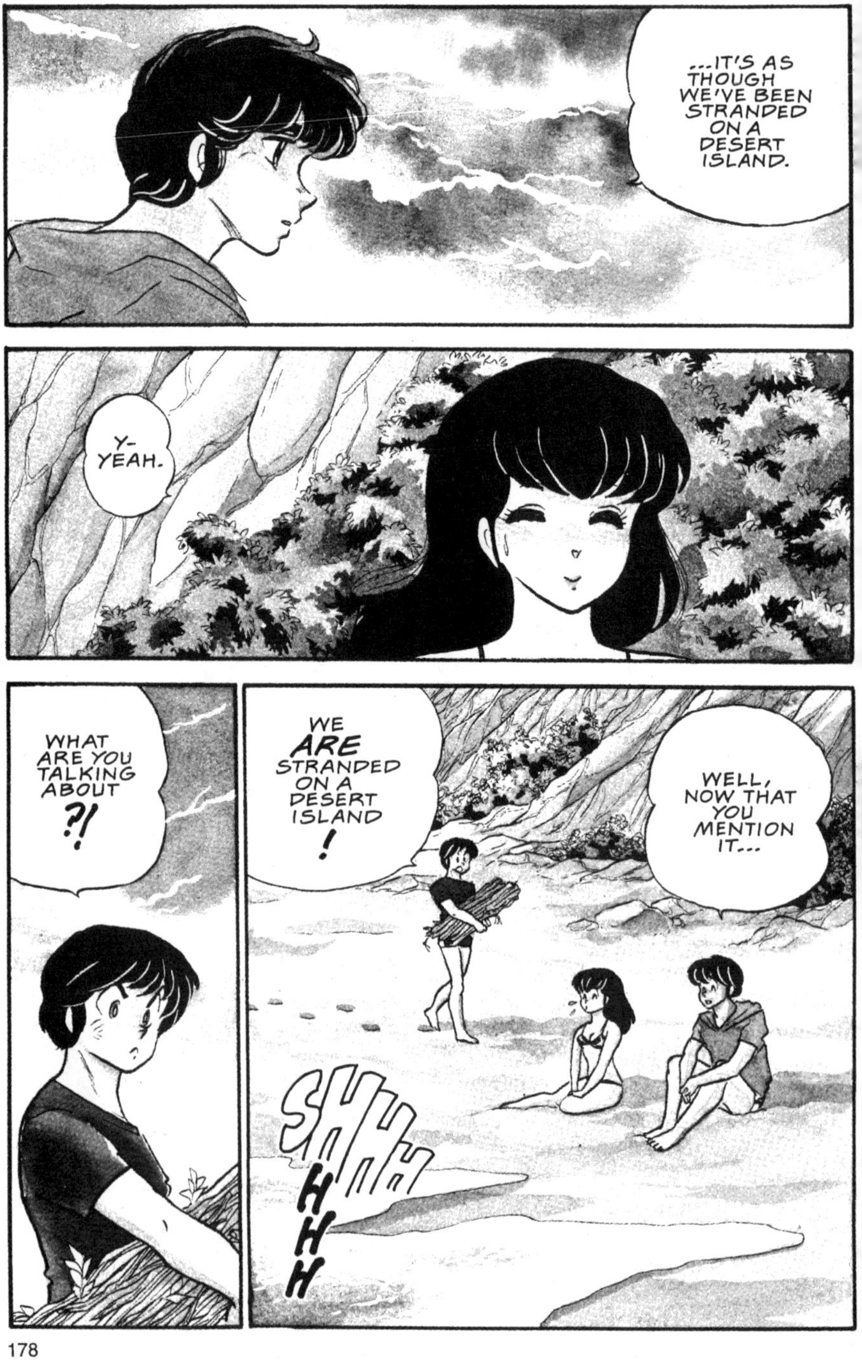
...IT'S AS THOUGH WE'VE BEEN STRANDED ON A DESERT ISLAND.
Y-YEAH.
WHAT ARE YOU TALKING ABOUT ?!
WE ARE STRANDED ON A DESERT ISLAND !
WELL, NOW THAT YOU MENTION IT...
SHHHH
HHHH

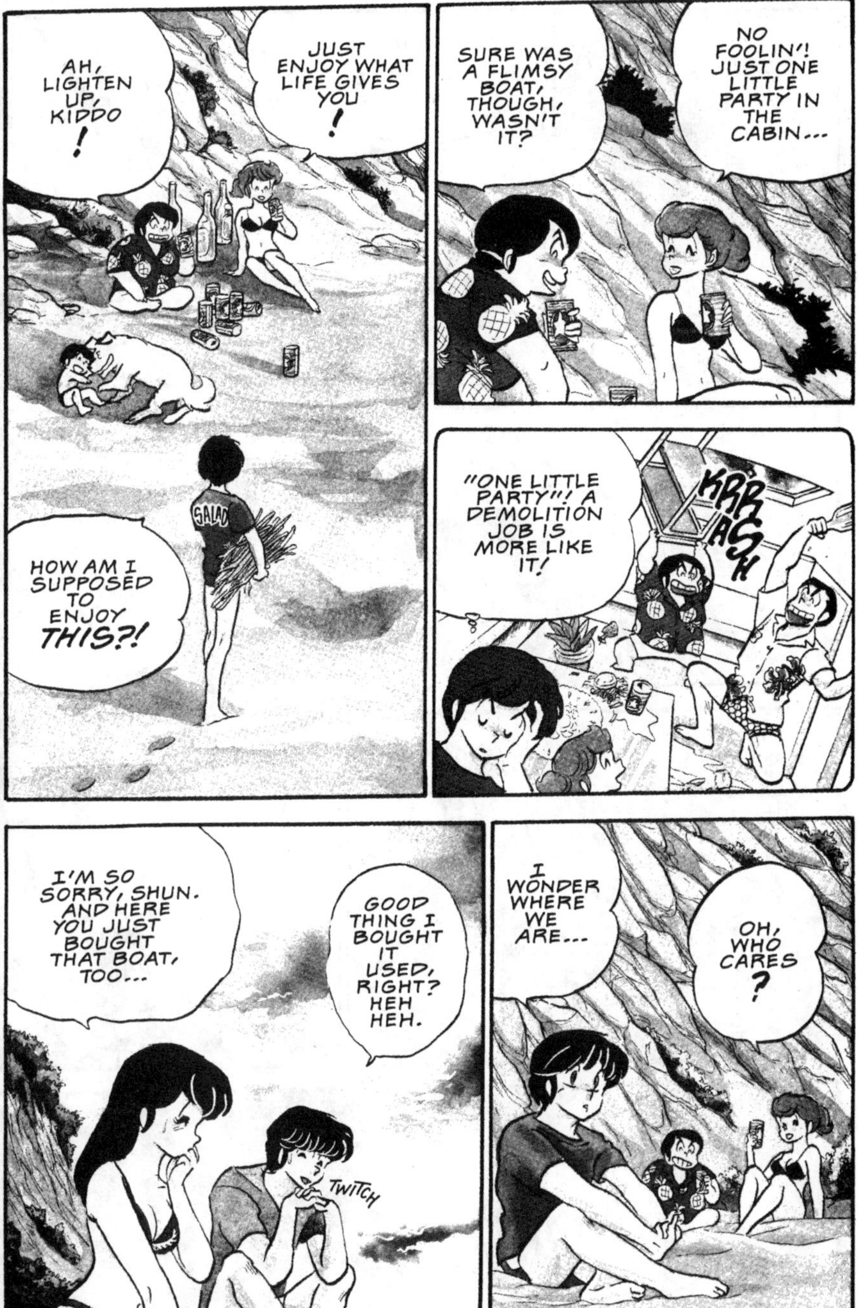
AH, LIGHTEN UP, KIDDO!
JUST ENJOY WHAT LIFE GIVES YOU!
SALAD
HOW AM I SUPPOSED TO ENJOY THIS?!
SURE WAS A FLIMSY BOAT, THOUGH, WASN'T IT?
NO FOOLIN'! JUST ONE LITTLE PARTY IN THE CABIN...
"ONE LITTLE PARTY"! A DEMOLITION JOB IS MORE LIKE IT!
KRRASH
I'M SO SORRY, SHUN. AND HERE YOU JUST BOUGHT THAT BOAT, TOO...
GOOD THING I BOUGHT IT USED, RIGHT? HEH HEH.
TWITCH
I WONDER WHERE WE ARE...
OH, WHO CARES?

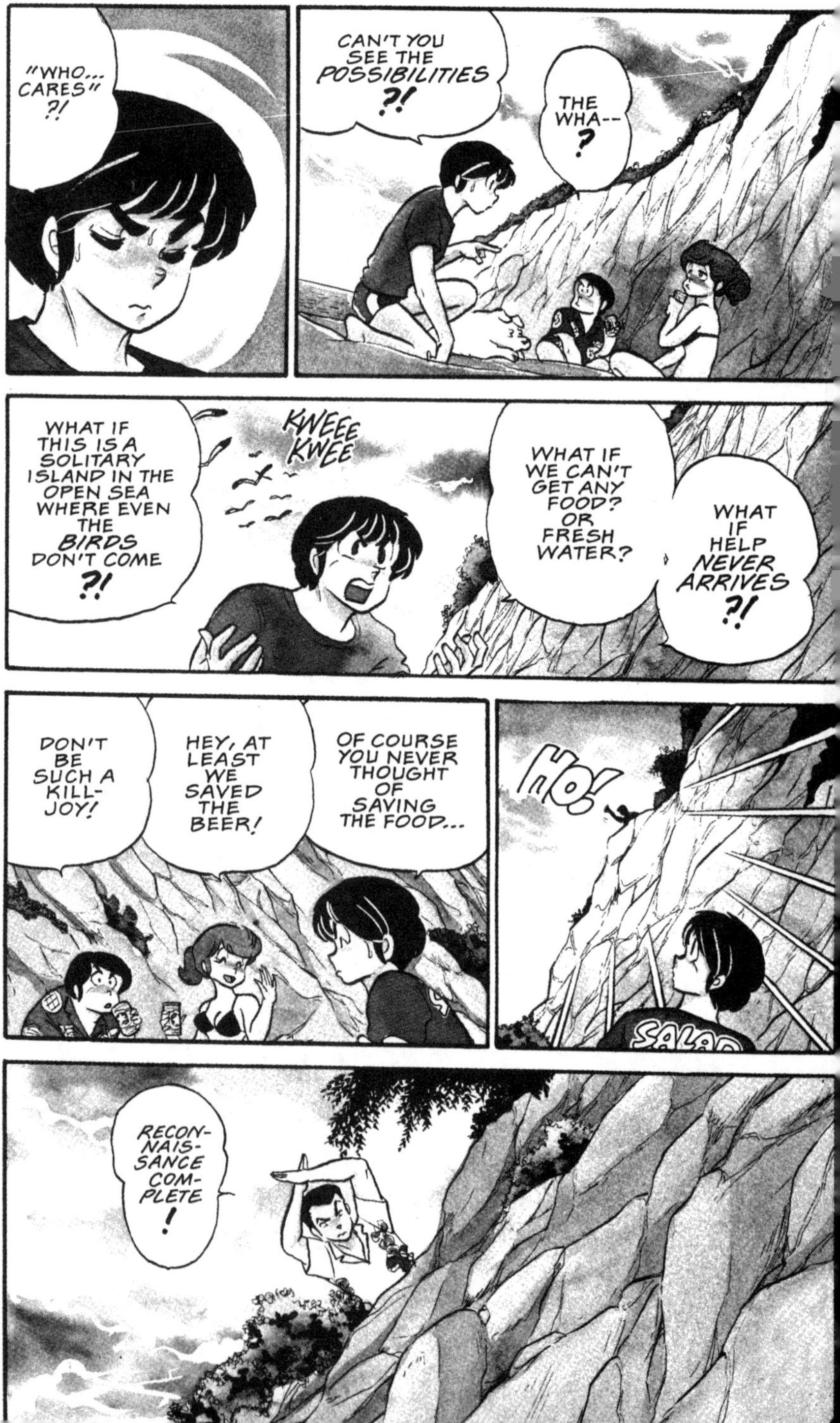
"WHO... CARES" ?!
CAN'T YOU SEE THE POSSIBILITIES ?!
THE WHA-- ?
WHAT IF THIS IS A SOLITARY ISLAND IN THE OPEN SEA WHERE EVEN THE BIRDS DON'T COME ?!
KWEEE KWEE
WHAT IF WE CAN'T GET ANY FOOD? OR FRESH WATER?
WHAT IF HELP NEVER ARRIVES ?!
DON'T BE SUCH A KILL-JOY!
HEY, AT LEAST WE SAVED THE BEER!
OF COURSE YOU NEVER THOUGHT OF SAVING THE FOOD...
HO!
SALAD
RECON-NAIS-SANCE COM-PLETE !

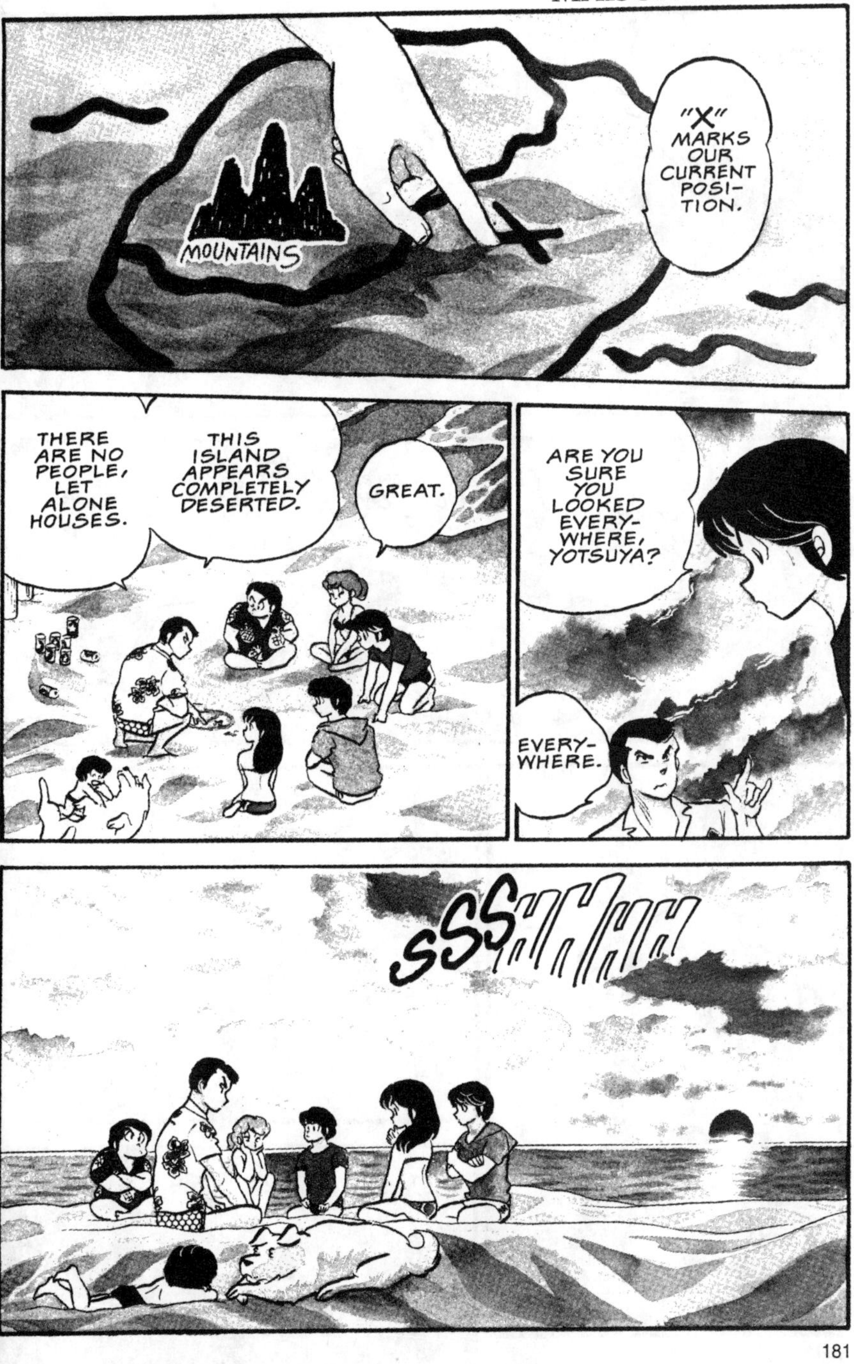
MOUNTAINS
"X" MARKS OUR CURRENT POSI-TION.
THERE ARE NO PEOPLE, LET ALONE HOUSES.
THIS ISLAND APPEARS COMPLETELY DESERTED.
GREAT.
ARE YOU SURE YOU LOOKED EVERY-WHERE, YOTSUYA?
EVERY-WHERE.
SSSHHHH

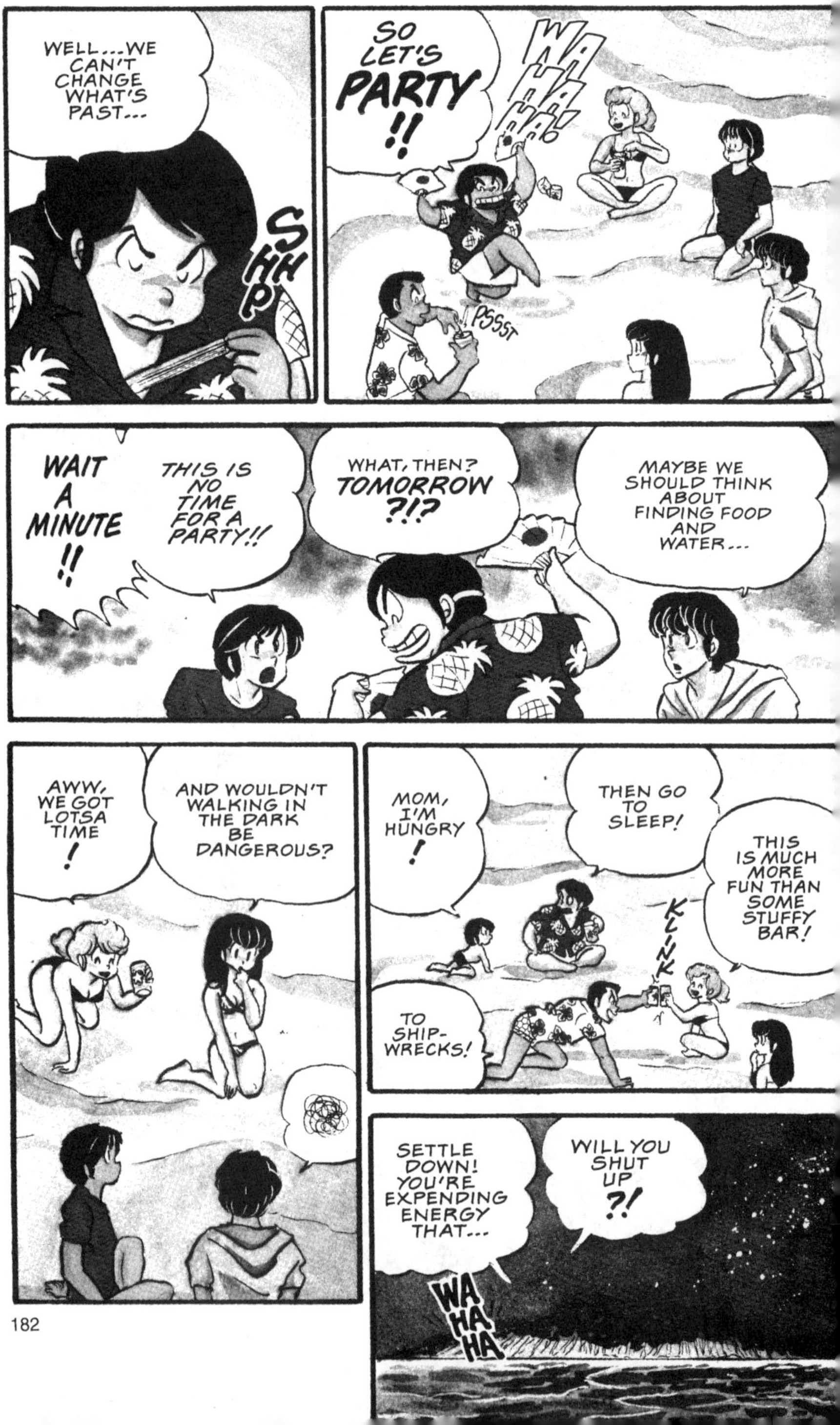
WELL...WE CAN'T CHANGE WHAT'S PAST...
SHHP
SO LET'S PARTY!!
WAHAHAHA!
PSSST
WAIT A MINUTE!!
THIS IS NO TIME FOR A PARTY!!
WHAT, THEN? TOMORROW?!?
MAYBE WE SHOULD THINK ABOUT FINDING FOOD AND WATER...
AWW, WE GOT LOTSA TIME!
AND WOULDN'T WALKING IN THE DARK BE DANGEROUS?
MOM, I'M HUNGRY!
THEN GO TO SLEEP!
THIS IS MUCH MORE FUN THAN SOME STUFFY BAR!
KLINK
TO SHIP-WRECKS!
SETTLE DOWN! YOU'RE EXPENDING ENERGY THAT...
WILL YOU SHUT UP?!
WAHAHA

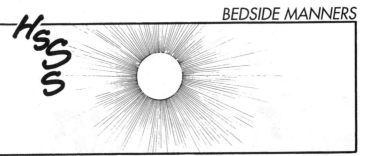

GET UP.

HEY, *GET UP!*

YOU'LL GET SUNSTROKE SLEEPING OUT HERE!

SNZXX!

LEA' ME 'LONE...

...I GODDA HANG-OVER...

HMM PH.

PLAY-TIME HAS TO END.

WILL YOU JOKERS LOOK AT THE REALITY HERE?!

WE ARE ACTUALLY STRANDED !!

SKRITCH SKRITCH

EEYAWW!

THIS IS NO TIME TO BE DRUNK ON THE BEACH!

HAIR OF THE DOG?

YOU SAID IT!

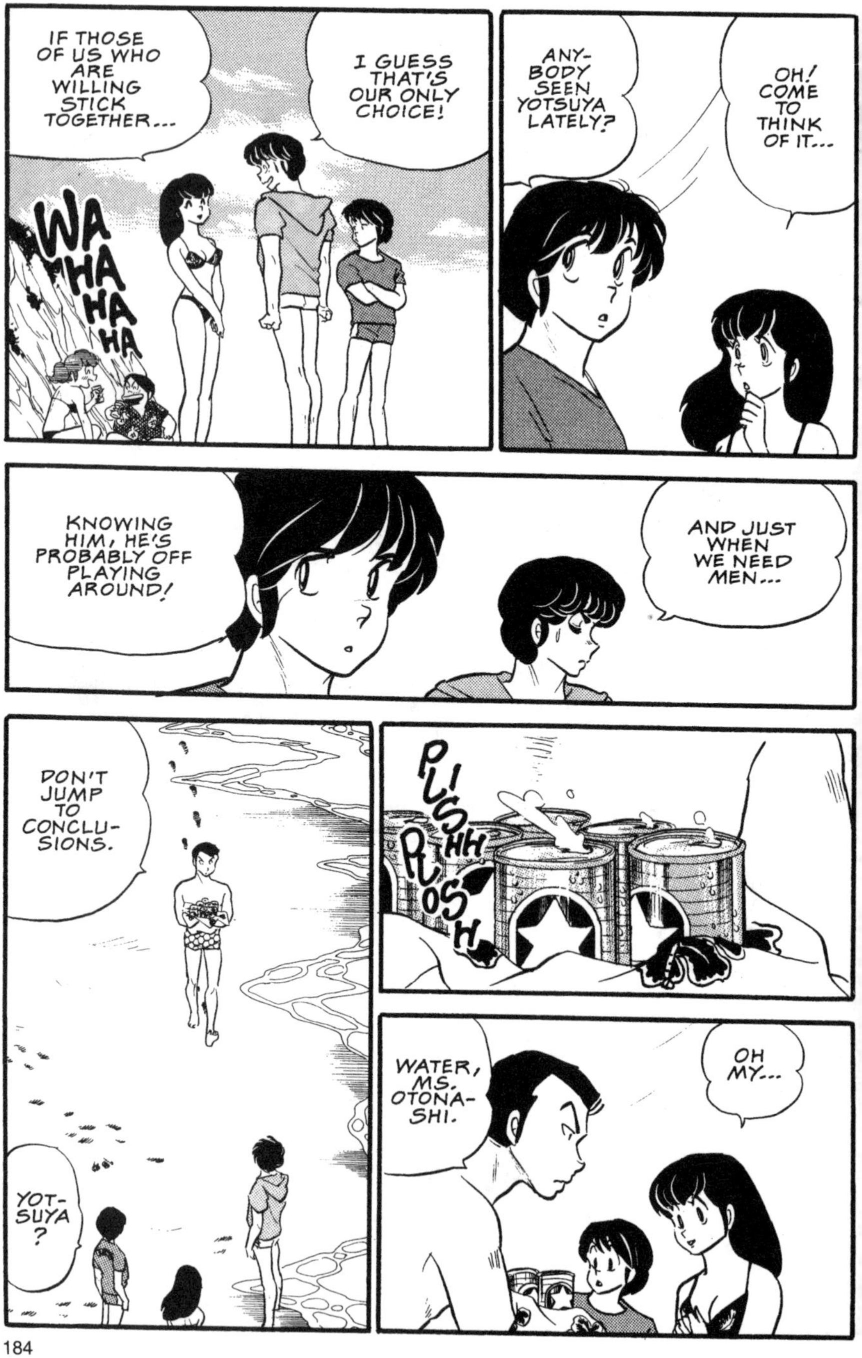
IF THOSE OF US WHO ARE WILLING STICK TOGETHER...
I GUESS THAT'S OUR ONLY CHOICE!
WA HA HA HA HA
ANY-BODY SEEN YOTSUYA LATELY?
OH! COME TO THINK OF IT...
KNOWING HIM, HE'S PROBABLY OFF PLAYING AROUND!
AND JUST WHEN WE NEED MEN...
DON'T JUMP TO CONCLU-SIONS.
YOT-SUYA?
PLUSHH
PLOSH
WATER, MS. OTONA-SHI.
OH MY...

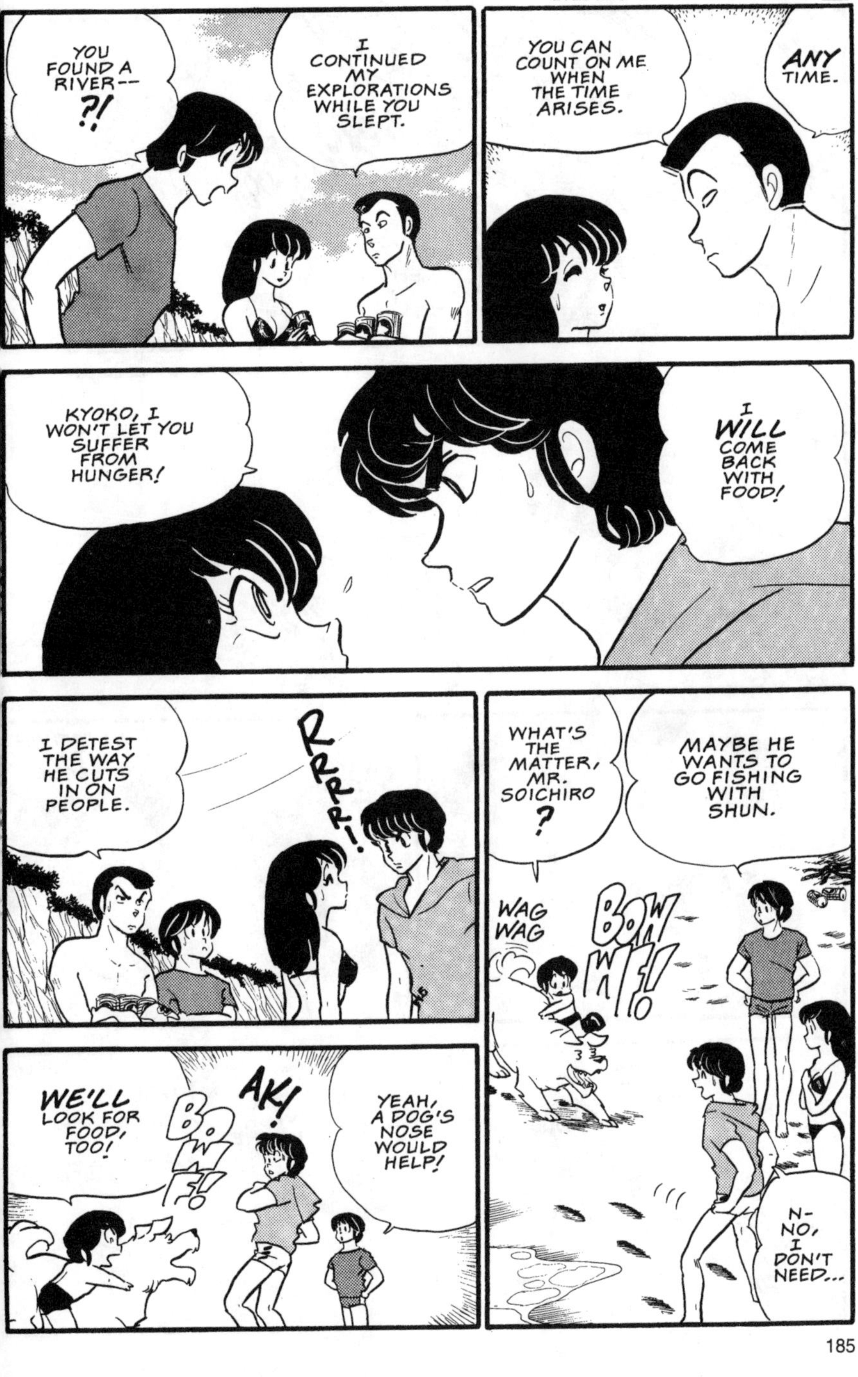
YOU FOUND A RIVER-- ?!
I CONTINUED MY EXPLORATIONS WHILE YOU SLEPT.
YOU CAN COUNT ON ME WHEN THE TIME ARISES.
ANY TIME.
KYOKO, I WON'T LET YOU SUFFER FROM HUNGER!
I WILL COME BACK WITH FOOD!
I DETEST THE WAY HE CUTS IN ON PEOPLE.
RRRR!
WE'LL LOOK FOR FOOD, TOO!
BOWF!
AK!
YEAH, A DOG'S NOSE WOULD HELP!
WHAT'S THE MATTER, MR. SOICHIRO?
MAYBE HE WANTS TO GO FISHING WITH SHUN.
WAG WAG
BOWWF!!
N-NO, I DON'T NEED...

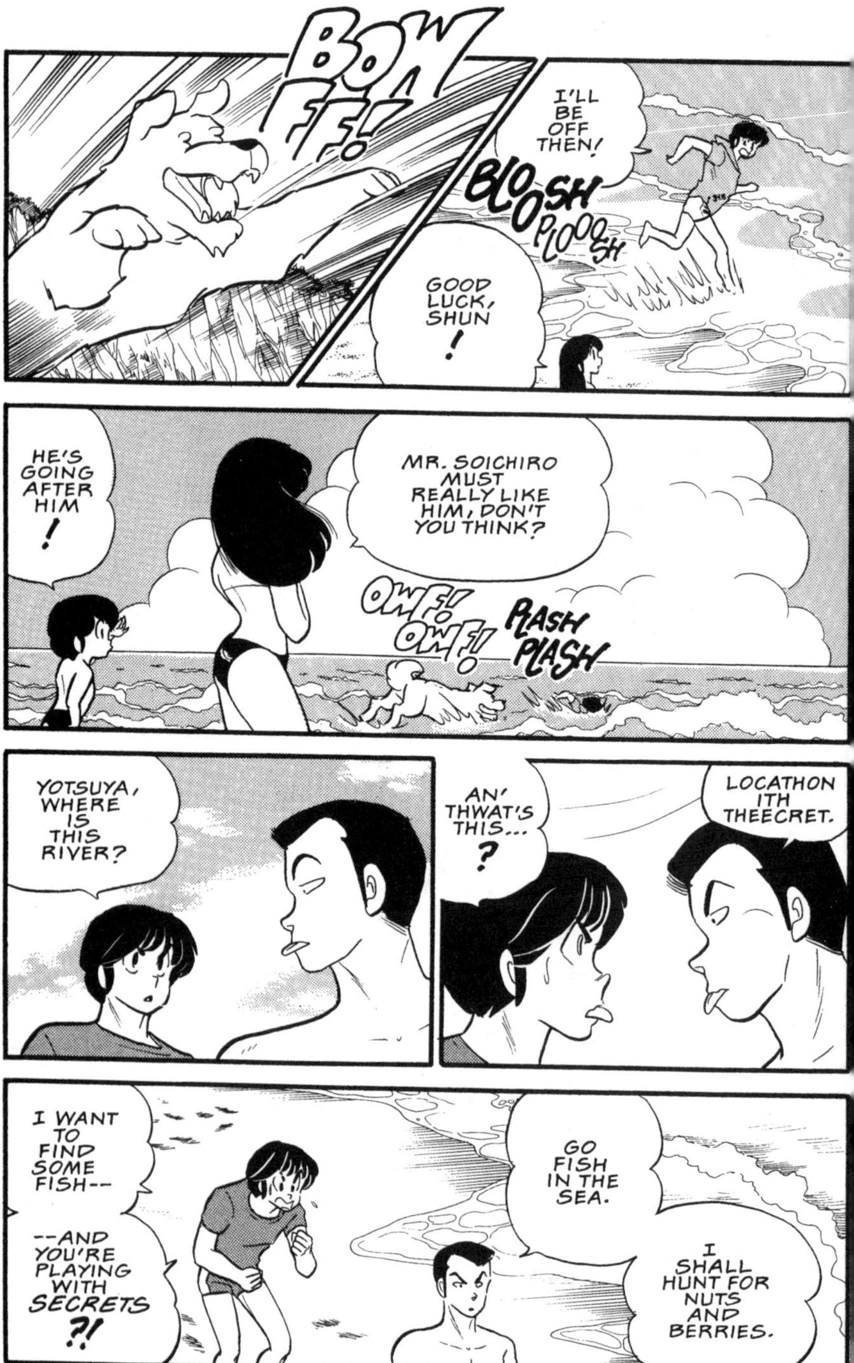
BOW FF!
I'LL BE OFF THEN!
BLOOSH PLOOOSH
GOOD LUCK, SHUN!
HE'S GOING AFTER HIM!
MR. SOICHIRO MUST REALLY LIKE HIM, DON'T YOU THINK?
OWF! OWF!
PLASH PLASH
YOTSUYA, WHERE IS THIS RIVER?
AN' THWAT'S THIS...?
LOCATHON ITH THEECRET.
I WANT TO FIND SOME FISH--
--AND YOU'RE PLAYING WITH SECRETS?!
GO FISH IN THE SEA.
I SHALL HUNT FOR NUTS AND BERRIES.

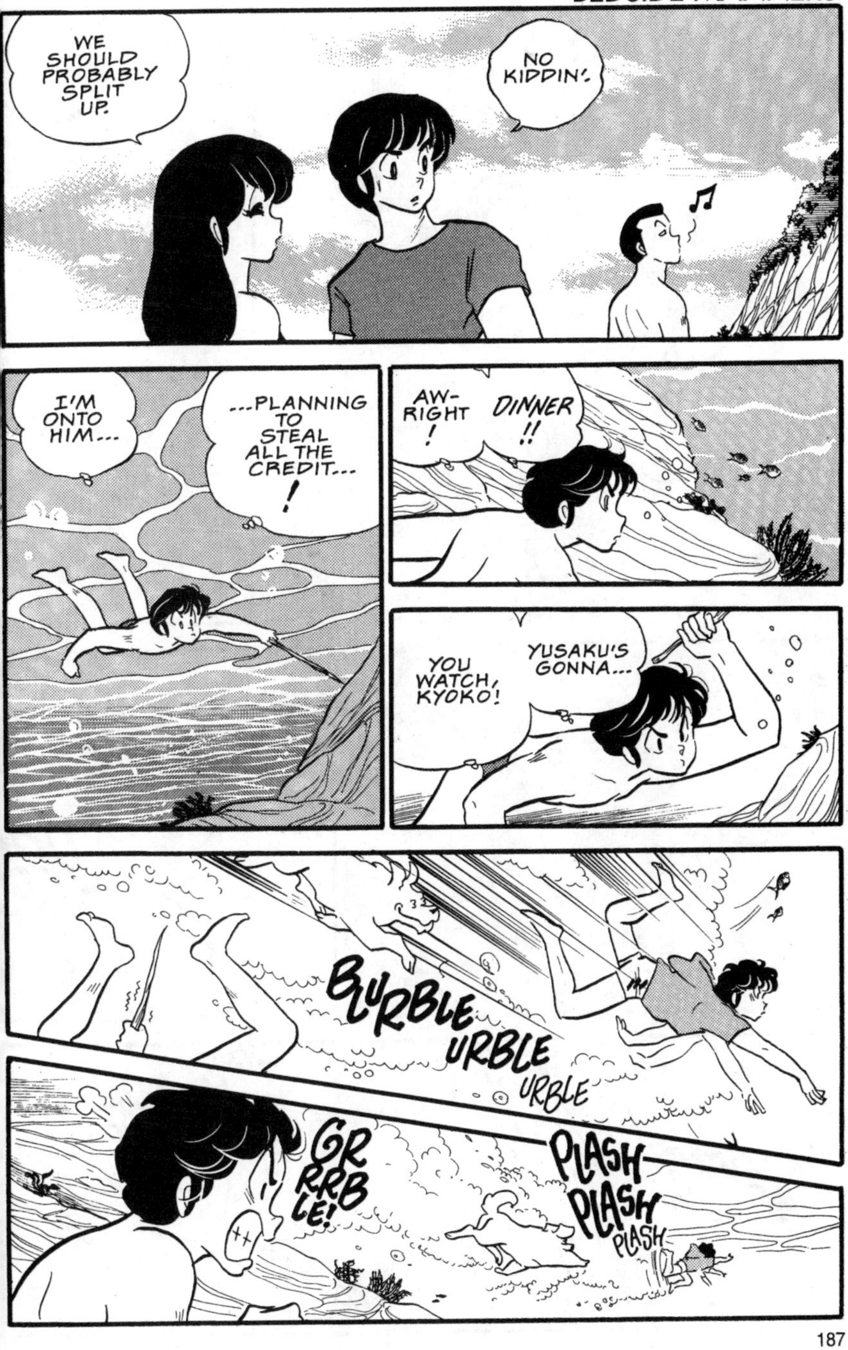
WE SHOULD PROBABLY SPLIT UP.
NO KIDDIN'.
I'M ONTO HIM...
...PLANNING TO STEAL ALL THE CREDIT...!
AW-RIGHT!
DINNER!!
YOU WATCH, KYOKO!
YUSAKU'S GONNA...
BLURBLE
URBLE
URBLE
GRRRBLE!
PLASH
PLASH
PLASH

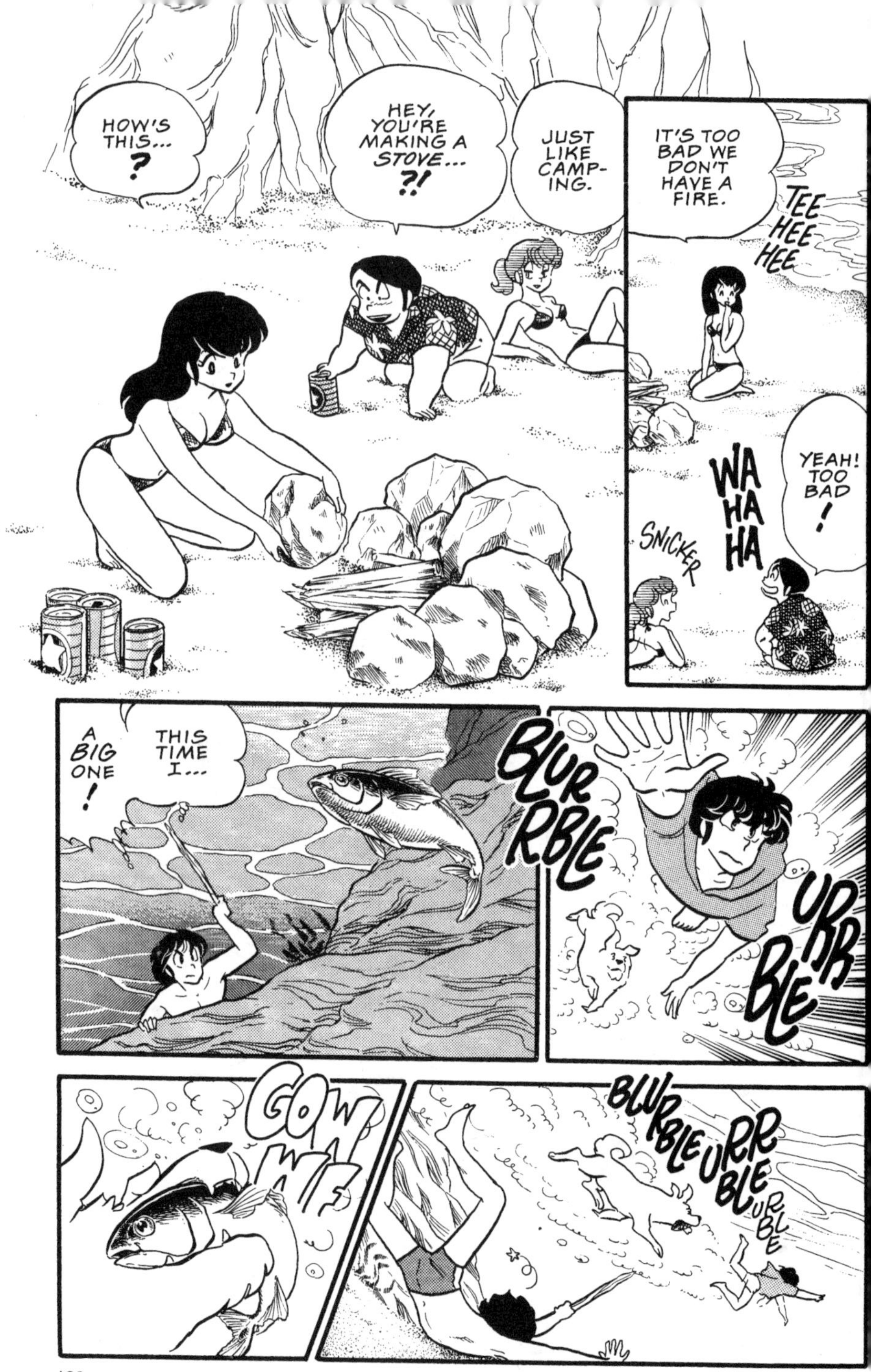

HOW'S THIS...?
HEY, YOU'RE MAKING A STOVE...?!
JUST LIKE CAMPING.
IT'S TOO BAD WE DON'T HAVE A FIRE.
TEE HEE HEE
YEAH! TOO BAD!
WA HA HA
SNICKER
A BIG ONE!
THIS TIME I...
BLURRBLE
URRBLE
GOWMF
BLURBLEURRBLEBLURBLE

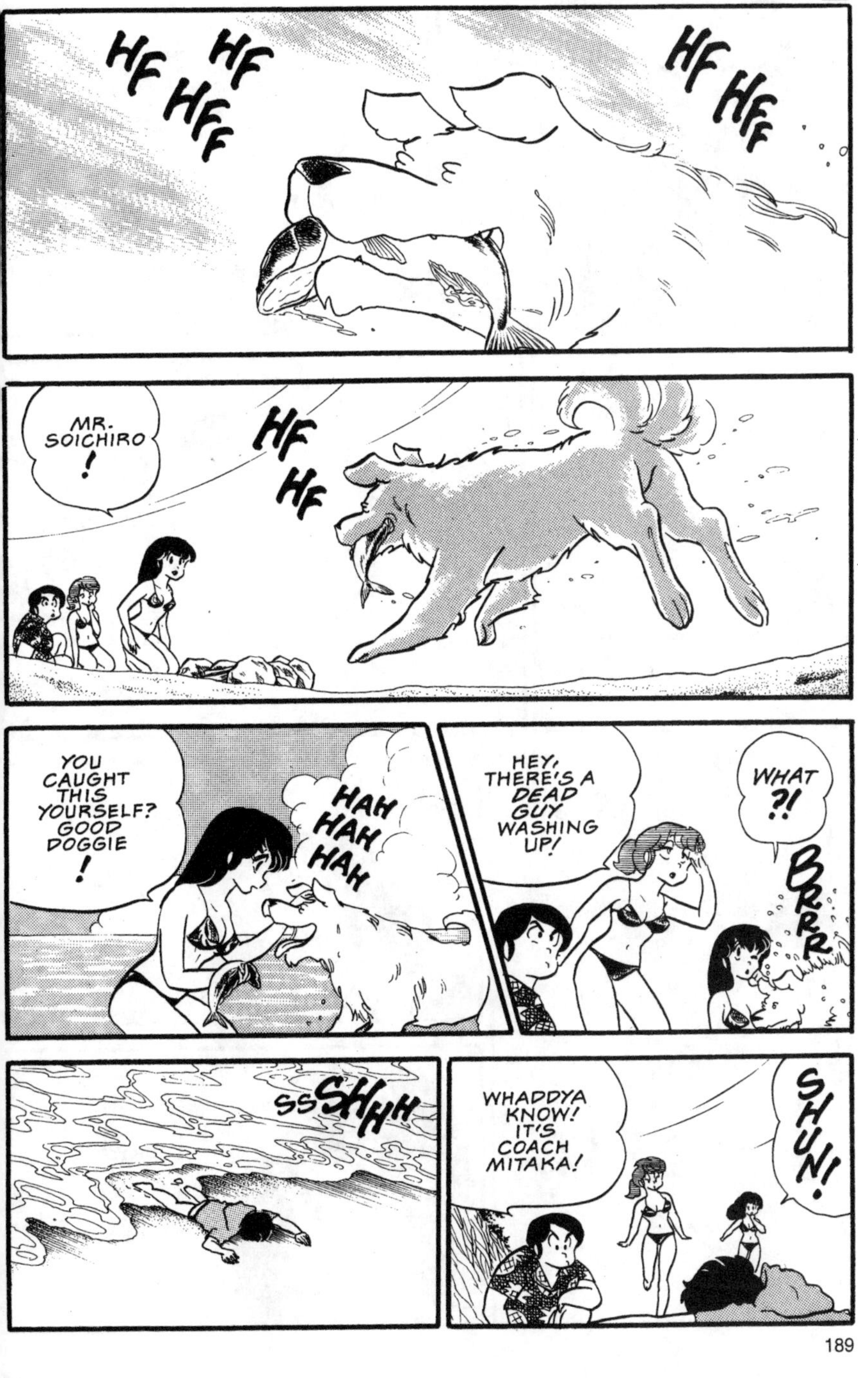
HF HF HFF
HF HFF
MR. SOICHIRO !
HF HF
YOU CAUGHT THIS YOURSELF? GOOD DOGGIE !
HAH HAH HAH
HEY, THERE'S A DEAD GUY WASHING UP!
WHAT ?!
BRRR
SSSHHH
WHADDYA KNOW! IT'S COACH MITAKA!
SHUN!

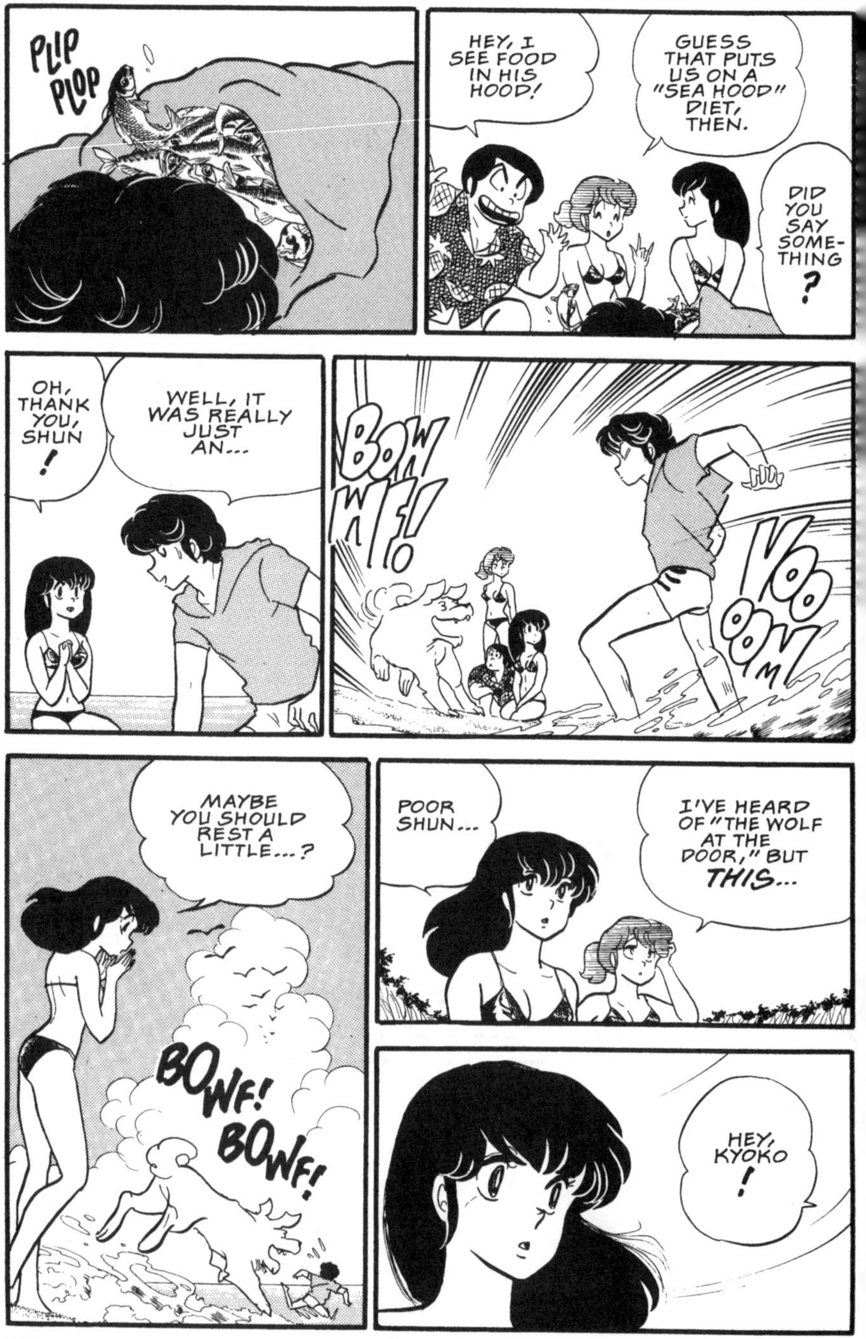
PLIP
PLOP
HEY, I SEE FOOD IN HIS HOOD!
GUESS THAT PUTS US ON A "SEA HOOD" DIET, THEN.
DID YOU SAY SOME-THING?
OH, THANK YOU, SHUN!
WELL, IT WAS REALLY JUST AN...
BOWWF!
VOOOOM
MAYBE YOU SHOULD REST A LITTLE...?
BOWF! BOWF!
POOR SHUN...
I'VE HEARD OF "THE WOLF AT THE DOOR," BUT THIS...
HEY, KYOKO!

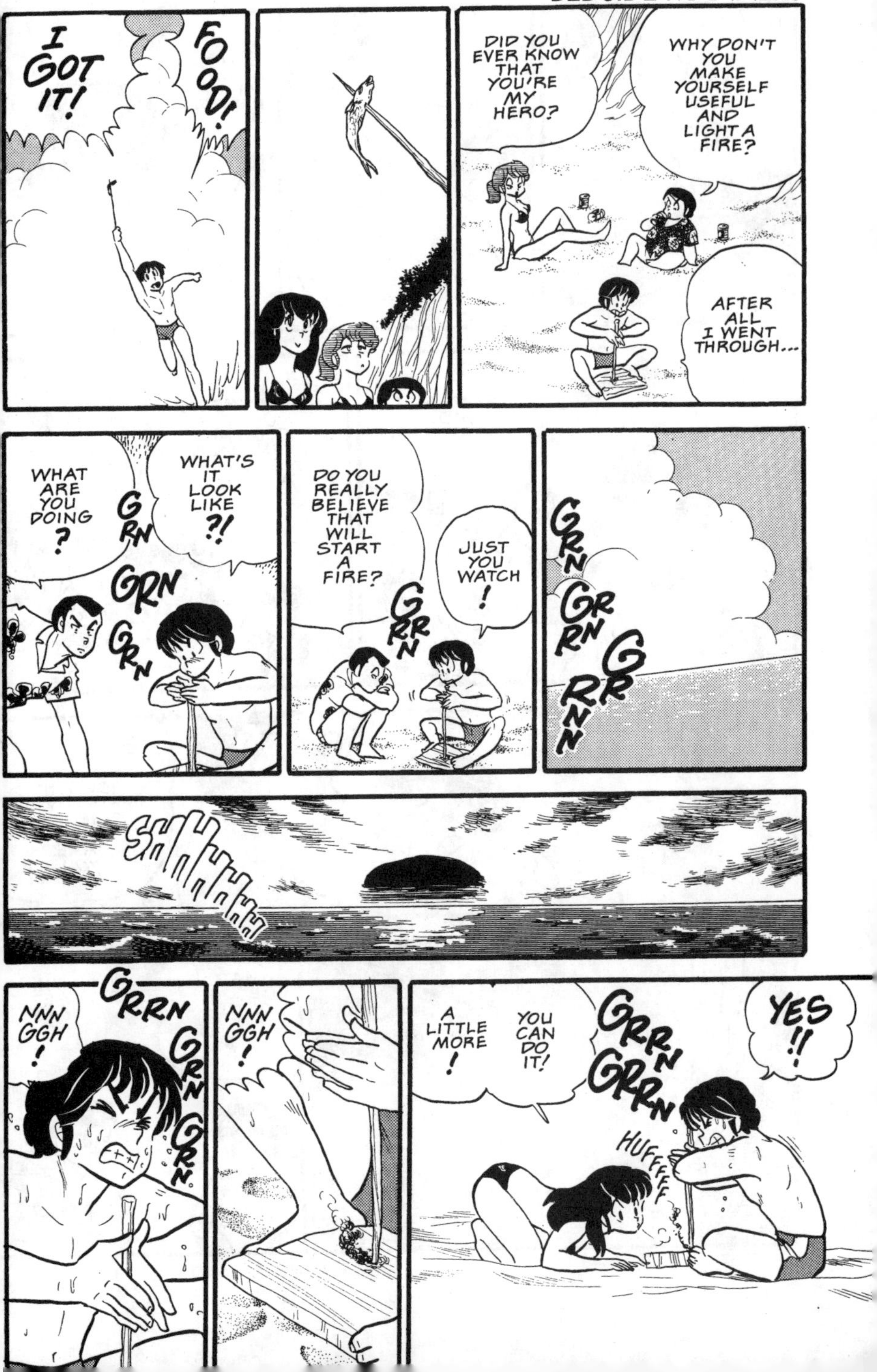
I GOT IT!
FOOD!
DID YOU EVER KNOW THAT YOU'RE MY HERO?
WHY DON'T YOU MAKE YOURSELF USEFUL AND LIGHT A FIRE?
AFTER ALL I WENT THROUGH...
WHAT ARE YOU DOING?
WHAT'S IT LOOK LIKE?!
GRN
GRN
GRN
DO YOU REALLY BELIEVE THAT WILL START A FIRE?
JUST YOU WATCH!
GRRN
GRN
GRRN
GRRNN
SHHHHHH
NNNGGH!
GRRN
GRN
GRN
NNNGGH!
A LITTLE MORE!
YOU CAN DO IT!
GRRN
GRRN
YES!!
HUFFFFF

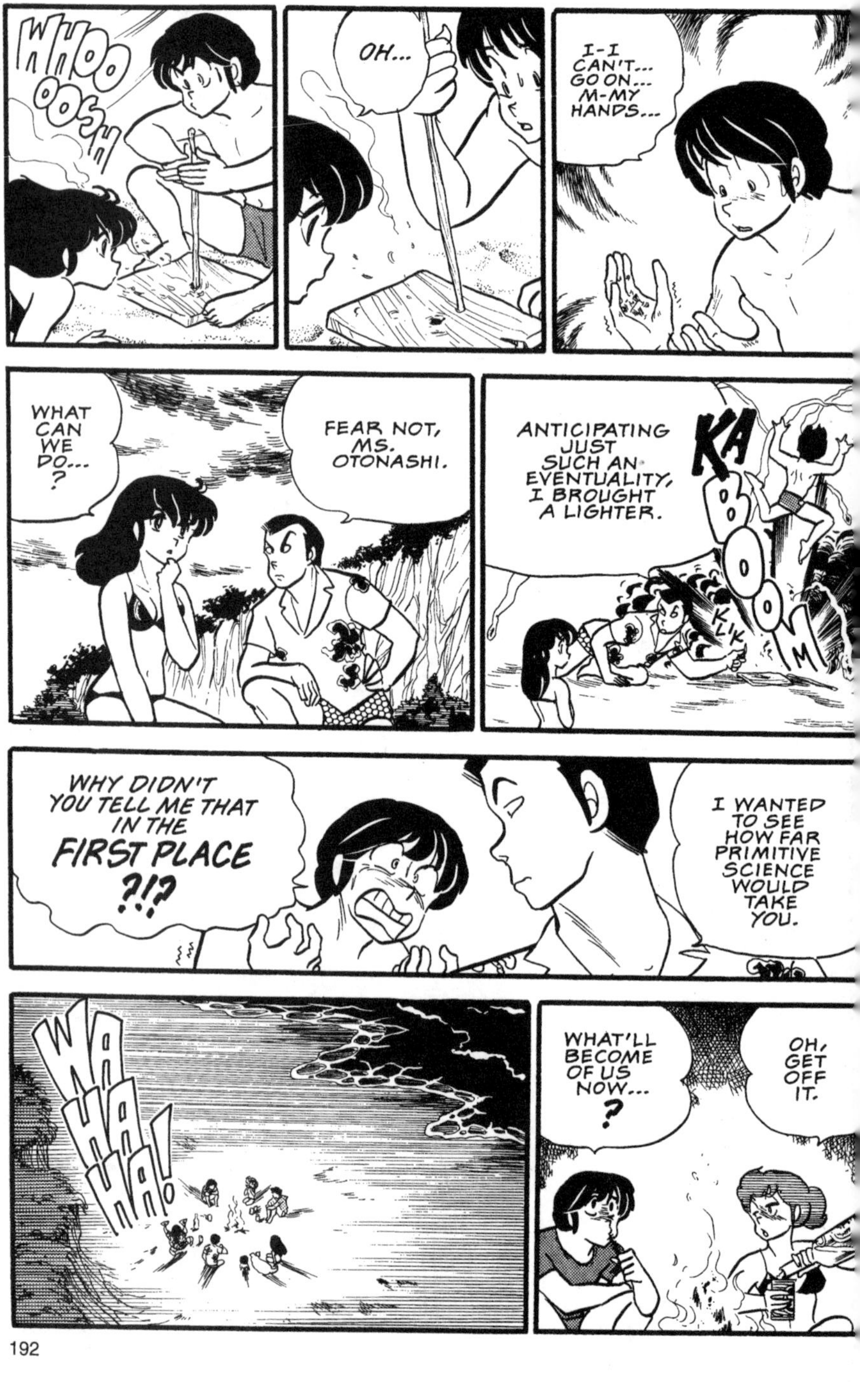
WHOOOOOSH
OH...
I-I CAN'T... GO ON... M-MY HANDS...
WHAT CAN WE DO...?
FEAR NOT, MS. OTONASHI.
ANTICIPATING JUST SUCH AN EVENTUALITY, I BROUGHT A LIGHTER.
KA BOOOOM
KLIK
WHY DIDN'T YOU TELL ME THAT IN THE FIRST PLACE ?!?
I WANTED TO SEE HOW FAR PRIMITIVE SCIENCE WOULD TAKE YOU.
WA HA HA HA!
WHAT'LL BECOME OF US NOW...?
OH, GET OFF IT.

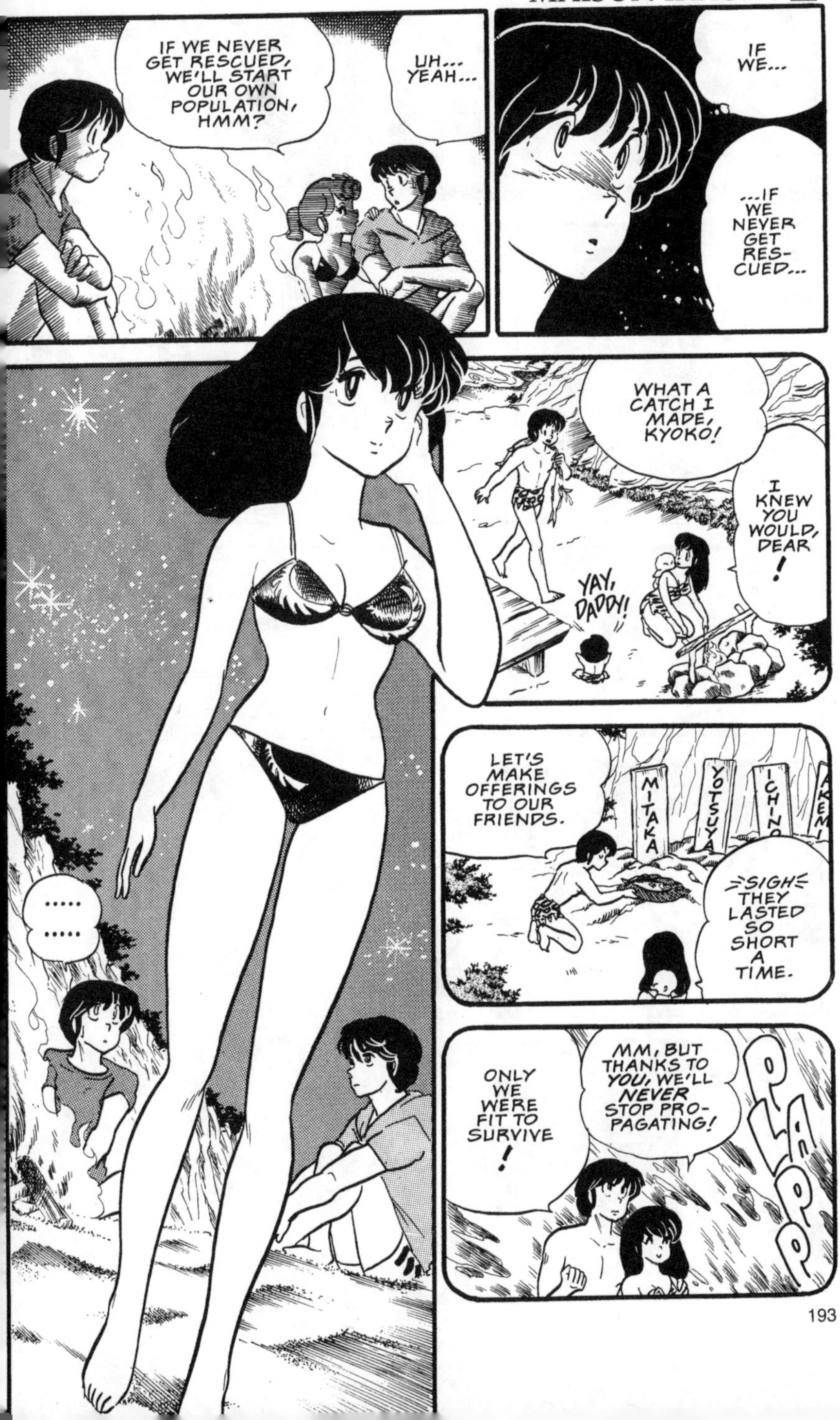
IF WE NEVER GET RESCUED, WE'LL START OUR OWN POPULATION, HMM?
UH... YEAH...
IF WE...
...IF WE NEVER GET RES-CUED...
......
......
WHAT A CATCH I MADE, KYOKO!
YAY, DADDY!
I KNEW YOU WOULD, DEAR!
LET'S MAKE OFFERINGS TO OUR FRIENDS.
MITAKA
YOTSUYA
ICHINO
AKEMI
≈SIGH≈ THEY LASTED SO SHORT A TIME.
ONLY WE WERE FIT TO SURVIVE!
MM, BUT THANKS TO YOU, WE'LL NEVER STOP PRO-PAGATING!

SSSSSSHHHHHHHSSSSSHHHH

SNRZZ

HMN
MN...
NN
MN...

ZZ
Z
Z
Z

I CAN'T
SEEM
TO
SLEEP...

F-FUNNY...
ME
NEITHER...

SHHHH

I CAN'T
BELIEVE
MY
GOOD
LUCK...

YES,
THE MEN
MUST
BE
ESPECI-
ALLY
TIRED.

THEY
WORKED
SO
HARD.

STAB

THEY'RE
ALL
SOUND
ASLEEP...
AREN'T
THEY?

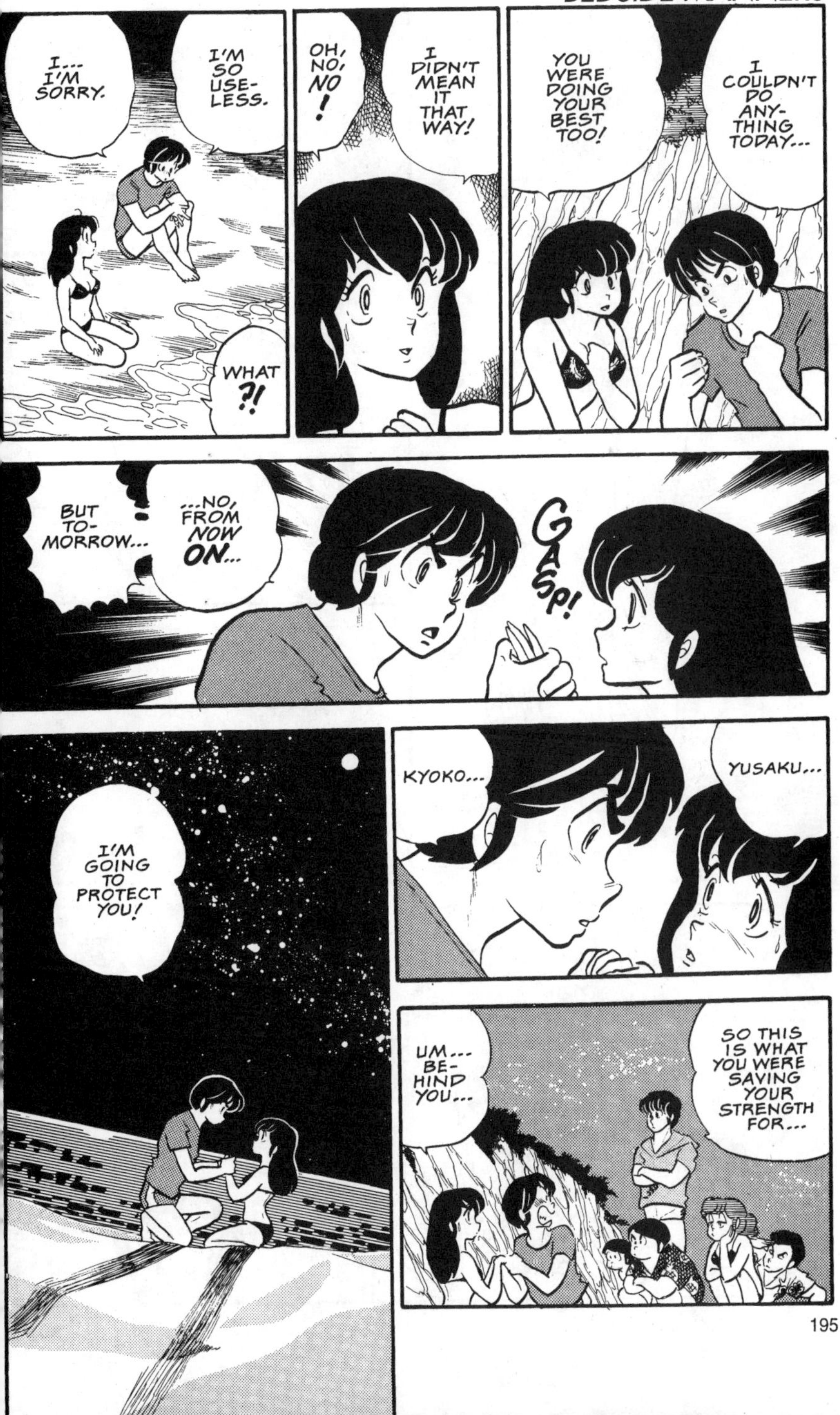
I... I'M SORRY.
I'M SO USE-LESS.
WHAT ?!
OH, NO, NO!
I DIDN'T MEAN IT THAT WAY!
YOU WERE DOING YOUR BEST TOO!
I COULDN'T DO ANY-THING TODAY...
BUT TO-MORROW...
...NO, FROM NOW ON...
GASP!
I'M GOING TO PROTECT YOU!
KYOKO...
YUSAKU...
UM... BE-HIND YOU...
SO THIS IS WHAT YOU WERE SAVING YOUR STRENGTH FOR...

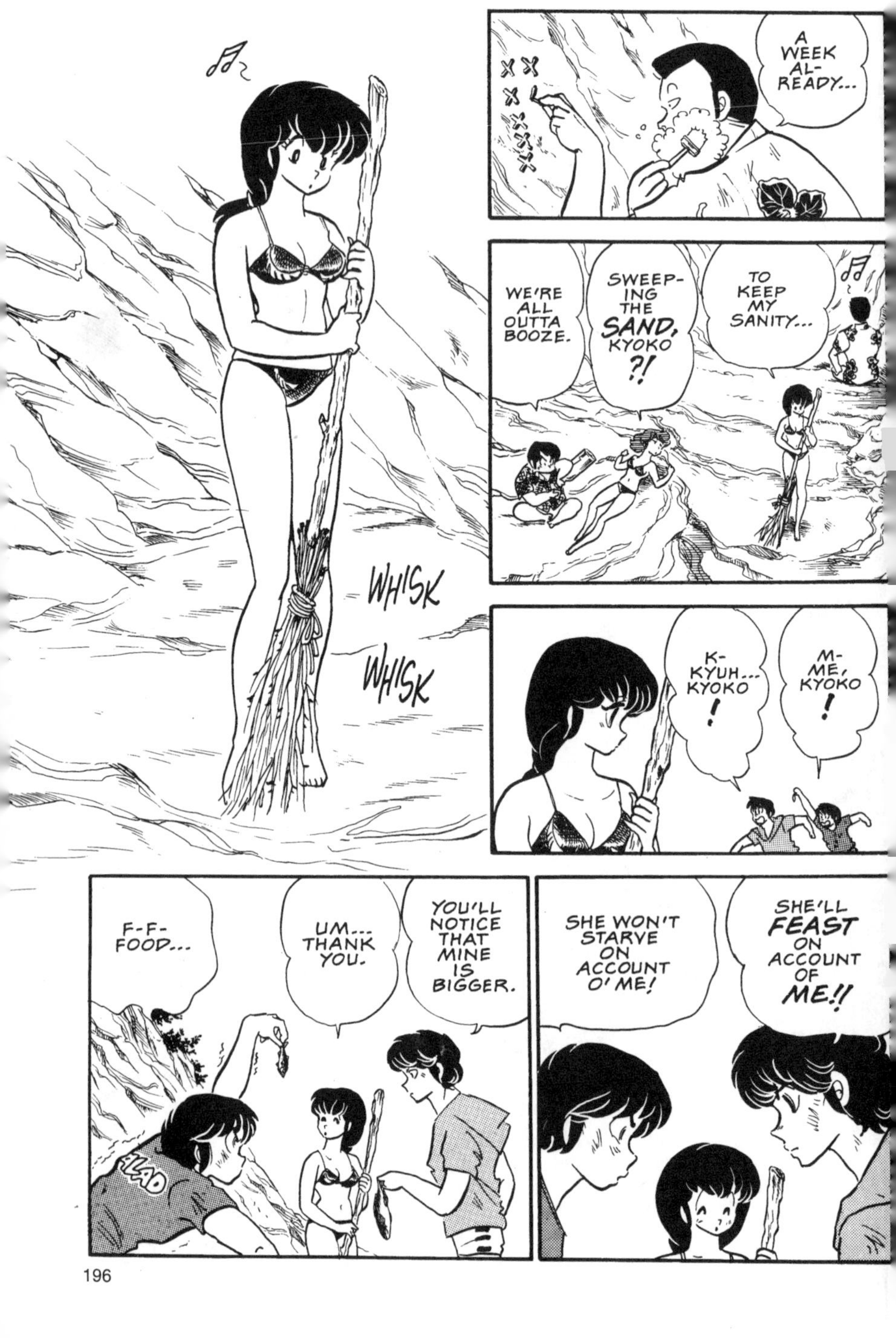
WHISK
WHISK
A WEEK AL-READY...
WE'RE ALL OUTTA BOOZE.
SWEEPING THE SAND, KYOKO ?!
TO KEEP MY SANITY...
K-KYUH... KYOKO!
M-ME, KYOKO!
F-F-FOOD...
UM... THANK YOU.
YOU'LL NOTICE THAT MINE IS BIGGER.
SHE WON'T STARVE ON ACCOUNT O' ME!
SHE'LL FEAST ON ACCOUNT OF ME!!

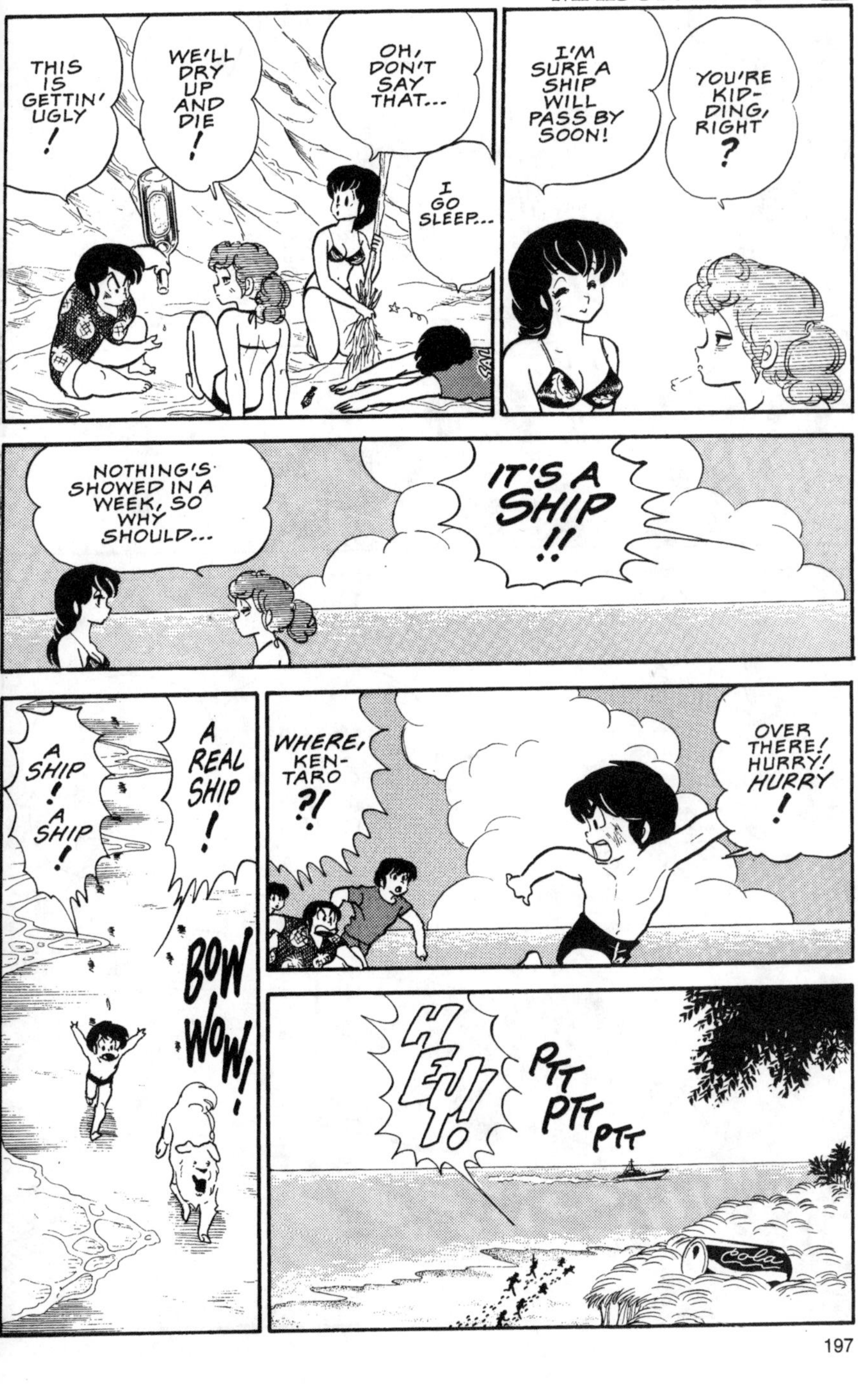
THIS IS GETTIN' UGLY!
WE'LL DRY UP AND DIE!
OH, DON'T SAY THAT...
I GO SLEEP...
I'M SURE A SHIP WILL PASS BY SOON!
YOU'RE KIDDING, RIGHT?
NOTHING'S SHOWED IN A WEEK, SO WHY SHOULD...
IT'S A SHIP!!
A SHIP! A SHIP!
A REAL SHIP!
BOW WOW!
WHERE, KENTARO?!
OVER THERE! HURRY! HURRY!
HEY!!
PTT PTT PTT

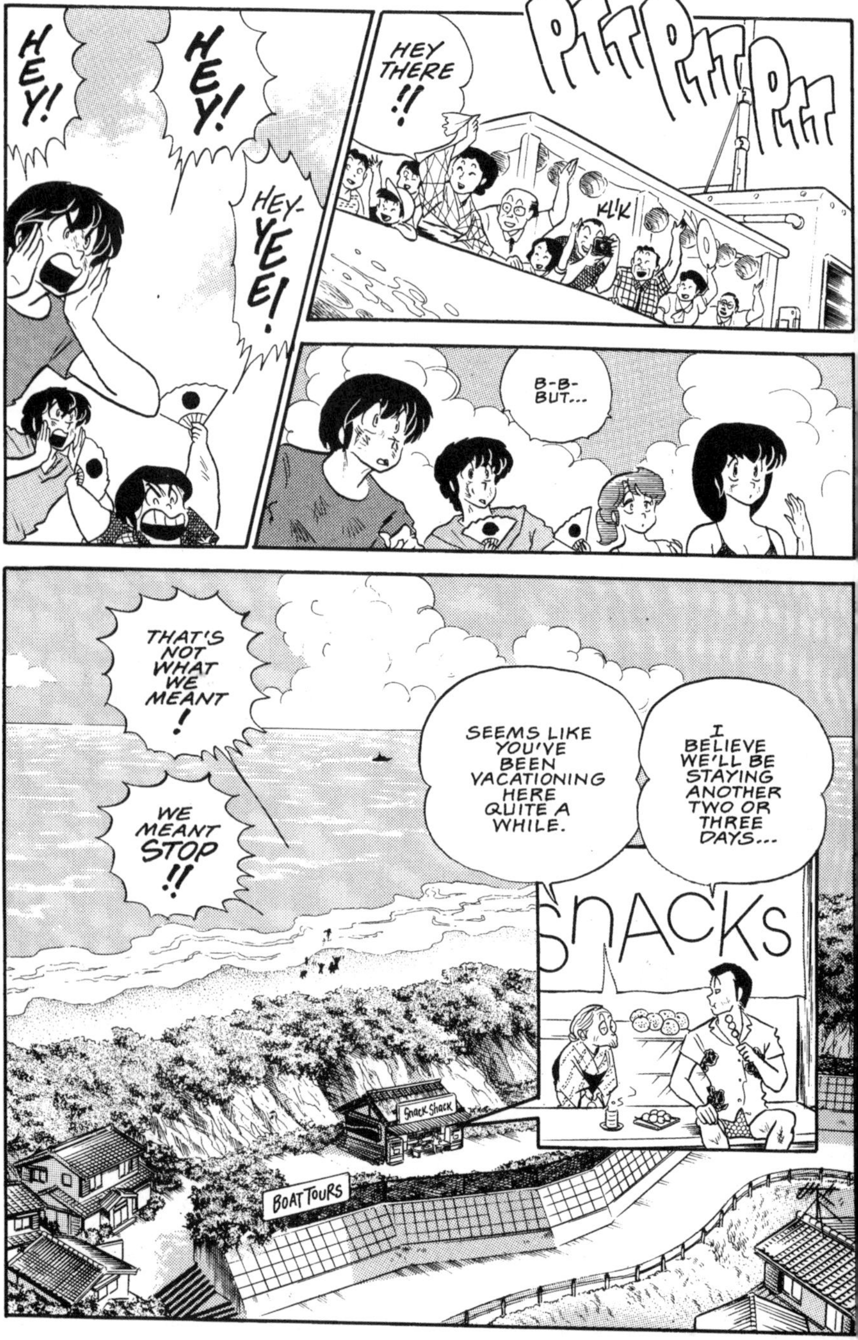
HEY!
HEY!
HEY-YEEE!
HEY THERE!!
PTTT PTTT PTTT
KL'K
B-B-BUT...
THAT'S NOT WHAT WE MEANT!
WE MEANT STOP!!
SEEMS LIKE YOU'VE BEEN VACATIONING HERE QUITE A WHILE.
I BELIEVE WE'LL BE STAYING ANOTHER TWO OR THREE DAYS...
SNACKS
Snack Shack
BOAT TOURS

TO BE CONTINUED...